CAPITAL OFFENSE

How Washington's Wise Men Turned America's Future Over to Wall Street

Michael Hirsh

WILEY

John Wiley & Sons, Inc.

Published by John Wiley & Sons, Inc., Hoboken, New Jersey
Published simultaneously in Canada

For general information about our other products and services, please contact our Customer Care Department within the United States at (800) 762-2974, outside the United States at (317) 572-3993 or fax (317) 572-4002.

Wiley also publishes its books in a variety of electronic formats. Some content that appears in print may not be available in electronic books. For more information about Wiley products, visit our web site at www.wiley.com.

ISBN 978-0-470-52067-3 (cloth); ISBN 978-0-470-76957-7 (ebk);
ISBN 978-0-470-76958-4 (ebk); ISBN 978-0-470-76959-7 (ebk)

Printed in the United States of America

10 9 8 7 6 5 4 3 2 1

For my parents, Charlie and Barbara,
and my sons, Evan and Calder

Contents

Acknowledgments

The bulk of this narrative was drawn from scores of interviews with the principal characters in the story, their aides—current and former—as well as their detractors and critics and close observers of the economic scene over the last two years. This was supplemented by reporting I have done going back some twenty years, mainly for *Newsweek* magazine but also for *Institutional Investor* magazine and the Associated Press.

I have had the great fortune to have been, as a journalist, a front-row witness to the rise of the post–Cold War world as well most of the financial crises that have plagued it since the Mexican peso crash of 1994–1995. I was able to cover most of the events described in this book in real time, as they were happening, and it has been fascinating and enlightening to return to them for a second look from the perspective of the biggest crisis of all, the financial meltdown of 2007–2009.

Unless otherwise noted, the events, scenes, and discussions described in the narrative are based on my own reporting and interviews. Some of the interviews were "on background," meaning the individuals would agree to speak to me only on condition that I not attribute any quotations to them by name in the text, but most were on the record. I would like to thank the following people who gave me their time, attention, recollections, assessments, and views. Together they contributed inestimably to whatever value this book may have.

They are, alphabetically: George Akerlof, Martin Anderson, Robert Auerbach, Sheila Bair, Peter Bakstansky, Roy Barnes, Charlene Barshefsky, Gary Becker, Ben Bernanke, Peter Beutel, Jagdish Bhagwati, Alan Blinder, Joan Blumenthal, Leonard Bole, Bill Brennan, Mark Brickell, Brooksley Born, James Bothwell, Chuck Bowsher, Barbara Branden, Nathaniel Branden, Charles Brunie, Michael Calhoun, Maria Cantwell, Chris Carpenter, Gerald Corrigan, John Dingell Jr., Randall Dodd, Kathy

Eickhoff, Stanley Fischer, Roberta Fishman, Barney Frank, Tim Geithner, Gary Gensler, Mark Gertler, Newt Gingrich, Harvey Goldschmid, Austan Goolsbee, Michael Greenberger, Rob Johnson, Sally Katzen, Ed Knight, Eric Kolchinsky, Jan Kregel, Anne Krueger, Marc Lackritz, Jim Leach, Arthur Levitt Jr., Iris Mack, Patrick Madigan, Reuben Marks, Janet Martel, Thomas P. "Mack" McLarty, Richard Medley, Leo Melamed, Tom Miller, Kevin Muehring, Paul O'Neill, Jonathan Orszag, Peter Orszag, Frank Partnoy, Hank Paulson, James Poterba, Lant Pritchett, Raghu Rajan, Robert Reich, Dani Rodrik, Kenneth Rogoff, Jim Rokakis, David Rubenstein, Robert Rubin, Anna Schwartz, Robert Shiller, George Shultz, Paul Singer, Roy Smith, Gene Sperling, Robert Solow, Anya Stiglitz, Eloise Stiglitz, Joseph Stiglitz, Larry Summers, Robert Teitelman, Sidney Verba, Paul Volcker, Dan Waldman, Timothy Wirth, Lawrence White, Jim Wolfensohn, and Edgar Woolard.

I want to reserve special thanks for the people who read early drafts of this book. They corrected many errors and gave me incisive and invariably helpful advice on how to make it better. Ken Rogoff, Rob Johnson, Steve Weisman, and Angel Ubide all took time out of their busy schedules to critique the manuscript in great detail, and they improved it in more ways than I could possibly enumerate. I will always be grateful to them. Frank Partnoy and Governor Roy Barnes read parts of the manuscript and also helped to make it more accurate. Michael Greenberger did so as well and was an infallible guide through the arcane netherworld of derivatives regulation. My *Newsweek* colleague Bob Samuelson, the great and humble dean of American economic columnists, has been a constant intellectual and journalistic mentor to me over the years, and he supplied some of the critical reporting details in the book, especially concerning the Jackson Hole meeting of 2005, which he attended.

Any mistakes or misjudgments in this book, however, remain mine alone.

I would also like to thank my editors at *Newsweek*. I did not take a leave of absence to write this book, and they were unfailingly sensitive and supportive as I tried to balance my time between authorship and my *Newsweek* work.

My editor at John Wiley & Sons, Eric Nelson, was a pleasure to work with from the start. Eric defines editing at its best. He dove into the manuscript with brio and proposed many changes, yet he didn't insist on a single one. I often pushed back, but in almost every case his judgment was right, and this is a far better book than it started out to be because of his handiwork in every chapter. Kimberly Monroe-Hill of Wiley unerringly supervised the copyediting, proofreading, and indexing of the book, along with everything else on the way from Word documents to printed copies. My agent, Andrew Stuart, helped enormously in refining the concept of the book, and when he eventually liked what he saw he set about selling it like a warrior. Andrew has been a constant source of support and advice.

Finally, I would like to thank my entire family, including the very earliest readers of my prologue, my sister Kim Hirsh and my brother-in-law Mark Widmann. My parents, Barbara and Charlie, have advised me well and lovingly on this project, as they have on everything else important in my life, and no thanks will ever be enough to convey the love and gratitude I feel. My sister Lisa Hirsh Schlossman has also always been there for me, and I would like to add a special thanks to her (and her husband Mark's) daughter and my niece Samara Schlossman, who is showing promise as a family historian and who thought it would be really cool to be mentioned in the acknowledgments. Thanks also go to Denise for understanding, and to our wonderful sons, Evan and Calder. They are the joy of my life, and for me the greatest pleasure while writing this book was to watch them growing up into the outstanding young men they are destined to become.

PROLOGUE

The Hippopotamus under the Rug

It was the last thing Bob Rubin needed that day, at that moment in history. It was April 21, 1998. Rubin, the Treasury secretary of the United States, was in the middle of a financial crisis that was toppling one Asian economy after another. So it really was not convenient to have this humorless, difficult woman, Brooksley Born, marching into his magnificent Greek Revival palace next to the White House, *his* Treasury Department, to lecture him about the dangers of derivatives. Born, that busybody from a minor regulatory agency. Born, with her pixie bangs and droning personality. Her ridiculous brown legal folder, from which she neatly extracted her talking points, and her litigator's demeanor. Born was most definitely not a member of the club; she had no sense of the smooth collegiality that characterized the top policy makers of the Clinton administration—what former Treasury secretary Lloyd Bentsen, with some exasperation, had once called the "meetingest" administration he had ever seen. So what if she was running a nominally independent agency? She had no sense of place, no respect for who they were. And it wasn't just the Clintonites. Over at the Federal Reserve a few blocks away, where Rubin's pal Alan Greenspan reigned—a man who for ten years had surgically thwarted every effort at regulation—staffers privately thought of Born as "a lightweight wacko," recalled a former Fed official.

Born was chairwoman of the little-known Commodity Futures Trading Commission (CFTC), an outlier agency that didn't even have its own federal building. It rented space in the commercial district of downtown Washington. Once Born had been on the short list for attorney general, but Bill Clinton had gone with Janet Reno for reasons Born never found out. This was her consolation prize. Still, she took her job very seriously. In recent years, she had grown increasingly alarmed by the ungoverned global trade in derivatives. Derivatives were market contracts that bet on the upward or downward movement of some underlying asset that they "derived" their value from, like interest rates or mortgages. Using derivatives, global companies could protect their overseas profits from market gyrations, and investors from all over the world could place bets on some country's currency, or get a piece of an entire state's mortgage payment stream. The geniuses on Wall Street were always finding new ways to repackage assets and sell them to new customers, and derivatives were the means. But Born, surveying the landscape she was now supposed to monitor for illegal or unethical behavior, began to get worried by the sheer size of the market in derivatives that were sold "over the counter"—or off any exchange and out of public sight. It amounted to multiple *trillions* of dollars in unmonitored trading, all happening completely without the knowledge of governments.

It was, in some senses, the most laissez-faire market in the world. And for the last year it had been giving Brooksley Born sleepless nights.

Rubin and Greenspan, however, were not terribly worried about this at the moment. And that is what counted.

By this time, in the late 1990s, Rubin and Greenspan were the lions of Washington. They were an odd but endearing pair, the rumpled, rheumy-eyed Fed chief and the slight, crisply barbered Treasury secretary. Many in the Washington establishment thought of them as the most effective Fed-Treasury team in the history of the nation, and there weren't many on Wall Street who would disagree. One man had begun his career as an Ayn Rand libertarian (Greenspan), the other as a liberal Democrat with deep compassion for the inner cities (Rubin). Yet it was in keeping with the times—if history had once produced a Bronze Age and an Iron Age, this surely could be called the Age of Capital—that they forged the closest consensus between the Fed and Treasury, and a Republican and a Democrat, that anyone could remember. Each man canceled out any doubts people might have had about the other; if Rubin and Greenspan agreed on it, it must be right.

Rubin was a natural; he fit the temper of the times perfectly. There was never any learning curve with Rubin. To his admirers—and they were everywhere—he had seemed to step into the role of Treasury secretary with the effortless grace of a Fred Astaire on the dance floor, or a Ted Williams in the batter's box. Treasury is the second oldest cabinet post, after State, but at this time it had become in many ways the most prestigious. Rubin's private office elevator took him right down to the East Wing of the White House. He and the president were never close, but Bill Clinton, as savvy a judge of political power as anyone could remember in Washington, trusted him implicitly, loved his dogged preparedness and passion for teamwork, and knew enough to keep Rubin out there as the public face of his pride and joy, the U.S. economy. Clinton also understood he had to keep Greenspan happy with a commitment to fiscal responsibility—and he did, in a way that was perhaps unsurpassed by any Democratic administration in history. Greenspan was then seen as the oracle of the age, the maestro of the 1990s boom. With each passing year at the Fed, Greenspan's runic pronouncements were waited upon more eagerly by the market. He was a living icon; even the fatness of his briefcase became a market indicator on CNBC: if it looked well stuffed on his way into the office, that supposedly meant he was preparing an argument that rates must go up (in truth, Greenspan later wrote, all it meant was that he'd packed his lunch that day).

Brooksley Born, on the other hand, was just a lawyer—a *Washington* lawyer. Worse, she was a woman, and to some of those involved that also played a part in what was to happen. There is no culture more macho than Wall Street's, which is why its heaviest hitters are called (or were, once upon a time) Big Swinging Dicks, and why a vast demimonde of massage parlors and escort services honeycombs mid- to lower Manhattan. Greenspan and Rubin were above all that, of course. They were soft-spoken gentlemen, with unimpeachable reputations; they had long since outgrown the grabbling ethos of the Street. Still, even though they had both worked in the nation's capital for years—Greenspan for more than a decade—both remained fundamentally Men of Wall Street. Wall Street was their spawning ground. Wall Street had given them their fortunes and their world views. It had shaped them. It grounded them.

Both Rubin and Greenspan were passionate about the key lesson they had learned from the Street and brought to Washington: finance must be allowed to flow, markets to operate unencumbered, and regulation kept at bay. Finance was the engine of innovation, America's greatest strength. Rubin and Greenspan may have lorded over economic policy making in Washington, but Wall Street—the bond and currency markets mainly—ruled Washington. Each day, the market signals emanating from the Street, reinforced by its army of lobbyists, transmitted to Rubin and Greenspan the basic operating instructions for the U.S. economy.

There wasn't a need for many instructions. The economy was for the most part booming on its own momentum. Sure, there were crises of capitalism: they were in the middle of one right now—the "Asian contagion," a broad collapse of currencies in the "Tiger" economies of East Asia. All the more reason why there was little time for Brooksley Born. But even now Greenspan, Rubin, and the latter's brilliant deputy, Larry Summers, were managing to smooth things out, giving heavy-handed advice to those wayward countries on why their currencies were crashing. Summers was in many ways the most cerebral of the three, a living repository of economic wisdom—he was the son of two economists and the nephew of two more, both Nobel Prize winners. He thought that if the East Asians would just do this, or that, behave more responsibly by opening up their financial sectors more, they might get their act together. Together the three of them were called the "Committee to Save the World"—*Time* magazine had lavished that title on them, with Rubin generously insisting that Summers be part of the cover story. And while all three had, blushingly, declined the encomium at the time, each man later hung a framed copy of the cover image on his office wall.

America's economy was the beau ideal of the globe, and they were running it. "We are currently enjoying the strongest U.S. economic performance in a generation," Summers had declared the year before, in a triumphal speech at the G7 summit in Denver. The Cold War was over, the Soviet Union gone from the scene. Its former satellites and republics were now humble disciples of the Western way. The American way. "The magic of the marketplace," as Ronald Reagan had called it in 1986, had performed miracles. The collapse of the Soviet Union had been only the beginning. It soon became clear that there was no competitor even on the horizon. Japan, which only a few years before had been seen as the up-and-coming superpower, fell into deep recession as its "bubble economy" collapsed. Post-Soviet Russia imploded into an economy smaller than Portugal's. The Europeans grew self-absorbed—even more self-absorbed than Americans—over their historic but still troubled experiment in combining national sovereignty with monetary union. China lumbered forward, a nation in transition, but it remained a developing country with its future as a putative superpower well ahead of it. No one was paying much attention to the Arab world, which mainly served as the gas station to the globe.

The United States, meanwhile, was enjoying the most capital spending in three decades, the lowest unemployment in a quarter century, and so little inflation that Greenspan seemed close to hitting the central banker's sweet spot—inflationary fears were no longer a significant factor in business decisions. America's techno-business titans, from Microsoft's Bill Gates to General Electric's Jack Welch, oversaw global empires. Wall Street, together with its Anglo-Saxon twin, the City of London, directed most of the world's increasingly privatized capital flows—diverting, in the process, a nice chunk of other nations' savings to help feed Americans' insatiable spending habits. America's economic performance, Summers said in his speech, gave "us a new authority on the world stage and an opportunity to shape a world of our making."

There was also a sense among the Americans that, despite the occasional financial crisis, the advanced economies had more or less tamed capitalism, introduced a new level of stability into the system. Volatility was down, risk was understood better than ever before and more diffuse. Some economists had even begun to suggest that if Americans hadn't defeated the business cycle, they'd at least gotten it under control. Sure the Asians had their issues, just as the Latin Americans had. But they would get there—to where we were—eventually. As the advanced economies became more service- and information-oriented—the International Monetary Fund (IMF) didn't even call them "industrialized" anymore—they grew less vulnerable to the supply shocks, inventory overload and overcapacity that triggered recessions past. Markets were becoming "complete," in the jargon of economists, and American-style financial innovation was leading the way. "Information is becoming cheaper and cheaper," Robert DiClemente, chief U.S. economist at Salomon Brothers, told me back then. "That's another way of saying that markets are becoming less and less imperfect."

Brooksley Born had always looked at all this triumphalism—especially Wall Street's—from afar. She had never really succumbed to the free-market religion. She just wasn't part of that world. If Rubin, Greenspan and Summers were shaped by the markets and driven by them, Born saw the markets as an animal force, necessary to our way of life but something to be contained by law and regulation. A West Coast WASP from a good family, she had a gentle laid-back manner that disguised, at least until you disagreed with her, a steely mind and an even harder will. She graduated high school at age sixteen and went to Stanford, where she was an English major and was considering medicine as a career until her mother, who remembered how argumentative she'd been as a child and how ferocious her sense of justice was, urged her to go to law school. She was the daughter of civil servants—her father had been head of San Francisco's Public Welfare Department—and the first thing she did out of Stanford Law School was to cross the country to clerk for a Washington, D.C., judge. She never left, fascinated by the public-policy challenges in a capital city full of wonks and intellectuals, where "everyone was just like me." As a result, Born came at the problem of derivatives from an entirely different direction. A different culture.

She was lovely as a young woman, which may explain some of the sexism. A photo of her as president of the *Stanford Law Review* shows an attractive, slim Born seated amid her male subordinates, gazing confidently at the camera. Her father had wanted a boy and liked the name Brooks, so Brooksley she became, and she grew up used to shoving her way into a man's world with that boy-girl name. Attending Stanford Law in the early to midsixties, she'd been stunned when at the beginning of her first year, one of the men in her class angrily told her she was doing a terrible thing because she had taken the place of some man who now couldn't get a draft deferment. Born's classmate said the anonymous male would probably have to go to Vietnam and he might get killed. "That was difficult to deal with," she recalled forty-five years later, still shaken by the memory. She graduated at the top of her class, which normally would have all but guaranteed a U.S. Supreme Court clerkship, but Justice Potter Stewart politely let it be known that he wasn't ready for a female clerk, so she had to settle for the Court of Appeals.

Afterward, she'd gone to work for Arnold and Porter in D.C. because it had the only female partner in town. Arnold and Porter was one of the great old white-shoe firms, as Washingtonian as, say, Goldman Sachs or Bear Stearns or Lehman Brothers were Wall Street. A&P was a New Deal creation founded by Thurman Arnold, FDR's trust-buster, and by Abe Fortas, a former assistant attorney general and undersecretary of the interior. (Fortas would later go on to become a Supreme

Court justice; after he was forced to resign in scandal, A&P refused his request to come back.) It was one of those monster firms that provided the corporate world with leverage in the world of patents, antitrust, and regulation, but it also had a proud reputation in public service, representing some of Joe McCarthy's victims in the early 1950s.

At Arnold and Porter, Born had watched the futures markets grow up from the 1970s, and her practice was built around mediating between regulators and players in commodities. Because of her clients, she knew how corporate players behaved. In the 1980s, Born represented a large Swiss bank after the Hunt brothers attempted to corner the silver market by investing heavily in futures contracts while they were acquiring millions of ounces of silver. A case of clear-cut manipulation, which was illegal. She watched on the front lines, knee-deep in the legal morass, as the commodities markets went from unglamorous trades like coffee and sugar to more difficult-to-understand products, such as energy and financial derivatives.

Born was a good litigator, making partner by 1974, and her reputation quietly grew in D.C. legal circles. Eventually, she came to be head of A&P's derivatives practice. She was also heavily involved in women's rights issues by now, meeting Hillary Rodham Clinton in the mid-1980s when Hillary chaired a "Committee on Women in the Profession" at the American Bar Association. By the time Bill Clinton came into office in January 1993, Born had developed a national reputation as a brilliant corporate lawyer and activist. She became chairwoman of the CFTC in 1996, and by that time the derivatives market was growing huge. But Born began to get worried very quickly. She was especially concerned by what her predecessors, Wendy Gramm and Mary Schapiro, were bequeathing to her.

Gramm, the wife of Texas senator Phil Gramm and a conservative Republican economist, had first cracked the door to unregulated derivatives trading in 1993 when, just as she was about to leave the CFTC, she issued two new rules sought by the industry. The effect of the two Gramm rules was to allow, for the first time, the trading of over-the-counter (OTC) derivatives without any oversight. And Gramm did one more thing before she left. She exempted Enron from regulation in some trading of energy derivatives. Then she joined Enron's board.

Born was especially worried about the scandals that began to crop up with greater frequency, like the first humid wisps of wind before a storm. Two years before Born became chair of the CFTC, Bankers Trust had nearly blown up two of its biggest clients, Procter and Gamble and Gibson Greeting Cards, by selling them complex derivatives products and, the evidence showed, falsely valuing them. P&G later acknowledged it didn't understand what it was buying at all. There was the Sumitomo copper scam, when the CFTC enforcement division found that the firm's chief trader, Yasuo Hamanaka, had been using over-the-counter derivatives contracts in copper to disguise loans, primarily from JP Morgan and Merrill Lynch, which were being used to finance enormous speculation. Hamanaka lost $2.6 billion in unauthorized trades, the largest derivatives loss up to that time. As Born saw it, that made it clear that OTC derivatives were beginning to play a role in manipulative activities, and also they could be used to disguise transactions on books of copper. To appear to be different in purpose from what they were. It was very close to what was later revealed to have happened at Enron.

For just about everyone in official Washington, the explosion of derivatives looked like a sophisticated new dimension to global finance, one that bore out yet again that markets would take care of themselves by finding novel ways to spread risk around, so that everyone took a piece of it. And indeed, for many global corporations, derivatives were often useful as a conservative way to reduce risk, especially when it came to currency swaps. But down on the trading floors of Wall Street, things looked different. The key to many other successful derivatives trades was, in truth, deception. Back then, in the mid-1990s, derivatives traders were already putting together deals that were precursors to the subprime mortgage-backed securities that would explode in our faces a decade later. "Quants" on the street—many of them former physicists or other math geniuses—were always finding complex new ways to repackage assets. The schemes usually followed the same theme: the key was to take junk investments—risky but very high-yielding bonds or securities denominated in pesos or Thai baht or Malaysian ringgits—and disguise them well enough so that pension investors or insurance companies or others thought they were buying investment-grade stuff denominated in dollars.

The payoff in fees for this confidence game was huge. A high-yield bond with an investment-grade rating was the Wall Street equivalent of having your cake and eating it too. It didn't really make any sense, since the only reason some bonds have high interest rates is that they're risky; if a bond gets rated at a high "investment grade," say AA and above, then those who issue it, like the government, don't have to pay out too much interest. The way the investment banks got over this problem was to make the rating agencies, mainly Standard and Poor's and Moody's, part of the scheme. With the right inducements, the agencies could be persuaded to look the other way at a low-rated portion of a hybrid bond, as long as it had a dollop or two of U.S. Treasuries as part of its makeup. The new derivative bond might be based largely on high-yielding baht-denominated Thai bonds, but if U.S. Treasury yields were also thrown into the mix then people felt better about it. The Wall Street investment banks often got the rating agencies to go along and label such a new composite derivative bond AA or AAA—the highest rating—even though a lot of the high-yielding product it was composed of was less than BBB, or junk. The banks achieved this by reminding the rating agencies subtly that they earned fees from every deal they rated.

Tempted by the high yields, state, county, and local investment funds that were supposed to be playing it safe began indulging in highly risky derivatives trades under cover. The temptation of showing great returns to one's board of directors, looking like a market whiz, was just too great. And one by one, they began going up in smoke. At one point, eighteen Ohio towns lost $14 million. City Colleges of Chicago lost almost its entire investment portfolio—$96 million. In 1995, the Wisconsin Investment Board abruptly announced a $95 million loss, $60 million of which was linked to investments in the Mexican peso. These state and local funds had no business investing their citizens' money in high-risk currency trades; in fact, most were banned by law from indulging in such speculation. But somehow they felt they could do it if they were packaged as derivatives.

Some of these scandals were so astonishing in scope and criminality that they should have raised at least a few warning flags in Washington. Orange County, California, under its treasurer, Robert Citron—a college dropout who consulted psychics and astrologers about interest rates—had lost a billion dollars and filed for bankruptcy in 1994. Again, it was a case of a Wall Street firm, Merrill Lynch, knowingly selling Citron investments that were so complex he simply could not comprehend them. But no one did anything. Born was worried that there were no controls on leverage and there was also no control on speculation—the way there was on a regulated exchange. On exchanges the authorities could place limits on speculative positions and use other tools to talk down or moderate speculative trading. As the speculative collapses continued, there were no rules in place to stop them—no requirement as there was on exchanges for marking to market or paying margin on a daily or intra-daily basis.

So Born began to ask the obvious: What did they really know about this growing market? They had some ideas about how big it was and who the major dealers were, but they didn't know how much speculation or fraud or manipulation was out there. They didn't know the extent of the private trading that was occurring out of sight. They didn't know how much "leverage," or borrowed money applied to trades, there was. Or whether the dealers were doing appropriate "due diligence" to find out whether their "counterparties"—those they did derivatives deals with—were who they said they were. "I realized how very little we knew and how there were these little tips of the iceberg, the mini disasters that were happening," she said. She hadn't had any particular epiphany. It was a cumulative realization that the commission had retained authority over what had become a $27 trillion market, but it wasn't doing nearly enough oversight.

Born also realized, to her distress, that the market had moved way beyond the exemptions that the commission had granted. The new exemption was supposed to be limited to "customized" products traded between large commercial firms. The industry promptly began ignoring that rule, and trading the customized derivatives instruments on the open market. Firms would get into deals where, if the original counterparty in a swaps trade no longer liked the terms, it would sell it—or "novate" it—away to another buyer, but without telling any regulatory authority. And because all this trading began occurring under the ever broadening "exemption," the CFTC was left without any tools to see how the market was working, whether fraud or manipulation was occurring.

For Born, there was a question of credibility too. You don't want to have laws on the books that markets and traders were routinely flouting, as they now clearly were. But the power shift in Washington was astonishing. Born first got some idea of what she was up against—the near-religious belief in markets that underpinned the men in power around her—shortly after being appointed CFTC chairwoman. Greenspan had invited her to lunch in his private dining room at the Fed. Just to feel her out. She described her legal concerns. "Well, Brooksley, I guess you and I will never agree about fraud," Greenspan told her. "What is there not to agree on?" Born replied. "Well, you probably will always believe there should be laws against fraud, and I don't think there is any need for it." Born literally couldn't believe her ears. But Greenspan, a decade before rampant fraud became the hallmark of the subprime mortgage bubble, was laying out his creed: the markets would take care of all, they would root out the fraud. Greenspan had written an article in Ayn Rand's newsletter back in 1963 dismissing as a "collectivist" myth the idea that businessmen, left to their own devices, "would attempt to sell unsafe food and drugs, fraudulent securities, and shoddy buildings." On the contrary, he declared, "it is in the self-interest of every businessman to have a reputation for honest dealings and a quality product." That was enough.

There were other developments equally disturbing to Born. She was running out of time. Bills had been introduced in Congress that would have deregulated exchange trading in further significant ways. She had to do some hurry-up research when she got to the CFTC as to what her reaction should be. And one thing that became clear was that many of the problems the futures markets had experienced were the work of large firms, the big boys of Wall Street. Bob Rubin's and Alan Greenspan's crowd.

Born, confident of her own judgment, pushed ahead. "It seemed to me I had three options," she later recalled. "One, to ignore this, as to some extent my predecessors had. We called it 'the hippopotamus under the rug.'" Another option was to head to the other extreme: to go "nuclear," asking her enforcement people to pursue, one by one, the big dealers who were violating the exemption terms. That would have meant endless and expensive litigation. The third option, which is the route she took, was to start afresh by finding out more about this totally opaque market. And assess whether there would be a better way to oversee it than a set of regulations that clearly had become totally worthless.

Aware that she was trying to stem what seemed an unstoppable tide, Born had her staff work up the mildest sort of proposal in March—what in Washington bureaucratese is called a "concept release." It was a thirty-three-page proposal suggesting that U.S. authorities begin exploring how to regulate the vast global market in derivatives. "We had no preconceived notions about how this should be done," said her deputy, Michael Greenberger. Then they sent the draft around to all the agencies.

That's when Brooksley Born really began to understand the nature of the forces arrayed against her.

The first sign came in March. She was in her office when the phone rang. At the other end was Summers, a former Massachusetts Institute of Technology (MIT) wunderkind known for his cutting arrogance. Though as deputy Treasury secretary he had no seniority over Born, an independent agency chief, Summers proceeded to dress her down, loudly. Greenberger walked in as the call was ending. "She was ashen," he recalled. "She said, 'That was Larry Summers. He was shouting at me.'" Summers, channeling the views of Wall Street's finest, had been alarmed that even a hint of regulation would send all the derivatives trading overseas, costing America business. It was the unspoken assumption in those years that what was good for Wall Street was good for the U.S. economy, and vice versa. Summers told Born that he had a bunch of trade association reps in his office saying that it was doing enormous damage to their business for her to ask these questions and he wanted to let her know she should just stop doing it. Born said: "I was astonished a position would be taken that you shouldn't even ask questions about a market that was many, many trillions of dollars in notional value—and that none of us knew anything about."

A few weeks later, it all came to a climax in Rubin's ornate meeting room on the second floor of Treasury, where museumlike displays of old currency are kept. The April 21 meeting of the president's Working Group on Financial Markets—which comprised Rubin, Greenspan, Born, and SEC Chairman Arthur Levitt—was supposed to be routine. That morning, Born had gotten a call from John "Jerry" Hawke, then undersecretary of Treasury for domestic finance. Hawke was no great ally—later on, as comptroller of the currency, he would also lead the fight against state efforts to regulate banks. But he was also an Arnold and Porter alumnus and a friend, he knew and respected Born, and he was also starting to get a little worried about how wildly leveraged banks were getting. He thought he should warn Born that she was going to run into a wall with Rubin. And so, with some trepidation, her talking points ready, she went into the meeting. With her was her deputy, Greenberger, and her general counsel, Dan Waldman, also an A&P grad.

It didn't take long. As soon as the meeting began, Rubin attacked the concept release. Being Rubin, he did it in a subtle way, calling Born "strident" about the position she was taking. Rubin insisted that Born could not go forward with the proposal. He also said the CFTC had no jurisdiction whatsoever over OTC swaps or options—though of course the commission had initially granted all those exemptions from its own rules. Rubin didn't bother to explain why, but he was channeling the same fears on Wall Street that Summers had conveyed in his phone call: just by virtue of putting out a concept release, Born could upset the markets. Rubin was afraid she might be signaling to market players that the CFTC had jurisdiction over derivatives bets. Giving the CFTC jurisdiction, in turn, would, Rubin thought, lead everyone to assume these contracts were "futures." Since futures were required, by law, to be traded on exchanges, all OTC derivatives bets could be thrown into a legal limbo. Traders on the losing side might decide they didn't want to pay off. Trillions of dollars were at stake.

It was, in truth, a silly overreaction. Born, who was stunned, spoke up. First of all, she said, she'd never heard or seen a legal analysis that suggested the CFTC did not have jurisdiction over at least a very significant part of this market. Rubin responded that, well, we have the legal analysis that demonstrates you have no jurisdiction. Born said that wasn't the view of the CFTC lawyers. They assured her she did have jurisdiction. Rubin replied: "Yes, but those are government lawyers. I think you should be talking to private lawyers, like bank lawyers."

Greenberger, sitting behind Born, jerked forward in his seat. It was unbelievable. Born had been president of the *Stanford Law Review*. Greenberger had been editor in chief of the *University of Pennsylvania Law Review*. Waldman had gone to another Ivy League law school, Columbia. They had all clerked for circuit court judges. They had all been in private practice in big firms until a year or two earlier. And here was Rubin telling them they weren't good enough? The Treasury secretary then asked for Born's assurance that she would talk to his general counsel, Ed Knight, before issuing the concept release. She agreed. Rubin no doubt thought that was that. He'd ended many other meetings in just this way, simply by expressing his opinion. But Born wasn't done. She spoke up again: "Well, we would be very interested in seeing your legal analysis," she said. To Rubin's aides, it was nearly an act of lèse majesté. "She came at Bob and Alan like a litigator," said one Rubin loyalist, still appalled by the spectacle ten years later. "It was as if she was suing them." Another Clinton official who was there said, "Everybody just kind of exploded at her." But he wasn't sympathetic. "There was so much going on then. Then someone comes up and says here's a non-problem, why don't we throw everything at it?"

Rubin would later argue, in his defense, that it wasn't just what he saw as a power grab by Born, one that would throw trillions of dollars of contracts into dispute. He also said the industry never would have stood for Born's idea of regulation; and he didn't have the political power to contain derivatives trading. But it was hard to believe. Rubin, along with Greenspan, was then at the height of his power and prestige in both Washington and New York. He could have had his way.

Oh, Rubin knew enough to be concerned about the uncontrolled market in derivatives. He was also a lawyer—he'd gone to Yale—but the law for Rubin was almost an afterthought. He'd always felt the lure of the markets, gravitated back to the Street. Rubin was cautious enough. He never entirely trusted models the way the most gullible Wall Street traders did. "Probabilistic" decision making was his creed: you're never quite sure of anything. He fit perfectly with the Goldman culture: take risks, but hedge, hedge, hedge, and carefully monitor your positions. But his bets usually paid off, no matter how speculative. Rubin had such fine antennae for market sentiment that he knew when things were over- heated, when risk was being undervalued. It was his evenhandedness that people remembered.

Above all, Rubin was mainly a man of capital, and capital had always done right by Bob Rubin. As Barney Frank, the brilliantly acerbic chair- man of the House Financial Services Committee, later summed up the Clinton administration's view to me: "The way to a good life was to leave capital alone. Do not tax it, do not regulate it. If you do that it will take care of you." This became known as the "Washington Consensus," a set of reform policies that Rubin and Company simplified into a three- pronged formula: rapid liberalization of markets, privatization, and a demand for fiscal austerity from governments. So by the time Brooksley Born was arriving at her conclusion that something had to be done about derivatives, Rubin had long since unconsciously adopted the view that whatever permits more capital to flow is good, and whatever stops it is bad. The flow itself was an organic, beautiful thing, a beneficent thing. And while everyone must share a little blame, the main thing that makes capital stop flowing is a government that makes wrong choices. Like Mexico during the peso crisis. Or the Asian countries, which had tried to get away with easy prosperity on big deficits and currencies casually linked to the dollar. Now here was someone who wanted to throw a net over this beautiful creature, the capital markets. Rubin was no ideologue like his good friend Alan. But Born's proposal—something that might send a chilling message to the markets—was the last thing Rubin needed right now. In the months leading up to the concept release, Rubin had been dealing with a global crisis unlike any the world had seen for quite a while.

He had handled that masterfully too. But the Asian contagion was still going on, and he hadn't had much time to reflect on what really caused it. Neither Rubin nor anyone else paid much attention to the fact that the Asian crisis was an early warning sign about the dangers of derivatives—and about the finance-dominated world they had cre- ated. Many Western banks had engaged in over-the-counter derivatives trading: Asian banks, like Mexican banks before them, had been mak- ing leveraged bets on their own markets and currencies using swaps, options, forwards, and other derivatives. One Korean investment firm, SK Securities Company, had bet with JP Morgan that the Thai baht would rise relative to the Japanese yen. When the baht collapsed, SK abruptly owed JP Morgan about $350 million and couldn't pay it.

There were a lot of deals like that; the suddenness and depth of the Asian crisis had much to do with these heavily leveraged derivatives trades beneath the surface. Rubin went in and got the big Wall Street banks like Morgan to roll over or extend their debt, but without asking too deeply about where all that debt had come from. He and Greenspan and Summers were trying to resolve a crisis that stemmed from the very prob- lems Born was concerned about, all without realizing it. Instead, thanks to Rubin's deft intervention—providing IMF and U.S. aid to national trea- suries, convening global conference calls—the crisis ultimately passed. And Rubin's reputation was further enhanced. People saw his profound understanding of international markets as a direct extension of his prow- ess at Goldman Sachs, where he made millions in risk arbitrage.

So Rubin could get tough on the Street, but it was always going to be a kind of tough love; and when the Street began screaming about Brooksley Born, Rubin's response was unsurprising. He would side with the Street. And he would tell Born where to get off.

The meeting at Treasury went on for about an hour and a half. Finally, toward the end, the Yoda of the group, Alan Greenspan, spoke up. He also told Born that just asking these questions would drive the business offshore. It was the same line that Summers had given her a couple of weeks before. Born responded that she wasn't aware of that, and it seemed to her that asking questions about the market would not have that impact. (In fact a later study showed that there was no loss of volume during that period.) But that was that. It was over, and they all got up and went back to their agencies. As far as Rubin and Greenspan were concerned, they had killed her plan. Born walked out pale-faced. It was so shocking and vehement a rebuff, particularly coming from the genteel Rubin, that Sally Katzen, who was a deputy at the Office of Management and Budget (OMB) at the time and dealing with her own terrifying case of breast cancer—she was noticeably gaunt at the meeting—called up Born afterward to sympathize. Katzen, who admired Rubin deeply, was also stunned by his manner, and what seemed to her to be a certain amount of sexism. Shortly after the meeting, Greenspan, Rubin, and Levitt, the head of the Securities and Exchange Commission (SEC), issued a joint statement highlighting their "grave concerns" about the CFTC proposal. Summers declared that it was "casting a shadow of regulatory uncertainty over an otherwise thriving market."

But they had all misjudged Brooksley Born. Toughened by a career confronting high-handed men, she only dug in harder when people tried to bully her. She had her general counsel, Dan Waldman, call Ed Knight up to ask for a copy of the legal analysis Rubin had mentioned—the one that barred the CFTC from jurisdiction. Knight didn't call back right away. "They can't pull this on us," Born told Greenberger. "They can't just not talk to us." The two sides went back and forth for a month, but it turned out there was no written legal analysis. Fed up, Born decided to publish the release and send it around *seriatum*—Washington jargon for getting sign-offs from independent agencies without holding a meeting. Born tried to stress to those who would listen that the concept release didn't make an overt play for control. Born, said Greenberger, was "completely flexible" about turf. "'If they want SEC to do this, we'll give it to SEC,' she said," Greenberger recalled.

It didn't matter. The powers that be were set against her. And Rubin was so infuriated by her decision to send out the release that he never spoke to her again. So Brooksley Born's proposal suffered the sentence of slow death that Washington's power elites mete out to undesirable ideas: they are simply ignored by the bureaucracy and shelved by Congress. She never heard back from any of the agencies about the concept release. But not before Rubin's Treasury made sure of it; according to Born, a White House aide was detailed to call one of her commissioners, John Tull, and express the administration's displeasure with the concept release. It was a seeming breach of ethics, interference with an independent agency. Born immediately complained to White House counsel Charles Ruff, who later dressed the aide down and indicated that Treasury had initiated the contact. But nothing, of course, happened to Rubin (who later said he couldn't recall doing anything of the sort).

For Born, the humiliations continued. On the day when her daughter was to go in for knee surgery at Georgetown, she was summoned abruptly by staffers for Jim Leach, the chair of the House Banking Committee, and the chair of the agriculture committee to appear on the Hill. At the moment they called, she was at the hospital and her daughter was about to enter the operating room. Her legislative liaison explained this to Leach and Company, but the word came back: you need to get here anyway. So Born called her husband, who was a partner at her firm, and told him he'd better get out of his meeting and get over to Georgetown. Leach had earlier raised serious alarms himself about derivatives, calling them "the new wild card in international finance," but he too was alarmed by the idea that the small and weak CFTC was attempting to seize control of the derivatives market. Leach and the others berated her for an hour over the concept release. Born sat there and numbly, once again, tried to explain about the dangers of a vast market that none of them had any information about. Other hearings were held and the pile-on continued: at least ten trade organizations, including the Futures Industry Association, were called on to berate Brooksley Born. The message was always the same: no need for oversight. They were big boys. Their members were large institutional entities capable of taking care of themselves.

Even as she was being slowly squashed in the vise between Treasury and the Fed, to little notice the derivatives scourge continued outside the Beltway. In the fall of 1998, as the Asian crisis was abating, Long-Term Capital Management (LTCM) collapsed under the weight of trillions of dollars in derivatives bets, and the Fed and Treasury had to bully New York bankers into liquidating its positions. This was exactly what Born had been waking up in the middle of the night in a cold sweat about: not just the size of the thing, and the near meltdown in markets, but the fact that it came out of nowhere. No one even knew it was happening until John Meriwether of LTCM called up the Fed and told them. In September, Rubin declared that "the world is experiencing its worst crisis in half a century." Even then Rubin refused to take Born's phone calls, said Greenberger. Greenberger called Gary Gensler, then Rubin's deputy, and pleaded with him to get Rubin to respond. Nothing happened. At that point Jim Leach, at least, began to see the light. He called a hearing on LTCM and opened it by remarking, "Well, I have to say, Ms. Born, you've been vindicated in your concerns." Born sought to seize the moment; in her testimony she compared the dangers of the OTC derivatives market to "the unlimited borrowing on securities that contributed to the Great Depression."

It was dramatic, but it wasn't enough. The momentum against Born was too great, the opposition of Rubin's Treasury and Greenspan's Fed too entrenched. Born later said she blamed Rubin more than Greenspan. Because he knew better that markets were imperfect, yet he had not the vision nor the courage to act. It was Rubin who had inspired his adoring underlings to compile ten principles—which they later presented to him in a frame—they called "the Rubin Doctrine of International Finance," the first of which was: "The only certainty in life is that nothing is ever certain," and the second of which was: "Markets are good, but they are not the solution to all problems." Rubin, knowing the markets, was a little queasy about derivatives, wondered if Treasury should do something about them on its own—far more than his deputy Summers, who with typical acerbity would make fun of Rubin for being a fogy who was still playing tennis with a "wooden racket." A year later, in one of his last acts as Treasury secretary, Rubin presided over a report of the President's Working Group on Financial Markets that hesitantly proposed, as a "potential additional step," the "direct regulation of derivatives dealers." Rubin himself would later insist that he'd always wanted leverage to be reduced too. But Rubin never did anything about these worries. The "potential additional step" was never taken.

Ultimately Brooksley Born was driven from office. In the fall of 1998, in the conference committee on that year's agricultural appropriations bill—which settled the CFTC's budget—a provision was mysteriously added, one that had never been discussed before or hadn't been in any of the bills before. No one knew exactly who introduced it, but the language was clear: the CFTC could take no action in the OTC derivatives market for six months. It just so happened that Born's term was up in six months. It had all been orchestrated to quash the concept release and ensure that Born no longer had any say. She was replaced by

Bill Rainer, the cofounder of Greenwich Capital Markets and an old Clinton crony from Arkansas.

Greenwich Capital Markets was later one of Wall Street's biggest bundlers of subprime mortgage-backed securities.

In the ten years after Born's 1998 proposal, the market in derivatives exploded from $27 trillion to one worth more than $600 trillion. By comparison, the entire U.S. economy was worth $14 trillion.

Even when Enron collapsed two years later, in 2001, under the weight of all those energy derivatives that Wendy Gramm had opened the door to, the result was similar. There were hearings. Congress passed a law, the Sarbanes-Oxley Act of 2002, that improved corporate governance. But there were no changes on derivatives. In fact, the rules for derivatives trading were loosened further during the presidency of George W. Bush, a free-market Republican who returned Reaganism to Washington. The amount of leverage that firms could use—the speculative bets they could make—was more than doubled.

But Born had long since gone back to Arnold and Porter, and few people ever spoke her name again. Until several years later, when her worst fears turned out to be crushingly real.

Why did Brooksley Born fail? Certainly, sexism must have played a part. So did the culture clash between Washington and Wall Street. But the main reason Born failed was that she was taking on the impossible: she was trying to turn back the tide of an entire era. She was defying the zeitgeist. She was fighting an idea so powerful, so intoxicating, that ten years later it required the worst crash since the Great Depression to tarnish it. And even then, it wouldn't quite go away. Much of this occurred to me in the fall of 2008, as I watched the financial system come apart and the greatest reputations of our time crash with it. As I listened to a living legend like Greenspan admit, shakily, that the assumptions of his career as an economist had been overturned, I felt that we were witnessing something that people don't often get to see: the end of an identifiable era—the era of free-market fundamentalism.

This book is about how an idea—that what's good for Big Finance is good for America—came to define this era and then spiraled completely out of control. It is about the men (they were almost all men) who made this idea the driving force of our times and lost all sense of proportion about it, to the point where the very notion of regulation and oversight became a kind of heresy. Crucially, they ignored the key differences between financial and other markets, which economists had known about for hundreds of years. Financial markets were always more imperfect than markets for goods and other services, more prone to manias and panics and more susceptible to the pitfalls of imperfect information unequally shared by market players. After the Great Depression, authorities had understood that the financial markets must be more regulated than other markets, not least because they supplied the lifeblood of a capitalist economy: capital. Yet that critical distinction was lost in the whirlwind of fervor that championed free markets and market solutions, especially in the minds of overconfident U.S. policy makers, after the Cold War.

Also lost was any sense of how much finance, when completely unleashed, had come to dominate the economy, rather than serve in its traditional role as a supplier of capital to the "real" economy of goods and services. It was another example of how the free-market fervor simply overreached, with no restraints in place any longer. Through most of the high-tech era of the last part of the twentieth century, the wizards of Wall Street were justifiably proud of the role they had come to play in providing venture capital to entrepreneurs. The ability of a smart person with a smart idea to turn it into a new company and new product in the United States was unmatched in the world. It was the heart of America's strength, and it was thanks in good part to the rollicking open markets on Wall Street.

But somewhere along the line, toward the end of this era—as the zeitgeist hit its peak and government regulators backed off completely— Wall Street became the master of Main Street rather than its handmaiden. Wall Street turned ordinary CEOs into stock watchers worried mainly about the performance of their options, and tied corporate time horizons to the upticks and downticks of the stock market. Venture capitalism transmogrified into speculative fever. Innovative ways of financing new business ideas evolved into vastly complex derivatives deals that added little or nothing to economic growth. During the latter part of the free-market era, for example, speculation in the shadowy derivatives market was permitted to drive up the costs of basic commodities, inflating the price of oil, rice, wheat, and corn despite plentiful supplies that normally would have kept prices low. A frenzy of buying and holding by Wall Street—and by its customers, funds advised to keep

10 percent of their investments in commodities—overwhelmed the physical supply and demand. As a result, in the eight years leading up to the financial crisis, "American consumers and businesses spent $1.5 trillion more on energy than they had to" because of derivatives trading, said Peter Beutel, who put out a widely read newsletter on the energy market.

So dominant and all-consuming was this free-market idea, and so admired were its champions, that it took special people to resist it, individuals of rare intellect, integrity, and courage. You needed a kind of immunity to it, as from a virus, while all around you were infected. Brooksley Born was one of those unusual people. Another was Joseph Stiglitz, the Nobel Prize–winning economist who in some ways was the John Maynard Keynes of his era. Stiglitz had grown up in Gary, Indiana—one of the grittiest industrial cities in the United States—and from the time he was a small boy he had begun to ask questions about why markets didn't work well. Like Keynes, who was ignored when he warned after World War I that the draconian peace imposed on Germany would lead to disaster, Stiglitz stood almost alone against the "Washington Consensus" lorded over by Rubin, Greenspan, and Summers.

A brilliant abstract thinker, Stiglitz sought to use the free marketers' own tools against them. He developed mathematical models that proved, paradoxically, that even if you assume rational human behavior, the economic outcome would often not be rational or reach equilibrium on its own. He showed that small changes in the free marketers' assumptions led to dramatic changes in outcomes, which they could not predict. But for nearly a decade Stiglitz was mocked as an extremist rock thrower and finally, like Brooksley Born, he was driven from the free-market paradise that Washington became. This book will be about him and others, such as Roy Barnes, a banker who became the governor of Georgia. Barnes saw, from the front end, the plague of predatory lending in his state that was driven largely by Wall Street's hunger for mortgages to slice and dice and package as securities. When he tried to halt the practice, he too was crushed by an army of lobbyists that invaded Georgia from Washington. It is a book about Frank Partnoy, a derivatives trader at Morgan Stanley who grew sickened by the kinds of scams he was engaged in and later became a Cassandra-esque crusader for regulatory reform. And it is about men such as Ben Bernanke, the Great Depression scholar and Fed chairman who finally saw the light—just in time to stop another Depression.

It's not as if the people who were the champions of the free-market ideal were bad men. They had their country's best interests at heart. They were, for the most part, outstanding public servants who performed as admirably as they did falteringly, mixing periods of triumph with vast errors of judgment that verge on tragedy, at least in the loss of their reputations. They did not seem to understand, until it was too late, that they were overselling an idea that modern economics had already proven to be fatally flawed: the idea that markets always self-correct, and finance was safe. Alan Greenspan, one of the chief characters of my story, was the most lionized Fed chief in history. Yet he later admitted he didn't understand the market system he had shaped and dominated for eighteen and a half years.

Robert Rubin—one of this new era's best and brightest—performed brilliantly as a crisis manager during the 1997–1998 Asian contagion; yet somehow he could not see or appreciate its deeper causes, just as he would later miss the crisis developing under his nose as a senior counselor at Citigroup in the 2000s. Rubin always had a big heart and a gentle manner: he was a liberal Democrat who, as a young trader at Goldman Sachs, used to show up at New York community meetings on the inner-city poor. Later on he opposed Bill Clinton's welfare "workfare" reform—a much-criticized compromise with the GOP—as too harsh. But he could not bring himself to lay a restraining hand on his former colleagues from Wall Street.

A decade after his star turn as Treasury secretary, as the floodwaters of the subprime disaster lapped at his executive suite high atop the Citigroup building on Manhattan's East Side, Rubin mulled over with me the consequences of what he had wrought. "We have a market-based financial system and yet we have a whole bunch of institutions that are too big or too interconnected to fail," Rubin told me in puzzled tones. "Yet the market-based system is the way to go. How do you reconcile all that? The fundamental theory of the [market] case is premised on the notion that failure or success reap their own rewards. But now that's not happening." Indeed, it remains the central pathology of our times: we have created a free-market system dominated by institutions so huge and systemically important that they no longer have to play by free-market rules. As this book will show, Rubin himself had been one of those who engendered this pathology, but somehow he couldn't own up to any responsibility.

It must also be noted that despite all the mistakes, these architects of the global financial system helped preside over a magnificent period of growth as well as a revolution in world affairs—the end of the Cold War. One of them was Milton Friedman, the great anti-Keynesian economist who is another key figure in this story. Friedman was right about much of what he said and wrote about markets, especially during the period when we were caught up in the great Cold War fight of freedom versus socialism. But he and his acolytes were so sure of themselves that they transformed that wisdom into a false sense of scientific certainty about the functioning of financial markets. Still, after the subprime disaster, one of Friedman's acolytes at the University of Chicago, Gary Becker, pleaded, "Don't kill the goose that laid the golden eggs." According to figures calculated by Becker and his own free-market acolyte at the University of Chicago, Kevin Murphy, from 1980 to 2007 the growth in world gross domestic product (GDP) was about 140 percent. Even if you assumed a depression—a world economy that contracted by 10 percent over the two years after the subprime disaster—"you still ended up with enormous growth, hundreds of millions of people brought out of poverty," Becker said. "So yes, markets are imperfect, but they deliver the lot."

Becker had an important point about a period loosely associated with freer markets. Still, he neglected to mention that the earlier period, from 1945 to 1976, when financial markets were tightly regulated, had shown even more robust global growth. And it was growth that was far more equitable, without the vast gaps in income between poor and rich—especially the financial rich—that marked the free-market era. In the latter stages of the era of free-market absolutism, the question was no longer what Friedman contributed to the triumph of market capitalism; he had clearly played a formidable role. It was whether Friedman and his acolytes had taken things too far. Every revolution tends to overreach. And so did this one.

Free-market absolutism was not a new phenomenon, of course; indeed, it was very similar to the laissez-faire thinking that led to the Depression and made Herbert Hoover such a disaster as president, and which FDR had to address with a Keynesian response (though he himself had little use for Keynes). The 1929 stock market crash had evolved into a terrible decade-long depression in large part because the Fed and Treasury at the time had thought the markets would correct on their own, even as a third of the nation's banks were collapsing. Andrew Mellon's infamous response after the 1929 crash was to allegedly declare: "Liquidate labor, liquidate stocks, liquidate the farmers." Hoover's Treasury secretary earned himself a permanent place in the annals of American villainy with those words. But all Mellon was doing was administering the standard laissez-faire wisdom of the time: allow the market to clear by selling. The problem was, things were probably too far gone for that to happen without a very painful depression. The Depression was the first large-scale demonstration in a modern economy of the economic wisdom that Stiglitz and others would later tease out with their mathematical models: that often, unaided by government, markets fail. It's what Bernanke had learned in his own studies, and why he revolutionized the Fed's lending practices in the space of six months in 2008 and early 2009, tripling its balance sheet to $2 trillion in an effort to keep Wall Street afloat. Bernanke was determined not to go down as the Fed chairman who had allowed a second Great Depression.

But at the height of the market hubris, in the 1990s and 2000s, much of that wisdom had been forgotten. In its modern incarnation, the reign of free-market absolutism began as the Reagan revolution of 1981, which launched a deregulation movement that unmoored much of the economy from government oversight and antitrust laws, creating the wild age of finance with which we've all grown up. From *Barbarians at the Gate* to *Conspiracy of Fools*, it was a decades-long spree of buyouts and swaps and crazy new collateralized instruments no one, in the end, could understand. For nearly twenty-five years, the facts on the ground seemed to bear out the idea that markets may overreach and go up and down, but they are always smarter than governments. The deregulatory 1980s were a boom time. The 1990s were better. The collapse of the Soviet Union in December 1991 seemed to prove, once and for all, the unworkability of "statism" and so-called command economies. Free-market absolutism went from being a mocked, maverick ideology—something identified in the 1960s and 1970s with Barry Goldwater and William F. Buckley—to a kind of national secular religion. It seized control of the national agenda and shifted the axis of the entire economic debate sharply rightward, turning ordinary Republicans into small-government zealots and liberal

Democrats into "Eisenhower Republicans" (that's what Bill Clinton mockingly called himself).

Then the phenomenon went global. Around the world, as well as in Washington and on Wall Street, free-market fervor produced an infectious passion for deregulation, especially in the early 1990s. On the advice of the U.S.-dominated IMF and World Bank, and under the tutelage of young free-marketers, many newly reformed nations began dancing to the tune dictated by the victor of the Cold War. Foreign-exchange controls were lifted worldwide, and in an astonishingly short period of time, a stream of private capital began circling the globe, fed by giant mutual, pension, and hedge funds and freed to roam at will by a worldwide telecommunications and computer network. Pools of globalized capital began moving from country to country, like some ectoplasmic monster, creating bubbles in one economy after another depending on which one looked the most inviting at the time.

The era continued through the Democratic administration of Bill Clinton, a centrist "New Democrat" who resisted the call of the market gospel at first but then succumbed; and finally right up until the final months of George Bush's eight years, when it all flamed out, forcing that conservative president to repudiate the market philosophy more totally than anyone since FDR. And we all came to realize—or should have—that the flaws in capitalism we once blamed on other nations like Mexico or Thailand or Korea lay at the heart of our own financial system and economic model for the world.

But not everyone has understood this even now—and among the most worrisome laggards are Barack Obama's chief policy makers, the architects of the solution, who by no coincidence helped to author the disaster. It is a role that few of them even now can bring themselves to admit. Some of the policy makers of the 1990s and 2000s have had a reckoning with themselves and admitted error. Most others have not. As Arthur Levitt, the SEC chairman who went along with the pillorying of Brooksley Born in 1998, told me ten years later: "All tragedies in life are always proceeded by warnings. We had a warning. It was from Brooksley Born. We didn't listen." Soon afterward, having heard about such comments, Larry Summers privately remonstrated with Levitt, telling him he shouldn't concede that Born was right.

That is the grave danger going forward. Wall Street is resurrecting itself. But it is too much the same old Wall Street, with too much of the same sense of certainty and too little concern, even now, about the impact it is having on society at large. In Washington, meanwhile, most economic thinkers continue to view the recovery of the stock market as the best measure of the health of the economy.

The subprime mortgage securitization scandal and the global crisis of capitalism that followed it had many proximate causes: a long period of loose credit orchestrated by the Federal Reserve; the "mega-expansion" of the financial sector, as Kevin Phillips called it, in which capital flows dwarfed trade flows; the vast power of the Wall Street and banking lobby in Washington, the extraordinary imbalance in global capital flows that "rained" money on Americans in the 1990s from places like East Asia and the Middle East, among other things. The explosion in derivatives trading connected up all these trends—making the ultimate failure a global one—and raised the stakes, because all these firms were using derivatives to double and triple down on their betting. But all these things are still only symptoms.

The main reason the catastrophe occurred is that the people in charge of our economy, otherwise intelligent and capable men like Greenspan, Rubin, and Summers—and later Hank Paulson and Tim Geithner—permitted themselves to believe, in the face of a rising tide of contrary evidence, that markets are for the most part efficient and work well on their own. Summers, for example, after the 1987 stock market crash, had written that it was impossible to believe any longer that prices moved in rational response to fundamentals. He even advocated a tax on financial transactions. Yet Summers, one of the world's most astute economists, later abandoned these positions in favor of Greenspan's view that markets will take care of themselves. How could such a powerful intellect continue to believe and advocate this view, despite the plentiful accumulating evidence that the "efficient market hypothesis" did not hold up, including *his own work*? Mainly because the near-religious attachment to free-market absolutism had become a ruling principle that no single senior official in Washington dared to contradict—especially if he was politically ambitious—with a few lone exceptions like Brooksley Born.

As John Maynard Keynes wrote, it is "the gradual encroachment of ideas" that matters in the end far more than vested interests; it is ideas that "are dangerous for good or evil." The Wall Street lobby could not have transformed Washington—and the economy—without the *idea* of free-market fundamentalism behind it. This book tells the history of how this idea took hold and very nearly brought down the global economy with it, along with what remained of America's global reputation as a beacon and a model. It is also about how, unless more fundamental rethinking of capitalism occurs, this could all happen again, sooner than you think.

1

The Most Certain Man in the World

There is a pecking order to history. Only the most influential figures merit an "age" all their own, for better or for worse. One thinks of the Age of Jefferson, or the Age of Augustus. So it was noteworthy when in 2009 Andrei Shleifer—considered one of the best economists of his own generation—published an essay calling the quarter century from 1980 to 2005 "the Age of Milton Friedman." Shleifer, a Russian-born, Harvard-educated wunderkind, described this period as one defined by the "acceptance of free market policies in both rich and poor countries" thanks in large part to the influence of Friedman. The biggest political figures of the age had themselves taken guidance from the great University of Chicago economist, Shleifer said. "Three important events mark the beginning of this period. In 1979, Deng Xiao Ping started market reforms in China, which over the quarter century lifted hundreds of millions of people out of poverty. In the same year, Margaret Thatcher was elected Prime Minister in Britain, and initiated her radical reforms and a long period of growth. A year later, Ronald Reagan was elected President of the United States and also embraced free-market policies. All three of these leaders professed inspiration from the work of Milton Friedman."

Shleifer was only echoing what his own mentor at Harvard, Larry Summers, had written a few years before upon Friedman's death at the age of ninety-four in November 2006. Summers wrote that Friedman's influence cut across all political lines, and it was not just theoretical but concrete. Friedman had opened up finance and currency trading. His ideas about freeing up markets had become almost a sacred totem for the Wall Street financiers who commanded ultimate moral authority in the global economy, and for the Washington policy makers who had promoted deregulation not just as a policy choice but as an economic necessity. "Any honest Democrat will admit that we are now all Friedmanites," Summers said, giving an ironic twist to the statement made nearly two generation's earlier by a Republican president, Richard Nixon, who had declared in 1971: "I am a Keynesian now." In the ensuing three decades, Friedman not only knocked the great John Maynard Keynes from his pedestal, but, Summers said, "he had more influence on economic policy as it is practiced around the world today than any other modern figure."

He certainly didn't fit anyone's idea of a revolutionary. He had started out wanting to be an insurance actuary. Tiny, bespectacled, and balding, Milton Friedman would have looked more at home in an anonymous office cubicle somewhere—an obscure worker bee in the vast hive of U.S. capitalism—than on the world stage. But that was just the point: Friedman's personal story embodied the American Dream that was the mainspring of all his economic thinking. He was the nobody from nowhere who on pure merit, left unencumbered by government meddling, became somebody. *Two Lucky People*, he and his beloved wife, Rose, titled their memoirs, and they believed it.

Born in Brooklyn, New York, raised in Rahway, New Jersey, and schooled at Rutgers University—where he matriculated at age sixteen—Friedman knew early on that he had an extraordinary talent for math. As a young man the only "paying occupation" he'd heard about that used mathematics was actuarial work and so, always practical, Friedman set about mastering the statistics of life and death. ("The most difficult exams I have ever taken," he said later.) But as word of his brilliance spread on campus—one year Friedman tutored so many students that he ended up running his own summer school—he caught the attention of Arthur F. Burns, later to become one of the nation's most eminent economists and chairman of the Federal Reserve. Burns was then teaching at Rutgers while finishing his doctoral dissertation at Columbia University.

Friedman had lost his own father at fourteen, and Burns became a surrogate dad to him and a role model. Burns, too, was the son of Austro-Hungarian Jewish immigrants who was determined to make good and did—living proof of the "human potential that a free society can release," Friedman later said. It wasn't long before young Milton switched his major from math to economics.

Economics would never be the same.

The next seventy years of his life were one long war, during which he won many intellectual battles. He became as famous for the manner in which he won them as for winning them. Even when he was in the minority—as he was for most of his long life—no one could out-argue Milton. "In a debate he could destroy pretty much anybody," recalled Gary Becker, Friedman's former student at the University of Chicago. "He was very quick and very insightful. He would restate a person's argument better than they had and then destroy it." Friedman's great friend, George Shultz, said that during the Reagan administration, one of the president's top aides, Bryce Harlow, used to insist that Friedman not be left alone in the room with the president "because he was just too persuasive. The saying is everybody loves to argue with Milton—particularly when he isn't there." Later, after Friedman won his Nobel Prize, George Stigler, a fellow free-market Nobelist and his dearest friend, told an audience at an event honoring him: "If Milton Friedman comes to you and says, 'Look, agree with me that night follows day. Or that two dollars is better than one dollar.' Don't do it. Don't agree with him. If you do, he'll inexorably lead to you to the conclusion that you'll have to do away with the Federal Reserve."

He was only five-foot-three, but his size never seemed to matter once he began to speak. "He had a certain kind of charisma that's hard to find in a man who's that short," said the much taller Robert Solow, his fellow Nobel Prize winner and longtime intellectual adversary. Miltonian battles were epic and memorable. To win an argument, Friedman would sometimes physically pursue a quarry across the room. At one faculty dinner party, Friedman began a heated discussion with Sidney Verba, a University of Chicago political scientist. Friedman was arguing that students protesting Vietnam were doing it only because they were "incentivized" by their fear of the military draft. Verba, a self-described "knee-jerk liberal," was outraged by the slur on the antiwar movement. He sought to leave the party in a huff, but Friedman—who remained spry and agile well into old age—cut Verba off by darting between several people and vaulting over a couch, drink in hand, as one witness described it. (Verba, asked about the incident four decades later, said he couldn't remember Friedman's acrobatics, but he did recall the argument and had since come to think that maybe Friedman was right: "Recently as I've watched on campus the reaction to the Iraq war, which was fought by a volunteer army, it made me think he had more of a case," he said in 2009.)

In the end, Friedman was the tiny engine of certainty who changed more minds than anyone else. He won his audiences over by turning the negative imagery about capitalism on its head. Whatever you thought was bad was probably good, Friedman said. He glorified the robber-baron era of the late nineteenth century, telling *Newsweek* readers in his regular column in 1976 that "there is probably no other period in history, in this or any other country, in which the ordinary man had as large an increase in his standard of living as in the period between the Civil War and the First World War, when unrestrained individualism was most rugged." He romanticized the struggle of his mother as a young girl in a Lower East Side sweatshop in the late 1890s, when New York was crowded with European Jews, describing it as a great place for an immigrant "to get started" because there was "no red tape."

"They're not going to stay here very long," the smiling Friedman declared to the camera in January 1980 in the opening sequence of his popular PBS series, *Free to Choose*, standing in a Chinatown sweatshop to evoke his fourteen-year-old mother's milieu ninety years before. "On the contrary they and their children will make a better life for themselves as they take advantage of the opportunities that a free market offers to them." He so identified himself in his thinking and work as a fortunate son of Hungarian immigrants that many decades later, at a luncheon honoring him at the White House, George W. Bush would sound the same note about Milton's mother and say how lucky America was that the elder Friedmans decided to get on that boat.

Friedman was the great nexus who dominated and changed the field of economics and then crossed over into American politics and changed that too—never ceasing to argue and fight even after his free-market ideas had gone from the margins to the mainstream. Among his many converts were such dominant figures of the free-market era as Phil and Wendy Gramm, Alan Greenspan, and Ben Bernanke, who has said that reading Friedman's and Anna Schwartz's *Monetary History of the United*

States "hooked" him on monetary economics when he was an MIT student. And, of course, Friedman later became Ronald Reagan's "guru," in the words of Reagan's loyal aide and attorney general, Ed Meese.

Friedman didn't gain his influence by ingratiating himself with those in power. He turned down all efforts to bring him to Washington in an official capacity. Above all what gave Friedman his sense of certainty was his conviction that the success of capitalism was a *moral* question as much as an economic one. Free markets were the only way to get people to cooperate in civilized fashion, without force, he said. One irony of Friedman's reputation as an unfeeling right-winger, especially in the 1960s, is that there was no one closer in spirit to the hippies who lived by the dictum, "question authority." Occasionally, there were moments when his liberal opponents realized he couldn't be fit into a conservative pigeonhole. Friedman relished telling the story of the liberal professor who began to quote derisively from Friedman's best-selling book, *Capitalism and Freedom*, to a crowd of students in the 1960s. Gradually the professor came to realize, when he got to a section about Friedman's support for a volunteer army, that the economist's ideas were winning the kids over. (Friedman also believed in legalizing drugs, or at least marijuana.)

Friedman was always consistent, and his unwavering beliefs in the free market led him to some maverick conclusions. His old friend Leo Melamed, the head of the Chicago Mercantile Exchange, recalled a scene toward the end of Friedman's life when Melamed had invited Milton to his house in Arizona: "He said, 'Let me see your Web site.' I said, 'I don't have a Web site.' He said, 'You've got to have a Web site! I want to read all those remarks, all those essays you do. Put them out there.' I said, 'I don't want to, I'm gonna be plagiarized all over the place.' He smiled and said, 'Of course. That's the idea. Then your ideas will be working. Plagiarism is good.' *Your ideas will be working.* It never dawned on me." (Melamed's Web site eventually featured a remarkable plethora of his speeches and observations, including a long account of his relationship with Milton Friedman.)

You can't have too much freedom, too much openness. It was the fundament of all his thinking, and it was simple enough for a child to understand. There were no philosopher-kings in history, he believed, so let's not pretend there are. Probably even Plato didn't really buy into all that nonsense (he was disappointed when he tried to train them). Indeed, beneath the math and the equations, a great deal of Milton Friedman's certainty sprang from common sense. He argued that politicians were as selfish and greedy as anyone else—maybe more so, since they were people who usually sought out power. So why in the world would you trust them with your lives and fortunes? "When a man spends his own money to buy something for himself, he is very careful how much he spends and how he spends it," he told guests many years later at his ninetieth birthday luncheon at the White House, summing up his life's philosophy. "When a man spends someone else's money on someone else, he doesn't care how much he spends or what he spends it on. And that's government for you."

Friedman, with that ungodly confidence, didn't care whom he offended in preaching his gospel. After Richard Nixon imposed wage and price controls in 1971, Friedman happened to be at the White House with George Shultz, who was then treasury secretary. Nixon, with his usual awkward humor, joshed to Friedman, "Now don't blame George for this." Friedman said, "I don't blame George, Mr. President, I blame you," dumbfounding Nixon, to whom the imperial presidency was a real thing. If government had to be around, Friedman wanted it to fail. Better that than to have it mildly ameliorate some situation and fool people into another misbegotten cycle of Keynesian government intervention setting them all back decades. Donald Rumsfeld recalled that when he was an assistant to the president under Nixon, he was placed in charge of administering phase two of the controls, even though he didn't believe in them. Shultz, who was also appalled by the controls, thought he was outsmarting Nixon. Rumsfeld, he knew, would do his best to undermine the new policy, and so he did, granting exemptions from the controls for small businesses, food industries, and so on. "I was kind of proud of the job we were doing, because we were doing as little damage as possible," Rumsfeld said. "Some time later I received an irate call from Milton saying, 'Stop giving exemptions. The more you do, the more the public will think controls worked instead of being an absurd idea.'"

He was Milton the subversive, always mistrustful of Washington in all its bureaucratic, vested-interest glory. To some degree, it was Friedman who engendered the enduring obsession of the Right with wanting government to fail. This was somewhat ironic, considering that he found his first employment in Washington in the hard-up 1930s. But Friedman always said the worst mistake he ever made was inventing the idea of the withholding tax when he worked for the Treasury Department during World War II. The tax was supposed to be temporary, a way to pay for the expense of the war. For Milton, it was an early and enduring lesson in how hard, if not impossible, it is to undo government programs once they're done. Gridlock was the best thing that could happen to Washington, he would say; the ideal combination was a Democratic president and a Republican Congress. "I say thank God for government waste," he would say. "If government is doing bad things, it's only the waste that prevents the harm from being greater." In an interview four years before he died in 2006, Friedman told me that the Nixon administration was "the most collectivist administration of the postwar period" because "it doubled the number of pages in the federal register."

"That's the real measure of government involvement," he said. "Deficits are irrelevant from my point of view. That has to do with the form taxation takes."

It was all about the size of government.

For most of those years of the Cold War, he remained the leader of a maverick insurgency, isolated and condemned even on the Chicago campus as the 1960s counterculture grew. There were times when no one would eat with him in the faculty dining room. At the campus bookstore Friedman's works were on a bottom shelf, far out of view of the Marx and Lenin posters on the walls. When he gave talks at other colleges, he would sometimes go in through the kitchen, the better to avoid protesters. Even to some who admired him, he was something of an oddity. "I had to see for myself what that black magician from the Middle West was like," one Harvard graduate student announced to him upon arriving in Chicago. It was a lonely time. Chicago graduate students couldn't even get placed, except at lesser schools. "We were on the outs, the East Coast and West Coast basically had no use for them," said Gary Becker. "Columbia was the exception; they were broadminded about it. But Harvard, MIT, Stanford, Berkeley, Yale, they were very hostile to all these types of ideas. We were considered extremists."

The long years in the ideological wilderness took their toll. Friedman never forgot the snubs. "You have no idea of the climate of opinion in 1945 to 1960 or 1970," he later told author Alan Ebenstein. *Capitalism and Freedom* "was not reviewed by any U.S. publications, other than the *American Economic Review*. It's inconceivable that at the time—I was a full professor at the University of Chicago, I was very well known in the academic world—a book on the other side by someone in that same position would not have been reviewed in every publication, the *New York Times*, the *Chicago Tribune*." Friedman grew so concerned about the stigma attached to his name in those years that he and his wife insisted that their son, David, a brilliant Harvard student who wanted to follow his parents into economics, study physics instead, so that he wouldn't suffer the same isolation as the son of Milton Friedman. It was a supreme irony for a man who despised paternalism in government that he was, in the end, something of an overbearing if loving father. As his coauthor Anna Schwartz recalled it years later, "The son never really got over the damage they did to his future. He wanted to be an economist and they said no, you be a physicist. And he got his Ph.D. in physics. But he never wanted to do anything with it. And because he didn't have a Ph.D. in economics it was hard for him to get a job to teach. Because an economics department doesn't want to say we have a physicist." David Friedman ended up teaching law at little Santa Clara University and rebelling rightward: he became an "anarcho-capitalist" with even more extreme libertarian views than his father.

But Milton Friedman turned out to be correct about a great many things, and eventually history started going his way.

Arguments about economics seem arcane, but they never change much. They are usually between those who advocate government intervention, on one hand, and those who argue that free markets operate better on their own, without government. Boiled down even further, these arguments are largely about the issue of human rationality versus irrationality. One side holds that markets are basically rational and efficient on their own—that they are an optimal way for societies to allocate resources—and governments only interfere. The other side holds that markets and the people who make them up often behave irrationally, inefficiently, and unjustly, and therefore the best course is to keep government involved at all times. In the most extreme interpretation of this view, put forward in the theories of Karl Marx and Soviet-style communism, this way of thinking led to the conclusion that markets left alone produce only social injustice, that "capitalists" always exploit "workers." Therefore it was better to have Kremlin apparatchiks at a

THE MOST CERTAIN MAN IN THE WORLD

"Gosplan," or government bureaucracy, organizing society's resources "scientifically."

Milton Friedman spent the twentieth century as the point man on one side of this long-running argument. The ghost of John Maynard Keynes was the other.

Most of what we now consider economic wisdom is the result of an end-less series of arguments and counterarguments, lasting several hundred years, around this question of human rationality in the marketplace. The Scottish-born founder of modern economics, Adam Smith, famously launched the rationalist idea in the late eighteenth century. In *The Wealth of Nations*, published in 1776, Smith wrote that the rational self-interest of the millions of individuals who engaged in markets turned a seeming chaos into social order. The process by which these individuals bargained and haggled over prices ended up placing a rational and fair value on goods and services for all. Society as a whole was thus led to greater prosperity and peacefulness as if "by an invisible hand" (though Smith had far more caveats about the dire effect of monopolies and other free-market ills than he's often given credit for). A hundred years after Smith, the French economist Leon Walras and his succes-sors began refining the idea of a free-market system, developing ever more elaborate theories of how markets operate rationally. They argued that markets reach "equilibrium" on their own, in which supply and demand come into balance, and society's needs are thus addressed in an optimal way.

But markets kept misbehaving and breaking down, leading to repeated crises; perhaps the worst of all of these was the Great Depression. As a result, 150 years after Smith there arose a counter-revolution in economics led by another brilliant Briton, John Maynard Keynes. A colorful polymath, Keynes did not dispute the idea that market-driven economies were vastly superior to Soviet-style "com-mand" economies. But living in a time of confusion and self-doubt about capitalism, Keynes argued that the irrational elements of human behavior—what he called "animal spirits," as seen in the mania and panic of financial markets—would continue to upset markets and cause them to behave badly. Having watched how savings had been used for stock speculation rather than sober investment during the roaring

1920s, Keynes was especially leery of the way Wall Street worked. That meant there was a need for constant government intervention.

Keynes also argued that markets often don't rationally self-correct themselves or automatically revert to equilibrium, as the free-market types believe. Instead, economies can sometimes get stuck in a recession or depression for a long period, contrary to *everyone's* self-interest. This happens if people respond to an economic slowdown by saving more of their money and spending less of it, and businesses produce less in response. Keynes called it the "paradox of thrift." The more that people respond to a recession by doing what seems to be the responsible and *rational* thing—spending less of their earnings and saving more of it—the worse they make the recession. That's because the less people spend, the less businesses invest; the less businesses invest, the less money they will have to hire or pay employees; the less money the employees have, the less they are willing to spend on buying things. And so the recession spirals downward in a vicious cycle, leaving everyone with less wealth. All these insights supplied intellectual heft to the Keynesian idea that government must jump in at such moments and stimulate the economy itself with spending, as well as to adjust interest rates and tax progressively. Keynes was, in effect, trying to save capitalism from itself; he wanted to "cure the disease" of terrible and socially destabilizing unemployment while "preserving efficiency and freedom," he wrote. But Keynes's critique also gave a new allure to socialism, which not coincidentally reached its height of popularity in the United States in the 1930s. (Keynes himself, while he never went completely pink, was a member of the Fabian Society who hung out with the Bloomsbury crowd, socialists all.)

For decades afterward, Keynesian thinking about government intervention came to dominate policy making. Washington's fiscal bureaucrats sought to tend to the economy like janitors puttering over a cranky boiler, one that often behaved irrationally but still functioned most of the time. Keynes and his followers, writing and thinking at a time when it seemed that market failure might be a permanent condition, believed that enlightened policy makers could thus "fine-tune" the whole contraption, throwing in a fiscal stimulus when recession loomed, and removing it when the economy heated up again. If you poured enough inflation in at one end, they thought, unemployment would go down at the other, and vice versa.

But beginning in the 1950s, Friedman began to raise major questions about this idea and to point the way back to the classical view of man as a rational actor and markets that function well on their own, without all that bureaucratic tinkering. At the time he began his journey to laissez-faire thinking, Friedman was still playing the field in economics, finding merit in both sides of the argument. As a sixteen-year-old freshman at Rutgers, he had devoured John Stuart Mill's *On Liberty* and had become entranced with Mill's idea that government's role should be limited to preventing citizens from harming each other. But he was mostly interested in following where the data led, and he actually liked some of Franklin Roosevelt's jobs programs during the Depression. In fact, he was "thoroughly" a Keynesian at the time, Friedman later wrote. On a personal level, the New Deal was "a life saver . . . the new government program created a boom market for economists." His brother-in-law, Aaron Director, a passionate libertarian even back then, kidded his sister Rose after she and Milton announced their engagement in 1937 that he wouldn't hold Friedman's "very strong New Deal leanings . . . against him."

Friedman came upon his new role as a market champion almost by accident. After World War II, he was working at the National Bureau of Economic Research, on one of several teams assigned to study business cycles. The task of Friedman and his study partner, Anna Jacobson Schwartz, was to study the role of money in the economy. "He wasn't even a market person until he became a monetarist," Schwartz recalled. The focus of economic thinking at the time was fiscal—in other words, what can government do by spending? To their astonishment, Friedman and Schwartz's research showed that economic rises and declines were closely linked to the amount of money supply. This was a huge revelation at the time because of the settled view that government could make a difference. "You had to confront the fact that the whole direction of economic thinking at the time . . . was about what the government was doing," said Schwartz. "And he was influenced by the current trends and thought of his associates. But once he was convinced that money was a central variable in what everyone was trying to explain in the way of not only business cycles but the ordinary operation of the economy, he changed his views."

More than that, he invented a new theory of economics: monetarism. Monetarism holds that the supply of money in the economy at any given time is the primary driver of prosperity and recession, and that Keynesian fiscal spending doesn't work. Government should therefore stay out of the way, other than to adjust the money supply. Like Keynesianism, monetarism was an idea that sprang directly out of the Depression. To a striking degree, most of the policy options we now discuss without even thinking about them—deficit spending, monetary policy, the role of the Fed, government intervention in general—come from what economists learned by examining that period. It was thanks to the Depression that Keynes created macroeconomics. And it was in response to the Depression that Friedman developed his theory of monetarism, rebutting Keynes. He and Schwartz, in their monumental *Monetary History*, argued that the Fed dramatically deepened the Depression by tightening money supply when it should have been doing the opposite.

Equipped with all these radical new ideas and an indomitable sense that he was right, Friedman began chipping away at Keynes. He developed a theory of a "permanent income hypothesis," which held that people made decisions about how to spend based on their rational perception of long-term income, not temporary disposable income. Later, in a famous speech in 1967 to the American Economic Association, he attacked the Phillips Curve, which had been in vogue for nearly a decade since the New Zealand–born economist A. W. Phillips theorized that there was a permanent trade-off between unemployment and inflation. When unemployment went up, inflation would go down, and vice versa. Friedman argued that over time people would build expectations of future inflation into their decisions—again, *rationally*. Workers would demand higher wages, and business owners, rather than hiring new workers, would sit tight. That would nullify any positive effects of inflationary policy on employment. Here again Friedman was moving away from the bleak, pathological view of markets held by Keynes and back into the sunlight of reason shed by Adam Smith. He was restoring economics to its default position, assuming that people will act rationally in the end and it's best just to leave them be.

In time he came to be seen as a prophet. At the generous suggestion of *Newsweek* columnist Paul Samuelson, the great postwar Keynesian economist, the magazine offered Friedman a regular column in 1966 in order to balance out Samuelson's views. In just his second column for the magazine, Friedman warned that year of an "inflationary recession" to come, even though he acknowledged that it sounded like a "contradiction in terms." It was the first foretaste of what was to become known as "stagflation," a condition of both high unemployment and inflation. Friedman was proved right, at least for the short term, and people began to pay attention.

In the late 1970s, the great Vietnam-era inflation, compounded of exorbitant spending on the war and Great Society–type government programs, left the economy mired in stagflation, with inflation rates of up to 15 percent and high unemployment. The double plague of inflation and unemployment seemed to undermine the Keynesian-style belief that the two problems neatly trade off with each other, and therefore can be managed by government policy makers. Keynes, or at least his policy-making acolytes, had misunderstood how hard it would be for politicians to eliminate such government spending programs once they were put into place, and how businesses and consumers would anticipate and work against such moves. These flaws contributed to the ever growing deficits and rising inflation, and this seemed to vindicate the Friedmanites.

The "supply shock" of the 1973 Arab oil embargo also "caught the Keynesian side of things with its pants down," said Robert Solow. Keynes had only addressed "demand"-side disturbances—what happens when there's a broad-based collapse of demand, as there was during the Depression. "Here was something entirely new," said Solow. "Inflation arising without any pull from the demand side. No one knew quite how to deal with that." Friedman leaped into the gap. The forty years of Democratic dominance in Washington, which had begun under Franklin Roosevelt as a revolutionary corrective to laissez-faire capitalism after the Depression, had clearly overreached. It was Friedman and his acolytes who, more than any other postwar economists, were responsible for putting John Maynard Keynes in the doghouse with policy makers, debunking the problems of statism and "countercyclical" intervention.

In truth, Friedman and his school were in some ways attacking a straw man. They were taking on what a then relatively unknown contemporary of Friedman's, a passionate devotee of Keynes named Hyman Minsky, called "bastard Keynesianism." Keynes himself had allowed this to happen to some degree, by leaving behind a series of vague observations and colorful sayings that summed up his views about government intervention without offering any overarching theory of it. His most remembered aphorism was, "In the long run we're all dead." In other words, yes, in the long run the market may well recover on its own, but we really don't know how long that will take. The long run is too unpredictable, too uncertain to worry about. And why go through the terrible suffering this will entail if the government can help in the meantime?

By contrast, Friedman's sense of the rationality of markets fed his sense of certainty about the system as a whole. And certainty had become necessary: the Cold War period was an absolutist death struggle between the ideas of freedom and communism, between capitalism and "command" economies.

Friedman relished every moment of it, of course. Seeing this as a battle royal for the nation's hearts and minds, he began to use the black-and-white rhetoric that has characterized American political campaigns going back to Adams and Jefferson. As his friend Stigler once said, "Milton wants to change the world. I only want to understand it." Friedman's political influence first surfaced in the early 1960s, when Barry Goldwater, leading his insurgent campaign to take over the GOP from the right, began to listen closely to him. Friedman's best-selling 1962 book, *Capitalism and Freedom*, advocated free-market solutions to schooling and medicine (even opposing the licensing of surgeons). "He was a libertarian to the point of nuttiness," said Samuelson, his Keynesian opponent. "I stayed on good terms with Milton for more than sixty years. But I didn't do it by telling him exactly everything I thought about him."

But grand economic movements are like nothing so much as religious movements, as the Nobel Prize–winning economist and columnist Paul Krugman later wrote. There's little room for subtlety in the heat of the battle. Keynes had led the reformation against the excesses of laissez-faire; Friedman led the counterreformation. It was all so exhilarating, and Friedman was the happy warrior. "The guy changed the world and did it with a smile," his old friend Charles Brunie said. In 1947, Friedman and his friend Stigler attended the inaugural session of the Mont Pelerin Society, founded by Friedrich Hayek to promote classic "liberalism" or laissez-faire views. At one point, Friedman recalled to Brunie, the tetchy Austrian economist Ludwig von Mises erupted at the group when the discussion took a turn toward discussing a reasonable role for government, saying, "You're all a bunch of socialists," before stalking out. "I realized then that you've got to get along with people," Friedman said.

He could be surprisingly gentle with ignorance. One time Friedman was at a cocktail party in New York. The next morning he was scheduled to appear at a "social investor" conference to debate James Tobin, the Nobel Prize–winning Keynesian who had proposed what came to be known as a "Tobin tax" on international currency transactions as a way of curbing "hot money." At the party a young man sought to challenge him on a financial question, and Brunie remembered how gracious Friedman was to him. The next morning Tobin asked the same question. "Milton went after Tobin like his fingers were around his throat," Brunie recalled. "I said, Milton, on that same question you were so polite to the young man. 'The young man didn't know what he was talking about,' he replied. 'Tobin knew it was an ambush question.'" "He had no guile," recalled Leo Melamed. "He would talk to a high school student with as much deference as he would to the president. He used language that everyone understood."

By the late Cold War period, Friedman's influence had helped to create an ideological divide in academia that no other discipline could claim to match. The field had split into what one economist in 1976 dubbed "freshwater" and "saltwater" economists. The freshwater economists were the market purists—the believers in market rationality—who tended to work at inland universities near the Great Lakes, starting of course with Chicago. The saltwater types kept their Keynesian skepticism about the functioning of markets; they tended to flourish in such seaboard universities as MIT, Harvard, Berkeley, and Stanford.

But in the post–Cold War period, saltwater thinking became much more freshwater. Various groups of economists who called themselves "neo-Keynesians" and "New Keynesians"— the latter, more recent group included Gregory Mankiw, later to be George W. Bush's chief economic adviser—developed a synthesis of views in which they conceded that theoretically, markets could break down during recessions. But most of them accepted the view that the economy should be left alone and financial markets were efficient. Keynes had, again, left this latter area of theory vague—though empirically he argued that financial markets act irrationally. That meant that even Keynesian economists had no "model" to explain how finance worked other than the rationalist one. Not surprisingly, rationalist views of the financial markets began to take over the entire policy-making arena, helped by a great deal of Wall Street lobbying. So in their zeal to keep up the fight, Friedman and his Chicago school sought to justify market solutions on all fronts, especially financial markets. Chicago school thinking provided the template for the rambunctious Chicago trading pits. "We are free-market fanatics," said Merton Miller, who won the Nobel Prize in 1990 for the work he and economist Franco Modigliani had prepared on the principles of leverage and the cost of capital. "I always say the Board of Trade practices what we preach." Not surprisingly, Miller later became a champion of unrestricted derivatives trade, and he pooh-poohed the idea of systemic risk, "the fear that a failure by one big bank will bring down another big bank which will bring down another until the world's whole financial system melts down in some cataclysmic Chernobyl. That can happen of course, but it's most unlikely." Miller argued that the global banks were "all very heavily capitalized, highly diversified in their portfolios, thanks in part to derivatives."

Friedman himself never bought into some of the more extreme versions of rational-markets theory that his own school spawned. But it was he, of course, who pushed to expand financial markets into ever newer areas. While he reshaped economics and advised presidents, this may end up being his most lasting legacy: turning the efficacy of capitalism on paper into a world of private financiers overseeing the economy.

Around 1970, Friedman wanted to bet on his negative view of the British welfare system by shorting the pound, but his banker laughed at the request to broker a transaction, according to Merton Miller: "Milton got very indignant, and he wrote a letter to some newspapers asking, 'Why is it that an American citizen can't sell the pound short?' Leo Melamed of the Chicago Mercantile Exchange saw the letter and said he had been thinking along the same lines."

Melamed idolized Friedman. A feisty immigrant from Lithuania who escaped the Nazis to become a great Chicago commodities trader, Melamed would even sneak into Friedman's lectures at the university to hear him expound on the glories of the free market. Melamed noticed that Friedman's name was popping in the news all the time in those years, as the author of essays in the *Wall Street Journal* and other publications against the Bretton Woods system. Friedman argued it couldn't continue, the United States couldn't continue to keep the gold window open. "It was like the match that lit in my being," Melamed recalled.

Friedman turned out to be right. The United States would no longer make good other nations' demands for gold in exchange for dollars—the heart of the fixed exchange rate system that had been set up after World War II to restabilize the global financial system. On August 15, 1971, President Nixon canceled the Bretton Woods Agreement and dropped the U.S. dollar convertibility to gold. (Friedman, of course, had advised him to do that from the beginning.) For Melamed, that was his opportunity to seize on an idea that he'd been thinking about almost from the time he was a boy, and which Friedman's commentary had inspired him to believe might be possible: a new market for foreign currency trading where the Chicago Mercantile Exchange would be the hub.

But Melamed felt out of his depth; he needed validation. This was going way beyond wheat and pork bellies, the traditional fare of the Chicago pits. He recalled:

> How could I, a lawyer turned trader cum financial innovator, really be certain that foreign currency instruments could succeed within the strictures designed for soybeans and eggs? Perhaps there was some fundamental economic reason why no one had before successfully applied financial instruments to futures. Indeed, on the eve of our currency launch, a prominent New York banker stated: "It's ludicrous to think that foreign exchange can be entrusted to a bunch of pork belly crapshooters." The good and great of Wall Street predicted that global banks wouldn't make much use of futures markets—and certainly not in Chicago. That was the habitat of Al Capone. Matters of finance belonged in the holy centers of finance—London and New York.

So Melamed approached Friedman, who by then was to Chicago traders a hero. He set up a meeting with Friedman, who was at his vacation home in Vermont, in the fall of 1971. Friedman came to New York and they met at the Waldorf-Astoria hotel for lunch. As Melamed colorfully told the story:

> I began by asking that he promise not to laugh. (At the time I had no understanding of what Alan Greenspan has described as Milton Friedman's utter disregard to status.) I held my breath as I put forth the idea of a futures market in foreign currency. "It's a

wonderful idea," he said emphatically. "You must do it!" Elated, I pursued, "Is there any reason foreign currency might not work in futures markets?" "None I can think of," he replied.

For a moment his words hung in the air. When my voice returned, I said, "No one will believe you said that."

Milton chuckled. "Sure they will."

"No," I boldly said. "I need it in writing."

He smiled. "Are you suggesting that I write a paper on the need for a futures currency market?"

I nodded.

"You know I am a capitalist?" Milton ventured.

We shook hands and settled on the amount of $7,500 for a feasibility study on "The Need for a Futures Market in Currencies."

The only question was convincing his board of directors. Using Friedman's paper, he did. Melamed later said the Friedman paper was crucial to selling the idea across the country and the globe. "It was magical," he wrote on his blog. "When we said the International Money Market was a great idea, the world yawned or laughed. When we told them Milton Friedman said so, the world took notice. When we were told fixed exchange rates were coming back, we responded, 'Friedman said they are not!' When we were told Chicago is the wrong place, we responded, 'Friedman is a Chicagoan!' When we were told that we were crazy, we responded, 'Friedman is one of us!' And each and every time, his name made the difference!" Melamed finally went to see George P. Shultz, who had just been appointed secretary of the Treasury. Shultz listened to his explanation, smiled, and with a wave of the hand said, "Listen, Mr. Melamed. If it's good enough for Milton, it is good enough for me." And so was born the financial futures market.

Yet after all that effort, Friedman turned out to be a "terrible trader," Melamed recalled.

The Canadian dollar was of great interest to Milton. Pierre Trudeau, a leftist, had just been elected prime minister. He thought Trudeau was going to bring down the Canadian economy. I had a trading firm and he called me up. "I want to go short the Canadian dollar," he said. So I looked into it. The Canadian dollar was in a bull market, it was on its way up from the 90s. I called him back and said, "You know there's a bull market. I don't see any reason to go short." He said, "I know what Trudeau is going to do. He's going to destroy Canada. How do I go short?" I don't remember how many contracts he sold. And we went short for him. The Canadian dollar continued to go up. When it reached 102, he called me up and said, "Get me out." About six months later, when it was making a top, I called him up and said I think it's topping out at 105, maybe you should think about going short. Friedman barked: "Don't talk to me about the Canadian dollar!" But in the end he was dead right. Eventually it went way down to 70 cents. He saw the truth of the economics that would unfold eventually. But his timing was terrible.

It was a movement, and it was catching. Friedman was a pragmatist and an empiricist. In the realm of pure economics, he was always careful. He knew markets were not perfectly rational. Practically, however, he said it didn't matter: the assumption of rationality in human behavior was still the best way of developing models about how economies performed. Starting from that assumption, others took his ideas beyond where he really wanted to go.

Robert Lucas, the inventor of the theory of "rational expectations"—the idea that rational market actors always anticipate government fiscal moves, rendering them useless—said that Friedman's courses on price theory at Chicago "changed my whole way of looking at economics and social science." Whereas Friedman only talked of a temporary trade-off between unemployment and inflation, Lucas later on propounded the idea that there was none at all: the populace was so rational it would anticipate all changes in economic policy, so there was no point to any. Friedman himself thought rational expectations were "bunk," Anna Schwartz recalled.

He also didn't have much patience for one of the brainchildren of rational expectations theory, the "efficient markets hypothesis" of Eugene Fama, said one of his students, Robert Auerbach. The "efficient markets" idea, which later provided the basis for much of the government's decision to leave financial markets alone, held that markets always arrived at the "correct" price for any good or service and they did it very quickly.

But Friedman knew enough to give his intellectual opponents a little credit. According to Auerbach: "I was in his workshop. He said, 'How could traders make any money if it's an efficient market, if all available information is instantly translated into price changes?' He said they must get some kind of feeling this is below normal."

Even so, to an extent he never fully realized, Friedman supplied much of the inspiration behind the "scientizing" of free-market economics. The sense of certainty that Friedman communicated about the moral triumph of markets and freedom over alternative forms of social organization only heightened the sense that financial behavior was rational and predictable. In a supreme historical irony, the most extreme champions of this sort of scientism about markets—inspired by Friedman—came to look like the mirror image of the Leninists and Trotskyists who sought to "scientifically" build socialism from the top down during the height of Soviet power. Not that they would acknowledge this. Friedman and the Chicago school "created a mind-set that policy is impotent to solve economic problems and that the system can do it on its own terms," said Stephen Roach, an economist with Morgan Stanley.

Much later on, the markets Friedman had done so much to set in motion—currency futures—became swaps and then credit default swaps, all in tune with the rise of the idea of efficient and rational markets.

Still, it was a long, slow slog into the hearts and minds of American politics. Friedman had been an adviser to Barry Goldwater in the 1964 presidential election, but the 1960s and 1970s were not ripe for him or for Goldwater. The 1964 campaign ended in one of the most humiliating landslides in U.S. history. The Arizona senator, despite his rugged man-of-the-West demeanor, was fairly inept as a candidate. His turquoise-studded cowboy boots kept landing squarely in his mouth. Only a year after John F. Kennedy's death, Goldwater told audiences that JFK had orchestrated the timing of the Cuban missile crisis to help his party during the midterm elections. He went to Boeing and blundered through a simple "thank you" to the company for the performance of its planes in wartime, saying that in his administration Boeing planes "will be doing so again." All of which, of course, played straight into the Democratic campaign's message that Goldwater was a warmongering extremist.

Goldwater's ideas about low taxes and small government, many of them given to him by Friedman, were much more reasonable. But they didn't resonate in that earlier time. The crushing defeat Goldwater endured at the hands of LBJ had much to do with the fact that the country just wasn't ready for that way of thinking. It was why his GOP successor, Richard Nixon, would later declare himself a Keynesian and push for wage and price controls. The rise of conservatism—its migration from the margins during the era of Goldwater to the mainstream under Ronald Reagan—would have to await the vindication that came with Friedman's dead-on critique of oversized government and the post-Vietnam stagflation.

What really turbocharged the process, however, was the abrupt end of the Cold War.

2

Triumph

By the time the Soviet Union finally went out of existence, at the end of 1991, its disappearance from the world map no longer seemed like much of a world-changing event. That's because it was only the last husk of the empire to crumble. In the late 1980s, a barrage of stunning headlines had signaled that the once-fearsome superpower was collapsing in on itself like a burned-out star. The Soviet military had retreated from Eastern Europe, whose republics were all in rebellion against their local communist overlords; the Berlin Wall had been joyously torn down; and in late 1990, West Germany had swallowed up its dysfunctional and unhappy Sovietized twin, East Germany. So it was no great shock when on December 26, 1991, the Soviet Union formally dissolved and a badly weakened and fractious Russia assumed all its debts and treaties. Even so, at that moment some profound sense of I-told-you-so satisfaction lodged itself in our collective consciousness as a nation. The cold war had ended not with a bang but with the biggest whimper ever heard from an expiring doctrine in recorded history. The United States of America was alone on the world stage.

Most of us quickly forgot how harrowing—and humbling—the Cold War had been in its worst years. For nearly four decades, America's existence was weighed against another species of social and political organization. Soviet communism denied everything we stood for: freedom, markets, democracy. The might of Soviet arms, the extent of the

USSR's reach, sometimes made Americans wonder whether Moscow was right. "The real question," as John F. Kennedy put it—tersely summarizing what was at stake in those grim years at the height of the tension, the early 1960s—"is which system travels better." For a long time most Americans really didn't know the answer. We were repeatedly reminded—through various crises, in countless books and popular movies—that we might even lose the Cold War. Though the Cold War never went "hot" (except when it was fought through proxies like the Koreans and Vietnamese), we knew that nuclear extinction could settle the contest at any moment. Our best minds and billions of dollars were devoted to studying how the Soviets could win with a massive first strike. At least twice in the 1950s, President Eisenhower rejected Pentagon proposals for a preemptive strike of our own. The hair-trigger calculus of deterrence—the so-called Balance of Terror—inspired annihilation dramas such as *Failsafe* and black-humored satires such as *Dr. Strangelove.*

Then we awoke one morning (so it seemed) to find that the Soviet Union had been, in effect, a fraud, a kind of ideological Ponzi scheme. As it turned out, Moscow had been quietly and desperately trying, and failing, to keep up with *our* system. The USSR had succeeded in becoming a superpower only by plowing vast amounts of its resources into its defense sector for seventy years while stinting on everything else: commercial goods and services, social welfare, civilian infrastructure. We had been in awe of the bristling outer face of the system: the five-thousand-warhead nuclear armada, the submarine fleet, Sputnik, Soyuz. But it was a system that had no internal integrity; it could not sustain its own home economy, much less an empire. Even Mikhail Gorbachev, the USSR's genial last leader, didn't understand what a hollow thing Soviet communism had become, and that he was trying to reform a scam economy that offered no incentives to work or produce. As the Russians ruefully joked among themselves, "We pretend to work and they pretend to pay us."

In the end, Moscow was essentially bankrupted out of existence. The Soviets just couldn't take the competition. The key to winning the Cold War, in other words, had been economics far more than pure ideology or sheer military might. The source of our strength had been democracy and openness, to be sure, but at its core, the engine room of our dominance was our market system and the vibrancy of the U.S. industrial base.

A strong, open, growing U.S. economy produced the taxes needed for the trillions of dollars consumed by the defense/industrial complex. It yielded the technology needed to outpace even the brilliant and well-resourced Soviet scientists. The ultimate victor in all this, it was clear, was freedom—and not some abstract concept of freedom written down on yellowing parchment, but rather the simple freedom to think of, build, and sell better stuff. It was a moment of history when the truth really did seem simple. The "end of history"—a time when all the big questions about how to organize human society had been settled—was close at hand, as philosopher Francis Fukuyama concluded in the great triumphalist essay of the era.

Initially as a foreign correspondent, and then as a journalist based in Washington, D.C., I was a firsthand witness to this broad transformation, and I too was caught up in the triumphalism. I too bought into the new zeitgeist and became a passionate devotee of free markets in the aftermath. How could one not? What choice was there any longer? I remember, in particular, visiting Vietnam, a Soviet client state, in that same late December 1991. It was just a coincidence that I happened to be there in the USSR's final weeks; I was living in Tokyo and was on a tourist trip with my wife and friends. But being a journalist, I spent my days talking to a lot of people. It was clear that the coziness between Moscow and Hanoi, once comrades, had curdled into mutual hatred. Throughout the country, but especially in the north, the Vietnamese had come to despise the large resident Russian population for their cheap spending habits and arrogance. Visiting Americans, by contrast, were welcomed with smiles ("Russians with dollars," we were called). Apart from stock phrases like "hello" and "thank you," I discovered that I really needed to learn only one line of Vietnamese to get along wonderfully wherever I went. I remember it to this day: *Toi la Nguoi My, khungfai Lien Xo* ("I'm an American, not a Russian"). On the day we visited the old U.S. embassy in Saigon—where some of those iconic photos symbolizing American defeat were taken—we discovered government workmen removing a tarnished copper plaque on the front gate. The inscription was in Vietnamese, but when we asked what the sign said, we were told that it commemorated the North's victory over the "U.S. imperialists." In the waning days of that epochal year, the 1970s-era propaganda against U.S. involvement in Southeast Asia was no longer politically correct. The new message from the aging communist mandarins in Hanoi was:

"Yankee Come Back" (and bring your investment and tourist dollars). Vietnam remained nominally communist, but Hanoi knew even then that it was an ideological relic surrounded by Asian capitalist "Tigers," all of them U.S. allies or dependents. The dominoes of the Cold War had fallen—but the opposite way.

All these victories, first the big one and then a lot of satisfying little ones—as onetime nemeses such as Vietnam and other former Soviet satellites eagerly sought to join the West—delivered a powerful sense of vindication to the Right in the United States. They ensured that the glow of Reaganism would last far beyond his presidency. The conflict with the Soviet Union was so black-and-white, so easy to see as a contest between right and wrong, that much like World War II, it solidified a sense in U.S. policy that the world isn't that complicated. Evil exists, and the best way to fight it is head-on. The more free the economy, the more successful the economy. It wasn't just a victory for freedom over fascism, or capitalism over communism. It was a victory for the very *idea* of freedom, and it was a final victory.

These lessons would be applied to future fights in the battle of ideas. The Left and the moderate middle had championed détente and conciliation, assuming the Soviets would be around forever. The Reaganite Right had pushed for confrontation and delegitimization of the USSR. It was no accident that two of the leading neoconservatives who would later dominate the era of George W. Bush, Paul Wolfowitz and Richard Perle, had both been passionate Reaganites with a fondness for black-and-white solutions. Perle had worked for Scoop Jackson, a super-hawk who in the late 1960s and early 1970s began preaching a kind of proto-Reaganism—throwing the first monkey wrench into the machinery of détente practiced by Nixon and Henry Kissinger. "Some people saw the principal Cold War issue as managing the relationship with the Soviet Union," Perle told me later. "Some of us took it differently that it was not so much to manage it, but to challenge the fundamental legitimacy of the Soviet Union." In the collapse of the USSR the Reaganite hawks and later the neocons found their triumphalist mythology. The arms buildup and democracy promotion of the 1980s had all seemed to work, and quite stunningly; the champions of détente with the Soviets were proven wrong. It was this hubris, this sense of certainty about the unique power of introducing freedom and democracy, that hawks like Perle and Wolfowitz would later carry into another war, in Iraq.

Nowhere was the sense of vindication greater, of course, than in one of the few places in the United States where there had been pockets of true believers all along, those who were certain that America and its market system would, ultimately, triumph as an economic and moral force. Not only had they been sure we would win, they had actually developed theories to explain *why* our system was superior. "The Cold War is over, and the University of Chicago won it," is how the columnist George Will summed things up in late 1991. He was exaggerating, of course, but it seemed churlish in the aftermath of the Soviet collapse to dispute that description. The Chicagoans should get their due, and they did. Over the years, the Nobel Prize Committee beat a path to their door— and the committee came calling so many times that one of those Nobel Prize winners, Gary Becker, proudly pinned an editorial cartoon to his office wall that pictured the University of Chicago economics department with a caption underneath reading, "Will the last one to win a Nobel Prize please shut out the lights?"

For Milton Friedman, the collapse of the Soviet Union brought, at long last, the kind of vindication he had never dreamed of in his wilderness years. Few other economists had dismissed, as completely as Friedman did, the idea that there might be something to the "command economies" of the Soviet bloc. After all, at the height of the Cold War, the Soviet GDP growth figures often seemed to outpace the West's. In the Soviet system, government bureaucrats developed five-year production plans for every industry: what they would make, how much of it, and who would get it. Even the Austrian free marketer Joseph Schumpeter, famed for inventing the idea of "creative destruction"— meaning the constant waves of innovation that are the great strength of capitalism—devoted a substantial portion of his classic 1942 book *Capitalism, Socialism and Democracy* to the question of why the Soviet version might work. Paul Samuelson, the dean of the era's dominant Keynesianism, entertained the same possibility.

But Friedman and his wife, Rose, who was also a libertarian economist, were certain that those estimates of real Soviet GDP growth, which came mainly from the CIA, had to be wrong. (Rose, who was even more right-wing and uncompromising about such things than Milton, later said that the only big issue they ever disagreed on was the 2003 invasion of Iraq; she was for it, and he was against.) Later on, when the wife of Friedman's friend Chuck Brunie (the couples were old friends) asked him what his biggest mistake had been, "he thought seriously, for a good forty-five seconds or more," Brunie recalled. "He said, 'I've always been too early, I don't understand why others cannot see what I do.'" The Friedmans insisted that the numbers coming out of Moscow didn't square with the hard data that existed on birth and death rates. And they told President Reagan so. "They said, 'Life expectancy is going down.' You cannot have 6 or 7 or 8 percent real GDP growth with declining life expectancy," recalled Martin Anderson, Reagan's top domestic adviser. Anderson said the president had come to many of his free-market beliefs on his own—especially the idea that the Soviet Union was an "evil empire" destined for the ash-heap of history—but Milton Friedman gave those ideas intellectual heft, bone, and muscle. Above all, he instilled in Reagan a sense of certainty. Reagan, said Anderson, "just could not resist Friedman's infectious enthusiasm."

The first green shoots of vindication had begun to appear in the success of the capitalist East Asian Tigers as early as the mid- to late 1970s. (Few economists or policy makers at the time appreciated that some of those countries, particularly Japan and Korea, had succeeded in part through a "mixed" economy of open domestic markets and strong government export promotion.) Said Becker, "The Tigers were more important in spreading these ideas than a lot of theories." So was the move away from command economics by Deng Xiaoping, the supreme leader of China, in 1978. At a key Communist Party plenary session in December of that year, Deng put forward the idea that economic modernization, not class struggle, would be the Chinese government's main focus. People, he said, should "seek truth from facts"—a quotation from Mao Zedong that Deng artfully twisted to stress that dogmatic Maoism was no longer de rigueur. It didn't matter what color a cat was, Deng said, as long as it caught mice. In the koanlike rhetoric of Chinese politics, that was a virtual revolution. Deng was saying that if private enterprise works, we'll try it. Soon he was allowing China's eight hundred million–plus peasants to plant vegetables on their own plots, the first private enterprise permitted anywhere in China in two decades. It was a tentative step out of the Maoist torpor and isolation following the nightmare of the Cultural Revolution and the horrors of the Great Leap Forward. Mainly what Deng was trying to do was to avoid the fate of the Soviet Union.

Final proof came in what for economists was the most perfect of all real-world laboratories: the comparative experiences of West and East Germany. Here were the same people, from the same culture, working and living right next door to each other, but with competing forms of economic organization. For economists, it was the closest thing possible to a sociological experiment with identical twins, wherein the variable of biological differences could be eliminated; this allowed scientists to assess the precise impact that different environments might have on development. For years leading up to the collapse of East Germany, economists had been noting its backwardness next to the shining cities of West Germany—as well as the steady flow of defectors across the Berlin Wall. But when it happened "it was overwhelming, the rapidity with which it came," said Becker. "We all believed it was right. But who could foresee the Soviet Union would just collapse like that? I took the train from West Berlin to Warsaw in 1989. You go through East Germany, you see so much government in command of everything, you want to get out. Then six months later it's gone. East Germany was considered the most successful bloc nation, but it was a complete failure in almost every dimension. That was very gratifying. Anyone who went to Chicago took a lot of heat. It had been very hard to get our grad students placed. And now to see all that changed. That was an amazing transformation."

In truth, West Germany had never been anything close to a free-market economy; its state sector was huge. Still, Friedman said that the fall of the Berlin Wall was worth more than everything he had said and written in his life. As he recalled to C-SPAN's Brian Lamb in 1994:

The collapse of the Berlin Wall . . . was undoubtedly the most influential action for the last hundred years because it put finis to an attitude. The general attitude had been that the future was the future of government, that the way in which you got good things done was by having government do it. I believe the collapse of the Berlin Wall and the exposure of what was happening in

Russia, the contrast between East Germany and West Germany, has been made a lesson; more recently, the experience of East Asia, of Hong Kong, of Singapore.

The rapidity of the Soviet collapse, the fact that no one expected it all to implode so quickly and reveal itself as a sham, contributed directly to the idea of "shock therapy" and a hell-for-leather conversion to markets for many of these newly freed up economies. The Friedmanites loved telling stories of how their ideas often carried the most weight behind the Iron Curtain—in other words, with those who had had to endure the reality of "command economics"—sometimes surprising left-leaning Americans. Vaclav Klaus, the Czech finance minister, said that during the Soviet occupation he and some other economics professors and students would gather in his attic and read banned copies of *Capitalism and Freedom* and Friedman's other work, according to Michael Boskin, the chairman of George H. W. Bush's Council of Economic Advisors. Becker, who was Friedman's student, recalled visiting Russia as late as 1989 with other U.S. academics to lecture to a group of a hundred Soviet students on why market economies were so good and why intrinsically command economies didn't work. As he spoke, Becker said he could see that a colleague they were traveling with, a prominent U.S. historian of the Soviet period, was increasingly uncomfortable with the lecture, the presumptuousness of it. "All of a sudden he gets up and tries to ingratiate himself with the audience, saying 'How about telling us all good things that happen here?'" Becker said with a laugh. "The audience—this was at the tail end of perestroika, when you could say such things again—started to erupt angrily. They said, 'You name one good thing! Just one!'"

Despite that, it was not the end of history for Friedman, nor would it ever be; he didn't accept the arguments of Francis Fukuyama. That was why Friedman always viewed himself as an insurgent athwart history—in the most profound sense, *not* a conservative at all. "I'm a liberal!" he would say, invoking the nineteenth-century sense of liberal, meaning in the direction of libertarianism. The thinking man's freedom fighter. Always an empiricist, and a student of history, Friedman knew that freedom was not the natural state of mankind, that coercive collectivism had dominated through the millennia. Just as the Founding Fathers had upset and confounded history by applying their ideas to a brand-new kind of country, so Friedman would stand up for the counterintuitive state of economic freedom. In late 1975, a year before his Nobel Prize, in the midst of the 1970s stagflation, he believed the world was heading toward serfdom. "You cannot find a date in history in which the greater part of the human race was not living in a condition of tyranny, misery and dictatorship," he said. He never stopped because he couldn't. The fight was never done.

In Ronald Reagan, Friedman found his perfect political avatar, a man passionate about freedom and relentlessly sunny about America's prospects. The rise of Reagan's political star paralleled closely the rise of Friedmanism, and the bankruptcy of big government; Reagan had made his name with conservatives delivering a powerful speech—now known just as "the speech"—on TV in late October 1964, but his move into the mainstream required popular dissatisfaction with the old Democratic model. After all, in that 1964 speech, Reagan sounded many of the themes he would later become known for: "Today, thirty-seven cents out of every dollar earned in this country is the tax collector's share, and yet our government continues to spend seventeen million dollars a day more than the government takes in," he declared. "We haven't balanced our budget twenty-eight out of the last thirty-four years." He inveighed against LBJ's then new "Great Society," a major government poverty-reduction plan. But most of the country didn't particularly see the need for radical cutbacks in goverment back then, not with low inflation and strong economic growth.

Sixteen years later everything had changed. By the time Reagan delivered his first revolutionary budget plan, with its giant tax cut, on February 18, 1981, the economy was in far worse shape. The new president "was speaking to an assembly of desperate politicians who had come into the chamber clutching the bloodied remains of their Keynesian and statist solutions," his budget chief, David Stockman, later wrote. "They knew they had lost their way—and now they were looking to him for a new way. They applauded him again and again that night, leaving no doubt that they were predisposed to grant him extraordinary latitude. . . . They were disposed to gamble, not because they understood the plan or even accepted it, but because they had lost all faith in the remedies tried before." Inflation was then at 13 percent, economic growth at zero.

As Reagan himself put it in his inaugural address that year, "It is no coincidence that our present troubles parallel and are proportionate to the intervention and intrusion in our lives that result from unnecessary and excessive growth of government." Goldwater had lost to Lyndon Johnson by 20 points; now his heir, Ronald Reagan, had defeated an incumbent Democrat, Jimmy Carter, by 10 points, 51 to 41. By the time he delivered his signature line at his inaugural—"Government is not the solution to the problem; government is the problem"—it resonated with a public tired of both double-digit inflation and high unemployment, the very "stagflation" that Friedman had warned of. Some historians compared the moment to FDR's inauguration in 1933—which was appropriate, since the earlier inauguration had ushered in the age of Keynesian tinkering and this one would start a whole new era of retreat from government.

Phil Gramm, then a congressman from Texas, was another one of the earliest and most powerful political torchbearers for Friedman's ideas in the Reagan era—and he would never give up the fight. Gramm had been elected to the House as a Democrat and only switched party affiliations in 1984, when the Reagan revolution was well under way. As a monetarist fully in the Friedman school, Gramm made up for lost time by becoming a passionate devotee of supply-side economics, which another passionate small-government advocate, Representative Jack Kemp, had pressed on Reagan while the California governor was a candidate. Along with David Stockman, Gramm became a hard-core believer in the true "revolution" that Friedman was trying to bring about—a reduction in the welfare state, both on the spending and on the tax side.

Even during the early Reagan era, however, there was only so far these would-be revolutionaries could go. For Reagan himself the get-rid-of-big-government impulse was mainly about reducing taxes anyway. And in the end, that's mostly what he managed to do: cut taxes—though even here his effect was limited; capital gains taxes remained high—without reining in spending. Indeed, Reagan blew out the budget as he increased defense spending in order to confront the Soviets. Deregulation of the economy was still a new idea then, and the Democrats were still in control of the House of Representatives (the GOP had taken over the Senate on Reagan's coattails in 1980). In 1982, John Shad, head of the SEC, went in to talk to then Representative Timothy Wirth about dismantling the Glass-Steagall Act. The Depression-era law separated commercial

and investment banking into two distinct industries as a way of preventing ordinary banks from becoming part of the Wall Street underwriting
and trading culture. Wirth called in his friend, Democratic representative
John Dingell, whose father had been one of the authors of Glass-Steagall,
and Dingell proceeded to tear into Shad, ridiculing the idea of a repeal.
Shad departed the office badly shaken. "He smoked about ten cigarettes
and left," said Wirth. As Dingell recalled: "They tried it, going back to
almost the first time I was on the committee. They couldn't get this thing
through my committee."

It was no contest, in fact. There wasn't much of a "Wall Street lobby"
in those days. The financial industry was much smaller and more staid,
less expectant of privilege from Washington. About ten firms controlled
about 75 percent of trading, and they could be watched every minute.
The talented graduates of Ivy League schools weren't going to Harvard
Business School; they were going to medical school and law school.
"Harvard Business School was not considered a sexy place," said David
Rubenstein, the cofounder of the Carlyle Group, who was Jimmy Carter's
domestic policy adviser. "It was then considered a place that you went if
you couldn't get into anyplace else. . . . People just didn't make that much
money on Wall Street." Regulators were then a different breed too; they
knew Washington's power structure had their back. For most of the
1960s and '70s the SEC's Division of Enforcement was led by Stanley
Sporkin, a fierce lawyer who instilled nothing less than terror in the
industry. "Sporkin used to go in and talk to these people, and it was said
that on occasion when they knew he was coming, or when he was there,
or after he left, they'd have heart attacks," said Dingell.

But the first cracks in the wall appeared in 1980, when Congress
passed a law phasing out Regulation Q, which had set limits on interest
rates for deposits. Then in 1982, Senator Jake Garn, Republican of
Utah, sponsored the Garn-St. Germain Depository Institutions Act,
which freed up the savings and loan associations to invest in whatever
they wanted—including a lot of bad real estate lending—still backed
by a government guarantee. The new law also ushered in the phenomenon of "brokered deposits"—money gathered up by brokers from many
different investors, which moved banks away from their traditional conservative depositor bases. "All in all, I think we hit the jackpot," Reagan

said at the signing ceremony. The deregulation of the savings and loan industry led to a period of reckless lending and investment that culminated in the worst banking disaster since the Depression, ending in a $160 billion bailout, most of which was paid by taxpayers. About two thousand institutions failed, and two of the three deposit insurance funds had to be recapitalized. This led to the invention of the securitization market as bad assets were separated from the banks that had to be rescued and sold off. It was a kind of microcosm of what was to come twenty-five years later with the subprime mortgage–securitization phenomenon, but by then the entire system would be infected.

In truth, when it came to pure economics as practiced inside academia, the fall of the Wall and the end of the Cold War didn't settle much.

"Nobody in the United States, outside of long-gone extremists, was a supporter of centralized planning," said Robert Solow. "So the notion that somehow Chicago was vindicated against Cambridge [home to MIT and Harvard] by the collapse of communism was pure propaganda."

The end of the Cold War, Paul Samuelson wrote, really only meant that "victory has been declared in favor of the market-pricing mechanism over the command mechanism of regulatory bureaucracy." The victor was plainly not pure laissez-faire capitalism but the "mixed economy" that had dominated U.S. and Western capitalism for most of the Soviet Union's history, Samuelson said—markets modified by government taxes and government-orchestrated transfers of wealth to limit inequality, and government monetary and fiscal policies to curb recessions and inflation.

But in the broad pendulum swings that mark the comings and goings of American political wisdom, such subtle distinctions no longer mattered much. What changed irrevocably was the public discussion. Behind the walls of academe, the "neo-Keynesians" such as Samuelson were still defending the idea of a proper government role to go with "the market mechanism," but outside no one in Washington really cared. In the years following the Cold War, any ideas for new government control became instantly backward and repulsive. Friedman himself, in his role as populizer of his ideas, took part in all this oversimplification, causing some critics such as Paul Krugman to accuse him of intellectual dishonesty. "In the aftermath of the Great Depression, there were many people saying that markets can never work," wrote Krugman, whose own classic work on currencies and trade over several decades had sought to find a balance between markets and government. "Friedman had the intellectual courage to say that markets can too work, and his showman's flair combined with his ability to marshal evidence made him the best spokesman for the virtues of free markets since Adam Smith. But he slipped all too easily into claiming both that markets always work and that only markets work."

Whereas once he'd had a few good things to say about the New Deal, Friedman later suggested that the Depression happened for one reason: poor behavior by the Federal Reserve. Markets and their leading players had performed just fine in the panic of 1907, when J. P. Morgan led a group of bankers to save the day by putting up money to keep the stock exchange afloat. Part of the mythology that Friedman built up was that the most disastrous shift came when the pragmatic interventionism of New York Fed president Benjamin Strong—a real banker, not a federal bureaucrat—was lost. Strong died of tuberculosis in 1928, just before the crash, and power shifted to the Fed in Washington.

But again, such distinctions were lost, just as people now tended to ignore the flaws in Friedman's work to the same extent as they had once ignored its virtues. Indeed, even as Friedman's theoretical pride and joy, monetarism, reached its heights of triumph, it was already being proved unworkable in crucial ways. Then Federal Reserve chairman Paul Volcker adopted monetarism in 1979, but abandoned it three years later when steady growth in the money supply failed to cure double-digit unemployment. And as the Fed adopted a more discretionary attitude of tweaking interest rates, in the 1980s, Friedman proved to be frequently wrong about the likelihood of a new inflation.

As is often the case with founders of movements, Friedman's thinking—as opposed to his public rhetoric—was more subtle than that of many of his followers. He knew, for example, that in practice it was simplistic to equate economic with political freedom. "Economic freedom is always favorable to political freedom. But political freedom can sometimes be dangerous to economic freedom" if it imposes the will of a big-government majority, he told me in the last years of his life. The political and civic culture was important: you might have nominal elections in India or Russia, but nondemocratic institutions could crush freedom. Friedman also acknowledged the paradoxical oddity that economies he cited as free-market models, Hong Kong and Singapore, were autocratic politically. He admitted to me that if he had to write *Capitalism and Freedom* again, he would develop the idea of "civil" freedom as well: "You have to distinguish between economic, civil, and political freedom. What impressed me was that Hong Kong had no political freedom whatsoever. As a colony of Britain, it had almost complete civil freedom and economic freedom, but you had to see that as a benevolent dictatorship. Much the same thing happened in Singapore under Lee Kwan Yew."

It was all too nuanced for the era of post–Cold War triumphalism. With the end of the Cold War, the Friedmanian fundament was the new floor, and so much else followed from that. As the economy sagged under the weight of government, the new trend had actually started under Jimmy Carter, who deregulated the telecom and transportation industries and began the deregulation of banking with the 1980 Depository Institutions Deregulation and Monetary Control Act, which lowered mandatory reserve requirements for banks, phased out interest rate ceilings, and raised Federal Deposit Insurance Corporation (FDIC) coverage insurance from $40,000 to $100,000. But it was Reagan, inspired by the Chicago school, who made deregulation the dominant paradigm of American politics. And because the Reaganite fever spread worldwide as the Soviet empire faltered and then failed, "competitive deregulation" became the order of the day. London's 1986 "Big Bang" created pressure back in New York and Washington to do the same, and all the way through the 1990s even Democrats such as Robert Rubin and Larry Summers would use the putative threat of freer markets overseas to turn back Brooksley Born and everyone else who sought to moderate deregulation.

But the sense of economic certainty that became the hallmark of free-market absolutism didn't have a single source, in Chicago or anywhere else. Instead it was a confluence of thought and experience that arrived at its moment in history from many different places. And while Friedman played the role of intellectual godfather from afar, ultimately the era came to be embodied in one man who ran things in Washington for nearly a generation—who dominated the economic agenda to an extent that few others had ever matched in the history of the nation. His name was Alan Greenspan. If Friedman was the man who led the theoretical assault on big government and spending programs, it was Greenspan who oversaw the rollback of government regulation. If Friedman dominated theory, Greenspan dominated practice. And unlike Friedman, who always resisted efforts to bring him into government—"we asked him many times," said Martin Anderson—and exercised influence from his ivy-covered aerie in Chicago, Greenspan was at the center of everything that happened.

3

The Stealth Ideologue

I t was strange that they were often lumped together as ideological soul mates, champions of the free-market ideal. Alan Greenspan was, in so many ways, the opposite of Milton Friedman. Friedman was the cocksure bantam genius, spouting certainties at people at campus cocktail parties. Greenspan, tall and reserved in manner, was always careful in what he said (even when he was a young man he spoke in cautious paragraphs, a hint of the Fedspeak to come) and all too aware of how little he knew. Greenspan was a connoisseur of uncertainty. He had built a career on being the guy who knew what he didn't know and freely admitted it. Long before he went into government, he would obsessively track down data that might give some hint of the direction of the economy. In fact, one of the things he loved most about running the Fed was his access to data, endless supplies of which he got from the two hundred Ph.D.s on his staff.

Greenspan started every day at 5:30 a.m. with a long bath. Engrossed, his thick eyeglasses steaming, he would pore over reams of statistics and enter a metaworld that only he seemed to understand, sloshing the sheets with bathwater. Greenspan once told me—as he did many others—that he always did his best thinking in the tub then, a time when, the Federal Reserve chairman said, his "IQ is about twenty points higher." Over eighteen years as Fed chairman from 1987 to 2005, he was revered as a man who had developed an almost intuitive understanding of the economy and feel for market conditions that seemed preternatural, deftly nudging rates this way and that, rarely appearing to guess wrong. "The data was his love," said his former wife and lifelong friend, Joan Blumenthal.

It was forever an unrequited love, which is what made it all so interesting for Greenspan: the data never lie, but they are always incomplete. One could never stop studying the statistics, the more obscure the better, and he had an uncanny ability to tie together seemingly unrelated phenomena in the economy. Greenspan, joked Frank Ikard, the Washington representative for the American Petroleum Institute, was "the kind of person who knew how many thousand flat-headed bolts were used in a 1964 Chevrolet and what it would do to the economy if you took out three of them." He loved tracking numbers like paperboard production as a "leading indicator" that augured ahead of time where the economy was going, because so many different kinds of products were packaged in paper boxes. He wasn't a theoretical economist—Greenspan barely earned his Ph.D., submitting as a thesis a collection of articles he'd written; it was more an honorary degree than anything else—but his amazing feel for the numbers that made up the blood and muscle of the economy was what made him so much in demand as a Wall Street consultant. Oddly enough, his firm, Townsend-Greenspan, didn't have a good forecasting record for inflation or GDP growth—in fact, it was downright "dismal," Senator William Proxmire noted at Greenspan's 1987 confirmation hearing. But projecting specific numbers wasn't really Greenspan's strength. His great talent instead was his gut-level feel for the inner health of the economy, the deeper trend lines. Because Greenspan saw things that no one else did; for example, he divined that increases in productivity would hold inflation down, allowing him to keep interest rates low. In so doing he kept millions of people working in the 1990s who might otherwise have been jobless.

Much later on, after the catastrophe of 2007–2009 had struck and its implications were well understood, Greenspan's role would still seem mysterious to many who had known this about him, how careful and deliberate an empiricist he was. Even after the markets crashed, and he was long retired, his reputation a shadow of what it once had been, the elderly former Fed chief would call up his successor, Ben Bernanke, to tell him about the rate of production on certain auto lines. How had a man like this missed the mortgage bubble? In truth, he hadn't; he just didn't think there was anything he could do about it. The markets must be left to sort things out.

But if Greenspan was a free-market ideologue, he had done a great job of disguising it. There was never any anger, or rancor. Never any of the ranting rhetoric or the reflexive identification with party agendas that characterized so many others in Washington. On the contrary, Greenspan had always demonstrated an impressive agility in getting along with politicians and policy makers of all stripes. While he ruled the Fed firmly, he still preferred to get consensus in meetings whenever he could.

He prized civility even above ideology. Greenspan began his Washington career as a campaign adviser to Nixon, who was, at best, a renegade conservative when it came to economics, having devalued the dollar and fixed wages and prices. Greenspan was impressed at first by Nixon's intelligence—the smartest president he knew, apart from Clinton, he later said—but he was appalled when Nixon, on the verge of winning the nomination in 1968, gathered his chief advisers together on Montauk, Long Island, and launched into a savage tirade against the Democrats. It was his first glimpse of the vicious Nixon, a man who used profanity that "would have made Tony Soprano blush," Greenspan wrote. "I never looked at him the same way after that." Disturbed by Nixon's dark insecurities, he declined to join his administration until his old mentor Arthur Burns prevailed upon him to become chairman of the Council of Economic Advisors. Later Greenspan worked closely with a centrist Democratic president, Bill Clinton, and with a Treasury secretary, Robert Rubin, whose views on many economic issues tended toward the liberal side. He had stood with them in some of the largest government interventions on record—the Mexican peso crisis of 1995, and the Asian financial contagion three years later. He even got along famously with Ted Kennedy, the über-liberal of the Senate. "It astonished me at the time," recalled Joan Blumenthal. "I remember asking him how he could agree with someone whose views were so different. 'I like him,' he said."

So like Kennedy, who at the time of his death from brain cancer in August 2009 was lionized as one of Washington's most effective makers of policy, Greenspan was a nice guy, a gentleman who reached beyond the rancor of politics. But in contrast to Teddy, Greenspan was very hard to know. "The irony is that Alan Greenspan is a very interesting person and a warm, wonderful conversationalist—who simply doesn't seem to like to have conversations," Laurence Meyer, a Fed governor who served under him, later wrote. If Ted Kennedy was a proud and vocal liberal, Greenspan the ideologue revealed himself in much quieter ways, only in the most subtle ways. He was a stealth ideologue. His ideology was defined in negative terms—in a mulish resistance to any policy that smacked of government regulation, and in a belief that the U.S. economy always returned on its own to equilibrium. In his own quiet way, during eighteen years in power that spanned from the end of the Cold War until the beginnings of the end of the great market mania, Greenspan did more than any other single person to shape the free-market zeitgeist in practice.

Much of this vision had coalesced in Greenspan's mind some fifty years before, in the parlor of a small apartment in the Murray Hill section of New York City, an East Side neighborhood of middlebrow brownstones just south of midtown Manhattan. It was there that, every Saturday night for a period of years in the 1950s, the young acolytes of Ayn Rand gathered to drink coffee and eat sweet pastries, read the latest pages from her masterwork in progress, *Atlas Shrugged*, and listen to the great woman speak. They called themselves, with self-regarding irony, 'the collective." It was a joke because Rand's whole life, her black-and-white view of humanity, was devoted to opposing collectivism and raising the individual capitalist to the heroic stature of a warrior in an ancient fable. Rand, in fact, made Milton Friedman look like a centrist by comparison.

Ayn Rand was a unique quantity, and there's never been anyone quite like her before or since in American intellectual life. She was born Alice Rosenbaum in St. Petersburg, Russia, the passionate, somewhat plain daughter of a well-to-do pharmacist. Her earliest memories were formed amid the brutal early days of leftist revolution against the czar. While her family went hungry in the Crimea, trying vainly to escape the civil war between the Reds and Whites, young Alice happened to take classes in U.S. history and she grew entranced by the elevation of individual happiness that was so central to the self-identity of that distant country. "I thought: *This* is the kind of government I approve of,'" she later said.

By 1921, the Reds were beginning to win, and they adopted appalling strategies like imposing a "week of poverty" to squeeze the remaining capitalist impulses out of the system. Those who had "too much," like her small-business father, had to give it up: in Fronz Rosenbaum's case it was a few bars of soap he had hoarded. Returning to her home in Petrograd after the final victory of the Bolsheviks, she experienced firsthand the dark years of "war communism," when all the country's productive resources were abruptly seized, and later the "New Economic Policy," the arbitrary arrests, the lines for food, the government-favored speculators called NEP men. Once the family had reached so low that all they had for dinner was a handful of dried peas, Rand later recalled, and she begged her mother for just one more pea that day.

Alice Rosenbaum saw, in other words, at the very start of the Bolshevik revolution—long before it grew shrouded in the kind of myth that led so many American socialists to apologize for it in later years—that it was a terrible injustice, an abomination. She saw that forced collectivism was a great evil, that those targeted as "bourgeois" were just as poor as everyone else. As a young girl, she could never rouse her father to passionate discussions of anything, but she later recalled how much she loved him when he finally took a stand for "self-esteem" and refused to work as a Soviet chemist. She came to hate everything about Russia, its glorification of tragedy and malevolence, just as she idealized America as a place where the talented individual could engage in a consummate act of self-creation, going from nobody to somebody as he could nowhere else on Earth, as Milton Friedman too had divined.

The soul of America was libertarian, in Rand's view, minimalist when it came to government, and that is how many people saw her, as a libertarian philosopher. But her ideas were more revolutionary and singular than that. Rand had a powerful and original mind, and she preached with the extra zeal of the converted. It wasn't enough to say that government didn't work in society, and freedom of the individual did—the traditional libertarian view. In Rand's eyes, individual achievement was the human race's *only* good; a man's reason and volition the *only* virtue. Altruism was "evil" because it undermined this virtue, distracted man from his true calling, and for the same reason so was collectivism and government interference in the economy. Much as Friedman stood the negative stereotypes about capitalism on their heads, Rand did the same with selfishness, redefining it as the highest good because it was the only way for people to fulfill their potential.

She called her philosophy "objectivism." It was based on the idea that all that was needed to understand man's place in the world was reason, which could on its own appreciate objective reality; and those individuals whose reason was superior to others' could, without guilt or shame about their selfishness and egoism, assume a place of superiority among their fellow men. It was a moral code to live by, and the simplicity of it was like a narcotic to many Americans for whom her philosophy was like smoking intellectual crack. For many on the Right, especially, reading Rand was akin to mainlining the distillate of the nation's revolutionary values about man's right to pursue happiness and maximize his freedom. She told Americans that their greatest glory was making money, and freed her followers from the guilt of getting rich.

The signature books she later wrote, *The Fountainhead* and *Atlas Shrugged*, both turned into best sellers, and Rand gained a cult following among libertarian Americans that continues to this day. Her proudest fictional character, John Galt, was the essence of American entrepreneurialism, a genius who stood for the concept that only creative individuals advance human progress, and against the idea that government ever could. "We are on strike against the dogma that the pursuit of one's happiness is evil," Galt declares in *Atlas Shrugged*, after he leads what is effectively a sit-down strike by the world's "men of the mind." "We are on strike against the doctrine that life is guilt." (Rand's ideas were so powerful that much later, after the Obama administration ratcheted up the market-interventionist policies begun by Bush, a "going Galt" meme began circulating among conservatives on the Internet who were outraged by the big government response to the financial disaster.)

Still, neither her ideas nor her literary efforts ever really gained mainstream respectability—and for good reason, since in her zeal to contrast the evils of collectivism with the glories of individual achievement, Ayn Rand threw out many ethical babies with the intellectual bathwater. Self-sacrifice for others is hardly the same thing as socialism, and government bureaucrats are not always Bolsheviks. Rand, who was childless though she was married for more than fifty years, never even gave any evidence that she understood the joys of parenthood, of moderating one's ambitions to focus on one's children. And her worldview reflected her very narrow real-world experience, broad though it might have seemed geographically in the long life journey she had made.

Yet Ayn Rand somehow had identified an untapped concept of greatness in capitalism and free society that intellects like Alan Greenspan, and others who grew up in such a society, could never have come to on their own. As with many strangers in a strange land—think of Alexis de Tocqueville explaining mid-nineteeth-century America to

Americans better than they could themselves—Rand divined something about the strengths of her adopted nation that no one else had. As an eighteen-year-old girl in St. Petersburg, later renamed Leningrad, Alice Rosenbaum drafted a story, a girlish tale of a heroic beautiful woman who gives herself to a genius, that was remarkable in its prescience about the titanic battle that was to shape the last part of the twentieth century. She later called the story "the grandfather of *Atlas Shrugged*," and it described how men of achievement all over Europe begin to disappear, led to the United States by the mysterious beautiful protagonist, who has persuaded them to break all ties with an increasingly collectivist Europe. The last genius to leave is a French inventor named Francis, and when he vanishes he turns up again as the leader of America and the protagonist's lover. All the refugee achievers then declare war on Europe, "which they conquer easily because all the machinery, the inventions and the brains are on their side," she wrote.

As a mere schoolgirl making up love stories, Rand had already grasped the stakes of the economic contest that would ultimately decide the Cold War nearly a decade after her death in 1982. It actually happened: men of brains and achievement began disappearing to the other side—read defectors (first Nazi scientists, then Soviet artists, and so on)—and in the end a system of free initiative produced both the money and the technologies that the Soviets could not match.

Alan Greenspan found himself at this strange but brilliant woman's side quite by accident. Photos from that time show the young Alan typically standing on the outside of the group, sometimes abstracted and unsmiling, as if he were never quite sure he should be there. In fact, he had been more or less dragged in. It's not surprising. Greenspan was always an introspective type, by his own admission, a boy of the Depression whose stockbroker father had left his mother, Rose, when Alan was two, and who buried himself in his dual loves: music and numbers. He was not much of a joiner of groups, but he did love women, and it's no accident that Greenspan was first introduced to the group by a gorgeous blonde named Joan Mitchell. She and others said Greenspan was standoffish at first when Nathaniel Branden, Rand's "heir" and secret lover at the time, sought to bring him to their regular gatherings. At the time his views, unformed though they were, were polar opposites of Rand's. She was a defiant egoist. "I'm not even sure I exist," he would joke in that honking voice, putting Branden off.

All he was then was a "26-year-old math junkie," as he later described himself. Greenspan had recently given up a career as a jazz clarinetist and joined the Conference Board. But he loved to read on his own time and considered himself an adherent of "logical positivism," a school of philosophy that depends entirely on physical evidence and rigorous proof for any and all conclusions, including existence, and rejects moral absolutes, finding the data invariably wanting. Even then, Greenspan spoke a kind of proto-Fedspeak, using complex sentence structure that was more a reflection of his own character than anything else. (Fed chairmen don't *have* to talk that way, as Ben Bernanke later showed.) Said Nathaniel Branden, "He was a master of elusive speech. We used to kid him about it." Branden, a psychologist, added that this may have been evidence of Greenspan's deeper uncertainties. "I'm inclined to be suspicious of that type of communication. If our thinking is clear, we should be able for the most part to explain."

It apparently ran in the family, Greenspan himself would later joke, when, as Fed chairman, he showed visitors a 1935 book, *Recovery Ahead!* written by his father, Herbert, with whom he had at best a distant relationship. Inside was an inscription to the nine-year-old Alan that the Fed chairman, later to be known as the Great Obfuscator himself, described as "somewhat mystifying:" "To my son Alan: May this my initial effort with constant thought of you branch out in an endless chain of similar efforts so that at your maturity you may look back and endeavor to interpret the reasoning behind these logical forecasts and begin a like work of your own."

Ayn Rand, on the other hand, spoke and wrote with a blinding clarity—a sense of certainty that, although it came from a very different place, was at least the equal of Milton Friedman's. And by Greenspan's own admission, she opened up to him a "realm" of human relations from which he, in his repressed, math-nerd way, had shut himself off. The first thing to go was his logical positivist view, which was all but shattered upon colliding with Rand's vehement brand of rationalism. "After listening for a few evenings . . . something prompted me to postulate that there are no moral absolutes. Ayn Rand pounced. 'How can that be?' she asked. 'Because to be truly rational, you can't hold a conviction without significant empirical evidence,' I explained. 'How can that be?

she asked again. 'Don't *you* exist?' 'I . . . can't be sure,' I admitted. 'Would you be willing to say you *don't* exist?' 'I might . . .' 'And by the way, who is making that statement?'" Rand asked. In his autobiography, written a half century later, Greenspan seemed a little embarrassed at recounting the episode—"maybe you had to be there," he wrote—but admitted that the "exchange really shook me."

He never seems to have won an argument with her. At the same time as he was working toward his Ph.D. at New York University and, by day at the Conference Board, analyzing the nation's air power capability in the middle of the Cold War, Rand was taking apart and remaking his world view in her little Manhattan apartment at night. "Talking to Ayn Rand was like starting a game of chess thinking I was good, and suddenly finding myself in checkmate," he wrote. Rand became "a stabilizing force in my life." But she was more than that. She gave a moral framework to the ideas that he was able to arrive at only empirically. "He was groping for a frame of reference," Rand herself recalled. "He had no fundamental view of life."

Others recalled a young man who came alive while reading and discussing Rand's ideas—and even broke into clear English on occasion. "Alan was a very repressed man," said Nathaniel Branden. "But he'd be sitting there reading *Atlas Shrugged*, so moved and excited. You'd see this guy suddenly now talking in simple, short sentences, full of joy and excitement. It was kind of charming." Branden's former wife, Barbara, who was also there, recalled Greenspan actually jumping up and down when they were all reading "the money speech" from *Atlas Shrugged*. In one of the long, passionate exegeses of her philosophy that Rand occasionally put into the mouths of her chief characters—making for powerful reading if not very good literature—Rand portrayed a scene in which Francisco D'Anconia, the brilliant copper magnate who is secretly working with John Galt, explains to a benighted socialite "moocher" at a party that money is not, in fact, the root of all evil.

Quite the opposite: it is the lifeblood of civilization and progress. And it is the avatar of America. "If you ask me to name the proudest distinction of Americans, I would choose—because it contains all the others—the fact that they were the people who created the phrase 'to make money,'" D'Anconia says. His—and Rand's—final words were words for a future Fed chairman to live by: "Whenever destroyers appear among men, they start by destroying money, for money is men's protection and the base of a moral existence."

They were powerful and dangerous ideas because of that. They inspired gifted amateurs, among them Jack Kemp, the former football star who found himself enthralled with the simple power of the message of *The Fountainhead*. Allied with supply-side economist Arthur Laffer, Kemp helped inspire Ronald Reagan to launch the tax-cut revolution. Greenspan himself, who knew better, never entirely drank the objectivist Kool-Aid. The aloof young man, while entranced, never became a cultist like the others. "He didn't make the same mistake as the rest of us," said Barbara Branden. Greenspan wasn't even aware of the huge scandal that erupted in the final years of the circle. Nathaniel Branden had been Rand's secret lover as well as her designated "intellectual heir" for years, but when she sought to renew the sexual relationship after a hiatus, Branden confessed to her he was in love with another woman. Rand responded by cutting him off forever, shattering her movement. But Greenspan managed to keep his relationship with Rand long after other acolytes had fallen from grace. "They had a kind of strange relationship. It was quite remarkable," said Joan Blumenthal. "They liked talking together, just the two of them. I think he was genuinely attracted to her way of thinking about things. He thought she was wonderful. He didn't really see anything else. I spoke to him once or twice about cooling down on the Ayn Rand stuff" after he became prominent in government. "Thinking about and talking about it. I hardly thought it would do him any good."

Greenspan pooh-poohed her concerns, and invited Rand to attend his swearing-in as the chairman of Ford's Council of Economic Advisors. Afterward, the guiding light of Greenspan's intellectual life gave him her highest accolade: "I think Alan is playing an heroic role," she said. Rand defined heroism for him. "When I met Ayn Rand, I was a free enterpriser in the Adam Smith sense, impressed with the theoretical structure and efficiency of markets," he once told my magazine, *Newsweek*. "What she did was to make me see that capitalism is not only efficient and practical, but moral."

Yet embracing that worldview had a subtle pitfall: if capitalism is not merely efficient and practical but a high moral good as well, then departing from its tenets is, in a way, immoral. Sure, it might be necessary to tamper with the markets at times, as he himself always conceded. But such departures are to be avoided at all costs. Greenspan, in other words, was a numbers-crunching realist when it came to gauging the direction of the economy, but he was a true Randian whenever he thought about the economy's social role and function. The tinkering that Greenspan became famous for at the Fed was a necessary sin, in his view, which the realist in him acknowledged was necessary. But he didn't like it, and it didn't feel right to him. It was like the way most of us stray from what we consider good behavior. We regret it afterward and try to behave better. We return, in other words, to the moral code. Greenspan always returned to his own personal starting point: the less government, the better.

In quiet ways that Greenspan almost never talked about publicly, that code became the moral framework for his life and business. In 1953, Greenspan had opened a consulting firm, Townsend-Greenspan, that specialized in detailed studies of industrial data. Yet even there the Randian ideas appeared as a stricture against regulation or even recommending it, said Kathryn Eickhoff, who ran the firm for him after he went to Washington and was another in a series of erstwhile Greenspan girlfriends. "Ayn Rand's philosophical theories were overriding," she said. "I viewed it as my responsibility to see to it that our commentary did not inadvertently imply that there should be greater government intervention." Another employee and economist, Lowell Wiltbank, put the same point a little differently: "There was an absolute rule at Townsend-Greenspan. No communication that came out of the firm should ever be interpreted to advocate any expansion of government interference in the economy. If we advocated anything in terms of government policy, it was deregulation."

For Greenspan, these Randian ideas acted like unseen roots; they were all but undetectable in the things he said during most of his time in Washington, first as chairman of the Council of Economic Advisors and then as Fed chairman. But they were always there, and they determined what he would do in government as much as the roots of a tree ultimately become its destiny; above the ground the tree might bend according to the vicissitudes of the wind and weather, but it would remain rooted to its spot. Greenspan himself later wrote that by the time he'd decided to join Nixon's campaign in 1968, "I had long since decided to engage in efforts to advance free-market capitalism as an insider, rather than as a critical pamphleteer."

Of course, he had always been a small-government guy. Greenspan first came to public notice in the mid-1960s, when a *Fortune* magazine

editor contracted with his firm to take a hard look at LBJ's numbers for
Vietnam. Greenspan found that not only had the president lowballed
the war seriously, "a revealing footnote" to the budget showed that the
administration was assuming, quite unrealistically, that combat operations would end on June 30, 1967. In 1976, when Gerald Ford was
preparing his State of the Union speech in the midst of the stagflation
era, Greenspan proposed they go back to the wisdom of the Founding
Fathers. But his suggestions sounded as if they'd been filtered through
Ayn Rand. "Freeing individuals is a fairly profound concept," he said.
"It involves reducing the size of government, reducing regulations, and
enhancing the status of individuals. A bicentennial theme for the State
of the Union could be the third century—the century of the individual."
As his biographer Justin Martin wrote, Greenspan's tenure as chairman
of Ford's Council of Economic Advisors was distinguished mainly for his
quietude. "With the exception of a minuscule tax rebate in the spring
of 1975, his counsel was almost numbing in its consistency—don't intervene, don't intervene, don't intervene."

It was advice of this kind that, in part, lay behind one of the most
famous newspaper headlines in history: "Ford to City: Drop Dead," in
the *Daily News*, as New York suffered through a fiscal near-meltdown.
And though Ford, tainted by the perception that he'd cut a deal to par-
don Nixon after Watergate, faced a major insurgent challenge from the
unknown but fresh-faced Jimmy Carter, and the economy fell into deep
recession, Greenspan's advice didn't change. On October 31, 1976, only
days before a close election, Greenspan appeared on *Face the Nation*
with Carter's chief economic adviser, the Nobelist Larry Klein of the
University of Pennsylvania. While Klein pitched a major stimulus,
Greenspan responded that "the best way to get unemployment down as
quickly as possible is to remove inflationary imbalances, and uncertainties in our system, and allow the private sector to rapidly create jobs."

Ford lost.

Even small innocuous pieces of regulation were thwarted. He always
gave Greenspanian arguments, of course, that were restrained and non-
ideological. It wasn't that regulation was all bad, it was more that in the
end it would do more damage than it would help, he would say. He was
hardly alone in believing that; economists such as James Buchanan and
Vernon L. Smith of George Mason University, building on the work of the
Chicago school, would later win Nobel Prizes for arguing that regulation

generated more costs than benefits, and markets worked better than governments in allocating resources and generating efficiency.

But it was more than just a stand against regulation. Greenspan brought a new philosophy to Washington, one that fit in with the emerging Reaganite zeitgeist perfectly. As he grew in power and prestige, supervisors slackened, regulators eased back. "It crept into the ethos," said one former Fed official who worked for many years under Greenspan. "Everyone became less affirmative, more reactive." It was apparent to those who worked with him in the forbidding building off the Mall that he had a kind of moral revulsion against regulation. At one point, in a major shift, the Fed under Greenspan stopped probing the loan books of banks and began to ask only if they had what they viewed as appropriate risk management policies in place.

Greenspan's emerging philosophy of conservative governance never took on the greater sophistication that allowed him to transcend the prevailing free-market view. Like Milton Friedman, he was no conservative of the Edmund Burke school, in which the task of government was "a perpetual act of compromise," as the writer Sam Tanenhaus put it, quoting Burke, "sometimes between good and evil, and sometimes between evil and evil." Government must always take the free-market view as its default position. His view was an oddly simplistic amalgam of soaring Randian idealism and down-in-the-weeds empiricism: more government was always bad, except when it was necessary. Then you would intervene, but afterward revert to an absolutist view of markets. There was no conceptual compromise to the ability of markets to work out their own problems. And he never really changed. Even much later, after the catastrophe, when he was long retired, Greenspan rejected the idea that he could have done anything more in a regulatory way. Regulation, after all, he pointed out, meant a "command economy. And command economies, we know, have always collapsed."

In truth, no one saw this strange divide at the time. Alan Greenspan edged his way into the confidences of powerful men in politics by being the voice of reason, the man who translated campaign promises into action. Still, his first practical connection to Washington came through a meeting with a fellow devotee of Ayn Rand: Martin Anderson, who was also an economist, with a Ph.D. from MIT in industrial management. The two met while Anderson was a professor at Columbia University and he, like Greenspan, used to make his way down to Murray Hill. From his own vantage point, Anderson was finding ways to attack Keynesianism and big government. In 1964, Anderson published a well-received book called *The Federal Bulldozer: A Critical Analysis of Urban Renewal: 1949–62.* That earned him a call from the Nixon camp, and Anderson persuaded Greenspan to join. "I thought he was the best economist I had ever seen. But he also had the best feel for what was politically correct to do," said Anderson. "He combined both." Greenspan may not have been a great admirer of Nixon's, but he was quietly running his domestic policy office in 1968, and he was getting noticed. After Ford's defeat in 1976, Greenspan again went back to his consulting firm and finally received his long-delayed Ph.D. from NYU. But Marty Anderson, his great admirer and now one of the coterie around the governor of California, Ronald Reagan, would not leave him alone. "Slowly he became lined up with Reagan," said Anderson. Together the two of them devised Reagan's first proposed budget in October 1980, even before the election.

Greenspan and Reagan were in sync, and while Greenspan did not have a lot of respect for Reagan's economic aptitude—unlike Anderson, who idolized Reagan and insisted that he had read all the works of Friedman, Hayek, and von Mises—Greenspan understood his charisma better than most. Reagan, he remarked at one point, was "psychologically a professional comedian," and that was a secret to his success. Greenspan's agility at crossing ideological and party lines also made him an ideal Reagan guy, especially when it came to bridging the divide between supply-siders and traditional fiscal conservatives in the administration. In 1983, Greenspan also chaired a commission on returning solvency to Social Security that became a model of bipartisanship in the eye of the Reagan revolution.

Having won over Ronald Reagan, Greenspan became the clear consensus choice to replace Paul Volcker as Fed chairman by the mid-1980s. The towering, cigar-chomping Volcker had earned the respect of the Reagan team, but he had been appointed by Jimmy Carter, after all. He'd been as tough as anyone could have wanted—perhaps too tough— in vanquishing inflation, but Volcker was most definitely not a Reaganite. "He won't take orders!" complained Treasury Secretary Don Regan, who didn't want him reappointed in 1983. Wall Street, at the time, had insisted: they loved the low-inflation environment Volcker was creating.

However, Volcker had a deep-seated fear of deregulation and unleashing Wall Street, and his influence was still deep, even among the Reaganites. With the Reagan administration's approval, Volcker's protégé, Gerald Corrigan, the president of the Federal Reserve Bank of New York, had managed to push through a pathbreaking agreement, called Basel I, in 1988, requiring international banks to hold substantial capital in reserve. But Volcker's time was ending, as was Corrigan's. In February 1987, shortly before the end of his term, the big Wall Street banks made the latest in a series of bids to unwind Glass-Steagall. The Glass-Steagall law had come under continual pressure as traditional commercial banks sought to follow their old clients into the capital markets, issuing stocks and bonds. Innovators such as JP Morgan had gone global while the law still reigned at home, becoming big in the Euromarkets.

At a hearing room in Washington, in one of his last acts as chairman, Volcker listened skeptically as Thomas Theobald, the vice chairman of Citicorp, argued that "the world has changed a hell of a lot" since the 1930s. Theobald argued that there were three new "outside checks" on corporate misconduct since then: "a very effective" Securities and Exchange Commission, knowledgeable investors, and "very sophisticated" rating agencies. Volcker stared gruffly at Theobald and the other two bankers who came to plead their case, he said sarcastically, as so "innocuous," so "sensible," that "we don't have to worry a bit." "But I guess I worry a little bit." Volcker worried aloud that without Glass-Steagall, lenders would begin recklessly lowering loan standards in order to win more contracts for public offerings of their borrowers' stock. He said that banks might start marketing bad loans to an unsuspecting public.

But Volcker was no longer in control of his board of governors. Reagan had named two free marketers, and so the Fed chairman found himself on the losing side of a 3–2 vote giving the bankers what they wanted. The new rules allowed Citicorp, JP Morgan, and Bankers Trust to move into some underwriting, including commercial paper, municipal revenue bonds, and mortgage-backed securities. It was the beginning of the process by which Glass-Steagall became effectively moot by the time it was formally repealed in 1999.

After Greenspan became Fed chairman in August, he permitted many more loopholes to be opened. The banks were allowed to begin dealing in debt and equity securities as well as municipal securities and commercial paper. Under the first loophole they were granted, back in 1986, they'd been restricted to only 5 percent of their business in underwriting; now they could go to 10 percent. Ultimately, Greenspan would allow the amount to be raised to 25 percent, effectively rendering large portions of Glass-Steagall obsolete. He later wrote that he didn't buy the conclusions of the Pecora Commission, whose investigation in 1934 led to Glass-Steagall, that "inappropriate use by banks of their securities affiliates was undermining overall soundness." In fact, it was banks with securities affiliates that "weathered the 1930s crisis better than those without affiliates," he said. Greenspan, ever the data hound, was at least partly right about that: later studies by Raghu Rajan of the University of Chicago, among others, showed there wasn't much evidence that banks with securities underwriting were systematically misrepresenting the quality of securities to the public before the Depression.

Still, while he quietly took a Randian ax to the regulatory thicket around him, his public face was as an interventionist. Greenspan believed that absent a gold standard (which he quietly still favored), a nation needs a strong central bank. And he turned the Fed into one. He faced his first major crisis just a little over two months after taking office. On Monday, October 19, 1987—another in a series of Black Mondays—the Dow plunged 508 points, or 22.6 percent, its worst ever one-day decline. He issued a strong statement saying he was ready to pump liquidity into the markets by opening the Fed up for loans. Critically, he also pressed Reagan to meet with Congress to address the huge budget deficit, which had brought inflation fears back to the market after the years in which Volcker had squeezed the stagflation out of the economy.

"Steady as she goes," Reagan had said after the plunge. "I don't think anyone should panic, because all the economic indicators are solid." Greenspan, fond of the phrase "history teaches us," had a flash memory of Hoover's infamous remark after Black Friday 1929 that the economy was "sound and prosperous," and pressed Treasury Secretary Jim Baker to set up a meeting with Reagan. The president offered to reach out to Congress on the budget, and the markets calmed. His performance in this first crisis immediately established Greenspan's interventionist bona fides. "Reagan thought Greenspan was terrific," said Martin Anderson. "[Reagan] thought for a long period of time that he was one of the best economists in the world."

But it wasn't until the single-term presidency of George H. W. Bush that Greenspan showed what a power baron he was really becoming in Washington.

Being Greenspan, he did it with gentlemanly style, of course. Greenspan became fast friends with Treasury Secretary Jim Baker after he went personally to deliver the bad news to Baker that the Fed had decided to raise the discount rate an entire half point just before the Republican convention of 1988. "I'm a believer in delivering bad news in person, privately, and in advance—especially in Washington, where officials hate to be blindsided," Greenspan later commented. "There's no alternative if you want to have a relationship thereafter." Indeed, one of the ironies of Greenspan's career was that while he maintained the image of a "purist" central banker uninfected by politics, no one was a savvier player in the Washington power game. As Steven K. Beckner wrote in a hagiographic biography, *Back from the Brink: The Greenspan Years*, the Greenspan Fed was crucial in stopping a number of wrong-headed policies such as talking down the dollar to ease the trade deficit with Japan, and in nudging a reluctant Bush administration toward budget reduction.

In fact, Greenspan's tightening in the late 1980s was largely responsible for President Bush's electoral defeat, and Greenspan made sure his successor, Clinton, knew it.

4

The Rise of Rubinomics

William Jefferson Clinton didn't start out as a free marketer. True, he'd run for president as a "New," or centrist, Democrat, but even then he was wary of alienating his liberal base. Clinton and his old schoolboy buddy from Hope, Arkansas, Thomas "Mack" McLarty, who had first managed a family service-station company and then a Fortune 500 oil concern, Arkla, had joined the Democratic Leadership Council together. The DLC was the Democratic Party's response to Reagan's defeat of Walter Mondale in 1984. It was the party's concession to the emerging zeitgeist: the new centrists would consciously and aggressively advocate "market-based solutions." Clinton "wouldn't have been elected if he hadn't run as a New Democrat," McLarty said. Still, during his days as governor of Arkansas, McLarty recalled, "Clinton used to ask me to speak to various business groups. I said, you just want me to be Jimmy Swaggart, you want me to give testimony here that you're governing as a centrist." It was McLarty who first recommended Lloyd Bentsen, a conservative Democrat, and Wall Streeter Robert Rubin as reliably pro-business advisers. "I said, you're not Dwight Eisenhower," McLarty said. "You've got to get some gravitas in here, some serious proven leadership. He agreed."

But Clinton had a strong populist strain; at heart he wanted to emulate FDR. He yearned to do something New Deal–sized and take the country in a new direction. He even quoted Roosevelt's call for "bold, persistent experimentation" in his first inaugural address, though that was rhetorical overreach: January 1993 was nothing like March 1933. Soon after taking office Clinton laid a wreath at Hyde Park; placed an iconic bust of FDR in the Oval Office; and in policy terms, one White House official later recalled to me, "talked far more about Roosevelt than JFK"—the president with whom, during the campaign, he'd hoped voters would identify him. These were different times, however. FDR had resorted to massive deficit spending to save the economy—and capitalism. But now, after a half century of New Deal thinking, the federal deficit was the biggest problem. The Reagan Revolution had deregulated and freed up the economy to market forces. But Reagan's halfhearted attachment to the theory of supply-side economics—his reluctance to cut government spending at the same time as he cut taxes, on the idea that lower taxes would unleash more prosperity—had left behind a fiscal disaster. So there was one major piece of the revolution unfinished: soaring government deficits of more than $200 billion a year. The result was that, even as the Fed under Greenspan began reducing short-term interest rates from 7 percent to 3 percent by the time of Clinton's 1993 inauguration, long-term rates were not following them down. The Reagan deficits, by creating huge government debt, had kept long-term rates high because the markets feared future inflation.

There was a gulf of suspicion between Wall Street and Washington, one that was even bigger than usual.

The new Clinton team believed that high interest rates, then a big drag on the economy, would not ease until the markets believed that Washington was going to do something to end the long era of budget deficits.

Like all incoming presidents, Clinton also badly wanted to avoid the mistakes of his predecessor, especially on the economy. George Herbert Walker Bush was a blue-blooded Texas transplant who always seemed to be trying to be something he was not, starting with the dubious claim that he loved to snack on pork rinds. Bush was in effect a transitional figure, a caretaker. He looked great on paper—former CIA director, ambassador to China, World War II hero—but he was uncharismatic in the extreme. Bush had never really been a Reaganite, starting from the moment he revealed his true colors in the 1980 campaign by mocking the tax-cutting fervor of the supply-siders as "voodoo economics."

Among those most suspicious of Bush was Milton Friedman, who said that Reagan's vice presidential selection was "the worst decision not only of his campaign but of his presidency." (Friedman wanted

Donald Rumsfeld instead.) Still, Bush eagerly signed on as the Gipper's vice president, and after eight years in the shadows he managed to ride Reagan's popularity to a win over the bumbling Michael Dukakis for the presidency in 1988. While in office Bush did many things well but in a managerial kind of way, and he never really won over the party of Goldwater and Reagan. The Reaganite hawks had, in their minds, won the Cold War.

George H. W. Bush had his moments as president. He stood down Saddam Hussein in the first Gulf War, after which his popularity reached its height of 70 percent. But the numbers quickly dissipated as the economy went into deep recession in 1991, thanks in part to Greenspan's interest rate hike. Fear and loathing of the Soviet Union, meanwhile, shifted to Japan, which had become an export superpower. Japan-bashing was at its height and America's dismal trade-deficit figures were bannered across front pages each month. "American jobs for American workers" became the new battle cry. "The Cold War is over, and Japan won," Paul Tsongas said during the 1992 election campaign, when a brilliant upstart named Bill Clinton began to exploit Bush Senior's out-of-touch persona with a singular campaign slogan: "It's the economy, stupid." Worst of all was the accumulation of giant budget deficits—supply-side economics had indeed been, to some extent, "voodoo economics," at least as it played out in practice. Beyond that, the nation needed to decompress. We'd had forty years of Cold War, and we were tired.

Nothing symbolized the mood of national exhaustion better than the day George H. W. Bush threw up in the lap of the prime minister of Japan, Kiichi Miyazawa. It was January 1992. The Gulf War was won, the USSR had winked out of existence the month before, but Bush was desperate to show he was taking command of the economic issues. American cars weren't selling well abroad, especially in Japan, so the president led the Big Three automakers to Tokyo, where they showcased their latest market-opening efforts. The mission was an utter failure, presaging Bush's astonishing election loss ten months later. The Japanese prime minister, a gentleman of the old school of postwar deference to Washington, urged his people to show "compassion" to the U.S. automakers. "I really don't want Mr. Miyazawa's sympathy," grumbled GM chairman Robert Stempel. Chrysler chairman Lee Iacocca was outraged at Miyazawa's presumptuousness. "We won the hot war, we won the Cold War; we're the leaders of the world," he declared. The bluster didn't work (and the Big Three never really did get over themselves, as we learned a decade and a half later). The most enduring image of the summit was that of the patrician President Bush, who towered over the elfin prime minister, lying helpless and gasping in Miyazawa's arms after vomiting all over him at a state dinner. (Bush had gotten dehydrated playing tennis during the day and fainted as the toasts were getting under way.) It was all very ugly.

Because he failed to inspire his Republican base, Bush always had razor-thin support during the 1992 election—the kind of support that could disappear if the economic numbers turned bad. And that's what happened. Texas maverick Ross Perot jumped into the presidential campaign; he argued for dramatic deficit reduction and played to the popular discontent by declaring that NAFTA (the North American Free Trade Agreement) would cause a "giant sucking sound" of vanishing jobs, siphoning what meager support both Bush and Clinton had in the moderate middle. Bush Senior lost the election in a landslide, getting just 38 percent to Clinton's 43 percent, with Perot amassing an astonishing 19 percent of the malcontent vote.

The political lesson to some was obvious: don't stray too far from movement politics; no one is inspired by a pragmatist or a caretaker. A popular president needs "the vision thing," as Bush Senior lamely called it. He had won only a half-victory in the Gulf War, leaving Saddam in place, and he had flip-flopped on taxes, pledging dramatically not to raise them ("Read my lips!" Bush declared, to his everlasting regret) and then doing so anyway. In truth, Bush had taken a brave stance in tackling the Reagan deficit, but in the public's mind there had been no higher principle at work in his administration, and no vision to inspire voters. Above all, Bush Senior seemed to waffle a lot, all too ready to see the world as gray rather than black and white. He had no sense of certainty. As much as the triumph of the Reagan years was a positive example, this was a negative example. Among those observing the lessons closely was the president's eldest son, George W. Bush, then a key election aide to his father.

The real reason for Bush's defeat, as Clinton divined, was the economy. And though Greenspan had actually loosened monetary policy as 1992 wound down, he had been uncharacteristically slow to recognize the recession. Had he acted sooner, the recovery might have begun early enough to help Bush. The Bush team, of course, was furious with him.

Treasury Secretary Nicholas Brady, in a fit of pique, stopped holding weekly breakfasts with Greenspan, and Bush himself never really forgave him. "I think that if the interest rates had been lowered more dramatically that I would have been reelected president because the recovery that we were in would have been more visible," Bush Senior told David Frost later in a 1998 interview. "I reappointed him, and he disappointed me."

But the experience only added to Greenspan's reputation in Washington as a man who could dictate the balance of power in Washington.

Bill Clinton, the new president, was absorbing all these lessons as well. For Clinton, avoiding Bush's mistakes also meant making sure that he avoided the ruinous infighting over the economy that had, in the end, destroyed Bush's presidency. A member of Clinton's inner circle recalled the candidate's reaction to a Bob Woodward story in the *Washington Post* in early October 1992, about a month before the election. The article exposed the bitter infighting between Treasury Secretary Nicholas Brady and Dick Darman, Bush's budget director, and Michael Boskin, the chairman of his Council of Economic Advisors. "President Bush's top economic advisers have worked for nearly four years without agreeing on an overall philosophy or plan and have been divided by personal animosity and turf fights that are fierce even by Washington standards," the story said. They were all sitting aboard Clinton's campaign plane when the candidate mentioned the story and said, "That's the problem with this administration." Clinton contrasted the Bush economic team to the smoothly running operation that Bush's national security adviser, Brent Scowcroft, was overseeing:

"They're behind in the polls, and his economic policy guys are fighting," Clinton said.

"But governor, the national security guys disagree with each other just as much," someone pointed out.

"You're missing the point," Clinton said. "With Scowcroft, it doesn't get out to the public."

That was the genesis of Clinton's idea to create a "National Economic Council" to coordinate policy and avoid the pitfalls of the Bush years. Clinton was enormously impressed with the way one of his advisers, Robert Rubin, had worked well as co-CEO of Goldman Sachs. After the election, he had Rubin fly down to Little Rock for an interview. The two bonded immediately when Rubin told Clinton that the difference between Drexel Burnham Lambert, the poster child for Wall Street dysfunction, and Goldman Sachs, the class act of the Street, was that Goldman's partners functioned smoothly as a team.

So Rubin was on board, and with him came a Wall Street sensibility that was to distinguish this new kind of Democratic administration for the rest of the decade.

Clinton's come-to-Wall-Street moment occurred even before he took office. It was at his opening act two weeks before the inauguration—the big economic powwow he held in Little Rock to fulfill his campaign promise of "putting people first." "Bob Rubin called me from Washington that morning," McLarty recalled. "It reminded me of the Houston-NASA thing. He said, 'Mack, we've got a problem.' And I said, 'What's the problem?' He said, 'The deficit is considerably larger than we thought it was going to be.' And what that really meant was the beginning of the hard choices [about whether to keep] the middle class tax cut he had promised, and some of the programs that our more traditional Democrats had felt were essential." Over the next couple of days, advisers such as Alan Blinder, an eminent Princeton economist, laid out the grim realities of what it would mean to cut a deficit this size. It was necessary to cut it, he said, because the vast amount of government spending that was creating the deficit used too much of the nation's savings, crowding out healthy private investment that was needed to boost the economy.

Unfortunately, as they cut the deficit the economy would contract, Blinder said. Clinton could face a recession not unlike the one that torpedoed Bush. The saving grace, Blinder thought, would come if the Federal Reserve and above all the bond traders on Wall Street cooperated by driving down interest rates. Most economists believe that large long-term budget deficits like the ones facing the Clintonites cause interest rates to rise. That's in part because the huge government spending behind long-term or "structural" budget deficits creates inflationary fears, and the Fed often reacts by raising interest rates. That chokes off growth and any recovery, Blinder said. But if the deficits were cut dramatically, inflation fears and therefore interest rates would begin to drop too, and that would spur economic growth, outweighing the contradictory effects of deficit cutting. Rubin, for his part, fretted about the problem from a trader's point of view: he feared that the federal government was so deep in the hole that bond traders would continue to perceive an enormous demand for capital and keep bidding up rates. But if they were reassured something was being done about the deficit, the market psychology would change for the better, he argued.

"You mean to tell me that the success of the program and my reelection hinges on the Federal Reserve and a bunch of fucking bond traders?" Clinton asked.

Blinder saw it as an epiphany: Wall Street (and the Fed) had taken command of the economy, and everyone up to the very top saw this now. Clinton accepted the idea, pushed on him by Bentsen, his new Treasury secretary, and Rubin, the head of the National Economic Council (NEC), that something had to be done right away. "The threshold issue had to be the deficit, and how quickly you gain credibility with the markets," Rubin told me, "since ultimately it's market interest rates that drive the economy." Interest rates had to come down for the economy to recover, and that meant the bond market had to be assuaged. The first weeks of the new administration were brutal. "We then spent this enormous amount of time in the Roosevelt Room," said McLarty. "To his credit [Clinton] went over that budget line by line himself. And those were long days. The reason is we had to cut that budget and reshape it." The decisive moment came in a hallway meeting with McLarty, Rubin, and chief of staff Leon Panetta outside the Roosevelt Room. Clinton popped out of the Oval Office and told them that of the three choices he'd been given, he wanted the one that would reduce the deficit the most. "He said, 'This is what we're going to do.'"

So Clinton, who had become a centrist, a DLC type, in order to get elected, began to tack even farther rightward on the economy. He was listening intently to Bentsen and to Rubin, who was listening to the bond market and to Greenspan.

With some bitter reflection, Clinton dropped his promised middle-class tax cuts and focused on the deficit. He understood the issues. As governor of Arkansas, Clinton himself had been bound by a revenue stabilization act that required a balanced budget. But he still wasn't happy at all about what he had to do. He kept coming back to his cynical wonderment at the power of the bond market. "Roosevelt was trying to help people," he said. "Here we help the bond market." At another point, as the debate turned increasingly to reducing the deficit, Clinton barked sarcastically to his aides: "I hope you're all aware you're all Eisenhower Republicans. We're Eisenhower Republicans here, and we're fighting the Reagan Republicans. We stand for lower taxes and free trade and the bond market. Isn't that great?"

For Clinton, it was a huge gamble. He was alienating his base, just as Bush Senior had done. The only hope was that his advisers were right on the economy, and if they were, he could recover.

Clinton was intent on following through with his campaign promises and promoting growth in other ways. He turned U.S. ambassadors into virtual salesmen for U.S. multinationals. They would now justify their paychecks by drumming for contracts. In Malaysia, Ambassador John Stern Wolf, a career diplomat, became a "one-man marketing organization," one American CEO told me at the time, landing multimillion-dollar contracts for McDonnell Douglas and General Electric. Walter Mondale, the former vice president, spent much of his two-year tenure as ambassador to Japan plugging for Motorola. Commerce Secretary Ron Brown, a close Clinton crony, transformed his backwater agency into a policy dynamo with trade-mission-a-month headlines, and even Secretary of State Warren Christopher declared that global economics was at the top of his foreign policy agenda. Clinton's combative trade representative, Mickey Kantor, said he wasn't interested in free-trade "theology" and declared that Americans would now behave like the mercantilist Europeans. "For years we have allowed our workers to be hurt and our companies to be left out because we wouldn't pick up the phone and ask for the order. Why shouldn't we?" he explained. Said Blinder, "Clinton had run in the 1992 campaign with more than a dash of Japan bashing, being critical of Bush Pere for not asserting rights. The one thing you learned in the early days of the administration is that contrary to popular myth, politicians take their campaign promises seriously."

In any case, the policy never really produced many jobs—the rules of economics, defined by national investment and savings, still governed—and after Ron Brown was killed on a trade mission too far, his plane crashing in the foggy mountains of Croatia, the new approach petered out. Very few people missed it.

One thing appeared to work well, however, the policy that his economic advisers had pushed: joint appeasement of the bond market and Alan Greenspan. The economy started picking up. Clinton and his top officials began to regain an attitude they had sorely lacked in those early days of giving up their campaign promises and moving toward deficit reduction: a sense of certainty. The markets were humming. The bond market had rewarded them. Greenspan had smiled upon them, avoiding a rate hike despite some incipient signs of inflation in the first months of Clinton's term.

Meanwhile, Clinton kept getting lessons in the failure of the traditional Democratic agenda. Robert Reich, his old pal from Oxford, advocated passionately for public support for an ailing middle class that had been undercut by job losses related to globalization. But in his post as labor secretary, he found himself cut out of the loop. Hillary Clinton, who had never completely bought into deficit reduction as the centerpiece of her husband's agenda, sought to reengineer health care from scratch. She succeeded only in destroying big-government politics for good. Hillary's 1,342-page health-care plan proved unpopular with insurance companies and patients as well as doctors. The backlash against "Hillarycare" led to the takeover of Congress by Republicans, who ended forty years of Democratic control of the House by gaining fifty-two seats (and five more from party switchers) along with eight Senate seats (plus two party switchers).

The period following the midterm elections was a decisive time for Clinton. In response to the Contract with America's Reaganite resurgence—calling for the complete elimination of welfare, among other things—Clinton triangulated further to the right. He began trying out a new phrase: "The era of big government is over," and it eventually became the most quotable thing from his 1996 State of the Union address. He stood up for Bush's North American Free Trade Agreement with Mexico and Canada, and pushed it through Congress. Although Clinton didn't realize it at the time, this amounted to the first major attack on the U.S. consumer and therefore on the world's entire post–World War II model of growth. American consumers were the world's buyer of last resort; now the wage base that underpinned this model of growth was being undercut. In later years, only an excess of consumer credit would keep Americans buying, and NAFTA would mainly benefit Wall Street and U.S. banks, which eventually took over most of the Mexican banks. (Little of this was apparent at the time, but the trade pact would do little to improve the job situation on either side of the border; the Mexican *maquiladora* factories—assembly plants along the border—had been operating under zero tariffs even before NAFTA.)

Clinton also brought in David Gergen, who had been an adviser to three Republican presidents: Nixon, Ford, and Reagan. And when it came to his agenda on globalization, it was all about promoting markets and democracy. Clinton, said Representative Barney Frank, became "a Reaganaut abroad."

But the new president was clearly on to something; he was getting out ahead of the emerging free-market mood. As Edward Knight, Rubin's general counsel at Treasury, later recalled, "We went through terrible times in '93 and '94. We had a vision that with encouragement of free trade, with fiscal conservatism, with a freeing up of capital for the entrepreneurial class, with the promotion of technology innovation, that perhaps this economy might get righted and have sustained growth. And lo and behold, it did."

There were other reasons for the mid-to-late-1990s boom. The post–Cold War opening to foreign markets and cheaper labor, especially in China, kept inflation from rising. The Fed could avoid raising rates, and the markets knew it. And the dot-com mania had begun. But as the economy began to recover, many in the Clinton administration and on Wall Street credited the good graces of the bond market, and a new power elite began to emerge in the Clinton administration. Sitting atop it was Rubin, a man who almost as much as Greenspan came to define the 1990s.

There was a style about Bob Rubin that everyone loved—judicious, calm, untouched by the rancor. He mastered a kind of political jujitsu that was very unusual in Washington, a city whose power structure is ever defined by jostling for rank, which meetings you're invited to join, and getting your allotted time. It never worried Rubin. He had impressed everyone right away with his tight command of the NEC, quashing the efforts of other agencies to establish an independent line into the White House. Rubin was "as close to anyone I've ever seen who came into a senior government job totally ready to do it," White House deputy Dan Tarullo, later to be a Federal Reserve governor, told me at the time. Clinton appreciated, above all, that Rubin took the new president's desire for teamwork seriously, and that he made the NEC into exactly what Clinton had wanted to create: a smoothly run policy coordination body where everyone got a voice, but the debates all stayed within the White House. "You can't have five different agencies with six different positions," Clinton would say, harking back to an infamous episode during the Bush administration involving what to do about the endangered spotted owl, when one agency did in fact put out two different positions.

And even as the young administration jostled internally over the economic trade-offs it faced—the fight over dropping middle-class tax cuts, how much investment in education and health care would have to be jettisoned to pay for deficit reduction—Rubin managed to keep the arguments mostly under wraps. Those who argued too vociferously, like Robert Reich, were gently edged out of the conversation and, ultimately, the administration. But no one could pin any blame for that on the low-key Rubin. He was known for giving up his daily brief with Clinton if he had nothing to say that day. Such regular demonstrations of self-confidence only enhanced his stature, of course. "Rubin will sit there at a cabinet meeting and say nothing while everyone else jabbers away," an administration official recalled to me at the time. "Then at the end the president will turn to him and say, 'Bob, what do you think?' And Clinton listens. It makes Rubin the statesman in the process."

He'd always been that way, always protesting that he wasn't the right guy, even while maneuvering to be the guy. When he was nine, Rubin's family moved from New York to Miami Beach. At North Beach Elementary School, Miss Collins, his new teacher, introduced him to the class by announcing: "Robbie Rubin has gone to a private school in New York and has never learned script. So let's all be very nice to him." As Rubin later remarked wryly, "As a result, I assume, of this suggestion, I was elected president of my fourth-grade class on my first day. My protests that I didn't know how to be class president fell on deaf ears." Even Rubin conceded in his memoirs that "you can draw a line from that day to my becoming Secretary of the Treasury forty-eight years later."

The son of a lawyer and investor who, like Warren Buffett, was a disciple of Benjamin Graham, the father of long-term investing, Rubin had grown up in upper-middle-class wealth and privilege, a milieu of golf and card games at the cabana club. He was a good but not standout student at Miami Beach Senior High School. Rubin was rejected at Princeton, but a friend of his father's helped him get into Harvard—the friend's friend just happened to be Harvard's dean of admissions and happened to be passing through Miami one day, so he met Bob. After an uncertain start—he feared flunking out his first year; and it may have been the last time he was ever completely unsure of his abilities—Rubin managed to graduate summa cum laude. He casually applied to Harvard Law School and to Harvard's Ph.D. program in economics and was accepted to both. Rubin decided on law, but after a few days there he walked into the dean's office and said he wanted to take some time off. He wanted to go to the London School of Economics and wander about Europe a bit.

There was always something of the bohemian manqué about Rubin. It was part of his charm. With that handsome, angular face, he looked and behaved like an ascetic, living apart from his wife at the Jefferson Hotel—a hater of Washington, she had stayed in New York to be near their younger son, Philip—lunching on carrot sticks, salad, and mineral water. In his professional life, Rubin had gone from success to success with seeming ease, but there was always the need to find some obscure stream to fish in, some place to hike to. He had no problem stretching out on his back on the steps outside the Oval Office as if he were lounging at the ol' swimming hole. At Harvard he had liked to go to coffeehouses, "liked the sit-around-and-ponder-the issues-of-life atmosphere," he wrote. Dreaming of escape was always a release valve for him.

So Rubin went off to the LSE and did the requisite wandering about Europe, reading Sartre and Camus on the Left Bank. When he finally came back, he went to Yale Law School, which seemed less structured than Harvard. Even then Rubin never really wanted to practice law. "I had a vague sense I wanted to do something financial," maybe real estate, he said. But he thought he ought to try out law for a while, "to see what it was like." His "career epiphany" came one day when young Bob was working on behalf of a Wall Street client called Hayden, Stone, the lead underwriter on an investment banking deal taking Comsat public. "When I'm forty, I thought, I want to be doing what those guys are doing, not what I'm doing," he wrote.

With his father's help, he got a job as a junior arbitrageur at Goldman, the primo firm on the Street. Rubin rose swiftly, impressing the firm's legendary top guy, gruff Gus Levy. In 1983, Rubin, then head of risk arbitrage, made what the *Economist* later called "arguably the single most influential decision of his long career" when he hired an economist named Fischer Black from the MIT Sloan School of Management in Cambridge, Massachusetts. An eccentric genius, Black had along with Myron Scholes developed a mathematical model for pricing options, opening up a whole new market that depended more and more on speculation and leverage. In light of what later would happen to him, Citigroup delving into complex derivatives that Rubin didn't understand, it was ironic that he helped set the trend in motion. "We will learn from Fischer," Rubin told his partners, "and he will learn from us." Classic Rubin: We're all in this together. Now let's make some money! When he arrived, Black was an efficient markets theorist. But, in fact, he did learn from the long-term success of Rubin and his fellow traders in foreign exchange that there must be some problems with that theory—because Goldman had made so much money outsmarting the markets.

As for Rubin, he may have been a believer in deferring to the markets, but he knew they weren't perfect. They couldn't be: he had gotten very rich by "arbitraging" price differences in the same assets, such as currencies, across different markets (say, in London and Tokyo). If the markets were perfectly efficient and transmitted price information instantaneously, the way some efficient markets theorists argued they must, then Bob Rubin would have been about $100 million poorer.

At Goldman Sachs, where he was co-CEO, he had developed a philosophy he called "probabilistic decision making." You played the odds; you were never certain; you were prepared to err, and so when you inevitably did you got out of the losing position fast and moved on with your life. Go with the flow, good or bad: that too was part of the Rubin charm, and he brought it with him to Washington. "The reason people listen to him is that he's not certain. He knows what he doesn't know. This is extraordinarily rare in this city," said an administration official. Rubin was also, as Jeffrey Garten, a senior Commerce official, described him during the Clinton years, "a fantastic listener. Everybody who advances a position is convinced they had their day in court." Rubin became the mature policy maker in the process, the grownup in the room, his judgment unsullied by ambition. And Rubin was no ideologue, at least he didn't seem to be; like Greenspan, he gave off an aura of measured deliberation, an openness to all ideas.

But behind the Rubin style, the humility and self-effacement, lay a hard ego and a set of very certain beliefs about the economy: Washington needed to have credibility on Wall Street. It became the defining principle of his tenure: globalized financial markets were simply too powerful, an elemental force that must be assuaged. Rubin became the schoolmarmish voice of the Street—and totally disciplined about not talking up the stock market or talking down the Fed. "To some extent once the administration took the position not to comment on or criticize the Federal Reserve you begin to be part of their team. Sometimes the president would pound the table, saying, 'How the hell can the Federal Reserve do this?'" former White House chief of staff Leon Panetta recalled. But "Rubin was very strict about paying attention to that rule." All were mindful of what Greenspan had done to the man they defeated, George H. W. Bush. And Rubin, who became Treasury secretary in January 1995 after the elderly Bentsen decided to retire, said the administration had no choice but to defer to the markets if for no other reason than that Clinton came into office confronting record deficits. Twelve years of business-friendly Republicans in the White House had done little to bridge the gulf between Washington and Wall Street.

When the stock market soared, so did Rubin's reputation, especially after Clinton's reelection in 1996. "The election was a vote of approval not only for Clinton but for Rubin and Greenspan," said Bob Hormats, an economic official under Bush I and later Obama. "For a long time there was a view that New York and Washington were two different worlds. I think he embodies the unification of those two worlds." Felix Rohatyn, the legendary investment banker and ambassador to France, thought that Rubin was precisely the right man for the time. "Modern global capitalism is a new animal. It's rather demanding and unforgiving. It requires fiscal discipline, high levels of investment, research, probably a strong currency. And he understands modern capitalism better than any government official I know," Rohatyn told me.

All these talents were put to the test in the decisive crisis of Clinton's first term: the fight over the budget. Newt Gingrich, the bombastic new Speaker of the House and the main author of the Contract with America, seemed to see himself as a Man of History and Clinton as an afterthought. Gingrich was supremely self-confident that his party's decisive takeover of the House represented a broad shift and a mandate for drastic cuts in spending and a balanced budget. Clinton, still triangulating, initially showed flexibility in negotiations, which only made Gingrich more self-confident that he could get his way. As the budget fight continued, Gingrich kept insisting on all of his program, including tax cuts for the wealthy and cuts in Medicare. After he hinted on *This Week with David Brinkley* that as Speaker he might refuse to raise the debt limit in April 1995, the political struggle erupted into open war.

Gingrich publicly threatened that the United States might have to default on its debt for the first time in its history. Rubin was appalled; the United States had just finished lecturing the Mexicans about what such an act would do to their credit standing in the world. Default would have jacked up interest rates, costing jobs, and it would have meant a devastating, perhaps permanent, blow to U.S. prestige. It was an odd reversal of roles, to be sure, with the Democrats deferring to Wall Street and the Republicans deaf to the Street's signals. After Rubin issued his warnings, Gingrich and other Republican leaders such as Senator Bob Dole began publicly questioning his credibility. But Rubin sensed early that Gingrich was overplaying his hand.

"The Republicans could have declared victory at several points—particularly after Clinton proposed a ten-year balanced budget, or after he later proposed a seven-year goal in exchange for the Republicans' relinquishing big cuts in social spending," Rubin later observed. "For some reason they never did."

Instead, Gingrich kept upping the stakes. He seemed to actually believe he was running the show, perhaps encouraged by Clinton's weak plaint to a reporter in April 1995, during the height of the Gingrich revolution, "Hey, the president is relevant here." Rubin bluntly told the president that a career on Wall Street had given him a lot of insight into the psychology of negotiation; and based on the way Clinton was behaving, he was hinting to the Republicans that they could "roll over you." The president at last stood firm, refusing to compromise on cuts in Medicare and other programs. Shortly after midnight on November 13, 1995, following an eleventh-hour nighttime meeting at the White House between the Clinton team and Gingrich, House Majority Leader Dick Armey, and Senator Bob Dole failed, a government shutdown of all but emergency services began.

It was a bitter, grim time for Clinton, during which the president came close to cracking, as his friend Taylor Branch later wrote. In the first two years of his administration his mother had died, and Vincent Foster, his longtime friend, had committed suicide. In November 1995, Israeli prime minister Yitzhak Rabin, whom Clinton considered a mentor and in whom he placed hopes for a historic peace deal while president, was assassinated. It wasn't long after that Clinton started his surreptitious sexual relationship with a flirtatious White House intern named Monica Lewinsky. "He felt sorry for himself," Branch said.

But Clinton eventually outmaneuvered Gingrich and humiliated him, and it was in large part because he had Rubin behind him. Rubin's reputation with Wall Street had sowed self-doubt among the Republicans about how the financial world might react to a U.S. default. And as the weeks passed, the Treasury secretary's deft efforts at easing the impact of the shutdown in the face of GOP intransigence conveyed a sense of confidence about the administration that hadn't been there before. First Rubin borrowed from two government trust funds, enraging the GOP members who hadn't expected the wily maneuver, some of whom threatened Rubin with impeachment. Rubin, cool as ever, joked that his wife, Judy, might be willing to testify in favor of impeachment—she wanted him back in New York anyway. Though neither side wanted to give in, polls increasingly showed that the public blamed Gingrich and the Republicans, especially after the Speaker revealed indiscreetly in an interview that he had been less inclined to be flexible in negotiations because Clinton had left him in the back of Air Force One on the trip to Israel to attend Rabin's funeral.

In the early months of 1996, things began to turn around for Clinton. Prompted by public warnings from Rubin, the two top rating agencies, Moody's and Standard and Poor's, issued a threat about cutting their triple-A ratings on U.S. Treasuries because of the greater possibility of default on America's debt. As businessmen started to get scared, the Republicans began to realize they were losing the support not only of the public but of Wall Street. The Gingrich insurgency started to crumble. The Speaker was no longer the cynosure of all headlines, and the media began to credit Rubin for standing up as the calm and commanding center of the Democratic resistance.

"Just possibly, Rubin-brand maturity may win Mr. Clinton a second term," opined the *Economist*. "Over the past few months, a cool temper has proved useful. As the Republicans in Congress have been refusing to raise the ceiling on the national debt, the Treasury secretary has been required to perform an alarming high-wire act. To induce the Republicans to relent, he has had to draw attention to the awful consequences that might ensue if the government is barred from taking out fresh loans: America might default on its debt, destroying its reputation in financial markets and so raising its cost of borrowing. Meanwhile, to keep the markets calm, Mr. Rubin has had to explain that default, though possible, is not really going to happen."

As public sentiment shifted, the Republicans caved on the budget, led by Dole, who began to grow worried about his prospects for the presidency in 1996. Gingrich would have a measure of vengeance later

on, when the Monica Lewinsky scandal came to light in early 1998 and
the House speaker led the drive to impeach Clinton. But his insurrection-
ary effort to eclipse the president in influence and prestige was over. Now
Gingrich was mocked in a cartoon on the front page of the New York
Daily News as a mewling infant, crying for attention at the back of Air
Force One. "What had been a noble battle for fiscal sanity began to
look like the tirade of a spoiled child," Gingrich's ally, House Whip Tom
DeLay, wrote. "The revolution, I can tell you, was never the same."

Rubin, by contrast, was seen as the adult in the room. The episode
cemented his reputation in Washington, though it also ingrained in the
public's mind the idea that being "grown-up" meant understanding
the Street and being understood by it—becoming a man of capital.

And as 1995 rolled into the election year of 1996, the economy began
to boom. The main measure was the stock market; the fact that wages
were moving up only very slightly seemed a secondary issue. Still, unemployment was dropping, and Rubin and the Clintonites took pride that for
the first time in years, compensation across all income groups was increasing. Now Clinton began to do something he had been unwilling to do for
most of his first term: talk about success, take credit for the economy.

His aide Gene Sperling recalled, "I remember I wrote up a statement on unemployment going down or something, and when I went into
the Oval Office he said, 'I don't ever want you to bring me something
again that somebody in the worst thirty economic counties in the country
would hear and think we've lost touch.' But by 1996 we started to take a
little bit of credit. Clinton said, 'You can finally go out and tell people.'"

Bill Clinton ran another election campaign on an "It's the economy, stupid" theme—but this time it was his economy, and Rubin's and
Greenspan's, and the news was almost all good. The president won a
second term running away against Dole, his aging GOP opponent.
Greenspan himself would later write mischievously, "I think Bill Clinton
was the best Republican president we've had in a while." By the end even
traditional Democrats like Paul Begala, a key Clinton aide, came to the
economic team and told them they'd been right to defer to Greenspan
and focus so monomaniacally on the budget deficit. "I thought you guys
were crazy for not beating up the Fed when they were raising rates. But
I have to admit, you guys were right," Begala told Sperling.

The Clinton era was, slowly but surely, turning into the Era of
Rubin. And the Era of Rubin was becoming an era of good feeling and

mutual understanding between Washington and Wall Street that was
almost unprecedented. For decades there had been querulous incom-
prehension between them—even during the Reagan era. "Washington
doesn't understand interest rates and Wall Street doesn't understand Washington," Stuart Eizenstat, a top domestic aide to Jimmy
Carter, would tell William Greider in *Secrets of the Temple*, his
1987 book on the Fed. "That two-hundred-mile gap is like a giant
chasm. They travel in different circles. They just don't speak the
same language."

Robert Rubin—a Democrat no less—changed all that.

5

Larry and Joe

Bill Clinton had anointed Bob Rubin, making him the administration's sole voice on the economy. But that wasn't the end of the story. There were still intense debates going on behind closed doors in the administration. They were largely academic, technical stuff, incomprehensible and dull to most people. But they were debates that would change the world, and the two economists who dominated them would come to represent two very different views of the post–Cold War era. Much as U.S. policy during the Cold War era toward the Soviet Union came to be seen by many as an intellectual tug-of-war between the views of George Kennan, the dove, and Paul Nitze, the hawk, this new economic age would come to be largely defined by the contending views of Lawrence Henry Summers and Joseph Eugene Stiglitz. Between Summers, the driver of markets, and Stiglitz, the skeptic of markets; Summer, the hawk, and Stiglitz, the dove.

Summers, for the most part, argued for freeing up the financial markets, confident that they would direct capital to where it was used most efficiently. Stiglitz was profoundly leery of the wisdom of Wall Street; he believed that in most cases capital would go to where it hoped to find the biggest short-term profits. The "smart money," he believed, was not nearly as smart as it was cracked up to be.

The two of them were little known outside their profession in those days. In fact, they weren't even very well known in Washington. But each man possessed a towering intellect with an ego to match. And each would come to carve out a vast sphere of influence for his ideas—one man in Washington, the other in almost every part of the world *except* Washington. The latter man, Stiglitz, was an outsider by temperament and would always remain one, though during the Clinton administration he had an office right next to the White House and would occupy senior positions elsewhere in Washington. Stiglitz's opponent, Larry Summers, was even then mastering the intricate politics of becoming a consummate Washington insider, and he was the man whom Bob Rubin came to entrust with big questions about the world economy. Rubin, after all, was no economist. Just as he had hired Fischer Black at MIT ten years earlier to bring the quant revolution to Wall Street, Rubin placed the big economic questions in the care of Summers. Soon he began bringing Summers along to his weekly lunches with Greenspan.

It was, by anyone's reckoning, a savvy choice. Summers was, like Stiglitz, emerging as one of the great economists of his generation. Both men were incredibly prolific and winners of the John Bates Clark medal awarded every two years to the nation's preeminent economist under forty (an award so hard to get that some economists say it's more prestigious than a Nobel Prize). But unlike Stiglitz, Summers had already left his academic work behind and had decided to put theory into practice in Washington. It was a role he would, in many ways, never relinquish.

Stiglitz, one of three members of Clinton's Council of Economic Advisors, was a Midwestern genius and an unlikely hero by any reckoning. Short and stumpy, he bore a passing resemblance to Mel Brooks, with perhaps a dollop of Chico Marx thrown in. Still, women were often attracted to him, and the feeling was mutual (he eventually married three times). Stiglitz liked to twirl a pencil in his ear as he talked, and he was so absentminded and otherworldly in manner that even friends and admirers in academe and government thought he wasn't meant for the practical policy-making world.

One time, discussing at a White House meeting how to respond to Norway's controversial hunting of minke whales, Stiglitz suggested that the U.S. boycott the 1994 Winter Olympics, which were being held in Lillehammer that year, to teach the Norwegians a lesson. Someone gently pointed out that it seemed like a somewhat disproportionate response— Jimmy Carter, after all, had boycotted the Moscow Summer Olympics after the Soviet invasion of Afghanistan. This was just about whales. Okay, Stiglitz countered, "Why don't we just boycott the events we're not good at, like that one with the skis and the guns?" By the end of his first year in Washington, everyone had a wacky "Joe" anecdote to tell.

"One time we went to Ukraine together," said Peter Orszag, who worked for Stiglitz at the Council of Economic Advisors. "We were preparing something for the next morning. It was running late. I called him on the phone about something." The two exchanged hellos. "Then he said, 'Peter, did I wake you up?' I said, 'Joe, I called you.'" Stiglitz also was known for falling asleep at the drop of a hat, even as a young man. Often it would happen when he was driving—and of course his family eventually kept him from driving.

He would write unceasingly, disgorging a stream of papers and memoranda that, one subordinate recalls, were "like one endless run-on sentence. . . . There would be ten pages with seven brilliant ideas and three flawed thoughts and a lot of other useful stuff. You just needed to find it." But Stiglitz had a grand passion, one that drove him in all his work. He would share a Nobel Prize in 2001 for showing mathematically that Adam Smith's invisible hand did not always work—especially when it came to financial markets. Stiglitz had demonstrated in his work that there were many cases when imperfect information led to less than perfect efficiency in markets—but even more than that, his mathematical models showed that the small digressions from rational behavior that Milton Friedman dismissed as unimportant were in fact hugely significant. They upset the proper workings of markets completely. Indeed, one of the ironies of the free-market 1990s is that, back in the cloisters of academe, the work of Stiglitz and a few others such as George Akerlof and Kenneth Arrow was beginning to show the fallacies in the Friedmanian ideal.

Stiglitz simply looked at the world in a different way from everyone else, Peter Orszag later said. After the S&L crisis and other banking crises of the 1980s, Stiglitz had concluded that there was likely something just plain irrational about the banking business, like so many other markets. He didn't know what it was, but it was there. Others, like Summers, observed the same thing in the papers they wrote, but moved on to other things. Stiglitz wouldn't let the idea go; he fit it into his larger emerging worldview about the imperfection of markets. "The evidence of the incompetency of banks is, by now, bountiful: a series of disasters—real estate loans . . . loans to Third World countries, oil and gas loans—provide a convincing case," he wrote in 1990. "This string of failures could, of course, simply be bad luck, but that seems an unlikely explanation." Stiglitz then issued a warning about a new, still-small trend: the securitizing of mortgages, turning home loans into bonds that would be sold around the world to buyers. Would that trend get out of control as well? he won-dered. Was the growth in securitization a good thing, evidence of greater efficiency and better technology in the markets? Or did it bode "an unfounded reduction in concern about the importance of screening loan applicants?" he asked. "It is, perhaps, too early to tell, but we should at least entertain the possibility that it is the latter."

The idea floated off into the ether, like so many others. And char-acteristically, Stiglitz later forgot that he'd even written that paper. (It turned up in 2009 after the subprime mortgage crisis, when he was col-lecting his *Selected Works* for Oxford University Press.) "Inevitably we'd find a paper he'd written in 1978 that he didn't remember. It's almost like he comes up with the thoughts anew, and doesn't remember that he had it," said Jonathan Orszag, Peter's brother, who also worked for him. Stiglitz's mind was so fertile and his pen so prolific that all the papers he'd written, if taken together, actually began to reinvent mod-ern economics in profound ways, undermining the prevailing doctrine of free markets as rational. But it was almost as if he was *too* prolific. No one could keep up with all the ideas.

Not even Stiglitz. He never managed to pull his insights together into an overarching theory. And he was so absentminded and scattered in his approach to policy that it would be years before people realized the full impact he had been having on the thinking of an entire generation. "Almost every time you dig into some sub-field of economics—finance, imperfect competition, health care—you find that much of the work rests on a seminal Stiglitz paper," the *Times* columnist (and fellow Nobelist) Paul Krugman would later remark, still sounding surprised. Even in the Clinton administration, people often didn't realize who Stiglitz was. As Jonathan Orszag recalled, "During one meeting, someone from the presi-dent's health-care task force was presenting something, and they used the term 'moral hazard' in a way Joe didn't agree with. Joe said, 'What do you mean by a moral hazard problem?' The person started explaining the con-cept of moral hazard to Joe. At which point somebody stopped the health person and said, 'Do you know you're talking to the guy who invented this field of economics?'"

Above all, Stiglitz was not really a debater. He was a thinker. He was so brilliant, some thought, that it was almost as if he expected everyone to see and agree with his arguments right away. They didn't, as it turned out—not by a long shot.

Summers, by contrast, was one of the best debaters Washington had ever seen. Only thirty-eight when he became undersecretary of the Treasury for international affairs, he was eleven and a half years younger than Stiglitz and he was, unlike his rival, to the manner born. Stiglitz was the son of an insurance broker who grew up in gritty Gary, Indiana; Summers was the son of two economists and the nephew of two more, both Nobel Prize winners who are considered among the greatest economic thinkers of the twentieth century: Paul Samuelson and Kenneth Arrow. He enjoyed a bucolic upbringing in suburban Philadelphia's Main Line, where his father and mother, Robert Summers and Anita Arrow Summers, taught at the University of Pennsylvania. It was an atmosphere of pure intellection—or in Larry's case, pure argumentation around the family table. His mother was the American-born daughter of Jewish immigrants from Romania. Robert Summers had the misfortune to be the lesser-known younger brother of the great Paul Samuelson. It wasn't surprising, perhaps, that he changed his last name. And it wasn't surprising that Larry Summers, despite the outstanding work that would win him the Clark medal, decided in midcareer that policy making was the way to go. As brilliant as he was, his academic work was never likely to rival the originality and impact of the work of Paul Samuelson and Kenneth Arrow.

He brought all his professorial habits to Washington. A heavily built former MIT prodigy and Harvard professor (at twenty-eight, one of the youngest ever to get tenure), Summers was also hopelessly absentminded. Unlike Stiglitz, he at least tried hard to clean up at Treasury, an associate remembers, but Summers still would forget to tuck in his shirt and look in the mirror after he shaved. "There were always patches left," the associate said. (Stiglitz avoided such pitfalls by growing a full beard.) Summers's table manners were atrocious; he was always stuffing things into his mouth. Chewing, to Larry, seemed an annoying nicety that would simply get in the way of another triumphant debate point to be scored at the dinner table.

Summers was the nephew of two great Keynesians, and ironically enough, he had made his name authoring a powerful series of empirical studies backing up many of the striking findings of a bold young economist named Joseph Stiglitz. In light of their later enmity, there were some ironic interconnections in the family stories of Summers and Stiglitz. At MIT, the older Stiglitz had been Paul Samuelson's protégé and the editor of his papers. Stiglitz later credited Summers's other uncle, Kenneth Arrow, with "opening up" the field of the economics of imperfect information that Stiglitz won his Nobel for in 2001. While Arrow won his Nobel for proving mathematically that the equilibrium of neoclassical economics can exist, under certain conditions, he later pronounced himself deeply influenced by Stiglitz.

During his whole career, Larry Summers found himself caught between these two traditions. He perfected both. In his academic work he "evolved from a focus on perfectly competitive models with fully informed, rational agents, to a greater consideration of models and theories that embody market imperfections and incomplete rationality," James Poterba, his MIT colleague and sometime coauthor, wrote in an appreciation after Summers won the Clark medal. Summers's career too embraced both ends of the spectrum. He went from serving a year as a senior staff economist on Ronald Reagan's first-term Council of Economic Advisors, to advising the liberal Michael Dukakis during his failed presidential bid in 1988. That's where he met Rubin, who had been raising money for Dukakis. Rubin later hired Summers as a consultant for Goldman Sachs. In fact, when Summers was appointed World Bank chief economist in 1990, there was an outcry on the Right. He was saved only by his Reaganite experience.

Summers developed an amazing facility, reminiscent of Milton Friedman, to argue both sides of a debate better than anyone—to the point where he could take either side equally well, depending on which way the wind was blowing. It made people uncertain about exactly where he stood—but it also turned Summers into a world-class briefer, a quality that Barack Obama, brilliant himself at detail, would later appreciate. Growing up in an academic bubble, Summers had no formative sense of certainty about the way the world worked. As the son and nephew of Keynesians, it was no surprise that his early academic work expressed a Keynesian skepticism. After the 1987 stock market crash, he declared that no one could think of the market as rational, and he made the case for a "Tobin tax" on transactions, a briefly popular idea meant to directly discourage the free movement of speculative "hot money" internationally, for the protection of fragile economies.

In one paper in 1988, he and James Poterba cast doubt on the efficient markets thesis, saying the evidence touted for it was flawed. "The freeing of financial markets to pursue their casino instincts heightens the odds of crises," he and his then wife, Victoria Summers, wrote in 1989. Two years later, Summers produced a remarkable paper that laid out how the next great financial crisis might unfold; he argued that the increased use of leverage on Wall Street and the advent of "financial innovation"—mainly derivatives—would exacerbate it. And when Robert Shiller of Yale held his historic first conference on "behavioral finance"—a new school of economics that, like Stiglitz's work, poked holes in the idea of rationally behaving markets—in July 1990, Summers was there in support. "I always thought of him as a kindred spirit," said Shiller. Summers not only showed up but he helped to advance the thinking in the new field, writing a memorable paper with his future Treasury subordinate, Brad DeLong, on "noise trading"—the way that investors irrationally responded to rumors in the market.

But Summers, as the undersecretary of the Treasury, was also fiercely ambitious. Even then he was telling friends he wanted to be chairman of the Fed some day. And he knew that Bob Rubin was going to be the arbiter of his destiny in Washington, which may help to explain his shifting point of view as the free-market zeitgeist took hold of the Clinton administration. And why more than a decade later, as the mortgage-backed securitization craze reached its lunatic heights, Summers would describe himself as a "repentant" former Tobin tax advocate who had learned "a lot" from Alan Greenspan. "I just want to try it," Summers would say, when he would make some flabbergasting argument that a fellow economist like Alan Blinder considered economically nonsensical. "Fundamentally he always remained the college debater he was," according to one economist who had known Summers for decades. "Once he knows the position he has to defend, he can argue and internalize that position better than anybody else."

Mainly what he was sure of, it seems, was himself. Larry Summers's sense of self was shaped by simply being, wherever he went, the smartest guy in the room. Even in rooms full of economists, he stood out. For many officials in Bill Clinton's Washington, the most terrifying prospect imaginable was to be on the other side of Larry Summers in a discussion about policy. In word and mannerism he specialized in making his debate opponents feel subhumanly stupid. It usually happened the same way: Larry would zero in on the perceived weakness in an argument, and then convey the idea that the victim's "error"—and it wasn't really always an error—was the final verdict on his life and worth. Summers was a polymath who mastered every argument. But growing up in an environment of pure academic discussion left him with few fixed points of belief about policy—until he met Rubin and Greenspan.

Summers understood as well as any economist alive that financial markets jerked this way and that in ways that often didn't reflect underlying economic fundamentals. But under the influence of Rubin and Greenspan, he came to adopt a view that he would consciously model after Winston Churchill's famous description of democracy—that it "is the worst form of government except for all the others that have been tried." Like Milton Friedman, Summers believed that markets were hardly perfect as allocators of society's resources, but they were generally much better than governments. They weren't that good at measuring the value of assets—Wall Street, he knew, was especially errant—but they'd still beat government bureaucrats just about every time. Summers also persuaded himself that markets had grown so huge and complex that a Tobin-like tax on financial transactions had become too difficult for government to administer. It was a feat of intellectual acrobatics that allowed Summers to land very close to where Greenspan and Rubin were on policy. And to get ahead, of course, that's precisely where Summers needed to be. According to a former Clinton administration official, "If you were undersecretary of the Treasury, a department which occasionally acts as a lobbying group for Wall Street, and you have in mind promotion, well then, if you have those ambitions you know where your bread is buttered. . . . He was thinking chairman of the Fed even then, that I know." (Summers later denied this to me.)

Summers's ruthlessness was often unconscious with him, the excess fervor of the competitive debater and the tireless truth seeker. Without even realizing it, Summers would sometimes annoy Clinton's first Treasury secretary, his sometime boss Lloyd Bentsen, by delivering his own explanations of what he thought Bentsen had meant to say— not the behavior of a guy trying to get ahead. He had a quick wit, so much so that Rubin, always looking for ways to improve his protégé's public image, would warn him against being "too colorful." There was an endearing side to his passion. Clinton's tough trade representative, Charlene Barshefsky, remembered when Summers, then Treasury undersecretary, humiliated a deputy of hers in a room full of staffers, telling the deputy that he would have flunked him as a student if he'd made arguments about a trade issue that were so weak. Afterward, the diminutive Barshefsky walked up to the hulking Summers and said, "If you ever do that again, I'll break your fucking knees." Summers was shocked, as if he'd just been told that he'd been sleepwalking through a dangerous neighborhood. "He didn't even know what he did," said Barshefsky. Summers later called up the aide to apologize, and they had a long talk.

While still in his twenties, just before his first marriage, Summers was diagnosed with late-stage Hodgkin's disease. He survived after a regime of chemotherapy and he rarely mentioned the experience again. But fifteen years later, when Clinton announced that Summers would be Rubin's successor as Treasury secretary, his voice broke in the Rose Garden as he alluded to the ordeal. It was a searing reminder that the best-laid plans of would-be Nobel Prize winners can go awry, and it added some much needed vulnerability to his personality.

He was an odd combination of social misfit who yet loved to be with people. Summers could be kind and supportive to those he liked and admired—loyal to a fault, in fact. As World Bank chief economist in 1991, he had signed off on a memo suggesting that the best place to send toxic waste, economically speaking, was to poor countries. It caused an uproar and enraged a certain environmentally minded senator from Tennessee who was to become important a year later, Albert Gore Jr. Summers hadn't written the memo himself; his subordinate Lant Pritchett had. Still, for years afterward Summers took responsibility for it, not even divulging who the author was, though the issue dogged him at every confirmation hearing and almost cost him a job in the Clinton administration. (Gore had objected vociferously to his hiring.) "The easiest thing in the world would have been to dump on that young kid," Pritchett recalled, referring to himself. "To say, 'I signed it by mistake, or I didn't really read all of it,' all of which I was recommending that he do." But Summers took the bullet, telling Pritchett, "Jesus, you got the politics completely wrong but you got a lot of the economics right." Pritchett later taught a Harvard course with him and was struck by how much time Summers had for his undergraduates, often taking them to lunch. "Larry really likes being around people who are smart and have new ideas. He's a socially awkward extrovert."

He was so absorbed in his work that the mundane facts of life often escaped him. "I don't mow the lawn," Summers told the *New York Times* when he first went to work for presidential candidate Michael Dukakis in 1988. "I certainly don't hang a picture. I hate it. I hate mowing the lawn. I love my work." "He's not a Renaissance man," William Niskanen, the Reaganite economist who knew Summers from Harvard, said drily.

Under Summers, the Treasury Department wanted to push to open up financial markets—especially Korea's. Summers met with fierce resistance from Stiglitz and another member of Clinton's Council of Economic Advisors, Alan Blinder, who was also deeply suspicious. Stiglitz wanted to see the evidence that this was going to be good for developing countries. He asked why they hadn't produced some research showing it was going to be good. "They said: we don't need research; we know it's true. They didn't say it in precisely those words, but clearly they took it as religion," Stiglitz said. Blinder felt that Treasury was "playing with fire. . . . We wanted to see much more developed capital markets, stronger, more regulated banks. I said that countries shouldn't adopt American financial practices until they were ready. Turns out we weren't ready either. The response was, it improves economic efficiency." Treasury was pushing the IMF as well, where senior officials such as Stanley Fischer, an eminent MIT economist (and onetime teacher of Summers's) wanted change, but much more gradually.

The Rubin Treasury was, in part, pursuing Clinton's policy of jobs, jobs, jobs, tied to his push for export promotion. And it wasn't as if the new administration didn't have a point. The United States had been trying to open up Japan since 1853, when Millard Fillmore's "black ships" first appeared in Tokyo harbor, demanding a parley. The Clinton team was merely pursuing an old U.S. objective. The Asians were flagrantly protectionist across the board, whether in finance, telecommunications, or goods. Summers insisted that his position was merely that he was opposed to discrimination against foreign financial firms in these foreign markets. "If a country wanted to maintain capital controls in a nondiscriminatory way, it didn't seem to me that that was something we should object to," he explained to me much later on.

Stiglitz and Blinder pointed out that since capital controls almost always favored the domestic firms, in practice the push to open up to foreigners amounted to almost the same thing as opening up the capital markets. Summers and Treasury "were arguing with a straight face that this was about creating jobs for Americans. Joe and I said, this is about derivative traders, how many jobs are you going to create?" said Blinder.

Part of the story, as one participant said, was that the administration "had to get money to buy their Treasuries" to pay off U.S. debt. A key way to do that was to induce foreign governments and firms to invest, and the only way to do that was to open their markets. But another part was free-market ideology that said that all markets should be open, period full stop, said Blinder. "And that innovations that come out of the financial sector have a strong presumption of being good things, which Joe and I characterized as making the world safe for derivatives traders."

The question of whether to open up capital flows—to make financial markets everywhere fully free—was actually a much more complicated issue than other trade issues. Economists—many of them, anyway—have always believed that financial markets behave differently from markets in goods and services. Things aren't quite as straightforward and simple. In 1983, a young Stanford economist named Ben Bernanke published the first of a series of papers on the causes of the Great Depression. The financial system, Bernanke said, was not unlike the nation's electrical grid. One malfunctioning transformer can bring down the whole system. (And, in fact, the deregulation of the electricity market later proved disastrous in states like California.) Bernanke showed that it was a broad-based collapse of the banking system that turned the postcrash downturn into the Great Depression. "I've never had a laissez-faire view of the financial markets," Bernanke told me much later, after the disaster of 2007–2009. "Because they're prone to failure." Even Milton Friedman, at one point, praised the idea of depository insurance. It was a lesson that William Seidman, the head of the Resolution Trust Corporation that unwound the savings and loan crisis, later noted began with Adam Smith: "Banking is different. . . . Financial systems are not and probably never will be totally free-market systems."

And unlike the trade in goods and services, short-term capital flows are haunted constantly by "panics" and "manias," as the economic historian Charles Kindleberger has written. Foreign money rushes into a country, often financing a binge of domestic consumption, then rushes out on a whim, leaving local banks to pay off short-term debt in dollars they no longer have. Countries are devastated by gyrations in interest rates, and recessions tend to be deeper after financial shocks. As far back as the Bretton Woods conference in 1944, when the United States and Great Britain teamed up to redesign the global economic system, John Maynard Keynes had remained haunted by the way these "hot money" flows wreaked so much havoc in the 1920s and 1930s. At Bretton Woods all agreed with the conclusions of a League of Nations study that some kind of protection was needed against "mass movements of nervous flight capital." Keynes declared in 1941 that the provision requiring capital controls was essential: "Loose funds may sweep around the world disorganizing all steady business. Nothing is more certain than that the movement of capital funds must be regulated."

The incredible prosperity that blossomed after World War II had been based mainly on goods trade, not flows of capital. In fact, as Stiglitz and Blinder argued, there was actually little evidence that free capital flows enriched developing countries the way open trade in goods and services did (although some studies showed a "deepening" of markets). Japan's postwar history was good evidence of that, as was China's later; in fact, all the East Asian "tigers" that Milton Friedman and his Chicago school were so fond of pointing to as examples of free-market success had done much the same. They promoted trade abroad aggressively but kept their banks and financial sectors closed to foreigners.

Beyond that, the work of Stiglitz and others showed that market efficiency is undermined by imperfect information, and there was no market more governed by information than finance. Information was, in fact, the main "good" or "service" that financial markets purveyed. Banks were not butcher shops, one economist wrote in a classic paper in 1985, pondering the failure of Chile to absorb the Friedman school's medicine. Supply and demand don't even work the same way in finance. In normal macroeconomics, higher prices usually lead to reduced demand. In finance, higher asset prices usually lead to lending, which in turn fuels more asset purchase. Before you know it, you have a mania and a bubble. By the same logic in reverse, falling asset prices and credit contractions reinforce each other in a downward spiral. In other words, there is no tendency toward equilibrium on the way up or down.

Some of the most brilliant and prescient work in this area was done by Hyman Minsky, an obscure economist at the University of California at Berkeley and Washington University who did more than anyone to flesh out Keynes's vaguely stated skepticism about financial markets. Minsky was an oddity in his profession. Born only a few years after Friedman, ironically enough, in Chicago, he was the son of socialist immigrants from Russia who became a bushy-haired dissident in economics, arguing in vaguely Marxian tones that capitalist markets sowed the seeds of their own collapse. But Minsky saw into the heart of financial market mania more deeply than anyone else, even Stiglitz. His "Financial Instability Hypothesis" held that success in financial markets always breeds its own instability. The longer a boom lasts, the less market players consider failure a possibility; as a result, careful borrowing, lending, and investment inevitably give way to recklessness and speculative euphoria. Margins and capital cushions come to be seen as unnecessary. At a certain watershed, or "Minsky moment," as it came to be called, the foreordained collapse begins. The most speculative bets crash, loans are called in, asset values plunge, and the downward spiral feeds on itself.

Yet amid the free-market triumphalism of the post–Cold War era, all this hard-won wisdom about finance was being forgotten or ignored. (An assessment of Minsky in 1997, a year after he died, concluded that his "work has not had a major influence in the macroeconomic discussions of the last thirty years.") It seemed silly and nitpicky to treat finance as a different animal. The dominant thinkers were the "rational expectations" economists of the Chicago school who simply assumed capital flows, no matter how open, would be stable. Rubin and the Treasury—all part of what economist Jagdish Bhagwati dubbed the "Wall Street Treasury complex" in honor of Eisenhower's warning about the "Military-Industrial Complex"—emphasized mainly the benefits of capital flows, and tended to ignore the mania and panic parts. "It never occurred to them that there could be a downside," said Bhagwati, and even as crises popped up, beginning with the peso crash of 1994, the answer was simply to give the IMF more powers to lift the hapless victims, like Mexico, out of trouble. But Summers and other economists "got caught up in it," said Bhagwati, who wonders to this day how someone of Summers's enormous intellect bought those arguments.

Summers began to betray his promarket bias even before he fell under Rubin's spell. As World Bank chief economist in 1991, he had engaged in the big argument getting under way about East Asia's success. East Asia was a strange outlier in the postwar world. After the Cold War, "command" economies were utterly discredited. So was big government in the United States. And in the developing world, government intervention—so-called "import substitution," meaning the support of domestic industry and the closing of trade barriers to foreigners—had also been an abysmal failure, especially in Africa and Latin America, leading to corruption and endemic poverty. And then there was East Asia. The East Asian "Tigers," inspired by the granddaddy of managed economies, Japan, had dared to tinker with market forces like demiurges playing with elemental fire, and they had largely succeeded. The East Asian insurgency was justified by Stiglitz's ideas, but it came out of its own orbit.

The fight began small in the Philippines in 1988, when the World Bank asked Japan to stop offering "concessional," or below-market-rate, loans to Filipino farmers. "That upset us very much," said Masaki Shiratori, Japan's executive director at the World Bank. At the time, Japan was emerging as the dominant economy, and Japan Inc., its unique mix of government-orchestrated finance and trade policy and aggressive export promotion, was seen as the reason. "Your next boss may be Japanese," shouted a *Newsweek* cover in 1989. Shiratori, sitting in his post in Washington a couple of blocks away from the White House, was appalled by the prevalence of what he called "neoclassical thinking" at the World Bank. "They say the market-friendly approach is the right approach," he told me in 1993. "But the market-friendly approach is applicable, by definition, where there is a market. I have asked many times, 'Where is the market?' In many developing countries, markets do not exist and the small entrepreneurs, small farmers, don't have access to credit. Or market failure is so great that the government should assist specific sectors. What kind of market is there, say, in Africa?" Shiratori lobbied passionately for a study of East Asia's unusual success, its unique and savvy combination of deft government promotion of markets.

Summers ordered up the study and asked Stiglitz to direct the financial markets part of it. The World Bank came up with one, 350 pages long, that hesitantly concluded that "market friendly state intervention" might sometimes work. But it was so heavily hedged that it had little impact. Many who agreed with Stiglitz thought the emerging "Washington Consensus" was uniting against another Japan Inc. model. Washington didn't want to risk turning countries like India into government-supported export giants with East Asian–style policies, especially when U.S. markets were already seen as being under assault and Clinton was preaching jobs, jobs, jobs. And they didn't want countries like Russia to find excuses for only half-reforming their way out of command economics. As Harvard's Jeffrey Sachs, then in full flower as a "shock therapist" (a description he would later disavow with great vehemence), told me at the time, an endorsement of Japan's industrial policy could be dangerous. Sachs said it might lead policy makers to forget about the free-market parts of Japan's success and the postwar Dodge Plan, an early form of shock therapy that called for severe fiscal belt-tightening to dampen inflation. "The booming parts of East Asia are based on private-sector growth," Sachs said. It was an approach he was then taking with Russia.

The historical tide for markets was in the end too powerful, and the Japanese too meek about asserting their views. Japan, as ever, was bad about "forming universal theories from the economic success of Japan," Naohiro Amaya, one of the country's legendary bureaucrats, told me in

1992 when I lived there. It was a culture of pragmatism; the Japanese had no Keynes or Marx of their own, not even a Stiglitz. And frankly, few bureaucracies were as savvy as those of the East Asians, with their agile technocratic class and Confucian tradition of service. India, for example, which had grown up with Nehru socialism, had suffered for decades under the "license raj." Every time you wanted to make any kind of foreign transaction you had to pay someone a bribe. In 1974, its FARA (Foreign Agents Registration Act) law had liberalized foreign exchange transactions, helping to open up the economy. But growth would come very slowly, very un-East Asia–like.

Summers, giving the World Bank's response to the East Asia study, said he would deemphasize the role of government, even in East Asia's case: "In the 1970s and 1980s, the World Bank was more inclined to accord government a strong role in industrial development. Experience, however, has led to a change in Bank thinking. . . . It appears that many developing countries do not have the capacity to pick winners. Consequently it appears that for most developing countries relying on imperfect markets rather than imperfect governments has a greater chance for promoting growth."

Stiglitz, of course, was allied with the proponents of the "East Asia model" who often cited his work. His work had shown "that with imperfect information the inner core of the neoclassical model was severely damaged," said Alice Amsden, a political economist at MIT who was deeply involved in the East Asia debate. Coming out of the Asia debate, some allies of Stiglitz voiced warnings about the new broader consensus to crack open capital markets. "As capital becomes internationally mobile, its owners and managers have less interest in making long-term investments in any specific national economy—including their home base," argued Robert Wade, a renegade World Bank economist. It was a forewarning of the out-of-control hot money that would later slosh back and forth, from the United States to Asia in the late 1990s and then back into the United States again in the 2000s.

The Asia debate was settled in favor of the free marketers. Japan, already in recession as its bubble economy collapsed in the early 1990s, lost the stomach for a fight. But the issue would come up again in the late 1990s as a new crisis began.

Just as important, the rising tide of Rubinism in the Democratic Party—as embodied in the shift in the thinking of the president himself—began to sap the vigor of populist opposition to market zeal. One example was the shifting attitude toward Glass-Steagall, which had been coming up for review since the Reagan era. In 1981, when John Shad first proposed Glass-Steagall reform, he had been excoriated by John Dingell. But now Dingell's brand of Democratic politics was dying. And more and more, the Wall Street forces that had met a blank wall in the 1980s, when Democrats were in control of Congress, found an open door in Washington.

As 1993 rolled into 1994 the headlines were, as usual, about political turmoil inside the Beltway: gays in the military, the stumblings of Clinton's young communications team, such as Dee Dee Myers and George Stephanopoulos, the rising Republican revolt. Within the administration, the arguments over forcing open financial markets around the world raged on, behind closed doors. First there were phone calls, and memos circulating that were drafted and redrafted. There were Summers and Stiglitz, each with their "seconds": Blinder, later to be vice chairman of the Fed, was in Stiglitz's corner; Jeffrey Shafer was backing up Summers. "I was Joe's cut man. Jeff was Larry's cut man," said Blinder. But the truth is that Stiglitz and Blinder never had a chance. Not only were they fighting the zeitgeist of what Stiglitz came to call "market fundamentalism." They were institutionally outclassed as well. The tiny Council of Economic Advisors could never stand up to the Treasury giant. "Remember, the Treasury is the big dog. Always. We're the Chihuahua nipping at the heels of the German shepherd," said Blinder.

Summers never stopped being a Keynesian. He advocated a fiscal stimulus in Japan. He remained somewhat skeptical of the usefulness of free-flowing capital "for its own sake." And the process of financial globalization was hardly Summers's brainchild; it had actually begun in Europe in the early 1980s. But now, whether out of ambition, or genuine belief, or a concession to the emerging zeitgeist, Summers came to be a fierce advocate of market liberalization, and he stayed that way for most of his time in Washington over more than a decade. It only heightened his profile, along with Rubin's. McLarty said that by the end of his first term, President Clinton himself was happy with his reputation as a market guy. "You've got to remember Bill Clinton started with 42 or 43 percent of the vote. Ross Perot got 19 percent. But that means 60 percent of the American people voted for change. But Bill Clinton did not come in with a strong mandate. My advice was people voted for change, but thoughtful change, not radical change. At end of first year, his approval rating was 65 percent. That was part of the trend line. He had co-opted the Ross Perot vote, at least on the deficit." And by championing the North American Free Trade Agreement that his predecessor had launched, Clinton showed he could stand up to traditional Democratic interests.

With Rubin and Summers making the arguments for him, it got to the point where Wall Street could no longer really tell the difference between Clinton and Reagan, Barney Frank later said. Soon enough this became known as the "Washington Consensus." The term had been invented by an economist named John Williamson and originally described a ten-point formula for reforming crisis-racked developing nations; but before long the Washington Consensus came to be seen as a synonym for market fundamentalism. It was oversimplified as "stabilize, privatize, and liberalize," in the words of Dani Rodrik. (Williamson himself, ironically, favored some controls on capital and lamented the misappropriation of his idea.)

Stiglitz and Blinder got nowhere. South Korea, feeling the pressure, proposed a five-year transition plan to market opening. That was considered much too slow by the Clintonites, just another delay tactic by the Asians. Even Stiglitz's mild proposal for a system of "prioritizing" market openings was swatted aside. Summers, Stiglitz later wrote, "adamantly opposed the exercise," saying it was unnecessary. And Rubin, as head of the NEC, decided the issue wasn't worthy of the president's attention. Summers would later come to say that whatever problems arose out of the liberalization of the Asian financial markets were really a question of how the Asians did it; he didn't expect it to be done so incompetently, he said. Unquestionably the market openings would have to happen at some point—"you can't tell a teenager they shouldn't grow up," as IMF chief economist Ken Rogoff later put it—and it's not that the Asian governments were entirely blameless. They wanted to continue to peg their currencies to the dollar while opening up to all that foreign capital, and that would prove a recipe for disaster in the late 1990s. But Stiglitz wrote "that was precisely one of the points [we] raised. It was very likely that a quick liberalization would be done poorly."

It was a long time before anyone came to appreciate the significance of those early debates. Much later, after the subprime mortgage disaster of 2007–2009, many Washington authorities would fret publicly over what they called the problem of "global imbalances" or the Asian "savings glut," as Ben Bernanke would describe it. In the 1990s, freed up by the rapid opening of capital markets under U.S. and IMF pressure, American hot money would begin to rush from Wall Street to "emerging markets" eager for bargains—especially Asia. A decade later, Asian money would rush back into the United States without restraint, helping to inflate the housing bubble. The truth is, much of the imbalance problem began with the debates of the early 1990s. "It created a global financial market," Stiglitz said. "It meant ultimately that savers in Germany or Norway could easily slosh money into the subprime market and blow it up. Anybody who says that global imbalances contributed to the crisis is saying that global capital market liberalization contributed to the crisis."

Bill Clinton himself never came to fully trust Wall Street, McLarty said. One of his proudest moments, in fact, came when for the first time he stood alone against the advice of Rubin and his economics team and vetoed a law, sponsored by GOP representative Christopher Cox, that would have made it more difficult for investors to sue over securities fraud. Cox had raised the bar: aggrieved investors now had to show malicious intent on the part of securities firms, not mere recklessness, to prove they had been defrauded. Clinton's veto, in late December 1995, was overridden. Beyond that the president worried privately that globalization, which he touted publicly, was getting out of control. "He always had a little bit of tightness in his stomach about it," McLarty said. "For all the reasons you now see. I think he had an understanding and a belief that both U.S. financial markets and world markets were going to dictate the flow of capital and interest rates. [But] should there have been just a little more tacking [left] at that point? Possibly."

Joe Stiglitz wanted more than mere tacking. He was profoundly worried that the rush to globalize markets was creating a deeper gulf between the haves and have-nots of the world, widening rather than narrowing income levels. The rapid opening up of markets worldwide, while doing nothing to boost the growing underclass, was creating a less fair world. Just as Keynes had searched for a way to save capitalism by curbing its worst excesses of income inequality and unemployment, Stiglitz was seeing the system as a whole and he thought it was in danger of failing. He saw that underneath the strong U.S. economy, a baleful dynamic was beginning to take shape. Income levels were widening. NAFTA and other agreements were further undermining America's industrial middle class by sending those jobs offshore. That in turn threatened America's ability to be the world's consumer of last resort. And yet—here was the rub—the world still depended on the United States to play that role. Rubin and Summers were worried about this as well, and they repeatedly urged other countries such as Japan and China to consume more. But Japan and China were reluctant to open up their economies and stimulate demand. And in the years to come, the increasingly hard-up U.S. consumer would be able to fill this role only one way: by taking on enormous debt—supplied of course by the rest of the world and brokered by Wall Street.

Stiglitz had a surer sense than did Clinton and his key economic advisers of why the system was creating an unsustainable dynamic—why all this deference to Wall Street was going to come to grief. He knew that there was something fundamentally wrong about the economic theories that were driving it all. The Washington Consensus was to become his bête noire. Eventually, it would drive Stiglitz out of Washington. But he would not go gently.

6

Portrait of a Contrarian

He was from Gary, Indiana. You couldn't understand Joseph Stiglitz without understanding that.

Some people are more shaped by their hometowns than others. The little girl who was to become Ayn Rand had pined for a way out of Bolshevik-besieged St. Petersburg. Sickened by the lies that haunted the days and nights of her youth—the sham that was Bolshevik collectivism—Alice Rosenbaum dreamed of a golden land, an America of free men and action. What she didn't find she invented, so powerful were the ideals she had passionately conjured in Petrograd.

Stiglitz was born in America, and in a place where the world wasn't golden at all but workaday gray, indeed notorious as one of the grimmest places in the United States. And in his own way young Joe Stiglitz grew to be just as uncompromising as Alice Rosenbaum became about what he had learned from the intrusions of the real world. In his case the lesson was almost the opposite. It was that markets don't work well at all in practice, at least on their own. Indeed, for all Stiglitz's brilliance at mathematical models, one could draw a direct line from his upbringing in Gary to his defiant declaration fifty years later in Stockholm, as he delivered his Nobel Prize lecture, that Adam Smith's "invisible hand" didn't exist at all—or if it did, it was surely "palsied."

Stiglitz, a fourth-generation American born in 1943, came from a Jewish family who were all Midwesterners. The Stiglitz family hailed from Belarus and other parts of Eastern Europe way back when, but was part of one of the earliest waves of Jewish immigration, settling in Cincinnati back in the 1850s. (Some kept going farther west: one of Stiglitz's great-aunts taught Ronald Reagan in grade school in Dixon, Illinois.) Stiglitz's parents, Nathaniel and Charlotte, both had been born within six miles of Gary, in 1903 and 1904, respectively, in the towns of East Chicago and Lyding. It was something of an irony that the adversaries Stiglitz later took on as an economist, the Chicago school, weren't really from Chicago at all, while he himself was a born and bred "freshwater" Midwesterner steeped in the problems of the industrial middle class that the Chicago school tended to ignore. The Chicago school, after all, was mainly Milton Friedman's progeny. Friedman had been born in Brooklyn and raised in New Jersey.

Stiglitz was also surrounded by immigrants when he was growing up. Many were Eastern Europeans who also had sought a better life, and many found it in the steel mills. But unlike Milton Friedman's mother, they weren't going anywhere, and they found themselves subject to the periodic layoffs that U.S. Steel and other giants imposed. For many in the industrial heartland, life never seemed to get better. His hometown, Gary, was invented by a classic American robber baron: Elbert H. Gary, the chairman of U.S. Steel, who founded the city in 1906 as the company's headquarters and decided to name it after himself rather than the president, W. E. Corey, to show who was in charge. Gary was a remarkable figure, a lawyer and judge who took a parental interest in "his" town and talked of cooperation with government but doggedly opposed labor unions. Vain about his ramrod posture and manicured mustache—and connections to European royalty—Gary declined to meet with labor representatives, whom he considered social inferiors. He constantly quoted scripture to support his policies, but refused to recognize the Sabbath as a day of rest for his workers. When Teddy Roosevelt accused U.S. Steel of being a "trust" and sought to break it up, Gary welcomed the description and then won a Supreme Court decision legitimizing the steel giant. By 1919, workers were comparing him to the German Kaiser, a local Indiana history recounts, after he stood against their demand for an eight-hour rather than a twelve-hour day. One cartoon juxtaposed the judge's statement, "The workmen prefer the longer hours," with pictures of tired, gaunt laborers.

By the time Stiglitz was growing up in the 1940s and 1950s, Gary had settled into industrial torpor even in the boom postwar years. "There must be something in the air here which leads one to ask questions," Stiglitz later said as he narrated an adulatory French documentary called *Le Monde Selon Stiglitz*—The World According to Stiglitz. "Poverty, discrimination, unemployment were all around us. These things mark a man for life and make him want to understand. Having seen the downside of a market economy, it would be impossible to be euphoric about its marvels." The railroad tracks ran next to his house, and the trains passed every thirty minutes. His own family life was a in state of constant struggle.

His father, Nate Stiglitz, a towering man who lived to the age of ninety-six, was not known for his business sense. He tried several different occupations before settling on insurance, which he sold out of a small office in the big bank building downtown, Gary's only "skyscraper." Though his father was a "Jeffersonian Democrat" who believed passionately in self-reliance and disliked big government, Stiglitz later said, "he had a deep sense of civic and moral responsibility. He was one of the few people I knew who insisted on paying Social Security contributions for household help—regardless of whether they wanted it or not; he knew they would need it when they were old." Nate kept the family in the black, and it wasn't a bad childhood, all in all. Stiglitz's mother, Charlotte, pampered Joe, his older brother, Mark, and their younger sister, Eloise, never asking them to help around the house or pick up after themselves. They managed to stay "middle class" and even had a maid. But the economically dispossessed, the truly poor, were never far away.

Stiglitz remembered his first dim realization that something was wrong with America: around the house and the dinner table. The Stiglitzes' maid, Minnie Fae Ellis, was from the South and had a sixth-grade education, and like the other inner-city blacks lived across the tracks from the Stiglitz home. "I remember thinking why do we still have people who have a six-grade education?" he recalled. Out in the streets, the cyclical layoffs were a constant presence, and pollutants clung to the wash that his mother hung out in the back yard. Visiting their cousins, the Fishmans in Chicago, they always were made aware they had less: fewer toys, and no summer home up on Lake Michigan like the others in the family. His sister, Eloise, who was six years younger, ran home one day to tell the family about the "cool rainbow" she saw in the Calumet River, only to be informed it was oil seepage. The ethos of the steel industry was everywhere, even in their religion. "Because of economic conditions and makeup of community, observing the Sabbath became very difficult," recalled Joe's older cousin Roberta. "Saturday was a big day for cleaning and laundering for people working in the steel plant. So orthodoxy diminished. My grandmother basically kept a kosher home." When young Joe and his older brother, Mark, came home from Hebrew school one time and said they wanted to keep kosher, their father said, "That's not going to happen."

As Stiglitz's father grimly prospered in his task as insurance salesman, the talk around the dinner table was about antitrust, fighting off the banks that tried to press insurance policies on their customers when they took out mortgages. It was no accident that Joe Stiglitz's early work on the fallacies of markets focused on the unequal relationship between insurance companies and those they insured, and the lack of good information shared between them. Those who seek insurance always know more about their actual health than the companies, which in response are habitually suspicious and always look for loopholes to deny coverage, like "preexisting conditions." Stiglitz's conclusion came to be that universal coverage is the only answer.

Above all there was his mother, who told him simply to "use your head and do service" for his career, advice that his sister, Eloise, would call a "fundamental guiding post" in his later work. Stiglitz would quote that line from Charlotte at her funeral. But he always had his feet grounded in the markets. As high school valedictorian in 1960, young Joe gave a speech praising U.S. Steel as a somewhat stable supplier of jobs. His uncle, Isidore Fishman, sitting in the audience, remarked, "Oh my God, I have a Republican nephew. Where did he come from?"

Joe, a middle child, was an academic phenomenon from an early age, becoming debating and spelling bee champ and winning the state math competition. He was often fired up by a rivalry with his older brother, Mark—also brilliant—that would later lead to an estrangement. Mark was tall, handsome, and four years older; some in the family, including Joe's cousin Roberta, recalled that Stiglitz didn't even speak at all until he was three and depended on Mark to represent him to the outside world. "Mark spoke for him. Joe would mumble something, and Mark would point to the cereal box," she said. Mark Stiglitz later graduated from Harvard Medical School; but as his brother's fame grew, he not only stopped translating for Joe, he eventually stopped communicating with the family altogether and changed his last name to "Lawrence."

At age twelve, Joe Stiglitz was already using college textbooks; off in a corner of the classroom, indulged by his overawed teachers, he would enter a world of his own dreaming. The family loved to tell the story of how, rushing off to school one morning, he got stuck in a mud patch and lost his shoe but ran on anyway so he wouldn't miss class. Like a lot of brilliant young men who later became economists, Stiglitz loved math but wasn't really attuned to the cloistered life of academe. He wanted to be a professor, but a psychological test at school concluded that he should "be a rabbi or a preacher," he recalled. In truth, he wanted to change the world, and for mathematically talented young idealists economics was the only choice, as Milton Friedman found out. Stiglitz's contemporary Paul Krugman, also later to be a Nobel Prize winner, had similar yearnings. He fell in love with Isaac Asimov's *Foundation* trilogy when he was a teenager because its hero was a brilliant "psychohistorian" who mathematically developed a science of history that allowed him to predict the future and save civilization. "I wanted to be a psychohistorian," Krugman once told me. "Economics is about as close as you can get."

A science to save civilization. It was the sort of grandiose self-regard that all economists seemed to have for themselves. The joke on economists, said one of them, Robert Johnson, "is that they model the rest of us as venal and have a blind spot regarding themselves. They see themselves as benevolent Martians who try to make the earthlings better off." The Friedmanites had modeled the rest of humanity as rational, self-interested actors, but failed to see that the way they squabbled over their own theories was itself evidence of how flawed that concept was. It was a phenomenon that Stiglitz would suffer with his own career: his "rabbinical" yearning to save the world like one of Asimov's psychohistorians would be frustrated by his own conclusions showing that economics could never, in fact, be certain about anything.

Stiglitz was accepted at Harvard but, on the advice of his brother—who, like him, was a National Merit Scholar and valedictorian of his class—felt it was too much of a "big-city" school. He turned down Harvard and went to Amherst instead. Soon Stiglitz was agitating, leading the antifraternity campaign there and getting himself elected president of the student council. The school's fraternities drew school financing to travel to matches and games during breaks, which Stiglitz thought was unfair. So he facetiously started a "caber-tossing team" and petitioned for money to go to Scotland. The school had no choice but to drop the subsidy program. Around the same time he took part in the civil rights march on Washington, D.C., in 1963 and heard Martin Luther King Jr. give his "I Have a Dream" speech. By his third year Stiglitz was renowned on campus as an academic superstar, and his professor was calling MIT and saying, "You've got to take this guy."

Gary never stopped haunting him. And he discovered that in a strange way, the example of Gary was haunting his chosen field of economics as well. At MIT in the 1960s Stiglitz came to realize that the Chicago school was already dominant, but few people outside Chicago took those perfect-competition models seriously. The problem was there was no real alternative to these models. So economists were simply using them because they had no other model.

Stiglitz, his liberal passions engaged as much as his intellect, grew obsessed with the idea that the perfect competition models couldn't be right. He saw, in his own hometown, the destruction of the industrial middle class unfold. And so, somewhat like Brooksley Born, who hadn't bought the free-market religion because she was a lawyer whose world view was shaped in Washington, Joe Stiglitz developed his own immunity to market fervor.

The models of the time assumed that where perfect competition failed to occur, these were minor flaws in the rationalist model. In fact, Stiglitz eventually showed, these seemingly small factors destroyed the model. The Chicago school thought that information was just another factor, another input, slightly altering the equation. Stiglitz's work showed that was wrong: even a small amount of imperfect information could destroy an economic equilibrium. Here Stiglitz was just describing what he'd seen in Gary and later on, in Africa: under the perfect-competition model, wages were supposed to drop during a recession, and employment levels would remain the same at lower costs. It didn't work that way in real life: Wages were "sticky," and didn't drop right away. At lower wages work habits also changed, to a degree employers didn't realize; workers would work less hard, leading to less productivity, which in turn deepened the recession. Things didn't simply return to "equilibrium" on their own.

Similarly, Stiglitz showed, banks would "ration" credit out stingily in tough times, fearing what they suspected but didn't know for sure: that borrowers were much less likely to be able to pay off, also prolonging a downturn. That undermined the perfect-competition model, according to which the banks should continue the same level of lending but simply raise interest rates to higher-risk borrowers. He showed that the efficient markets hypothesis, based on the idea that the stock market fully reflected all information, didn't add up for the simple reason that if it did, there would be no incentive for anyone to pay money to get information. Stiglitz and his academic allies also demonstrated the flaws in Joseph Schumpeter's famous thesis of "creative destruction," which postulated that healthy capitalism inevitably produces innovative entrepreneurs who destroy monopolies; Stiglitz showed that monopolies could persist indefinitely by blocking the entry of competitors.

The free-market school believed that Adam Smith's "invisible hand" always guided behavior correctly; unemployment shouldn't exist at all if the market was left to work properly. Stiglitz, raised in an environment of chronic unemployment, saw it didn't work that way, and he concluded that the only agent powerful enough to correct the failings of the market was government. To make his case, once again he began to use the rationalist school's own tools against them. He constructed an elegant mathematical model showing that if one assumes rational expectations of the future among market participants, not only would unemployment persist but government spending programs could be even *more* effective in reducing it (because the rational expectation of higher income from government programs translated into more consumption in the present). In more practical terms, Stiglitz wrote a paper showing, for example, that World War II was not just a pick-me-up from the Depression; it represented extraordinarily successful industrial policy too, getting people off Depression-ravaged farms and into factories, permanently upgrading the U.S. economy.

The skepticism engendered in Gary was deepened when he went off to Kenya to study after graduation in 1969. What he saw there confirmed what he had experienced as a boy in Gary. All markets did not, in fact, "clear"—with buyers and sellers finding each other at the right price—on their own. Sometimes they would just stagnate. His longtime friend George Akerlof, with whom he shared the Nobel Prize, later said that for both of them the time spent studying in desperate Third World economies changed their views forever. "The year after I went to India, he went to Kenya," recalled Akerlof. "We basically did the same thing . . . and somehow we see the world a little bit differently. Life isn't so much what it appears to be. We knew that capital account liberalization was a bad thing" because so few developing countries were even close to being ready for flows of sophisticated capital.

And more, they saw that the details of markets and the peculiar conditions of individual countries mattered. "I had seen cyclical unemployment—sometimes quite large—and the hardship it brought as I grew up," Stiglitz later said in his Nobel lecture, "but I had not seen the massive unemployment that characterized African cities, unemployment that could not be explained either by unions or minimum wage laws (which, even when they existed, were regularly circumvented). Again, there was a massive discrepancy between the models we had been taught and what I saw."

Milton Friedman loved to point to Hong Kong as a nearly perfect free market. Stiglitz wrote a paper on Hong Kong at one point, showing that the role of government was actually pretty large in what Friedman considered to be the "freest market on earth." In his Nobel lecture Stiglitz said that may be true, but "the government was the major provider of public housing and it had a lot of influence on rule of law. The free market operated within the context of a positive government."

Paper by paper, Stiglitz and his colleagues began to prove, in effect, that market failures happen all the time, and government intervention is needed on a regular basis. The myth of perfect markets was just that, a myth. Stiglitz wanted a "third way" that found a balance between market forces and government oversight. His sense of certainty about these results made him out of joint with his times. While the Reagan revolution was taking off, Stiglitz and his colleagues were already starting to win Nobel Prizes for demonstrating the fallacies of free markets. And there was no real critique of this approach from the Right.

What the Right did was to ignore the Stiglitz critique. The Friedman school never developed an overarching theory to counter Keynes. Instead, Stiglitz would complain, conservatives only employed the *rhetoric* of theory in the debates over public policy. After all, their ideas were far easier to explain to the public, and their policies—simply let the market rip—were far easier to think up and enact.

As Stiglitz worked prodigiously in developing his theories, his reputation grew within academia. He won the Clark medal. And then one day a call came from Little Rock. Laura D'Andrea Tyson, the newly named chairwoman of Bill Clinton's Council of Economic Advisors, wanted him on board.

• • •

Stiglitz was excited about going to Washington. He was eager to "test his theories to see if they worked," recalled his sister, Eloise. "I remember him saying how interesting it was to figure out a strategy to get your idea across. . . . Political gamesmanship to get your idea accepted. At first he really enjoyed it. Then he reached the point where he didn't."

Stiglitz's early introduction to the Clinton administration was congenial. There was an enormous sense of possibility about what government could do. The failure of health care, the 1994 Gingrich revolution, and the rise of the Wall Street-Treasury axis were still ahead of them. Stiglitz had been chosen, after all, because he specialized in finding fault with markets and where government could help. No one really saw him as arrogant then. They only saw his lovable, absentminded side. At one early meeting of the economic team, twenty minutes in, the budget director, Leon Panetta, who had been staring at Stiglitz, jumped up, exclaimed, "I can't stand it anymore!" and walked over behind him and fixed his tie, which Stiglitz had put on top of his collar rather than beneath it.

But the bonhomie didn't last. When Stiglitz went to Washington, even after he took over the chairmanship of the Council of Economic Advisors in 1995 when Laura Tyson decided to return to California, he found that no one cared about his findings. Efficient markets theory ruled the landscape. Stiglitz quickly saw that Rubinomics—and the Washington Consensus—was turning into the law of the land. Stiglitz would find himself getting increasingly agitated as he sought to argue that markets don't solve all problems at once. Globalization had enormous benefits, but he knew it had also destroyed the steel industry and with it Gary, Indiana—the very neighborhoods he'd roamed as a boy. The jobs were gone, and there was nothing to replace them. This was happening all over the country to America's industrial middle class, the very consumer base that the rest of the world relied on.

For Stiglitz, his early 1990s debate with Larry Summers over capital liberalization was only the beginning of what was to become an epic rivalry—and a fairly faint beginning compared to what was to come. Before long, Stiglitz found he was taking on all of Washington.

The keepers of the Washington Consensus existed—and still do—in a four-block bastion of economic orthodoxy in downtown Washington.

It lies physically on Pennsylvania Avenue between Fifteenth Street, home of the U.S. Treasury Department, and the Nineteenth Street headquarters of the International Monetary Fund, with the Eighteenth Street building of the World Bank in between and the Federal Reserve a couple of blocks to the south. Though the World Bank and the IMF are made up of economists and policy makers from more than a hundred countries, as the 1990s went on most of them began converging around the same post–Cold War market consensus that Rubin and Summers were part of. Prodded by the American policy makers a few blocks away, animated by the same free-market evangelism, the IMF was intent on dictating when and how nations would open their markets, how small and austere they would make their national budgets, and so forth. The fund's economists forbade alternative approaches, like the East Asian "model" of maintaining partially closed economies and promoting exports during a country's development phase, before it hits full industrialization. This was used to differing degrees not only by such major nations as Japan and China but by the United States itself during its own developmental period in the nineteenth century.

The Washington Consensus, even more than Larry Summers, would become Joe Stiglitz's nemesis.

After capital liberalization, Stiglitz's next big fight was over Russia. Once again he was alarmed by the rush to open things up. Soon after the Soviet Union disappeared from the map in the early 1990s, Moscow heard a lot of blithe, promarket rhetoric from the Bush and Clinton administrations, and it was the subject of much high-minded tinkering by the free-market consultants at the Harvard Institute for International Development, as well as the IMF. Citing their Western-trained advisers, both former Soviet leader Mikhail Gorbachev and his successor, Russian president Boris Yeltsin, confidently predicted a two-year transition to a market economy. But Washington didn't provide much help or support in institution building; its rather poor substitute was to ally itself with the power base of an increasingly addled Yeltsin. Privatization of the former communist production system quickly degenerated into what the Russians called "grabitization," the unfair seizure of old state assets by party apparatchiks-turned-oligarchs with insider connections. When the West did finally send over boatloads of IMF assistance, things were so far gone that the aid only led to massive capital flight. World markets attacked the ruble, and Russia fell into a long economic slide.

"By paying insufficient attention to the institutional infrastructure that would allow a market economy to flourish—and by easing the flow of capital in and out of Russia—the IMF and Treasury had laid the groundwork for the oligarchs' plundering," Stiglitz wrote later. "While the government lacked the money to pay pensioners, the oligarchs were sending money obtained by stripping assets and selling the country's precious national resources into Cypriot and Swiss bank accounts."

Stiglitz debated Summers and Harvard economist Jeffrey Sachs, a leading proponent of fast marketization, on this issue at the beginning of the 1990s. "They thought you needed to pursue privatization rapidly and that infrastructure would follow," Stiglitz said. "It was a divide then. You can't talk about property rights in the absence of rule of law. In Russia, you gave them control rights. In fact, with capital market liberalization, it was the worst of all possible worlds." In other words, the Russian apparatchiks-cum-oligarchs were using their power to steal state assets and then, with open capital markets, to ferret that huge amount of wealth safely offshore. "At least if you stop capital flight they would say, we'd better invest here," said Stiglitz. "It was an intellectually incoherent view."

The irony was that, at home, it was not as if the U.S. government suddenly threw off the welfare state and let markets rampage. U.S. policy makers hadn't truly practiced laissez-faire economics at home since Calvin Coolidge's day. Again, even Ronald Reagan ran record deficits in order to support FDR's welfare state. Indeed, government spending as a percentage of GDP actually rose during his term. Nonetheless, when it came to promulgating U.S. economic ideas abroad in the post–Cold War era, America's top policy makers ended up giving different advice abroad than they would have at home. There may have been an entrenched welfare state in the United States, but developing economies, especially newly enfranchised economies such as post–Soviet Russia, provided a clean slate for rapid marketization.

Jeff Sachs was no free-market ideologue, but he too got caught up in the furor. In the immediate aftermath of the Cold War, Sachs had stopped hyperinflation in Bolivia, then in Poland. But privatization of the former Soviet economy was a bridge too far into marketization. In the summer of 1990, Sachs and his colleague David Lipton were invited into the once-cloistered sanctum of Gosplan to talk about reform. "In my own thinking I had treated Russia like Poland, only four times larger and perhaps ten times harder," he wrote. Moscow hired Sachs and Harvard's Institute for International Development, but the level of corruption and the lack of preparedness for capitalism were much greater in Russia, which hadn't ever really experienced it, having gone almost directly from serfdom to socialism. Sachs also came to believe that Washington was not nearly as eager to help Russia get on its feet as it was Poland, which was welcomed into Europe and NATO. He finally quit in early 1994, fed up with the endless turf-fighting between "reformers" and the communist old guard and blamed the lack of Western aid support for his failure.

Later on, after the disaster of grabitization, even Milton Friedman would come to agree that Stiglitz's more subtle analysis had been largely right. Stiglitz and Friedman came to have enormous respect for each other and sometimes saluted each other across the gulf of economic war. "I'm very much on his side," Friedman eventually told me in 2002. "You need more than privatization. What you need as a basic element is the rule of law. I don't go all the way with Joe. He stresses the problem of providing a safety net. Which will enable people to own property. Take the Russian case, even today most land in Russia will not be privately owned. It's interesting China is doing much better on that issue than Russia. You do need rule of law." In the immediate aftermath of the fall of the Soviet Union, Friedman said, "I kept being asked what Russia should do. I said, privatize, privatize, privatize. I was wrong. He was right. What we want is privatization and the rule of law. I remain persuaded that free markets are a necessary ingredient of the solution." Then he added: "One of the things Joe tends to stress that I would disagree with is the need for regulation."

Despite their early tussle over liberalization, it wasn't until the mid- to late 1990s that the Stiglitz-Summers rivalry grew explosive. Things came to a head soon after Stiglitz moved over to the World Bank as its chief economist in 1997. In early July of that year, the government of Thailand abandoned its long-standing policy of fixing the value of the baht against the dollar, and the baht began plunging. It was the beginning of the Asian contagion, and its outcome was to change the lives of both Stiglitz and Summers.

Thailand, like a lot of East Asian countries, had gotten fat and lazy on enormous inflows of eager Western capital looking to pile onto the

"Asian miracle." The Asians had been doing fine before with their own high domestic savings rates, but capital liberalization precipitated a rush of Western money. In the mid-1990s, a strengthening dollar made Thailand's roaring export industries more expensive—because of the fixed currency rate—and exports fell off. Meanwhile, the Thais kept borrowing all those dollar-denominated debts, doing heavily lever-aged derivatives trades with Western banks, and piling up a trade deficit. Thailand, of course, was one of those countries that had opened up to foreign capital. In late 1992, Bangkok created a new foreign banking center intended to attract capital from around the globe. Thai banks paid higher interest rates, which made it an attractive center, and the fixed exchange rate meant no worries about fluctuations.

Thai borrowers meanwhile paid lower rates if they borrowed in dollars, and they took on a lot of short-term debt in dollars to invest in the overheated Thai real estate market. In early 1997, rumors began spreading that many Thai borrowers were near default, and Western hedge funds began selling the baht short, betting that Bangkok couldn't maintain the link to the dollar. When a government ties its currency to the dollar, it has to maintain a huge surplus of dollars. To make good on its promise that the two currencies are interchangeable, the government must have enough dollars on hand to trade them with any investor who wants to hand over his baht. But now speculators were betting that the government would run out of dollars. Many Thai firms began trading their baht for dollars in order to pay off their dollar debt. The baht sales became a torrent. The IMF orchestrated a $17 billion bailout on July 2. A little later, Indonesia found itself in similar trouble and got a $42 billion rescue.

In return, though, the IMF insisted on even more financial openings. And it jacked up interest rates to make the currencies more attractive, stopping the outflow. The Asians themselves were stunned: they had high savings rates, disciplined budgets. Why would their currencies suddenly collapse? To many observers at the time—including me, covering it for *Newsweek*—it was the latest evidence that U.S.-style economic thinking was elbowing out the once championed "Asia model." Robert Solomon, a former Federal Reserve official, noted wryly to me that "for some inexplicable reason, every Anglo-Saxon economy in the world is doing well now"—free-market countries like Britain, Canada, Australia, and New Zealand.

Stiglitz, more than most, saw that there was something different about this crisis. Everyone knew that the countries in East Asia had low inflation and, as Stiglitz put it in a feisty speech in April 1998, "a fiscal stance and public debt-to-GDP ratios that were the envy of even the most responsible industrial economies." This was not the Latin American or the peso crisis. Wasn't it a bit odd, he asked, that only a few years earlier Western economists were praising the Asians for their willingness to compete openly in international markets, and now they were saying these economies weren't open enough? For the past several decades, the East Asian "model" of relatively open trade and government-controlled capital markets had "delivered the most impressive level of increases in GDP that have ever been attained in such a short span," Stiglitz said. Now they were being belittled as "crony capitalism." Strange.

Beyond that, if financial markets were so often irrational and therefore it was difficult to say what might restore confidence, then how was it the IMF was so certain that its remedies would do so? Stiglitz grew contemptuous of the IMF's staff economists, and he would later make many enemies there by publicly calling them "third-rank students from first-rate universities." He was convinced they didn't understand the underlying problems—the so-called microeconomics that explained how market participants like households and companies actually made decisions—and that the single biggest problem was capital market liberalization. He pushed for a deeper analysis more attuned to the specifics of Asia, and its relationship with the big banks.

Stiglitz thought that the IMF's conditions were simply causing a lot of unnecessary pain. Once again, his own work guided his way and gave him the backbone to stand up to what seemed all of Washington. Stiglitz's theories had shown that it was far too simplistic to assume that higher rates will attract foreign investors and lenders—or will stop them from fleeing. His work showed that in the absence of good information—and there wasn't much of it in those hectic months—investors and lenders can't discriminate well between good and bad deals; in the fog of a crisis, higher interest rates might simply signal that those paying them are more likely to default. At the same time, higher interest rates would do long-term damage, putting banks out of business. The resulting deeper recession in the country would just make foreign capital flee faster, defeating the original purpose of raising interest rates.

Stiglitz preferred capital controls to jacking up interest rates. Why not just make it a little more difficult to trade all that hot money by placing a tax on it, or putting a time limit of, say, a year on investments before they could be pulled out of the country? That's what Malaysia did. When speculators began selling the Malaysian ringgit, the country's outspoken prime minister, Mahathir Mohammad, tore into George Soros, calling him a "moron" and saying that all foreign money traders were "racists" and "wild beasts." Mahathir then imposed capital controls. It was, of course, just a reassertion of the alternative model of development that all these countries, beginning with Japan, had represented. But that was now heresy against the Washington Consensus and Summers; it meant that *government* somehow knew better than the financial markets, and that was impossible. So it was never even considered.

Larry Summers never bought completely into the idea of strict "conditionality" for the Asian economies in return for bailouts. Privately he was more willing than Rubin to simply prop them up with funds without asking for political concessions in return, but once again Summers went along with the prevailing wisdom. Still, Stiglitz was angry about the way the debate had narrowed, that the East Asia model was being ignored. Sensible solutions left behind by the rigid Washington Consensus were no longer even considered. He was appalled by all the unnecessary pain. Banks were defaulting, and they would continue to default at a greater rate if interest rates were raised to keep capital flowing in. People's lives were being destroyed by a wrong headed idea. And of course there was his personal pique at the idea that the IMF had slighted his own vast body of work.

Stiglitz could no longer contain his outrage. In September 1997, at the annual meeting of the IMF and World Bank in Hong Kong, Stiglitz committed his first act of what would later be seen as ideological treason by Summers and others. He met privately with a group of East Asian finance ministers, and urged them to push ahead with a plan to impose capital controls. They never went ahead with it, except for Malaysia.

Jeff Sachs was on Stiglitz's side now. Sachs had never lived down his checkered experience with "shock therapy" in the early 1990s—which worked brilliantly in Eastern European countries like Poland, but proved disastrous in Russia. Indeed, Sachs disowned all responsibility for what happened in Russia, to the point where he would erupt at anyone who brought the subject up, as I learned when I moderated a panel discussion including him at Harvard in 1999. I asked him what I thought was a delicately phrased question: whether his experience at shock therapy had "informed" his new work as a development economist in the poorest nations in any way. Sachs erupted in anger, calling the question a "cheap shot." But of course it was just an uncomfortable reminder. (After he calmed down, Sachs did admit that his new work represented "an evolution of my personal efforts since the mid-1990s.")

The Asians never forgot Stiglitz's support. Later on Stiglitz would be criticized for being too passionate in defense of his theories when practical solutions were needed. "Joe's brilliant. But his problem is that he tends to leap to the conclusion: okay, this market isn't working very well. How can government make it better?" said one of his allies. "He doesn't pay enough attention to the possibility that government will get it wrong." But Stiglitz also saw that something much larger was going on: What was emerging on the global stage was a great test of alternative theories to economic development. The Cold War had not been just a contest of Soviet-style command economics versus free markets for goods and services. There was also the Chinese middle way out of communism, a way that had been paved by Japan's postwar "mixed economy." Those economies benefited from market discipline, but they didn't embrace fully free trade and capital. Yet almost no one was paying attention to these nuances or taking lessons from them. Fifteen years on, the Chinese experiment seemed to be succeeding brilliantly, just as Japan once had, bringing double-digit growth every year. Stiglitz understood that the dramatically different approaches to reform taken by communist China and Russia—gradualism versus shock therapy—were "one of the most important sets of economic and social experiments ever conducted," as he said at the time. There was, Stiglitz believed, a genuine alternative model to growth being born in Asia.

Summers was still going in the opposite direction. That same month he called Eisuke Sakakibara, Japan's vice minister for international affairs, and angrily protested that he'd just heard of the Japanese minister's plans for an Asian Monetary Fund. Sakakibara was one of Asia's intellectual champions for an alternative model. "This is not an Asia crisis, it is a crisis of global capitalism," Sakakibara warned me. "Global capital markets are responsible to a substantial degree. If you look at the so-called Asia crisis, the root cause has been the huge inflow of capital into

Malaysia, Thailand, Korea and China," Sakakibara told me around that time. "And all of a sudden, due to some trigger mechanism, all of that has [fled] from those countries. Borrowers have been borrowing recklessly, and lenders have been lending recklessly. And not just Japanese banks. American banks and European banks as well."

Sakakibara was actually in league with Stiglitz and Sachs. (Interestingly, Mahathir and Soros were also later to join forces and condemn the system of capital flows that the Clinton Treasury Department had sponsored.) Summers was alarmed by this unexpected insurgency: the idea of an Asian Monetary Fund raised the prospect of an alternative power center, one where the Treasury and IMF conditions for reform might be thrown out or undermined. "You would have competing IMFs," Rubin said later. "That would be used to lessen conditionality"—removing Washington's leverage. So Summers sprang into action, squelching the idea in a series of meetings in Asia. Rubin and Greenspan also wrote a letter denouncing the Asian Monetary Fund. The hubris of the Washington power elites in economics during this era was not unlike that of the Bush administration in the national-security realm after 9/11. For Summers especially, Stiglitz's constant kibitzing—and his habit of taking sides with the Asians—was getting a bit much to take.

7

Children of the Boom

Milton Friedman was the exception. It's more typically the fate of economists—especially great economists—to be ignored in Washington. Their advice is usually too nuanced, too unpleasant, or simply too hard to understand for politicians who are worried about the next election. That's what Larry Summers seemed to know and Joe Stiglitz did not. Summers, the economist-turned-Rubin-acolyte, was quickly becoming a key player on the global stage in the 1990s by mastering the nuances of the policy-making process. Stiglitz, for all his noise and brilliance, was just a gadfly, much as John Maynard Keynes had been little more than an annoyance to Franklin Roosevelt in the 1930s. After their first meeting in 1934, Roosevelt dismissed the economist as too abstract and intellectual, according to Robert Skidelsky, Keynes's biographer, and Keynes himself often fretted that Roosevelt was not spending enough to bring the United States out of the Depression.

Stiglitz had even less credibility now than Keynes had had then: as the 1990s moved on to the millennium, Stiglitz was proving to be naysayer to a global economic boom. He was, frankly, annoying people.

The roaring 1990s now belonged to Robert Rubin and Alan Greenspan and their protégés. There was, in those years, almost no daylight between the three of them—Greenspan, Rubin, and Summers. It was almost unprecedented for a Fed and a Treasury to be so simpatico—as if, on Capitol Hill, the Republicans and the Democrats had declared a holiday from politics and were caucusing together. But why should they argue, when everything seemed to be going so well? For four and a half years the three of them met weekly for breakfast, and nothing they said to one another ever leaked out. And that meant no cause for jitters in the markets. They even conferred on how to word statements about the dollar if it took a tumble in the currency markets.

Greenspan was clearly the presiding spirit of the decade. These were the years when Greenspan could seem to do no wrong. At his Humphrey-Hawkins testimony in 1997—shortly before the Asian financial contagion, when Rubin and Summers would share the cover of *Time* with Greenspan as part of the "Committee to Save the World"— then Representative Michael Castle, chair of the House subcommittee, compared Greenspan to a Roman general at a triumph. The committee, Castle said, was like the servant holding a laurel wreath above his head and whispering in his ear, "Remember, you are only human." Even Milton Friedman, who had become his great friend, was impressed. Friedman had built his reputation on proving the inefficacy of the Fed, but he conceded that Greenspan had the magic, that he was the greatest Fed chairman ever. "In the first seventy-five years of its history, the Fed was a major negative feature in the economy. We never would have had the Great Depression if there hadn't been a Fed. I had very seldom had anything good to say about the Fed before the 1980s. But since Alan Greenspan took over, I have had very little but good to say."

Greenspan seemed to have helped to fundamentally alter the economic culture in the United States. Building on Volcker's work, his mantra was to seek an "inflation rate so low that it is no longer a factor in economic decision making." By keeping prices consistently low, he created stringently low expectations among businesses, wage earners, and consumers who, a couple of decades earlier, had seemed resigned to constant inflation. In the eyes of many, what distinguished Greenspan most from Volcker was his extraordinary deftness, an approach to monetary policy that was almost like the improvisational jazz Greenspan had dabbled in as part of the Henry Jerome band. Whereas Volcker savagely pounded down inflation—which he had to do, since he caught the worst of it—Greenspan seemed to outfox inflation.

The signature policy move of the Greenspan era became known as the "preemptive strike." That meant raising rates *before*, rather than when, inflation shows up in the numbers. The reasoning is obvious: nipping inflation in the bud means you don't have to be as severe as when it actually appears. Inflation became such a nonfactor during his tenure that it soon became received wisdom that Greenspan wouldn't tamper with the rise in asset or stock prices by raising interest rates. He would only seek to lower rates if a market downturn hit, as he did in 1987 and again during the Asian contagion. By the end of the 1990s, this became market folklore and was known as the "Greenspan put"—a "put" is a reverse option used to hedge against a downturn. It meant that market players could place a dependable bet on Greenspan's reluctance to inter- fere with rising values while he would move quickly to stem a downturn. The Federal Reserve chairman himself was the best hedge against a market decline.

This was all music to the ears of Bob Rubin's Treasury Department, for which every upswing in the stock and bond market meant that the Clinton administration would get credit as the author of a historic eco- nomic boom.

It was Greenspan, however, who was the first to understand the broader picture of what was happening in the 1990s, in the post–Cold War era, better than most of his colleagues. His primary achievement was not the one he typically gets credit for: keeping unemployment low. At that crucial moment in history, Greenspan saw that inflation would not be the danger it formerly had been; productivity was increasing enormously as a result of new information technologies and as three bil- lion people who formerly had been contained behind the communist bloc were released as a productive force in the world. As a result, the U.S. economy could be allowed to grow faster without risk of inflation. Greenspan, to his credit, saw this first. Repeatedly, Fed staff and the regional governors—who tended to be conservative—warned Greenspan that the low unemployment numbers signaled that inflation pressures were rising. Time to raise rates. But he saw something in the numbers they did not: improved productivity was keeping costs and prices down. "Let's wait awhile," he would tell his staff.

It was Greenspan's incredible affinity for data. It seemed so hope- lessly optimistic that Rubin and Summers played the Grinch, resisting the idea at first. Once again, they had a remarkably topsy-turvy rela- tionship: Treasury was supposed to be the one pushing the Fed to keep rates low, not the other way around! But they were all so comfortable with one another. Greenspan would "show up at breakfast and ask what I thought about the latest railcar shipments of some kind of wheat I had never heard of," Rubin recalled. "I'd say, 'I don't know how I missed that figure in the paper, but I did.' He would have worked out a whole hypothesis around it. Greenspan was the first of the three of us to reach the tentative conclusion that . . . the speed limit on economic growth was higher than we'd thought." Summers, ever eager to thrash out new ideas, would joust with Greenspan over the issue, questioning whether the surge in productivity was temporary. It was the topic du jour through the entire decade, said a former Fed official who served under Green-span his entire eighteen years. "You would never expect a guy like that to come down on the side of unemployment, and not on the side of sta-bility. But he was right. We were wrong," said the Fed official. Critics would later dismiss Greenspan's low-interest-rate bias as merely a tool for juicing up the stock market, but many who worked for him, like this official, disagreed. "The 1990s was his baby. Alan Greenspan did great things for his country. Millions of Americans owe their jobs to him. If he had listened to us, and to the other Fed governors, he would have raised rates and caused more unemployment. It's a shame, because he will be remembered more for what he didn't do, on the regulatory side."

Still, there were some disquieting signs of what was to come. Ed Gramlich, a little-known University of Michigan academic, had been appointed to the Fed by Clinton. Assigned to oversee consumer lending, he grew concerned about unregulated mortgage originators growing out of control in the late 1990s. Knowing Greenspan's aversion to regulation, Gramlich gingerly approached him on a one-to-one basis, suggesting that the Fed use its discretionary authority to send examiners into the offices of consumer-finance lenders. Greenspan turned him down. Gramlich later resigned and died of leukemia just as the mortgage market was overheating.

In 1994, Congress had given the Fed authority to write new rules regulating unfair and deceptive practices related to mortgage loans under the Home Ownership and Equity Protection Act (HOEPA). None were ever written during the Greenspan era. As Greenspan later recalled it, Gramlich came in and mentioned to him that there were a lot of these egregious practices going on and maybe the Fed should do something about them. Greenspan replied that he didn't think such efforts could succeed and in fact they might make things worse, because subprime lenders would then put signs in their windows pro-claiming they were "supervised by the Federal Reserve." "They would have been far more egregious in their actions and basically done far more damage," he said. Testifying later before Congress, Greenspan would defend himself by saying he "voted for virtually every regulatory action that the Federal Reserve Board moved forward on." But that was disingenuous: he himself stopped the Board from moving forward on most things.

It wasn't just Greenspan, of course. Most of his Fed Board also took a very traditional view of the Fed's role in overseeing the banking system. On January 12, 1998, the Federal Reserve Board voted "to not conduct consumer compliance examinations or, not to investigate consumer complaints regarding, nonbank subsidiaries of bank holding companies." Later, when Gramlich led efforts to take away the regulatory powers from the Fed, Greenspan blocked the effort—but only so he could ensure there was no regulation. And when someone suggested protections for Habitat for Humanity homeowners, who had a lot of equity but tight finances and were being targeted by subprime lenders, the Fed proposed new protections but then mysteriously backed off. "They just didn't want to use their authority," said Michael Calhoun of the Center for Responsible Lending. James Bothwell, author of a 1994 General Accountability Office (GAO) report on the dangers posed by derivatives, recalled being "dumbfounded" hearing Greenspan speak out against margin requirements. Once, at a lunch held by Chuck Bowsher, who was comptroller general of the GAO, Bothwell heard Greenspan say, "I don't know why the Federal Reserve has regulatory authority over banks." "Truth be told," Bothwell said, "he wanted more because he didn't want to use it." Greenspan occasionally spoke out against predatory lending. But he also gave lenders the go-ahead to do more adjustable-rate mortgages, which later became notorious.

At another point, to prevent any tampering with the banks, Greenspan did something he almost never had to do—he stood against his entire board. In the mid-1990s, it came to the attention of the Fed board of governors that the "average percentage yield" that banks used to advertise their certificates of deposit was based on an erroneous formula. Banks were forced to publish the numbers under the Truth in Savings laws. Alerted to the error, the securities industry threatened to sue the Fed, because the mistaken formula was making the yields on the long-term CDs the securities firms were trying to sell lower than they really were. "Several of us thought we ought to change the formula," Alan Blinder recalled. "Not Greenspan. His attitude was, yes, you're right in principle, but we shouldn't bother the banks about this." The board, remarkably, outvoted Greenspan. But the chairman wasn't finished. He called in the Fed's chief counsel, Virgil Mattingly, who gathered the dissident governors together and pressed them to agree to put the vote on hold "pending further study." Greenspan "managed to deep-six the whole thing," said Blinder.

But this was all happening out of the headlines.

If Greenspan was the overarching presence, Rubin was the confident public face of the era—the "glass of fashion, the observed of all observers." People loved calm in the face of crisis, the Hemingwayesque ideal of grace under pressure—like Reagan's wisecracks after being shot—and Rubin had that quality in spades. But behind Rubin's effortless persona, he was also a demon for preparation; his staff had a saying: "One hour of preparation for every minute of time on the Sunday shows." On October 27, 1997, propelled by the Asian crisis, the Dow Jones average tanked 554 points, its largest ever single-day drop. The percentage decline was only a fraction of what it had been on the "Black Monday" a decade before, when the Dow dropped 22.6 percent in a day. Rubin hesitated over whether to say something. After consulting with Greenspan, Summers, and Gene Sperling—they spent four hours on it—he settled on a brief statement of faith in the fundamentals of the economy. Standard stuff, and not unlike what Reagan had said in 1987 that so worried Greenspan in his first crisis. But again, the Rubin style had a lot to do with the reassuring impact the statement had. He orchestrated a simple walk down the Treasury steps, delivered the statement, then turned on his heels and walked back up the steps as the mass of reporters shouted questions at his back. That was all. It was all in the way the moment was handled, as Rubin himself later noted: "One advantage of avoiding frivolous market commentary is that one builds and maintains a credibility that can be drawn upon when it is really needed."

Rubin handled the Asian crisis the same way.

Even during what should have been a restful time—the last week of December 1997—Rubin didn't have much time to stop and think about the long-term impact his deregulatory approach was having on the global system. At some point between Christmas and New Year's that year, Rubin found himself standing, like some sort of globo-plumber, knee-deep in the middle of a country with a huge leak—South Korea—and wondering how to plug it. South Korea's currency and banking system were in the middle of the most catastrophic collapse in history. For the Koreans, once proud standard-bearers of the Asian miracle, it was the worst moment of national humiliation since the Japanese had forcibly colonized their country nearly a century before. As Rubin recalled it in an interview with me several years later, Korea at that point had only about $4 billion in reserves left, "and they were being used at the rate of a billion a day. You can do the arithmetic." Now the markets were panicked, a sentiment exacerbated by the Korean government's unwillingness to reveal how much it had left in reserves. Rubin's job was to somehow stop the outflow.

There was only one thing left for Rubin to do: interpose himself, personally, between the fleeing capital and the Koreans. Rubin would need to use the prestige he had won as the commanding and graceful Treasury secretary who had presided over the high-growth, low-inflation U.S. economy of the 1990s. "So what we did," Rubin said—it was always "we" with Rubin, though he was the guy on the spot—"was we got on the phone with the major money centers—London, Tokyo, Frankfurt, Paris—and spoke to the appropriate officials and authorities and asked them to work with their banks, as we were going to work with our banks, and try to put in place a voluntary standstill."

There was no one better at this sort of thing than Rubin. He wasn't actually in Korea at the time, of course. Rubin took care of it over the phone from ten thousand miles away. He had flown to the Caribbean to eke out a few days engaging in his favorite recreation: bonefishing. That week turned out instead to be the climax of the six-month-long Asian contagion, and Rubin spent most of it on secure phones in his hotel room before flying back to Washington to continue his round-the-clock manhandling of the world's leading bankers. It was a close-run thing. "I think there was a real possibility that there was nothing we could do to stem that flow. The question was whether we could reestablish enough confidence so that Korea would not run out of reserves, which could have caused the private banking system in Korea to have to default on its interbank credits," he said.

Cajoling, joking, always with that verbal jujitsu he liked to use— "Well, I don't know exactly what will happen, Jim, but I'll tell you what could happen, and what I think will happen"—Rubin proved to be, by all accounts, masterful that week. It turns out there were a few big banks that did not want to extend their credit lines to Seoul's thinning treasury. "There was one in particular who didn't see quite why he shouldn't cut and run," Rubin related wryly, "but after a long discussion he decided to remain part of the global community." Translation: He, Bob Rubin, had suggested in genteel terms that doing business in the future might become a tad *complicated* for the prodigal banker if it became known that he had refused to help. It was a show of calm mastery that made Rubin an awesome figure to his young acolytes, among them Larry Summers and Tim Geithner. "They all said it was an amazing performance," recalled one former associate of Geithner's—the equal of anything Greenspan once did.

No one dwelled on the fact that much of the extraordinary indebtedness of the Asian banks had a lot to do with heavily leveraged derivatives trades between Western and Asian bankers. Or that the market breakdown—the plumbing problem Bob Rubin had attended to—might have been a problem with the system itself. If there was no need for capital controls, then why did Robert Rubin, Alan Greenspan, and Larry Summers need to be a "Committee to Save the World" and impose ad hoc capital controls? These were not questions most people were asking at the time. In the immediate aftermath of the Cold War, it was simply an intellectual beat too far—a conversation stopper—to suggest that there might be some fundamental problem with markets. By the end of the 1990s, the global economic system looked like such a reliable provider of growth, and financial markets were so sophisticated, that the era would soon become known as the "Great Moderation." And Rubin had the biggest fan club in Washington. He had become a heroic mover and shaker of the global economy, while back at home skeptics like Joe Stiglitz and Brooksley Born were trying to throw monkey wrenches into the works. That's what I told Rubin when I first sat down to interview him around that time. Seated beneath the giant oil portrait of Alexander Hamilton in his office, I opened up the interview with: "Mr. Secretary, some people are saying, even now, that you may be the best U.S. Treasury secretary in memory." The response was classic Rubin: he arched his eyebrows high and averted his face with a comical grimace. "I just don't think those kinds of comparisons are useful," Rubin snorted.

Through it all Rubin remained something of a puzzle. Nothing seemed to fit exactly right in the picture. He had come from Wall Street, yet he had gone in his spare time to community development meetings in the outer boroughs of New York City. Liberal Democratic sentiments were "deep inside his soul," Mickey Kantor, another liberal, told me at the time. He had proposed that executive pay over $1 million be paid in stocks and options, leading to a dramatic upswing in compensation levels and appalling house liberals Robert Reich and Leon Panetta, then White House chief of staff, who affirmed to me in the late 1990s that "Bob has certainly always presented that [Wall Street] viewpoint." At the same time that Rubin strenuously defended the interests of high finance, he opposed Clinton's plan for "workfare"—a major reform of the welfare system, requiring evidence of job hunting before payments were made—as too harsh on the working class. He also opposed capital gains tax cuts even though his fellow Wall Streeters loved them (Rubin felt they did not increase savings or investment). "I'll reconcile it for you," Rubin said when I asked him about the paradox of views he seemed to represent. "The answer to that is that the best social policy is a strong economy." He and Clinton, he said, "deliberately" decided to try to approach inequality by "equipping people to be effective in the modern economy, but obviously with a safety net," rather than the traditional Democratic means of redistributing income through government spending and higher taxes on the wealthy.

One of Rubin's favorite sayings was a phrase he adapted from John F. Kennedy: "A rising tide lifts all boats." The problem was, it wasn't quite true. While real wages were edging up, the larger trend during the Rubin era was always to favor capital at the expense of labor. There seemed to be one rising tide for Wall Street, and another for everybody else.

That was a big change. During the high-growth decades after World War II, labor and capital had existed in an uneasy but prosperous equilibrium. Even during the earlier golden age of globalization before World War I, labor and capital had meshed well on a worldwide scale. As free trade supplanted mercantilism in the mid- to late nineteenth century, barriers to trade and immigration fell at roughly the same time. "Unproductive Polish or Portuguese peasants who could not compete with Canadian and Argentine grain farmers," Jeffry Frieden wrote, "became productive urban workers in Warsaw and Lisbon or emigrated to become productive factory workers in Toronto or farm workers on the pampas." Streams of investment followed. But after the Reagan years, the balance of power between labor and capital shifted dramatically, between groups that had the advantage of international mobility and those that didn't. Investment capital could move at blinding speed, while labor still had to go by boat, train, and plane—and that's if it was lucky. With much tougher immigration restrictions than existed a century before, labor was more often confined to its home markets, forced to wait anxiously to see if globe-hopping capital deigned to come its way.

The growing power of financial capital explained a lot of the phenomena of the 1990s and 2000s: why Wall Street became the accepted arbiter of corporate performance; why the gap between executive and worker pay had widened to record levels; why the U.S. labor movement was a pitiful shadow of its former self, the victim of a "China price" set half a world away by a seemingly limitless supply of cheap labor. A new jargon entered the corporate lexicon, terms like "downsizing," which became routine, "employee empowerment" (read: think like a boss, get paid like a worker), and of course the all-embracing "corporate reengineering" (read: Our bottom line stinks. Rethink all costs. Start with labor.). "The bad guys won," Richard Bensinger, chief organizer for the AFL-CIO, America's leading labor federation, told me in the late 1990s. "The anger at capital, at employers and bosses, is greater than I've seen in twenty-three years of doing this."

The unease was global. In Germany especially—perhaps the most protectionist developed economy after Japan—there was tremendous pressure to rethink *Ordnungspolitik*, its policy of managed competition. Major corporations, such as Hoechst, began lining up to list on an exchange in New York, lured by the big investment banks, which had become adept both at spotting underperformers around the world and finding potential bidders from anywhere in the world. This created pressure worldwide to adopt the Anglo-American focus on short-term results and promote the happiness of shareholders to the exclusion of both workers and communities. While Wall Street had always thought this way, the entrenchment of Friedmanian thinking in Washington—and the growing fealty of the Clintonites to it—meant there was no shortage of experts who argued that this was at once efficient, just, and better for everyone.

At Deutsche Bank, the lion of German universal banking, there was a frenzied shift into U.S.-style investment banking and a new brand of advice being dished out to its corporate charges. Deutsche Bank executive Kurt Kasch told me flatly at the time that Germany must become more like the United States: "Despite their unpopularity, massive cost cutting, lean production and wage discretion are clear necessities." In the developing world too, on the advice of the U.S.-dominated IMF and World Bank, newly reformed nations were playing America's tune.

In Latin America, *yanqui*-hating dictators in epaulets were replaced by technocrats trained at MIT, Harvard, and Stanford. It was no surprise that by the late 1990s the backlash had begun to set in, erupting in massive antiglobalization protests in Seattle in 1999. On the Left, astute writers such as Robert Kuttner and William Greider began to warn, to no avail, that "scores of nations . . . have been taken hostage" by Wall Street, as Greider put it in his brilliantly prescient, if occasionally overwrought, 1997 book, *One World, Ready or Not*.

Alan Blinder, one of the few dissidents along with Stiglitz, finally left Washington in 1996 after an unhappy stint as vice chairman of the Fed. From his rearview mirror, Blinder liked what he saw less and less. "I think when historians look back at the last quarter of the twentieth century, this is going to be the number one focus: the shifting from labor to capital," he said. "They will see it as very major, almost unprecedented shift of money and power up the income pyramid, and they will marvel at the equanimity with which it was accepted."

Not just accepted—but actively encouraged by the men in power. Rubin and his acolytes, again, worried about how the U.S. consumer could continue to drive the world economy. But they did not seem to understand the extent to which their own policies were fatally undercutting the American consumer. In a conversation that Rubin later had with British publisher Harold Evans, the Treasury secretary remarked that U.S. auto companies could never develop "five-year plans." If they did, he said, they'd be laughed out the door. But that was because Wall Street would not tolerate five-year plans. It was too long a time frame; quarterly returns were what counted now.

But how had we gotten ourselves to that pathological place—where long-term strategic planning and concerns about employee welfare had gone out of fashion? How had the short-termism of Wall Street come to have the whip hand over the economy? As he did in so many other areas, Rubin played an important but quiet role in making this happen. In 1993, outraged by high executive salaries, Congress passed a law limiting to $1 million the amount of senior-executive base pay a corporation could deduct for income taxes. But Congress, in a compromise, exempted compensation that was a reward for performance in higher sales or profits. According to Leon Panetta, then the White House chief of staff, it was Rubin who came up with the compromise, which led to a furor to link executive pay to stock prices and options as a way of getting around the law. (Rubin later told me he "couldn't recall" proposing that provision.) As with so many other congressional actions, what was actually enacted was the law of unintended consequences.

In the space of a few years, stock prices and quarterly profits became the main barometer of corporate success, not only on Wall Street but on Main Street. Much-watched executives like Jack Welch of General Electric began to boast about how much "market cap" they had created; if the company's stock rose by $50 billion in value the CEOs took credit for it, and before long no one was terribly embarrassed at extracting a $20-million or $30-million-a-year slice of that leap in market cap, even while their corporate subordinates were making $150,000. Top executives began measuring their pay packages against other top executives across the country, informing their boards that if they weren't in the top 50 percent, then the "market" would begin to lose confidence in the company. "It was a frigging game," said Ed Woolard, the former chairman of Dupont, one of the few to resist such practices and restrict his top executives' pay to no more than 30 percent of lower-level, non-stock-optioned executive pay. "There were so many big stock option packages that people were driven to drive up the stock as fast as they could, to get big payoffs. And they began to take more risks to get the stocks up to get the payoffs."

Rubin did little to stop this. "He could have been bully-pulpiting the boards, asking them how they could allow the CEOs to run away with executive compensation," said Woolard, who considered himself a friend of Rubin's. "He never did. No one did. Why would he? The Treasury was filling up with revenues. Everybody thought Rubin was a genius. Rubin thought Rubin was a genius."

There were other lingering doubts about the impact of Rubinomics. Had deficit cutting really led to the 1990s boom, as they all claimed? Among the skeptics at the time was my *Newsweek* colleague Robert Samuelson, the famous economic columnist, who was one of the few in Washington who remained immune to Rubin's charm. Samuelson, a genial, soft-spoken man with a superbly economical writing style, was as much a master of data and statistics as Greenspan was. "It's simple arithmetic," said Samuelson. The cut in the budget deficit and the 1990s boom had very little to do with Clinton's budget plans and almost everything to do with the death of inflation and the post–Cold War peace dividend, especially cuts in defense. "The real roots of the economy's resurgence date to the early 1980s when the Federal Reserve suffocated double-digit inflation with the harsh 1981–82 recession," Samuelson wrote in a lukewarm appraisal of Rubin's tenure in 1999. "It is often said that smaller federal budget deficits—and now surpluses—propelled the economy forward. Just the opposite is true: the economy helped erase the budget deficit." Even Samuelson conceded that Rubin "projects calm and inspires confidence," but he said that Rubin's real legacy would await future judgment on "the outcome of the global financial crisis that started in mid-1997. Rubin helped shape the response, and if the crisis recedes, he will deserve much credit."

By the time Rubin finally laid his plans to leave Washington, the crisis did seem to be receding. And Samuelson was in the minority; few people disagreed with Clinton's effusive description of Bob Rubin, in his parting statements on the White House lawn, as "the greatest Treasury secretary since Alexander Hamilton." Rubin badly wanted to return to New York to be with his wife, Judy, and his family. And as far as he was concerned, there was only one possible replacement: his brilliant and loyal fellow commissioner to save the world, Larry Summers.

Rubin had made known as early as December 1996, just after Clinton's reelection, that he wanted Summers to replace him. Stiglitz was moving over to the World Bank as chief economist, leaving the chairmanship of the Council of Economic Advisors open, and Summers was tempted by the post even though it would almost certainly take him out of the power loop. It was a chance to run something on his own. But Rubin couldn't bear to lose him, so he cut a deal with Erskine Bowles, then Clinton's chief of staff: Rubin would leave midway through the second term, and Summers would replace him. Clinton, eager to give Rubin whatever he wanted if he would stay on, grudgingly agreed.

Still, it wasn't going to be an easy transition. Rubin was everything that Larry Summers still was not—and wanted to be. The way Rubin addressed the Wall Street bankers as peers, knew their business from the inside out, could walk that rhetorical tightrope between cajoling and pushing them with billions of dollars at stake—that was something Summers had never quite gotten the hang of. So Rubin began to play a kind of benign Svengali to his ungainly protégé, constantly pushing him into the limelight, sending him abroad to dicker with prime ministers before the cameras, missing no opportunity to credit him for policy successes. In 1997, Summers began

to work hard at winning over the Senate, knowing he would face confirmation hearings later on. To everyone's astonishment, he would go up to
the Hill and patiently answer the senators' often economically illiterate
questions about how currency crises occurred. At the same time Rubin
worked on Summers's personality flaws, deflating his ego by poking fun at
his high-handedness. (Rubin delivered a last shot in the Rose Garden, saying that one of the true pleasures of being secretary of the Treasury was to
"laugh at Larry.") In an interview just before Summers took over for him
in 1999, Rubin continued to tirelessly shape his protégé's image, especially Summers's main weak point: his lack of market experience. Rubin
described first meeting Summers on the trading floor at Goldman Sachs
in the mid-1980s. "I thought even then," he confided to reporters, "he has
a feel for this."

On policy, Rubin and Summers achieved a kind of mind meld during
their years together, by all accounts. Associates said that Summers also
worked hard to remake himself in Rubin's image. "I think he made it a
personal mission to learn from Bob," said Gene Sperling, Clinton's former economic adviser. Said another former senior U.S. official, "From
the beginning of his life Larry was the best student in his class. That is
true here. He realized that if he was going to achieve his goal, he would
have to become more even-keeled in discussions, more socially adept,
not walk into meetings and blow everybody away with how brilliant he is
and indicate his utter contempt for their existence." At the Rose Garden
ceremony in 1999 when his appointment was announced, Summers
was smooth and diplomatic, hitting his speech lines like a pro—even,
amazingly enough, evoking sympathy. Summers nearly broke down as
he humbly thanked his parents, his family—and Rubin, "from whom
I can't begin to describe how much I have learned." Still, the "new Larry"
could never completely eclipse the old Larry. As he took over, he mock-
complained to his aide, Howard Schloss, that replacing Rubin "is a little
like following Joe DiMaggio in center field." Schloss replied, "Larry, you
know who followed DiMaggio—Mickey Mantle." Summers, a baseball
fanatic who was born in Yankee country—New Haven, Connecticut—
replied with a grin, "Yeah, I know."

Another young aide to Summers had also learned at the feet of Rubin:
Timothy Geithner. He was the perfect protégé, Geithner, born to inter-
nationalism and public service, always a young man on the move, full of

high earnestness. His father, Peter Geithner, had been head of the Ford Foundation in Asia. In the late 1960s, around the same time little Barack Obama was running around the muddy alleyways of Jakarta—Obama and Geithner are almost exactly the same age, each born in August 1961— young Tim was spending his formative years, from six to eleven, going to an international school in New Delhi. Foreigners from advanced countries are always horrified to distraction by the poverty of India, the kind of desperate, almost medieval poverty that exists nowhere in the West—families living in garbage cities, children with horrific disfigurements forced to beg by their parents in the middle of the streets of its major cities, such as Delhi and Mumbai. As Peter Geithner recalled, young Americans usually reacted to this culture shock by going to one extreme or another. Either they poured out their empathy and sought to become more like the Indians, or they isolated themselves as much as possible behind the walls of their international settlements and clubs. Tim Geithner did neither: even then he was a middle-of-the-road guy. He mainly wanted to learn. And he would remain cautious in the extreme about taking sides.

It was part of what helped him bond with Barack Obama later on. "We had the same piece of experience in a narrow sense of growing up outside the United States, looking at the United States from afar," Geithner told me afterward. "I decided I wanted to work for my country after seeing how it was perceived by the world." It was in Jakarta that Obama came to appreciate both the powerlessness of his native companions and the status that came from having a white American mother, Ann, who worked for the U.S. embassy. (Obama and Geithner later learned, to their mutual astonishment, that the president's mother had met Geithner's father when she was a researcher working in Jakarta.)

Geithner had a similar epiphany. When the Geithner family moved to Bangkok in 1976 and Tim was a young teen, he would also make his way over to the U.S. embassy as a mystical locus of power. Mort Abramowitz, who was then the U.S. ambassador to Thailand, used to give lectures at the embassy on the Indo-Chinese refugee problem in the aftermath of the Vietnam War, which is when he first met Geithner. It is somewhat ironic in view of all the aspersions thrown at him during his first months as Treasury secretary—that he was too young, too scared of the spotlight—that at fifteen Geithner was already mature beyond his years. "He was an avid listener," recalled Abramowitz. As Geithner later said at his Treasury swearing-in: "My father gave me, among many wonderful things, the important gift of showing me the world as a child. . . . It was that experience—seeing firsthand the extraordinary influence of American policy on the world—that led me to work in government."

It also led him to see the world in gray and to never stray too far from the status quo. Geithner went to Dartmouth and then almost immediately headed to Washington to work in government. He became a man of the establishment, always trying to fix problems—yet always deferring to the reigning zeitgeist. And in the late 1980s and early 1990s, during Geithner's formative years as a policy maker, the reigning zeitgeist was Wall Street's. His first big assignment was Japan, as an assistant Treasury attaché in the waning days of the bubble economy. It was the heyday of Western finance. I was in Tokyo around the same time as Geithner—from 1990 to 1994—and I, like Geithner, saw an economy being strangled by overregulation, especially in its financial sector.

It was, of course, yet another iteration of the old East Asia debate. The "model" that looked so promising in the early 1990s now, with the contagion, looked old and corrupt. The problem wasn't just that the mandarins in Japan's all-powerful Ministry of Finance dealt with the collapse of their bubble too gingerly, refusing to let debt clear. It was that they failed to deregulate their financial system. Summers, on his visits, was often compared to General MacArthur or, worse, Commodore Perry, who commanded gunboats sent by President Millard Fillmore to Tokyo in the mid-nineteenth century and issued the first in a long and often futile series of demands on the Japanese to open their markets. A popular book around Tokyo in those years was called "Citibank Is Definitely More Profitable"—a how-to guide on getting better returns on your yen with Western banks. The hauteur of American financiers visiting Japan in the late 1990s was striking—a complete turnabout from the fear and loathing of Japan in the 1980s. In February 1998 I ran into Sandy Weill having breakfast at Tokyo's plush Okura Hotel. Weill, a legendary acquirer of new companies, was then chairman of Travelers Group and was about to gobble up Citibank. He had come to Tokyo to inspect the damage and to stroll among the ruins of the Asian contagion. "It's a good time to start looking" for distressed financial assets, he told me as he spooned up some fresh papaya. And what properties might he be interested in? I asked. Weill swallowed some more papaya, grinned, and cracked, "How about the post office?" It was a good joke. Japanese citizens kept trillions of dollars in post office savings accounts at low interest rates simply because it was safe. Japan's postal savings system was perhaps the world's single largest pool of private capital.

These were the views that Geithner, like his mentors Bob Rubin and Larry Summers, fully embraced. And the lesson that Geithner, like me, took away from that was that Japan's overregulated economy was to blame for Asia's ills at the time. The freer its financial markets, the better off it would be. Later in the 1990s, Geithner wrote what was widely considered a brilliant analysis of the South Korean financial crisis that Rubin had helped to solve. After Rubin elevated him from a deputy assistant secretary, Geithner traveled with the Treasury chief everywhere and came to be seen as a zealous protector of his reputation—the perfect protégé. In later years, after Rubin went back to work on Wall Street and Summers returned to his natural milieu, academia, Geithner would stay in government, and the Rubinesque interventions of the Asian crisis (big, but temporary, leaving Wall Street intact in the end) would continue to be a model for him in the years ahead. "I think he was persuaded that what the Treasury and the IMF had done in Asia had worked. He was oblivious to the criticisms," said an economist who worked with Geithner later on. "He was competent, and he knew how to take control of a meeting. But he would never be bold. He would not tamper with the balance sheets of the big banks."

They became a cabal of sorts. And soon there was no discernible difference in views between them—and between them and Greenspan. If only the Asians would learn to emulate Wall Street!

But we were all caught up in it; we were all children of the boom. In June 1995, in the aftermath of the Gingrich takeover of the House and with the advent of a new generation of Republicans sworn to a platform of minimizing government, I authored a cover story for *Newsweek International* headlined "Does Government Matter?" "A brash new world economy is shoving the old statist structures aside; it is private, it is fast-paced and it is, by and large, averse to government meddling," I wrote in the breathless tones later adopted most famously by *New York Times* columnist Thomas L. Friedman in his own paean to the new capitalist world order, *The Lexus and the Olive Tree*. "The libertarian 'digitocrats' who are creating the Information Age, the young Republicans in Washington who are dismantling the New Deal–engendered welfare state, the swaggering investment bankers and fund managers who command the fawning attention of Third World finance ministers are all part of this phenomenon."

More than ten years before Friedman's bestseller, *The World Is Flat*, I declared in another *Newsweek* cover story in October 1994: "Whereas individual economies once had climates of their own, like mountain hollows, the simultaneous lowering of market barriers worldwide has transformed the economic geography into a broad plain, and the market winds howling across it are molding once-protected markets into a common shape beyond their will. Wealth, like so many peoples around the world, has broken free of government restraints. . . . Fickle and not particularly patriotic, this capital stops and pools where it pleases. . . . In the years ahead nearly every economy—whether industrialized or emerging—will find itself jostling thirstily with rivals to feed at this global stream."

We were all of us somewhat skeptical of how healthy this was, this scramble for free-flowing capital. But on the whole, most of us thought it was a good thing, and we believed that it was inevitable. Globalization seemed to be working. And for all the Clintonites—Rubin, Summers, Geithner, and others—their mutual pride and joy had become this roaring global economy. Clinton's and Rubin's concept of an economic policy from which no one dissented only gave further encouragement to the free-wheeling markets, and that was good for everybody. "We felt gratified," said Ed Knight, Rubin's general counsel at Treasury. "We felt that part of this was innovation in the financial markets, and also because the financial community was producing instruments allowing for better management of risk, putting risk in the hands of people who could manage it."

There were still some dissidents around, but as the 1990s boomed on, their voices were growing fainter. Among those who were most aghast at the change in the zeitgeist was, of course, John Dingell Jr., the feisty Democratic chairman of the Commerce Committee. Dingell, then nearly seventy, was the son of Representative John Dingell Sr., who had helped draft the House version of the bill that Senator Carter Glass of Virginia and Representative Henry Steagall of Alabama had pushed through in 1934.

The Glass-Steagall law not only separated commercial from investment banking, it also established the Federal Depository Insurance Corporation guaranteeing bank deposits. In other words, the guys who were supposed to be careful with other people's money were given federal guarantees, but they were told that in order to get them they had to remain separate from the fellows who gambled in speculation in stocks. It was tough stuff, but the issues had been clear-cut back then. From

1932 to 1934, the Senate banking and currency committee held hearings on the 1929 crash and found that commercial banks had misrepresented to their depositors the quality of securities that their investment-banking sides were underwriting and promoting. Among the culprits, according to the FDIC's history, was First National City Bank (later Citigroup), which was found to have repackaged the bank's Latin American loans and securitized them without disclosing its own confidential findings that the loans posed adverse risks. Dingell Junior had been a wide-eyed kid listening to his father discuss these stories around the dinner table. "I was one of the few people around here who remembered the New Deal," he said. The banks had gambled recklessly, and Roosevelt had to close ten thousand of them, allowing only seventy-five hundred to reopen. To get people to put their money back into the banks FDR would introduce the federal guarantee for deposits, but that also meant the institutions that enjoyed this would have to be segregated. Wall Street screamed, but it had no standing any longer. Pure, white-hot outrage, Dingell knew from stories he'd heard as a child, was what drove people in Washington then: "Dad lost $7,500, his whole worth in a bank that closed. Roosevelt closed it. Dad wasn't mad at Roosevelt. Americans all hated the damn bankers, they hated Wall Street. We had more communists in this country than in the Soviet Union because of them. They all hated those people that brought them down."

Now, no one was left to remember the outrage, except maybe old John Dingell.

Yet even then, there were signs that something else was amiss, that maybe the zeitgeist had overlooked something important after all. In early 1998, I went to Japan to try to elicit some remorse among the Japanese for being so backward, so out of touch with this wondrous new global economy. They were using their capital inefficiently, it was said. They were slowing things up. Not all of Japan's capital was used badly, of course. Much of it had helped create the Asian miracle in the first place. And some $270 billion worth was funneled into U.S. Treasuries. But the lion's share still sat in low-interest accounts, or was tied up in loans, many of them gone bad, funding skyscrapers and infrastructure boondoggles across Japan and Asia.

Some Western analysts blamed the Asian crisis, or its beginning, on Japan. Larry Summers certainly did. After the bubble economy of the late 1980s, Tokyo could have restructured its banking system and turned its savings into consumption. Instead Japan merely exported its cheap capital to Southeast Asia. That led to a huge buildup of overcapacity there. (German and French banks—like Japan's, relatively inefficient— piled yet more bad loans into the region.) "In many ways," Summers said then, "the Asian crisis is a reflection of nonmarket finance—the allocation of capital on bases other than where it will find the highest return."

It's not as if some in Washington didn't look inwardly by then and get a little queasy at the size and speed of all this superfast global trading emanating from Wall Street and the West. That was certainly the reaction after riots broke out in Indonesia while I was traveling around Asia. For any smallish country, no matter how healthy its economy, a negative turn of the markets had become an utterly unequal contest, like Godzilla stomping on a kiosk. By the late 1990s, $2.5 trillion was being flipped daily in world currency transactions, more than twice the GDP of the entire Third World. Greenspan himself had recently remarked that the Asian economies were incapable of absorbing such a "surge in funds." And Rubin found himself blindsided by a minirebellion by Democrats led by then House Democratic leader Richard Gephardt of Missouri, Democratic Whip David Bonior of Michigan, California representative Nancy Pelosi, and Massachusetts representative Barney Frank. They threatened to hold up IMF funding over the U.S. and European plan to amend its charter to make the liberalization of capital movements one of the fund's chief goals. Rubin agreed to shelve the charter change for the moment.

But it was just a pause. That's all everyone was issuing at the time: caveats. No one was paying much attention to Stiglitz and other critics. With both parties so clearly in agreement about the wonderful functioning of high finance, it seemed perverse to spend time thinking about a different system entirely.

Even Japan's Eisuke Sakakibara, notorious for being outspoken (and beloved of journalists as a result), was reluctant to criticize the IMF directly, other than to suggest mildly that it was imposing deflation on many of the economies of Asia. "You disagree with the IMF approach?" I asked him. "I cannot openly disagree with the fund. I am a responsible G7 official," he replied with a laugh. The reason was that zeitgeist again, always omnipresent. The prevailing wind was still for financial-market liberalization. Yes, "the capacity of governments has lagged behind the integration of global capital markets," a senior Treasury official conceded to me at the time, but that doesn't mean "it is an attractive or viable option to cut off capital flows." The solution instead, he said, was to push for sounder banks and market surveillance. Yet few of us noticed at the time that banks were getting into more proprietary trading, and derivatives were exploding beyond anyone's ability to monitor them.

As Stiglitz had suggested, there really wasn't much evidence that all this liberalization of capital was doing these countries much good. And in fact, much later on, one of Stiglitz's harshest critics, IMF chief economist Kenneth Rogoff, would mount a massive study showing that the expected benefits hadn't really shown up, just as Stiglitz had suspected. Most bizarre of all, some economists were beginning to show that countries that relied less on foreign capital tended to grow more rapidly. But Stiglitz was out of touch with his times, and few people were listening anymore, especially as the Asian crisis appeared to peter out in late 1998 with little recessionary impact in the Western hemisphere. Stiglitz had been forecasting annual doom and destruction since the early 1990s, his longtime academic collaborator, Columbia's Bruce Greenwald, conceded with a laugh. It just wasn't happening, at least not on the timeline Stiglitz laid out.

For the Committee to Save the World, all this was under the radar. The main problem was always with the other guy, the other economy. A reckless pool of hot capital had been loosed upon the world. Now it was Western capital flooding Asia. Later it would be Asian capital flooding the West. The system was at fault, was in fact out of control, but it would require several more data points a decade away before that became clear.

The denial of U.S. culpability grew into a pattern, a mantra of Washington-centered hubris. When Baring Brothers collapsed in 1995, my reaction along with other journalists was to say that the old merchant bank didn't have the risk management systems that Wall Street did. A rogue trader, Nick Leeson, had staked huge amounts of capital at its Singapore office on derivative bets and broke the bank. For most of the globalization crowd, the explanation was that the hoary British bank's merchant banking culture—its advisory business—was still too dominant in its approach. The Baring "toffs"—those English upper-class types—just didn't understand trading, that was it. Summers had a favorite analogy, one he would use often. The arrival of global finance was like the invention of the jet engine. Transportation was vastly improved and made much more efficient, but the crashes when they came were much bigger. The answer, he told the *New Yorker*'s John Cassidy in 1998, was to lengthen the runways, not to try to uninvent the jet engine. Adopt American-style legal and banking systems. Copy us.

Summers in particular, with that debater's edge of his, seemed to relish the idea that his opponents in the great debate had been proved wrong, especially after the Asian crisis had passed. "He would always go at me, saying twenty-five years from now, they'll wonder why Bhagwati went bananas on capital account liberalization," recalled Columbia University economist Jagdish Bhagwati, a free trader who sought to argue that finance must be treated differently from other markets. "He'd say, 'There'll be a footnote on you.'"

Summers himself would get more than a footnote, but not necessarily for the right reasons. With his zeal of the convert, he often outdid his teacher, Bob Rubin, in his enthusiasm for markets, in particular when it came to derivatives.

The booming derivatives market was the Great New Fact about the financial world in the 1990s. Derivatives had been around in some form for centuries; the first standardized futures contracts traded on an exchange can be traced to the Yodoya rice market in Osaka, Japan, in the mid-1600s. For most of their history, derivatives were uncontroversial and generally considered safe. This was true well into the 1980s, when many international companies began using what was called the "plain-vanilla" swap. If a corporation wanted to lock in a fixed rate of financing but realized that it could raise money more cheaply by issuing a bond with a floating rate, it found that with derivatives, it could do both. The corporation would agree to make regular fixed-rate payments to a "swaps" dealer; in return it would receive payments on a floating rate so it could make its bond payments. As companies did more business around the world, derivatives provided a way to hedge many risks, including the fluctuations of currencies. In the 1970s, the invention of the Black-Scholes option pricing model (named after the same Fischer Black whom Rubin later hired at Goldman) gave the financial world a tool for pricing options in a standardized way that allowed them to be widely traded.

The superfast, mind-bogglingly complex derivatives market as we know it today didn't really take off until the 1990s. That's when the business moved from careful corporate hedging to widespread betting. Rather than just a hedge on risks, derivatives became a game of financial roulette, a side bet on all manner of assets—currencies, oil, loans, mortgages.

This was accomplished through "structured finance," or the repackaging of assets in clever ways, and "securitization," which meant turning these same derivatives, or packages of derivatives, into new types of securities that could be sold and traded on markets as straightforward bonds once were. Ironically, securitization took off in the aftermath of the S&L crisis, when the assets of failing companies needed to be stripped out and sold off. A government agency created to unwind the bad banks, the Resolution Trust Corporation, effectively invented the market for securities backed by nontraditional assets such as commercial and nonperforming mortgage loans. That led to a whole new industry of securitizing, and combined with structured finance, which involved the repackaging of financial assets to reallocate risks and gain higher credit ratings. These were often turned into securities and resold, and soon investment banks were looking for newer and more complicated ways to securitize loose assets, which were connected less and less to the individual and companies that once owned them. They were bought and traded off balance sheets, which meant a bank didn't have to report them because it didn't carry them on its books. By the mid-1990s, the market in all these derivatives had exploded to a much larger size than stocks and ordinary bonds, some $60 trillion in face value. According to the prevailing theory, this provided liquidity for some, stability for others, and huge profits for those willing to manage the risk.

At the time, this innovation was viewed by some as devoting too much of the world's money and brainpower to risky paper swapping. To others, it was a shining example of American financial ingenuity, a harnessing of expanding computer power to make markets even more efficient and risk-free. What matters, though, is that the leading pundits in Washington—in politics, business, and the media—all agreed it was the latter.

Many of the derivatives bets were placed with foreign banks, thanks in part to the loosening of capital restrictions. That was the untold story of both the Mexican peso crisis of 1995 and the Asian financial crisis. Rubin, Summers, and others rarely talked about it, but the reason those crises unfolded so much more quickly than international financial crises had in the past—for example, the Latin American debt crisis of the 1980s—was the explosion in derivatives. Western banks had sold derivatives to their counterpart banks, often in highly leveraged ways, as a way of placing bets on exchange rates. When the Asian currencies dropped, the banks suddenly owed hundreds of millions of dollars in margin calls overnight. This wasn't like a traditional loan, which takes ninety days or more to mature. That's why when the Mexican government tried to do a managed devaluation of 10 percent, it got swamped by sellers.

Similarly, the Asian crisis was exacerbated by this reversal of short-term bank lending, and most of the banks' initial losses were related to derivative-based credit swap contracts, economist Jan Kregel later wrote. This was a lot of the reason for the urgency of the bailouts: to pay off this sudden and huge debt, the Asian banks had to begin selling vast amounts of collateral. That in turn led to "contagion," causing the crisis to spread fast. But because it was all happening off the balance sheet, because most of these derivatives bets were outside the purview of regulators and supervisors, there was scant information about it and the extent of the damage was not seen.

But the derivatives world was becoming a shadow world. That's why, when Rubin and other officials later discussed the Asian crisis, they talked in general terms about loan defaults, without getting too much into the mechanics. And as more and more things were "securitized," there was no longer any meaningful connection between the users of assets, like those who took out mortgages for a home or a student loan, and those who came to own those assets. The sense of credit and trust that had once depended on an eye-to-eye relationship between, say, a lender and borrower at a bank, was becoming vested in the market system itself. The theory was that all these risks were now being spread around, in a kind of global portfolio diversification. Broadly speaking, the creators and the owners of assets were like a married couple who get divorced and move to different countries, remaining connected only by the tenuous link of an alimony or child-support payment.

Rubin, knowing the excesses of financial markets, was worried about these new trends. As far back as the 1987 market crash, he'd been concerned about the role played by traders shorting stock index futures, another form of derivatives. He was especially worried about the amount of leverage involved in derivatives bets and how that might blow up if there were another crash. Rubin would occasionally suggest that new restraints were needed, such as higher margin requirements that would dampen derivatives trading somewhat. But he always found too much resistance among his friends on the Street. Indeed, throughout his time in office in the 1990s Rubin never sought to apply new rules to the market. There just didn't seem to be any urgency, with everything going so well. Perhaps it was because his economics ace, Summers, the man he relied on most for a second opinion, felt differently. As Rubin later wrote in his memoir, *In an Uncertain World*, "Larry thought I was overly concerned with the risks of derivatives." "You're playing tennis with a wooden racket," Summers would josh, ribbing him about how long it had been since Rubin had done risk arbitrage at Goldman. Sure, Summers had his own concerns about risk and leverage, but he thought his boss was too obsessed with derivatives alone. Rubin, on his way out of Washington, was of another generation. The old man worries too much, Summers thought.

8

The High Tide of Hubris

Gerald Corrigan was worried about derivatives, even if Larry Summers wasn't.

Corrigan was exactly the sort of man Wall Street and Washington power brokers loved to look down on. The bluff big-shouldered president of the Federal Reserve Bank of New York was something of a throwback. Born to a working-class family in Connecticut, educated at the decidedly non–Ivy League Fairfield University, Corrigan didn't act or talk like a central banker. He was profane and blunt and looked "like he'd be more at home in rugby scrum," his former aide Peter Bakstansky said. As a young central banker in the early 1970s, Corrigan had been asked by his boss and mentor Paul Volcker, then head of the New York Fed, to take over the Fed's accounting department, which was having a great deal of trouble keeping track of its various accounts with banks. Corrigan was nonplussed at first, feeling slighted. He was an economist, after all. "I said, 'The accounting department?' I had this vision of green eyeshades. I didn't know a damn thing about accounting."

But it was, for Corrigan, a life-changing experience. Unlike many of his central banking colleagues he became known as a "plumber," a man who knew how to get his hands dirty with the inner workings of finance—how back-office payments are made and such, how to keep the financial system running in a crisis.

In Corrigan's world—the real world of banking—even the smartest and most sophisticated banks screwed up.

He'd seen it himself many times, and he was never shy about demanding information from his charges, the elite bankers under his supervision. "He's got this Irish gruffness, this Sergeant Friday demeanor: 'Just the facts,'" said Marc Lackritz, the former longtime head of the Securities Industry Association and a longtime industry lobbyist. But Corrigan was also highly intelligent. In 1982, three years before he became head of the New York Fed, he'd written a seminal report titled, "Are Banks Special?" Of course they were, he concluded: they can't simply be treated as another business. They were transmission belts that kept the rest of the economy going; and they were the primary source of liquidity for other businesses. They had a higher responsibility to the economy, he believed.

Corrigan had spent his career fretting over systemic breakdowns of the banking system—and, bit by bit, putting in fixes. For Corrigan and others of his generation, the Bank Herstatt crisis had been formative. Herstatt was a German bank that, one day in 1974, had suddenly found itself unable to convert deutschmarks into dollars because of time-zone differences and had to cease operations. The bank was liquidated. Suddenly every banker in the world was worried about being caught short in an international settlement. Shortly after Corrigan took over as president of the New York Fed in 1985, the Bank of New York—the supersophisticated, fabled bank of banks—suddenly suffered a computer failure one day. It ended up owing $23 billion—a huge amount of money in those days—that it couldn't pay because it couldn't exchange its government securities. That afternoon Corrigan, worrying as always, told his general counsel to create a special loan agreement that would stake all of Bank of New York's assets—"even the flower pots"—as collateral. It was an amazing piece of foresight, because at one thirty in the morning the next day, Bank of New York suddenly found it needed every penny. For Corrigan, it was a high-wire act, because it turned out that Bank of New York had only $15 billion in assets to pledge. But in the end the debt was paid off.

As the crises multiplied—the 1987 stock market crash was a big one—Corrigan had begun to worry, all by himself, about what banks were doing with derivatives, though they weren't even called that back then. He realized that even then, banks were having a hard time keeping track of all their swaps trades, and he was obsessive about the idea that a bank should always know its exposure at any given moment. This, of course, was exactly the sort of "perfect information" that the efficient markets types thought was out there but didn't exist in real life. In late 1991, seeking to assuage Corrigan, the major banks asked their top derivatives traders to go see him at the Fed. Among those called in to deal with Corrigan's concerns was said to be a vice president at JP Morgan named Mark Brickell, a diehard free-market ideologue as well as a successful trader. Brickell, not quite realizing who he was dealing with, launched into a monologue about how everything was going to be okay, this is a new world now in which global firms are big boys and can hedge their own risks according to two people privy to the conversation.

His tone implied, "This stuff's beyond you, old man."

Brickell (who later said he couldn't remember going to the meeting, and thought it was another trader at JP Morgan) apparently addressed Corrigan somewhat in the same way Robert Rubin would later treat Brooksley Born. As he delivered his smug, free-market message to Jerry Corrigan, the Fed president got redder and redder and the veins in his neck began to pop. Finally Corrigan could take no more.

"Listen, you little fuck," he interrupted, "I'm not a Boy Scout," and then he went into his experiences with bankers during the Herstatt and other crises. Recalling the episode to a journalist friend of mine a year later, Corrigan crushed his spoon into his grapefruit as if the fruit were the Morgan man's head.

Shortly after that, on January 30, 1992, Corrigan made a speech before the New York Bankers Association. Corrigan told his audience they'd better "take a very, very hard look at off-balance-sheet activities," adding: "I hope this sounds like a warning, because it is." Over-the-counter derivatives, he said, "must be understood by top management, as well as by traders and rocket scientists." It was astonishingly blunt for a central banker—and Corrigan's staff tried to get him to take the line out. He refused.

There were other old lions of Wall Street who were worried, among them Lazard Frères's Felix Rohatyn, who warned in July 1992 that "twenty-six-year-olds with computers are creating hydrogen bombs." (That was strikingly close to the truth, since many of the numbers wizards who were creating this stuff on Wall Street—known as "quants"—were actually former physicists who might have otherwise been making hydrogen bombs if the Cold War were still on.) But Corrigan, in taking a public stand, "was actually the first dissenter about the whole thing," said Marc Lackritz.

A month later, Corrigan gave another big speech in which he warned against pay "being lower for people who oversee risk than people who are creating the risk."

His warnings, more than six years before Brooksley Born took on the issue, came to nothing. Corrigan was a fearless and resourceful regulator in the grand tradition of Ben Strong, the no-nonsense New York Fed chief who had died of tuberculosis in 1928 and whom many, starting with Milton Friedman, felt might have averted the Depression had he lived. But now, with free-market fundamentalism in full flower, there was something that felt antiquated about Corrigan's—and Strong's—approach to supervision. It suggested that banks needed to have their hands held—and of course they occasionally did, as the Bank of New York episode showed. But that kind of deeper knowledge, another way of acknowledging the imperfections of markets, was just out of keeping with the times.

Even so, down in the canyons of Wall Street there were many who knew that Corrigan had reason to be afraid of derivatives—very afraid. One of them was a derivatives trader named Frank Partnoy. At around the same time that Corrigan was blowing up at JP Morgan and other banks and delivering his "warning," Partnoy was hard at work at his trading desk at Morgan Stanley in New York. A Kansas-born math whiz who had gone to Yale Law School, Partnoy was living out Jerry Corrigan's and Brooksley Born's worst fears—and Joe Stiglitz's theories. After Yale, Partnoy had clerked for Judge Michael Mukasey, later to be George W. Bush's attorney general. Partnoy was fascinated by the Street, so close yet so far from New Haven, Connecticut, and Mukasey reluctantly told him to go ahead and give it a try. After a time at First Boston, a second-tier firm—during which Partnoy's most enduring accomplishment was to invent a supercool poker program—he made it to the promised land: Morgan Stanley, the most prestigious house on Wall Street.

Morgan Stanley had once been the ultimate "white-shoe" firm, the blue-blooded offspring of JP Morgan after Glass-Steagall legally separated commercial and investment banking. For four decades, from behind their antique mahogany desks, the bankers of Morgan Stanley underwrote the securities for and dispensed investment counsel to America's corporate finest. The firm did not even have a salesman or trader on its staff until the mid-1970s. But more aggressive firms like Salomon Brothers and Goldman Sachs began to earn more money as the leveraged-buyout 1980s began, and Morgan found itself dropping in the "league tables," which is how the investment banks ranked themselves. The "pivotal point," as Partnoy described it, came when Ron Perelman was readying a junk-bond-funded takeover attempt at Revlon, which had long been a Morgan client. The temptation was too great: The firm jumped in, earned $25 million in fees, and soon included among its clients some of the biggest takeover pirates of the era, including T. Boone Pickens.

Not that this trend was all bad. Through the 1980s and into the early 1990s, the changing nature of Wall Street still benefited the larger real economy. Capital was becoming more available to wider sectors of the economy. Back in the nineteenth-century world of J. P. Morgan, capital had been scarce and Wall Street had been controlled by a stodgy few. Morgan himself held major stakes in the railroads, which together comprised some 60 percent of the New York Stock Exchange, and stock issuance was a closely held right granted to only the most blue-blooded of corporations. But now the IBMs and the General Motors didn't need Wall Street as much as before; their corporate ratings were often better than those of the investment banks and they sometimes had their own financing units. They could easily tap the commercial-paper market on their own. So whereas in the old days prestige came to those firms that worked their way up the credit scale to the blue chips, now firms like Morgan Stanley had to look for less creditworthy new clients.

That was Michael Milken's great insight at Drexel Burnham in the 1980s as he began finding ways to issue "junk" bonds for buccaneering entrepreneurs, people who in previous periods would not have warranted a second look from the Street. The ever-escalating race to finance less creditworthy borrowers proceeded through the biotech bubble and the high-tech bubble of the 1990s, but at least Wall Street ended up financing some great companies of enduring value. Google. Yahoo! Genentech.

The derivatives selling craze that Frank Partnoy was part of was beginning to take on a wholly different quality. At some indefinable point, in its desperation for new sources of profit, Wall Street crossed the line from innovative if sometimes reckless financing of new ventures, and

the hedging of them, into practices that were purely about speculation and scamming. It was yet another example of how finance simply
operated according to different market rules than the rest of the economy when left to its own devices. As Ron Chernow, the historian who
chronicled J. P. Morgan's career, put it to me: "In most businesses, competition is beneficial and healthy. On Wall Street, competition always
waters down standards." As a new trader at Morgan Stanley, Partnoy
realized that the business was now mainly about finding complex new
packages of debt obligations and interest-rate payments to foist on
customers who barely understood them. By the time Partnoy arrived
in mid-1994, "any evidence of the old, stodgy Morgan Stanley had been
washed away. The new firm was a turbo-charged profit machine." Sales
and trading drove most of its revenues, and "its engine was fueled by
derivatives." Morgan's CEO was now John Mack, a legendary trader
known as "Mack the Knife," whose oft-repeated order to derivatives
traders was: "Let's go kill someone."

The only difference between Partnoy and his colleagues on the trading floor seemed to be that he was, oddly, afflicted with a conscience
about how top Wall Street firms had changed from suppliers of capital to sellers of financial snake oil. Partnoy knew the theory of efficient
markets—how the market would always sift out the good from the bad.
And what he saw on the derivatives trading floor at Morgan Stanley was
nothing like the theory. He was having a kind of Joe Stiglitz experience.
"The thing that was most stunning to me was the disconnect between
the theory of the way markets work and what was on Wall Street," he
said. *Dispersing risk?* Give me a break, Partnoy thought. Sure, derivatives were useful on a company-to-company basis as a way to hedge the
risk of going into a foreign market: you would buy a futures contract in
the foreign currency at a certain price to make sure you weren't hit hard
if the currency rose or fell. But in its later stages, much of the explosion
in the derivatives business was more about structured finance—math
whizzes who came up with Rubik's cube combinations of new types of
securities to entice investors in search of higher yields. It had turned into
a way to find new things to bet on. Wall Street was becoming Las Vegas;
it was becoming something worse, actually, since no one had a real sense
of the house odds and how they were being fixed. Now the game was all
about taking a plain vanilla product, something with a quarter of a point
interest "spread"—meaning the difference in interest earnings between

what Morgan Stanley paid out for it and what the firm eventually sold it for—and repackaging it together with riskier products so that Morgan could sell it for a five-point spread. That gave his investment bank a big payday.

This is why the banking industry resisted all efforts in the 1990s to "standardize" derivatives and allow them to be traded on an exchange. For the banks, the more custom-made the derivative, the harder it was for investors to figure out its fair value and real risk—and the easier for the banks to increase their profit margin. Partnoy realized that what Morgan's derivatives department was doing was taking risky but high-yielding bonds from "emerging markets" that paid out in, say, the Thai baht or the Russian ruble, and mixing them in with safer, dollar-denominated bonds that were AAA-related in order to create a new security. Often the investor was sold on the idea that he was buying the highly rated safe part, while the fact that he was taking a risk with a dubious foreign currency was hidden in the finest of print in the "term sheet" that came with the purchase. The name "emerging markets" was itself an invention of a World Bank economist that was turned into a derivatives marketing tool by CS First Boston. "It wasn't clear what 'emerging' meant, or how these markets might 'emerge,'" Partnoy later wrote. "Still, it sounded awfully good, and it helped cloud the fact that the emerging bond an investor bought actually was a Peruvian loan that hadn't paid any interest since the 1800s." The outcome was a derivatives salesman's dream: eager but often unsophisticated investors would think they had found a magic instrument that was both safe and high-yielding.

It was a trend that led to huge losses among unsuspecting customers as disparate as Orange County, California, and Procter and Gamble. But the Washington regulators never really caught up.

The real key to turning these risky derivatives deals into a big payday for Morgan Stanley was twofold. First, make them very complex so that most customers don't understand them and then, using large amounts of leverage, issue huge amounts of them and sell them to deep-pocketed pension funds, money market funds, and insurance companies. The problem: the bylaws governing these funds required them to invest in safer, investment-grade bonds, ones that were fairly assured of not defaulting. So the investment banks needed to fool not only their customers but also the rating agencies into giving a risky new security an "investment grade" rating. Often this was done by bullying the rating agencies, reminding them that they earned their fees from the deals they rated. Combining a risky foreign security with an AA or AAA U.S. security "was like baking a cake and then adding icing," Partnoy later wrote colorfully. "The cake was crap. But the icing [the AA or AAA part] was real chocolate. The icing persuaded the ratings agency to call a crap cake a chocolate cake."

The alacrity with which the rating agencies often went along was a big change in corporate culture for them—as big as Morgan Stanley's conversion from staid stock-issue underwriter to trading dynamo had been. The three largest agencies, Moody's, Standard and Poor's (S&P), and Fitch, were quasi-governmental organizations. They had been anointed by the SEC as the arbiters of what is considered "investment grade"—or safe—securities appropriate for conservative investors like pension funds and insurance companies. The prominence of these firms in the financial landscape was an ironic result of the government's efforts to fix the system during the Great Depression. "Back in 1936, the bank regulators told banks if you are going to buy bonds, and have them in your portfolios, those bonds cannot be speculative. They must be investment grade. Who is the arbiter of what is speculative and investment grade? These handful of rating agencies," said Lawrence White, a financial expert at New York University. "In essence, the bank regulators were outsourcing this safety decision. The rating agencies' judgments secured the force of law." Later on, in 1973, the SEC formalized the role of the rating agencies in the system by designating them "Nationally Recognized Statistical Rating Organizations." Only these firms could decide what was safe or not.

That system worked fine in the days of ordinary corporate or municipal bonds, when the agencies' rating assessments were publicly available and could be checked against performance. No rater wanted to be embarrassed by being exposed giving a faulty rating. So the agencies were more immune to pressure from the investment banks to rate bad deals. But as the era of structured finance took off, debt began to get packaged and repackaged in ever more complex bundles of securities. It became harder and harder to double-check the ratings within those bundles. Every rating company had its own methodology; it wasn't standardized as methods were in accounting. In the end there was no longer any public accountability— the embarrassment of getting a rating badly wrong—to weigh against the temptation of fees from big deals from the issuers, like Morgan Stanley.

At first subtly, then profoundly, that began to corrupt the integrity of once respectable rating agencies like Moody's. They became vassals of the Wall Street firms they were rating, and once again, neither the Fed nor the SEC was closely watching the change. Neither the public nor even sophisticated investors could check the ratings. And barring some catastrophic market collapse—which was highly unlikely—there was almost no way for the agencies to be caught out on the derivatives deals they rated, even as they enjoyed the government's protection.

As long as investment banks like Morgan Stanley could secure the blessing of the nationally recognized rating agencies, they could sell anything to anybody. And they pretty much did. Those who invented, packaged, and sold the same derivatives, for the most part, if they thought about it—and they rarely did—laughed at the idea that most derivatives served a public good at all, or that you were fine-tuning risk. Partnoy remembered going, like a man with a guilty secret, to a conference on derivatives sponsored by the *Wall Street Journal* in the mid-1990s. He knew that most of the derivatives deals he had been involved in by then were nothing less than scams. The "pervasive information gap" that Stiglitz had warned about was "not just a gap, it's a chasm," Partnoy said. Partnoy cadged an invitation to the conference, hoping that someone was on to them. They weren't. "It seemed to me from the low level of debate at this conference that no one was likely to find out about trades, ever," he said.

Jerry Corrigan had divined all this in his speech back in January 1992. If derivatives like swaps were all about securing a hedge against interest rates, he asked archly, then why was it that there were so many more swaps than there were interest-rate deals to swap about? "The interest rate swap market now totals several trillion dollars. Given the sheer size of the market, I have to ask myself how it is possible that so many holders of fixed or variable rate obligations want to shift those obligations from one form to the other," he said. Corrigan was as much a capitalist as anyone on Wall Street, yet he was now worried that the allocation of capital was no longer efficient; it was no longer contributing to economic growth. It was becoming pure speculation.

Despite Corrigan's warnings, an era of fecklessness followed. Both regulators and big institutional investors got lazy, relying on these risk-laden time bombs they thought were safe simply because Moody's or S&P had slapped a AA or AAA rating on them. No one seemed to notice that the number of AAA-rated securities, which used to be but a handful of companies and bonds like Treasuries, expanded enormously in the 1990s. The big institutional investors were behaving somewhat like a handful of "feeder funds," passing on money to an investment manager named Bernie Madoff in those years; they took fees for doing it and then simply didn't pay attention to what Madoff was trading in (as it turned out, nothing).

The real answer to countering the growing complexity of these deals, it later became clear, was to force big investment managers at the banks and pension and money market funds, and the regulators who oversaw them, to simply get more involved. Pressed by Washington, these big institutional investors could have been induced to double-check the deals and the ratings that were placed on them, perhaps by using the plethora of smaller rating companies that didn't earn their fees from the investment banks. But no one in Washington wanted to do "plumbing"; no one wanted to get down to that level of granularity, whether it was looking closely at the new derivatives deals or the rating systems used to rate and monitor them. Above all the regulators didn't want to impede the industry and its innovation, to second-guess whatever ways the markets were evolving.

Just before she left to join Enron's board, Wendy Gramm had issued her two exemptions of OTC derivatives. One permitted so-called hybrid instruments to be treated not as futures and options—which the Commodity Futures Trading Commission controlled—but as securities or debt obligations. Since they weren't futures or options, which the CFTC oversaw, that would make them exempt from any regulation at all, under Gramm's new rule. The other new rule exempted from regulation some "swaps" between companies that were traded "over the counter"— or off any exchange—as long as the deals were "customized," or simply agreed to privately between two companies. Swaps were the most heavily traded contracts in the world; again, the idea was to hedge risks. If one company had a lot of debt in fixed interest rates, and another had a lot of debt in adjustable rates, or if one company did heavy business by borrowing rubles and another relied on Mexican pesos, they could "swap" some payment obligations so that neither would be wholly dependent on the fixed rate or the adjustable rate, or on the fortunes of the ruble or the peso. Corporations prefer to customize such contracts because it allows them to tailor a hedge to a firm's specific needs for a certain time period—a company might bet, say, against the possibility that the ruble will fall in the next six months if it's selling insurance in Russia.

But if derivatives are not traded on exchanges or in clearinghouses—which require firms to put up capital for each trade—then they face no restraints at all, and no accountability. And now the big firms had poured like an invading army into the gaps Gramm had created, finding new justifications for "customized" deals that were exempted. It's what Rubin and others failed to understand when they dismissed Born's 1998 concept release as a power grab by the CFTC. Ironically enough, part of the hunger for derivatives was driven by the responsible fiscal policies of the era. Interest rates were still low through the decade, a result of the Clinton-Greenspan entente on spending and the deficit, and the productivity boom that Greenspan had divined. That meant safe investments such as government bonds had low returns. Portfolio managers were desperate for better yields. Morgan Stanley loved Mexico. Mexican banks were thoroughly corrupt, and loved to take on risk. Morgan supplied it.

Much of this trend was also a somewhat ironic outcome of the end of the Cold War and the collapse of the Soviet Union. Because creating derivatives this complex required major-league brains. And now they were available. Particle physicists weren't needed as much after the Soviet threat disappeared, so many of them headed for Wall Street. One of them, Emanuel Derman, came to Goldman in 1985. He eventually took over from Fischer Black, who had been hired away from a full professorship at MIT by Robert Rubin. Members of the "quant" influx were being referred to as "POWs"—physicists on Wall Street. What Wall Street really wanted, said one of them, Andrew Lo, was not so much quant Ph.D.s as PSDs: people who were "poor, smart and with a deep desire to get rich." This trend brought two new big things to Wall Street: a whole new level of intellectual horsepower—the upper reaches of the IQ scale—and a new layer of important players who had no reason to doubt that markets worked as formulaically as the weapons systems they had once puttered over. The quants could take the science of designing new securities and derivatives to dizzying new heights. What they didn't have was self-doubt or any experience of market failure. "They didn't have the skill of remembering there were human beings in markets," Paul Volcker said afterward. "These things were not natural events, independent of observation. It's not like a physicist looking at some event that follows a nice normal distribution curve."

Longtime market players like Bob Rubin and Hank Paulson knew that, as Rubin wrote, formulas only take you so far, and in the end a trader's judgment is what counts. "Entranced by the model, a trader could easily forget that assumptions are involved and treat it as a definitive," Rubin warned. But Wall Street's new elite were not traders; they were scientists. And few of their bosses, the longtime market players who now ran the big firms, really understood any longer what their scientists were doing, which made it all but impossible for them to keep tabs on it.

Washington had an even bigger problem. The tragic, almost cosmic disconnect was that at the precise moment in history when a deep rethinking of regulation was required, the free-market fundamentalism had reached its height and the economic mind-set had grown dead-set against regulation.

As far back as Corrigan's warning, regulators knew they were being outstripped by the unique complexity of derivatives, and the fact that everyone was getting into it at once. Even in the best case, the regulators would have had a hard time keeping up with those genius quants. They knew then that the hodgepodge of agencies—the Office of the Comptroller of the Currency, the SEC, the CFTC—were being outmaneuvered like cavalrymen trying to face down an armored blitzkrieg. They knew that the entire legal structure would have to be rethought. But there was no impulse to do it in Alan Greenspan's and Bob Rubin's Washington.

On the contrary, things went in the *opposite* direction as Greenspan's stealth efforts at gutting and blocking regulation and oversight continued. At the upper levels of government, the deeper pragmatism of a Corrigan or a Volcker was no longer practiced. Regulation was becoming a lost art. During the era of free-market fundamentalism, Corrigan later reflected, there was a "growing flaw in what I like to call the philosophy of prudential supervision." Regulators began to rely on mechanical oversight, and lost the sense that every bank and situation had to be dealt with on a case-by-case basis, he said. There was, because of the zeitgeist, a growing unwillingness to delve into the workings of markets. The market function had become a totem, a sacred and elemental thing that one dared not tamper with. The job of regulation, ill-paid, disrespected, became a fool's profession, reducing the general competency level, as Bernie Madoff found out when he kept his Ponzi scheme going long after it should have been discovered.

The supercomplex derivatives that Partnoy and his colleagues were creating in this laissez-faire environment in the early 1990s were the forerunners of what would ultimately become notorious as the "collateralized debt obligation," or the CDO. As people realized after the subprime mortgage crash, CDOs had taken derivatives to a whole new level of complexity. These securities were no longer based on an underlying asset but instead on other derivatives—"tranches," or slices of mortgage-backed securities that were traded around and repackaged, with some buyers getting good mortgages and others getting subprime junk. There were even weirder, synthetic derivatives—"CDOs squared"—that allowed the CDOs themselves to be sliced up and repackaged and resold, so that the values were now several times removed from any actual assets underneath.

Some of the books that came out after the financial disaster would encourage the myth that CDOs were, for Wall Street, a uniquely complex and deceptive practice—and that therefore the subprime mortgage crisis was also a unique disaster. "The collateralized debt obligation may well go down in history as the worst thing anyone on Wall Street has ever thought up," wrote David Faber of CNBC in one quickie book, *And Then the Roof Caved In.* That may be true. But Faber's description slighted the long lineage that Corrigan had fretted over, Partnoy had lamented, and Washington had ignored. As the years had gone by, the only change that had occurred despite the regular blowups—Orange County! Long-Term Capital Management! Enron!—was *even more* deregulation. No wonder that the subprime securitization mortgage market later took off the way it did, leading to the bizarre world of CDOs. After all, at the start, CDOs were only the latest, "improved" version of a model long in the making, the process of turning dubious or bad assets into better-seeming securities while the adults weren't watching, while central bankers were no longer getting their hands dirty with worrying about exposure, as Corrigan had. Wall Street's whizzes were getting better and better at making crap cakes, in other words. It was a process that was possible only with derivatives, when buyers were increasingly distant from the underlying asset, and when no one was monitoring production.

In his public comments, Greenspan kept saying again and again that derivatives were just diffusing risk through the system, parceling it out in little pieces, making everyone individually safer. That was true, but this process was also *infecting the entire system* with risk, and thereby making the total risk greater. Trade by trade, instrument by instrument, through CDOs and credit default swaps and the rest, every major market player was becoming systemically linked up with everyone else. It was only much later, in an interview on CNBC, that Greenspan admitted he himself hadn't understood CDOs at all. He had the theory of derivatives right from thirty thousand feet, but because he profoundly disbelieved in interfering with the market he was never in a position to see what derivatives had become in practice. Said Greenspan, "I didn't understand what they were doing or how they actually got the types of return out of the mezzanines and the various tranches of the CDOs that they did. And I figured if I didn't understand it, and I had access to a couple hundred Ph.D.s, how the rest of the world is going to understand it sort of bewildered me."

But he didn't speak about his bewilderment at the time.

Partnoy eventually resigned from Morgan Stanley in disgust, and wrote a book exposing the reality of the derivatives market. It sold well, but made not a dent in Washington's complacency. Through the decade, Partnoy kept expecting someone to catch on. He wrote another, fatter book. After Enron, he testified before Congress, and he thought he was "making some progress when Senator Fred Thompson reacted to questions he had raised about footnote 16 of Enron's annual report, which contained cryptic disclosures about some of the company's most opaque and horrific derivatives deals."

Thompson piped up, "I'm very familiar with it."

Partnoy got all excited—someone was paying attention! "If you can tell me what's going on—" he started to say.

"Just kidding," Thompson replied, with that camera-ready drawl.

Again, it's not as if everyone was asleep. In the mid-1990s, the blowups that precipitated Brooksley Born's concerns—Orange County, P&G—created some legislative brushfires. Representative Edward Markey, head of the House subcommittee on telecommunications and finance, asked Congress's General Accounting Office to draw up a report in 1992, around the same time Corrigan was venting his worries. The nine-hundred-page report came out in May 1994, and in it Charles Bowsher, head of the GAO, warned that "the sudden failure or abrupt withdrawal from trading of any of the large U.S. dealers could cause liquidity problems in the markets and could also pose risks to others, including federally insured banks and the financial system as a whole." He suggested that could mean a big taxpayer-funded bailout. Greenspan slapped that reasoning down; in his congressional testimony a week later, he said the risk of a bailout was "negligible": "There is no presumption that the major thrust of derivatives activities is any riskier, indeed it may very well be less risky, than commercial lending."

Among those who were most alarmed was Representative Jim Leach, who would later berate Born. But Mark Brickell, it turned out, had not been humbled at all by Jerry Corrigan. As head of the International Swaps and Derivatives Association (ISDA), he led every effort to stop the legislation, and at every turn he succeeded. "They did a very effective job of putting their heel on the throat of the legislators," said Lackritz. On July 12, 1994, at a hearing of Leach's committee, the congressman blew up at Brickell just as Corrigan had two years before. Leach, believing that there needed to be a statutory change and not merely an expansion of regulation, had proposed a "Federal Derivatives Commission" to regulate the markets. Leach accused Brickell of making false statements, citing his quotes in an article in *American Banker* to the effect that banks would become liable for every derivatives contract. "I would like to know where in the bill it says that!" Leach yelled. "That is a very powerful statement and one that is false." Brickell simply worked around Leach, and he soon got the help of, of all people, Jerry Corrigan, who joined Goldman Sachs in 1995, two years after leaving the Fed, and soon became cochairman of an industry entity called the Derivatives Policy Group. It was pushing for self-regulation as a way of throwing sand in the government regulatory machine, and that is ultimately what happened. In March 1995, the Derivatives Policy Group agreed to a "Framework for Voluntary Oversight." Two months later, in May, Corrigan testified alongside Brickell's boss, Dennis Weatherstone of JP Morgan. "I am hard pressed to think of sensible things that might be done through legislation that would better equip the Fed or other bodies to cope with a financial disruption of consequence," said Corrigan. It was testimony that, years later, he would come to regret.

• • •

Into this zeitgeist the issue of Glass-Steagall repeal reemerged—and this time the advocates of repeal found they were pushing on an open door. Opposition to repeal had all but vanished. The axis of debate had moved that far rightward, uniting the New Democrats with the free-market zealots of the GOP. Bob Rubin, even when he was at Goldman Sachs, had pushed for Glass-Steagall repeal well before many of his fellow investment-bank CEOs, who in the early days of the debate were leery of the change for fear that their firms would be eclipsed by the commercial banks. "He was viewed as a sellout" for a time, before the other investment banks came on board, said Suzanne Nora Johnson, a former Goldman vice chairman. In late February 1995, less than two months after he became Treasury secretary, Rubin again proposed that Glass-Steagall be bank dismantled. Some commentators noted that his speech came only days after the failure of Barings Bank—but again, that was *them*, not us. "The more diverse banks are by geography and by product, the better off the banking industry will be," Rubin said at a luncheon in New York. He pointed out that "no other industrialized countries have the rules we have separating our commercial and investment banks, our insurance companies and our other financial industries." That was true, although it was also true that none of those other countries had financial markets as freewheeling and unregulated as America's.

Rubin also called for repeal of the Bank Holding Company Act, passed in 1956. The law had effectively barred most financial concerns from owning both commercial banks and insurance companies. Revoking it was the ultimate lurch rightward for a president who had once embraced FDR. Even Jim Leach, the Republican, criticized Rubin's plan for not being stricter in preventing federally insured deposits to be used in areas outside commercial banking. Taking a lone stand, Leach insisted on a rule that kept commerce and banking separated: he deeply feared that companies such as Microsoft or Wal-Mart would end up owning federally insured banks. Both the Treasury and the Fed ultimately agreed to the Leach rule.

But one by one, the dissidents who could still make a difference, who held positions of authority, were being eliminated. In June 1995, a lawyer who worked for the New York district attorney's office, John Moscow, was hired by the New York Fed. Soon afterward, he published an op-ed piece in the *New York Times* against the dismantling of Glass-Steagall, saying "the results could be catastrophic. . . . Nobody could regulate a company this big." A month later, Moscow resigned under pressure from Washington—from Greenspan's Fed. Around the same time, Joseph Stiglitz warned that "when enterprises become too big, and interconnections too tight, there is a risk that the quality of economic decisions deteriorates, and the 'too big to fail' problem rears its ugly head." Unfortunately, Stiglitz wrote, his worries "were quickly shunted aside" by the Clinton Treasury team.

While other progressive voices in the Democratic Party were still there, they were increasingly treated as wild-eyed rock throwers, easily dismissed as old-fashioned 1970s-style liberals or knee-jerk anticorporate agitators. Among them was John Dingell, the man who had stood down and humiliated proponents of Glass-Steagall reform in the 1980s. Now Dingell was the desperate minority. As repeal passed on an overwhelming vote in 1999, Dingell declared in a speech on the House floor: "What we are creating now is a group of institutions which are too big to fail. . . . And under this legislation, the whole of the regulatory structure is so obfuscated and so confused that liability in one area is going to fall over into liability in the next. Taxpayers are going to be called upon to cure the failures we are creating tonight, and it is going to cost a lot of money, and it is coming. Just be prepared for those events." Wall Street responded with a smirk and a spate of Brobdingnagian mergers. As finance morphed into ever bigger entities creating ever more complex instruments, the regulatory structure stayed the same as it had been since the 1930s. But the problem actually was much worse than that. Because even that meager, outdated regulatory structure was being denuded, gutted by Greenspanism. "I remember saying at the time, people don't get it—the level of missed opportunities to address some of these problems," said Annette Nazareth, then the SEC's head of market regulation. "It was an absolute siege on regulation."

Much later, after the crash, many experts would conclude that the repeal of Glass-Steagall had little to do with it. After all, *everybody*, investment banks, nonbanks, insurance companies, had gotten into trouble—firms, in other words, that were not ostensibly changed by the repeal. Some would even argue that the absence of Glass-Steagall made the cleanup easier: after all, it allowed Bank of America to buy Merrill Lynch and save that famous broker from oblivion.

But this argument missed a larger point. The blinding complexity and interconnections created by derivatives—precisely because they were going to overwhelm government supervisors—demanded that there be strong firewalls and capital buffers between Wall Street institutions and their affiliates, and between banks and nonbanks and insurance companies. Otherwise there would be no more islands of safety—no one to come and rescue things as commercial banks traditionally had done since the days of JP Morgan's famous bailout in 1907. The repeal of Glass-Steagall took things in precisely the opposite direction, once again. Systemic failure was entirely forgotten.

9

The Last Guy at the Alamo

By the late 1990s virtually every dissenter was being ignored, like Joe Stiglitz and Frank Partnoy, or pushed from office like Brooksley Born, or co-opted like Jerry Corrigan. The zeitgeist had become almost a religion, the hounding of dissenters very nearly inquisitorial. And the phenomenon was going global; it was no accident that much later on the chairman of Great Britain's Financial Services Authority, Adair Turner, would describe himself ironically as "high priest of a particular religious cult." The cult's central tenet was that financial innovation was perfecting capitalism and that tampering with that process was a form of apostasy. Whether you were Brooksley Born or Joseph Stiglitz—or even Jerry Corrigan—you eventually found out you were taking on an entire era, a mode of thinking that permeated the times and simply didn't allow any doubts to surface. Wall Street lobbies had always been persuasive—campaign contributions often make an argument more compelling—but now they were making their arguments in an environment in which people really did believe the Wall Street way was always the smartest way. In that environment the Mark Brickells would always win against the Jim Leaches.

And now these forces were emanating from Washington into the rest of the country. It was there, out in the heartland, where individuals like Roy Barnes would make the last stand against the financial free-market revolution.

Barnes was a self-described "small-town lawyer" from Mableton, Georgia, just outside Atlanta, with a mane of silver hair and an Andy Griffith drawl. Like Ben Matlock, the TV character he resembled, Barnes was the farthest thing from a rube. He had come from a family of bankers and described himself as "a capitalist through and through." And as early as the 1980s Barnes saw, long before many in Washington, what was happening as deregulation took lending farther from the local banks and gave it to mortgage brokers and Wall Street, where no one cared much if the loans were good or bad as they were bundled into securities sold around the world. Georgia, like other states, had tried to fight off predatory lending. Barnes had led the effort, earning himself statewide fame when in 1993 he successfully won a $115 million settlement against Fleet Finance over abusive lending practices in poor neighborhoods in Atlanta, a precursor of the subprime mortgage contagion.

Barnes managed to turn the fame of his Fleet Finance win into a successful run for governor of Georgia in the late 1990s. It was a time when he was seen as among the most promising of a new generation of Southern politicians. But Barnes saw there was more to the problem than just the usual mortgage scamsters. They now had a great power behind them—Wall Street. It would be a long time before Barnes would understand just how great a power that was.

Wall Street was becoming a different place. The transformation of Morgan Stanley that Partnoy had described, from the white-shoe restraint of yore to the blood-in-the-water culture of John Mack, was typical of what was happening to all the firms. The profits from derivatives and proprietary trading were too staggering. The competition was too intense. And in the low-interest-rate environment of the Great Moderation, investors were looking for new ways of obtaining higher yields. Now even traditional banks like Citigroup felt they had no choice but to go the same way as Morgan Stanley and the rest.

Robert Rubin himself helped to make that happen too, even after he left the Treasury Department.

Just a month after he departed Washington in July 1999, Rubin agreed to go to work for Citigroup as "chairman of the executive committee." It was a largely ceremonial post in which Rubin would be used as a meet-and-greet eminence to snare big clients around the world. Still, the move shocked some of his biggest fans, who felt that the widely admired former Treasury secretary ought not to allow his pristine reputation to be tied to any particular corporate name. Rubin had been wooed by the irrepressible co-CEO of the giant bank, Sandy Weill. A shark for big opportunities, Weill had cornered Rubin almost immediately upon his return, at a "Welcome Back to New York" party thrown at the Metropolitan Museum of Art by Rubin's wife, Judy.

Rubin wasn't interested at first. He had not been entirely happy about the creation of financial supermarkets in his waning days as Treasury secretary. In a rare, perhaps unprecedented, public disagreement with Greenspan, Rubin had insisted that the Treasury retain regulatory control after Glass-Steagall repeal by placing the new bank powers in affiliates overseen by the Office of the Comptroller of the Currency (OCC). Greenspan wanted control through the bank holding companies, which the Fed regulates. Rubin expressed concerns about the way the law was written—just as he would worry aloud about derivatives, hedge funds, and leverage ratios. But the bottom line for Rubin was always the same: he didn't take a firm stand when it came to standing in the way of Wall Street.

And now Weill made Rubin an offer he couldn't refuse: At Citigroup there would be global travel and access to all the real-time data he had once enjoyed as Treasury secretary, unlimited time to go fishing, and $33 million a year in salary, bonuses, and benefits. Above all, there would be no line responsibility; he wouldn't be running the firm. "I had had thirty-three years of operating responsibility at that point and I simply didn't want to have it anymore," Rubin told me later on. At the same time, Rubin badly wanted to stay atop the global economy; his position at Citigroup would allow him to know what was happening in China and elsewhere while taking it easy.

For Weill it was a bargain. He had built an investment banking and insurance empire, gobbling up Smith Barney, Salomon Brothers, and Traveler's Insurance; his $76 billion merger with Citi the year before had been a final assault on Glass-Steagall. Weill and Citicorp chairman John Reed had done the deal betting that congressional repeal would happen, but now they had to wait it out. So bringing the world's most respected financial official on board was an unmistakable message to the power barons in Washington, especially Rubin's former protégés at Treasury and his admirers on Capitol Hill: finish off Glass-Steagall and permit the total crossover of traditional banking, investment banking, and insurance. "Snaring Bob was big news," Weill wrote. "The press had been relentlessly calling into question our merger progress for months, and hiring someone as widely respected as Bob translated into a highly visible public endorsement." Weill later proudly hung a giant wooden sign on his office wall with his picture on it and the words: "The Shatterer of Glass-Steagall."

Rubin also played a critical role in the final—and ultimately near-fatal—evolution of Citigroup. Bit by bit, year by year, the dominant way of thinking in finance had been moving from traditional banking to investment banking, and then from investment banking to trading. By the time Rubin came on board, it quickly became clear to top officials at Citigroup that the co-CEOs, Weill and Reed, were hopelessly incompatible personally. Each represented a different and once incompatible culture that symbolized the strains between traditional banking (Reed) and investment banking/trading (Weill). The board of directors was divided between Weill appointees and Reed appointees.

The cerebral, conservative Reed, who had spent three decades rising through the ranks at Citibank, had rescued the bank from the debt disaster left by his predecessor, Walter Wriston, who engulfed Citi in defaulting Latin American loans. Reed rebuilt Citi's brand around the world, creating a globe-dominating giant whose automated teller machines revolutionized consumer banking. Reed's dream was to turn Citi into a global brand name, the Coca-Cola of finance. "I viewed Citigroup as the best bank in world," said Edgar Woolard, who joined the Citicorp board in 1988 under Reed. "John Reed had us travel to Asia, South America, and Europe, and I saw how powerful Citigroup's brand was in foreign countries. It was very profitable because the deposits were strong and lending was strong."

But the merger hadn't been working smoothly. In part it was because Weill was far less interested in building brand names than he was in increasing the new conglomerate's stock price. "My interests are the shareholders," he said. In part it was because traditional commercial and retail banking was an alien thing to Weill. "Sandy Weill had grown up in an environment where he had built a company that had businesses that weren't regulated at all, whereas banks are heavily regulated. I could just see the tenor of the company changing to, 'Let's not worry so much about regulations,'" said Woolard.

At the time of the merger, Weill and Reed had agreed to retire together after two years as co-CEOs. One of the men, at least, had to go, and Reed had indicated a desire to fulfill his part of the retirement plan. Weill wanted to stay on. At a seven-hour-long meeting one Sunday afternoon in February 2000, the Citi directors hashed out who should take over as sole head of the company. Rubin—who at one point had been offered the post himself and refused it—was called in to mediate.

As Woolard recalled it, "Sandy's outlook wasn't looking too good" until Rubin came in the room and pulled off one of his classic acts of political jujitsu. Rubin disarmed the Reed supporters by announcing at the outset, "My beliefs and philosophies are closer to John's than to Sandy's." But then he added: "If John wants to retire, I've heard the names of the people who might replace the two of them, and in my opinion keeping Sandy is better than bringing in any of the [outside] candidates we talked about." Rubin's remarks swiftly stunted a discussion about bringing back a brilliant young executive named Jamie Dimon, whom Weill had earlier fired, as the replacement CEO. Said Woolard, "That was an enormous factor in the final outcome, in my opinion." The board anointed Weill sole CEO.

Bob Rubin had paid off again for Sandy Weill, the shatterer of Glass-Steagall. Sandy Weill would never take that sign down, while John Reed would one day apologize for helping to dismantle the law.

With the final eclipsing of Glass-Steagall—and the extinguishing of the last vestiges of Depression-era caution about finance—all the remaining divides between traditional retail banking and investment banking and other firms disappeared. The trend toward combining formerly separate financial sectors was vastly accelerated by the new mining to bundle loans into securities and sell them around the world. Global banks that had jumped without restraint into investment banking now also opened a vast conveyor belt of securitized loans from local towns to world markets. People by now had forgotten about the dangers of hot money, and they had also completely forgotten that the two cultures—investment and retail banking—used to be hostile to each other, that traditional banking was supposed to be meticulous and cautious, while investment banking and trading was buccaneering and bold. Now the bankers were overwhelmed by the buccaneers, who took over the ship. By the early 2000s, recalled financier Doug Hallowell, "being a traditional banker at a Wall Street firm was like being the last guy at the Alamo."

At the same time, there was a desperate search for the next big trade. After the dot-com bubble burst in 1999, corporate profits and stock prices had remained fairly flat. Interest rates were still low; Greenspan deliberately had kept them low after 9/11, and while he would be harshly criticized for that too in later years—helping to inflate the housing bubble—he felt it was necessary to help the nation get back on its feet. But persistent low rates meant safe investments like government bonds continued to have low returns.

The only thing that still seemed to be going skyward in the early 2000s was housing. And with the derivatives industry now full of experience at basically converting *anything* into a bond to sell, the most tantalizing stuff around for investment managers seeking an edge was mortgage-backed securities based on high-interest residential junk loans. Wall Street always had a euphemism, of course. Just as it had once euphemized the Third World as "emerging markets," now it euphemized bad credit risks as "subprime borrowers."

The subprime concept was fairly straightforward: hard-up borrowers who didn't qualify for normal, low-interest loans would have to pay off their mortgages at high interest, and those paybacks were funneled to the owners of the securities. While these risky mortgages once had been shunned by the Street, the ever appreciating real estate market meant that even indigent mortgage holders could always refinance. There was almost no requirement to put money down, so when subprime borrowers found they couldn't keep up with their mortgage payments they simply took out a new subprime loan to pay off the previous one—and Wall Street, of course, snapped up the new loans and bundled them into yet a new round of securities. After the mortgage refinancing boom of 2003–2004, demand for fresh subprime "product" grew so intense that lending standards disintegrated altogether. Frank Partnoy's old firm, Morgan Stanley, even sought to cut a deal with New Century, one of the giant nonbank mortgageurs that emerged in those years to slake the Street's thirst, to buy $2 billion a month in subprime loans, no questions asked. To meet these needs, lenders kept reaching lower and lower down the scale of quality in both property and borrowers until the street hustlers jumped in to offer up their "product." Wall Street held its nose and calculated that as long as house prices went up, even bad loans could get paid off. Most of them, anyway. In the late stages of the mania, the investment banks and hedge funds began playing a new game as well: creating synthetic CDOs actually *designed to fail* so that their creators could sell them short and bet on the collapse of the bubble. This meant that Wall Street firms were actively *soliciting* bad credit borrowers out in the heartland so that short sellers could make money on their defaults.

The major banks also began to buy up the nonbank mortgageurs themselves, the ones that were operating in states such as Georgia. One by one, the banks used them as a pipeline for more assets to securitize. Why not control the whole pipeline?

Down in Georgia, Roy Barnes—then newly installed in the governor's mansion—wasn't fully aware of how crazy things were getting in New York, but he had some idea. Mainly, he was worried about the way lending standards were dropping precipitously, especially in inner-city Atlanta. By this time, driven by Wall Street's interest in securitization, many banks and other lenders were eager to find new markets, and the once-shunned inner city was a prime spot across the United States. That in turn led to the phenomenon of "reverse redlining." Whereas back in the 1980s, the big story was the "redlining" of low-income, often African American neighborhoods by banks that refused to lend there, now the opposite happened. According to two major lawsuits later filed by Baltimore and Buffalo, banks now began to "discriminate" against these inner-city neighborhoods by making them particular targets of predatory lending.

Around the same time, Barnes was growing more and more concerned about the sheer volume of high-interest debt that Wall Street was securitizing. At least Fleet Finance had kept most of its paper on its books. Now all that bad paper, with Georgians signed onto at one end of the mortgage, had no responsible party on the other end. "I started seeing how securitization was really running rampant and taking away accountability for the banks," Barnes said. By 1999 "I was convinced there was a calamity coming." So Barnes decided to push through the toughest antipredatory lending law in the country. The bill made everyone up the line, including investment banks and rating agencies like Standard and Poor's, legally liable if loans went bad in Georgia and were shown to have been fraudulently or recklessly issued. "There has to be accountability," Barnes told me. "You have to be able to say, do I want to make this loan, because I may have to eat it."

As the bill made its way through the Georgia legislature, the stalwarts of the Washington zeitgeist began arriving in Georgia, eager to offer Barnes advice. At first they were friendly, if condescending. Major rating agencies such as Standard and Poor's and major mortgage issuers like Ameriquest let Barnes know in no uncertain terms that he was something of a "country bumpkin" when it came to banking, said his legislative aide, Chris Carpenter. "They treated us like mice interfering with this vast financial system." Suddenly, the governor found himself besieged by lobbyists from major banks and national regulators—as well as Fannie Mae and Freddie Mac, the national mortgage issuers whose mandate was to help people obtain affordable homes at fair prices. What really agitated Fannie and Freddie, as well as the major banks, mortgage issuers, and rating agencies, was the idea that those who turned loans into securities and sold them around the world might actually be legally on the hook—liable—if the mortgages went bad. "They would say—and Fannie Mae and Freddie Mac were part of it—this is a complex market that has many levels," said Barnes. "If you start interfering with the free flow of money, then Georgia will become an island that has no credit. I kept telling them, 'You're in for a crash here.' 'Oh no, we're not,' they'd say. 'You're a politician, we're the experts.'" The well-heeled Washington lobbyists stood out in the state hallways in their expensive suits and alligator loafers. "I began to get paranoid, thinking everyone I saw was a lobbyist," said state senator Vincent Fort, an early backer of Barnes.

When Barnes insisted on passing the law anyway, things got a lot less friendly. The advice turned to outright threats. Standard and Poor's promised, in a letter, that it would rate no securities that contained Georgia loans. Ameriquest and major banks followed. Freddie and Fannie first asked to be exempted altogether, and then threatened to pull their business out of the state. No matter. Finally, Barnes had his triumph. On April 22, 2002, he flew through the state to sign the landmark legislation in seven different cities in front of TV cameras. Not only did the new law make buyers of loans liable, it mandated counseling for purchasers of "high-cost" predatory loans. "A victory for Georgia consumers," the *Atlanta Journal-Constitution* editorialized on April 23, 2002, praising Barnes for drawing "on his political clout to stave off bank opposition." Said Barnes, "It was hardest thing I ever tried to pass."

But the governor and his comrades in the legislature had underestimated the determination of Washington to quash regulation of subprime lending, especially when it came from the states. The Washington interest groups feared the Georgia law would become national precedent. To permit liability even for fraudulent loans would be devastating to the global mortgage machine that had been set up. The industry gave up trying to strong-arm Barnes and sponsored fund-raisers for Barnes's GOP opponent, Sonny Perdue. After Perdue upset Barnes in November of that year—largely, it is believed, because the Democrat removed the Confederate flag from the Georgia capital—his successor sponsored a much weaker law that removed the liability provisions.

The decisive moment in Georgia's legislative debate came when a Republican senator stood up on the floor and declared that he was about to receive a letter from Freddie Mac threatening to cut the state out of its loan business. The speech applied the coup de grace to Roy Barnes's law. "It broke my heart," said Barnes. For a time after leaving the governor's mansion, he went to work for Legal Aid, defending indigent mortgage holders.

That moment in the Georgia statehouse didn't happen by accident. It was orchestrated by Freddie's Washington lobbyists, who brazenly organized fund-raisers for members of the House Financial Services Committee, which has key jurisdiction over legislative issues relating to Freddie Mac, at posh D.C. restaurants like Galileo. A senior Clinton administration official said both Freddie and Fannie were powers unto themselves in forestalling additional regulation, thanks in large part to their lobbying power. "These guys are like the worst things I saw when I was in Washington. They are the singular embodiment of special interests and rent-seeking, with $170 million in lobbyist expenses, and every lobbyist in town on the payroll, with jobs for all folks in Congress after they leave office." They virtually captured Congress, the official said—preventing any efforts at reform—with a brutal style of our-way-or-the-highway lobbying. "They basically make it clear there are two ways we can do it: if you vote with us, we'll put on a big fund-raiser, and make you out to be a 'hero of housing.' That's path A. Path B is we'll do anything to get you defeated, we can send out twenty thousand pieces of mail to your district. So take your choice." That view was endorsed by Representative Richard H. Baker, a Louisiana Republican who was chairman of the House subcommittee that oversees the companies: "When their interests are threatened, the response is almost armylike. They're tactical, and they're everywhere."

The lobbyists were helped by the Washington regulators and the free-market mentality that prevailed. The OCC issued a preemption order saying the states did not have the authority to enforce laws against abusive national lenders. Tom Miller, the Iowa attorney general, said the comptroller of the currency, John "Jerry" Hawke, was spending all his energy on fighting state efforts to regulate, without paying attention to what the banks were doing in subprime securitization. "He kept saying the states are too strong in regulation, and telling the banks, 'We're not going to be as tough on you.'" The OCC was helped by the U.S. Supreme Court, which ruled for Wachovia Bank and its mortgage subsidiary in 2007 and against a Michigan state official, Linda Watters, who had claimed that federal law preempted her authority to regulate subsidiaries of national banks. Nowhere was the sense of state impotence greater than in California, which later became ground zero for subprime defaults. Most of the biggest abusers such as Ameriquest were headquartered there, yet the state repeatedly failed at making its own firms legally liable for poor or crooked lending practices. When the feds tied the hands of the locals, "it was clear this was the Wild West, and there's no sheriff in town," said Jim Rokakis, the treasurer of Cuyahoga County in Ohio, who was also early to see the predatory lending problem. "If you're a lender, there's nobody who can stop you. The only difference is that in the old days people robbed the banks. Now the banks were robbing the people."

There were a few doubters left in Washington. At the FBI in Washington, a senior agent named Chris Swecker began to get concerned about the level of fraud. "Based on various industry reports and FBI analysis, mortgage fraud is pervasive and growing," Swecker, then assistant director of the criminal investigation division, told a House subcommittee in October 2004. It had "the potential to be an epidemic," he said. But Swecker remained a lone voice. What prevailed was a simple disbelief among the feds and most of the Wall Street elites that there could be something that badly wrong with the market.

Even Alan Greenspan, in a speech to the Credit Union National Association in late February 2004, said that U.S. household finances appeared to be generally sound, despite rising debt levels and bankruptcy filings. The Fed chairman suggested that more consumers ought to take advantage of the "adjustable rate mortgages," or ARMs, that were central to the subprime pyramid, because they allowed indigent borrowers to get a low initial interest rate in exchange for possible higher rates later on (it was okay as long as they could refinance on the basis of those constantly escalating home prices). "American consumers might benefit if lenders provided greater mortgage product alternatives to the traditional fixed-rate mortgage," Greenspan said.

It didn't seem to matter that out in the country, at around the same time that Greenspan spoke, state attorneys general were fighting the deceptive lending practices behind these ARMs. In late 2005, forty-nine states and the District of Columbia won a class-action suit against Ameriquest over its deceptive lending practices, getting $325 million in compensation. Later on, Patrick Madigan, an assistant attorney general in Iowa—one of the states that led the Ameriquest case—was on a conference call with a senior official of one of the government-sponsored enterprises (GSEs), along with someone who had recently retired from a high position in one of rating agencies. Madigan was explaining to them what the attorneys general were finding at Ameriquest—that Ameriquest was engaged in widespread fraud. Systemic fraud. "One said to us: 'What you are saying cannot possibly be true.' Not 'you're wrong.' It just can't be true. . . . The reasoning was, one, if what you're saying is true, it means massive amounts of fraud. . . . Two, it means we're screw-ups."

Greenspan worshiped the wisdom of the markets, but in truth he was mainly a real-economy man. That was his expertise. He didn't really comprehend how complex things in finance were getting, how the instruments were so complex that even the CEOs of the firms didn't understand them anymore. He occasionally agreed to intervene, but that was only in cases where foreign governments had botched things—Latin America, Asia.

Even in December 1996, when Greenspan had issued his famous warning against "irrational exuberance" as the tech bubble grew, he was prodded into it by his staff, which drafted the speech for him. "How do we know when irrational exuberance has unduly escalated asset values, which then become subject to unexpected and prolonged contractions?" he asked. It was meant to be a message to the markets. But he never really followed up, and later he disowned the idea that the Fed could do anything about it anyway. He didn't really want to believe the markets were overpricing, weren't working. And when the tech bubble burst and the economy didn't crash, it was some vindication for Greenspan. His Fed elevated into a doctrine the idea that it can't deflate bubbles, but it can reinflate the economy when the bubbles burst. In 1999, an obscure Princeton economist named Ben Bernanke would supply the mathematical ammunition for that view and in so doing make himself the front-runner to succeed Greenspan. Irrational exuberance was a problem, perhaps, but not nearly as big a problem as any government solution to contain it. Similarly the Long-Term Capital Management bailout was evidence that banks could take care of their own problems.

In 1999—just as the housing market was beginning to take off— Greenspan gave up worrying about asset bubbles and told Congress "that the Fed would not second-guess hundreds of thousands of informed investors. Instead the Fed would position itself to protect the economy in the event of a crash," he related later in his 2007 memoir. "'While bubbles that burst are scarcely benign, consequences need not be catastrophic for the economy,' I told legislators." After all, markets in the long run were rational, and smarter than governments. Gerald Corrigan, by contrast, felt there could be a "tilt" to interest-rate policy to deflate bubbles; the Fed had a whole variety of supervisory tools. The Fed could, for example, impose higher capital requirements on banks, which would have dampened mortgage lending. Summers sided with Greenspan, in a 2004 interview with *Business Week*, about the Fed's helplessness in dealing with asset bubbles.

Corrigan, from his perch at Goldman Sachs, continued to push for better risk management—and his work as cochairman of Goldman's risk management committee would pay off later on. But he found that Washington was no longer interested. Six months after the Long-Term Capital Management disaster, Corrigan had overseen a report recommending enhanced regulatory reporting—frequent reports that would give firms' exposure on trades, including over-the-counter derivatives. "We worked like hell," he said. But Rubin, Greenspan, Summers, and the other officials in Washington rejected the idea. And Corrigan himself, representing now his investment bank's interests, began to shrink from more aggressive proposals for a clearinghouse—which he later admitted was a mistake.

By the late 1990s, it sometimes seemed as if the only dissident left was Joe Stiglitz, the gadfly who wouldn't shut up. Stiglitz tried again to do for the developing world what Roy Barnes had tried to do for Georgia— to put a brake on the excesses of finance capital. In a landmark speech in April 1998—around the same time that Brooksley Born was being silenced over at the Commodity Futures Trading Commission—Stiglitz sounded what was to be his valedictory warning about the dangers of too much certainty about free markets. Stiglitz made a grand plea to move beyond ideology, the black-and-white, markets-versus-government debate of the Milton Friedman era and the Cold War. He was appalled at the way the alternative Asian model had simply been buried, cast aside, reinterpreted so that even successful government restraints on capital flows were dismissed as aberrations not worthy of Washington's attention. Stiglitz asked for a reasonable amount of scientific second-guessing when it came to the please-the-market prescriptions that the great institutions of Washington were handing out to the world. He harked back to the debate over capital account liberalization—still part of the conditions laid out for U.S. and IMF aid—declaring that the "scientific foundations" for opening up financial markets were just "not very sound." He pointed out the differences between free trade in goods and services and free trade in financial markets. He noted that "empirical evidence, as well as recent experiences in East Asia and Africa, buttress the theoretical propositions that economies can suffer from too little regulation, just as they can suffer from too much or the wrong kind of regulation." The biggest problem: the evidence for widespread economic gains was not really there, while there was considerable evidence that "opening up the capital account may subject the economy to more systemic risks."

Stiglitz called for the champions of the Washington Consensus to be more sensitive to the very real differences in interests between, say, Wall Street investors and workers. A Wall Street investor is going to see the trade-off between inflation and unemployment much differently than a worker will; the former will fear the loss of value of his assets from inflation, while the worker is likely to be much more concerned about rising unemployment, and he won't mind inflation if it helps to erode his debt. The government needed to be mindful of both views, Stiglitz said, if it was to get a social consensus for moving forward that would endure. But he kept going back to the theme of uncertainty, how much there was of it, and that "this uncertainty should, at the very least, induce a modicum of humility on the part of advisers."

It was powerful stuff, but by then many of his opponents in the Washington Consensus saw only arrogance in Stiglitz. Why else would the man keep speaking against them? He just couldn't admit he was wrong. He was too unrelenting in questioning them. At the Treasury Department and the White House, the view was that Stiglitz was impossible, a huge ego strutting around Washington who wouldn't listen to anybody. By the time the Asian crisis seemed to pass, Stiglitz was being belittled all around town. In his book *The World's Banker*, *Washington Post* economic columnist Sebastian Mallaby captured the view of Stiglitz that prevailed then, as an ineffectual rock thrower whining about market failures. "He was like a boy who discovers a hole in the floor of an exquisite house and keeps shouting and pointing at it. Never mind that the rest of the house is beautiful," Mallaby wrote. His foes at the IMF turned on him with a vengeance, especially after Stiglitz suggested that senior IMF official Stanley Fischer, an eminent and much-beloved economist, had embraced Rubin's policies in return for a fat job at Citigroup later on. Fischer's former student at MIT, Ken Rogoff, the chief economist at the IMF, angrily accused Stiglitz of hurting the very people he purported to want to save by kibitzing. "In the middle of a global wave of speculative attacks, that you yourself labeled a crisis of confidence, you fueled the panic by undermining confidence in the very institutions you were working for," Rogoff wrote in an "open letter." "Do you ever lose a night's sleep thinking that just maybe, Alan Greenspan, Larry Summers, Bob Rubin, and Stan Fischer had it right—and that your impulsive actions might have deepened the downturn or delayed—even for a day—the recovery we now see in Asia?" Rogoff concluded: "Joe, as an academic, you are a towering genius. Like your fellow Nobel Prize winner, John Nash, you have a 'beautiful mind.' As a policy maker, however, you were just a bit less impressive."

It was odd, because everywhere else around the world Stiglitz had a reputation as a great listener. "The main thing about good economists, like good doctors, is empathy. I may not agree with you but I'll listen to your point of view. He does that," said Malaysian economist Andrew Sheng. Stiglitz's family was also baffled by his reputation as a strident ranter in Washington. Every time they all took a trip together, Stiglitz would spend the whole time asking fellow tourists who they were and what they did for a living.

In the end, the enmity between Summers and Stiglitz grew too intense. The town really wasn't big enough for the two of them, and Summers continued to have the upper hand in seniority, just as he had all decade. So what if Summers had been rejected at Harvard, and Stiglitz had gotten into Harvard but had turned Harvard down for Amherst? Or that Stiglitz's work in economics was deeper and vastly more influential than Summers's? Larry Summers had his hands on the levers of power, and no one in Washington really wanted to see Joe Stiglitz anywhere near the levers of power any longer.

Over at the World Bank, Stiglitz suddenly found himself frozen out of his job. By 1999, Rubin had left and Summers had taken over, as part of the deal worked out with Clinton, who took Rubin at his word that Summers was the only man who could replace him. Around the same time Stiglitz's boss, Jim Wolfensohn, was looking for another term as World Bank president—a decision the Treasury secretary usually influences. But there may have been a price. In 1999, Wolfensohn genteelly asked Stiglitz if he might tone down his criticisms somewhat if he were to stay on as chief economist, and Stiglitz refused and resigned. Stiglitz was convinced that his old rival, Summers, had orchestrated his departure. Summers later denied it, and Wolfensohn told me, "I put no pressure on him to resign and, to the best of my recollection, was never put under any pressure by Treasury to bring about his departure, although I was of course aware of the tension that existed." In a last parting shot, Stiglitz told the *New York Times'* Louis Uchitelle that there was an "intellectual gap between what we know and what is still practiced" at the Treasury Department and the International Monetary Fund.

Wolfensohn announced Stiglitz's resignation in November 1999. That same month, the great event that so many in the financial world had been working toward for almost two decades finally took place. Bill Clinton's new Treasury secretary—the man who had once mocked financial markets as irrational—gave his approval to the historic passage of the Gramm-Leach-Bliley bill, which overturned Glass-Steagall. The new law allowed securities firms and insurance companies to buy banks, and it allowed the banks in turn to underwrite securities and operate brokerages without having to create nonbanking "affiliates." Gramm-Leach-Bliley also effectively put in place voluntary regulation, since it did not provide for any SEC oversight of investment bank holding companies. Investment banks eager to buy up banks could decide to police themselves—or not. But Treasury Secretary Summers didn't mention that in his statement that day. "Today Congress voted to update the rules that have governed financial services since the Great Depression and replace them with a system for the twenty-first century," he said.

"This historic legislation will better enable American companies to compete in the new economy." Among those enthusiastically applauding was Summers's fellow Democrat, New York senator Charles Schumer, the man who twelve years before had warned against repeal by saying it would turn the banking industry into a casino. "We've been working towards it for eighteen years," Schumer declared, saying, "the future of America's dominance as the financial center of the world is at stake. . . . If we don't pass this bill, we could find London or Frankfurt or years down the road Shanghai becoming the financial capital of the world."

Like so many others, Schumer now thought it was obvious why New York would want to be the financial capital of the world. What terrible consequences would come from London taking over went unsaid.

Summers wasn't blind to the inequalities being created in the economy—the kinds of issues that Stiglitz was talking about. During his brief eighteen months as Treasury secretary, Summers cosponsored, with Andrew Cuomo at the Department of Housing and Urban Development, a pathbreaking report on predatory lending in inner cities. It was a report that would later catch the eye of a Bush administration official named Sheila Bair. And, smart economist that he was, Summers kept warning of overconfidence in the markets, saying colorful things like, "The only thing we have to fear is no fear itself." But for the most part he still thought the future lay with even more deregulation. Shortly after he took office, in late 1999, Summers signed off on one more major new policy. He approved a President's Working Group report in support of the deregulation of derivatives, a report that led to the most significant change of all. And since it occurred in the middle of the most dramatic and most serious constitutional crisis since Watergate, almost no one was watching.

10

Reaganites Redux

You could hardly be surprised that no one was watching. The date was December 15, 2000. Holiday parties were in full swing, schools were closing, and Congress's Christmas recess was just hours away. Three days earlier, in one of the most dramatic and debated decisions in its history, the U.S. Supreme Court had handed the U.S. presidential election to George W. Bush in a 5–4 vote that ended the recount in Florida. For more than a month the entire world had been gripped by the spectacle of Bush v. Gore, the razor-close contest that had turned into an unprecedented constitutional crisis. Now every talk show and newspaper would obsessively parse the Supreme Court decision for weeks. The celebration on one side, and the blame and recriminations on the other, began in earnest. For the Democrats, the Clinton era was finally and bitterly over. Conservative Republicans were planning their joyous return from long exile. The nation was turning a major corner.

That certainly was the intention of George W. Bush and his ultraconservative vice president, Dick Cheney. In the alphabet soup that is official Washington, with its multiplicity of agencies and bureaucratic jargon, the new approach of the Bushies quickly became known as ABC, or Anything But Clinton. Bush scarcely ever mentioned Bill Clinton's name after he took office, but the new president made clear, through his actions, that one of his overriding goals was to be the un-Clinton. Every opposition-party candidate running for office seeks to distinguish himself from the incumbent, whose lack of vision and poor policy choices have, invariably, led the nation to the precipice of disaster. But Bush went about this obligatory political task with a special vengeance in his heart. Clinton, after all, was the man who had deprived his father of a second term, and who then had soiled the great office that the patrician Bush family—with its odd mix of Yankee rectitude and Texas regular guyness—had worked so hard to dignify. "If I know anything about George W. Bush, it is that one of the psychological themes in his soul is settling scores. Anything to do with Clinton gets his antennae up," one Republican senator who talked with the president frequently told me at the time. "I think he took the last eight years as a personal affront to his family." On foreign policy, on taxes, on defense and national security—the new Bush administration swiftly lurched in the opposite direction.

Yet there was one exception to the ABC rule: their attitude toward Wall Street. Bush did not tamper with what Clinton had done there— he only accelerated things. And the best example was the quiet handoff between administrations that occurred in that tumultuous December.

No one took any notice at all when in the early evening of that Friday, December 15, Senator Phil Gramm of Texas sought to complete what his wife, Wendy Gramm, had started seven years before. While serving as Ronald Reagan's chairwoman of the Commodity Futures Trading Commission (CFTC), Wendy Gramm had been the first one to exempt some over-the-counter swaps from regulation in 1993. Now in her husband's hand was a letter from Larry Summers; the departing Treasury secretary had given his imprimatur to new legislation that would do much more to liberate Wall Street on the global stage.

Phil and Wendy Gramm had been a team, philosophically and romantically, since they met in 1969. He had interviewed her for a job at Texas A&M University, where he was teaching economics. "As a single member of the faculty, I'd be very interested in having you come to Texas A&M," Phil told the young Korean American woman from Hawaii. "She looked up at me and said, 'Yuck,'" as he told the story. But Phil Gramm was a bulldog in everything he did, and they were married six weeks after her arrival.

Phil, who had a drawl as long as his Southern lineage—he'd grown up in Fort Benning, Georgia—had once made a run at the presidency himself. He'd brought in a lot of funding support—among his chief supporters was Ken Lay of Enron, who served as regional chair of the Gramm for President Campaign—but he got nowhere in the polls, and he later joked that he was "too ugly to be president." The son of an army sergeant who died when he was fourteen, Phil had failed the third, seventh, and ninth grades, but went on to get a Ph.D. and a full professorship by age thirty. He'd been elected to the House as a Democrat and only switched party affiliations in 1984, when the Reagan revolution was well under way. A monetarist fully in the Milton Friedman school, he made up for lost time by becoming a passionate devotee of supply-side economics, which he declared "is a new term for common business sense." He was always consistent and never—if the public record is any indication—uncertain.

Gramm began pushing aggressively for deregulation, even while enjoying a career at the government trough. Gramm has said his tendency to view issues starkly came from his mother, Florence, a retired practical nurse who taught him: "Take a stand. Don't weasel. Everything was basically black and white. A guy was either honest or a crook," according to his half-brother Don White. Gramm adopted a policy of opposing all expansion of government, but getting in on the take when he could. "If we should vote next week on whether to begin producing cheese in a factory on the moon, I almost certainly would oppose it," Gramm once said. "On the other hand, if the government decided to institute the policy, it would be my objective to see that a Texas contractor builds this celestial cheese plant, that the milk comes from Texas cows, and that the Earth distribution center is located in Texas."

He was known for his abrasiveness and once joked in a dinner speech that he does have a heart: "I keep it in a quart jar on my desk." He once sent a longtime foe, Representative Chet Edwards, a Democrat from Waco, a card that proclaimed, "I feel so sorry for your many problems, but you deserve them." He also left a legacy: among his former students was Jeb Hensarling, later to become a leading voice for deregulation in Congress after the crash of 2007–2009.

Wendy Lee Gramm was just as uncompromising, and her husband used his presidential jump-off bid in New Hampshire to brag about how she'd lived the American dream. The three-generation tale of the Lee family was, like the story Milton Friedman loved to tell about his mother, evidence that all one needed was a place to start. Wendy's grandfather had been a laborer in Hawaii's sugar cane fields; her father had risen to become the first Korean American officer of a U.S. sugar cane company. So when Reagan named her chairwoman of the Commodity Futures Trading Commission, she was regulating the nation's entire trade in the same crop, sugar cane. "That's America in action," Phil said.

Wendy had made an impression fast in Ronald Reagan's Washington in her first big job, heading the Office of Management and Budget's (OMB) Office of Information and Regulatory Affairs. Her task was to decide what else in the economy should be regulated, and she was unerringly consistent. Everything not *proven* to be deadly, she believed, should be left to market forces. She spent several years thwarting every new regulation in sight, especially on health and safety issues, leading the *New York Times* to describe her in December 1987 as "one of the Reagan administration's most vigorous deregulators." It was around then that Reagan himself called Wendy "my favorite economist." So she was only acting out of principle when, after being named to head the CFTC, she excused Enron's energy derivatives from regulation, freeing the company to become a massive fraud. Enron collapsed while she was on its board, but she never expressed regret over what might have been and she opposed a new rule that would have opened up corporate boards to smaller shareholders.

Phil Gramm was nearing the end of his political life—he would choose not to run again in 2002 and joined UBS soon afterward. Now, with almost no discussion, at his urging the U.S. Senate tacked on a 262-page amendment to its 11,000-page government reauthorization bill, which it was rushing to pass before the recess. Gramm was one of the few senators to bother to speak about the amendment, also known as the Commodity Futures Modernization Act. Taking its cue from Summers's November 1999 President's Working Group report, it essentially forbade any regulation of the derivatives "swaps" market. The nation, Gramm said, was about to turn away "from an outmoded Depression-era approach to financial regulation" and position its financial services industry "to be world leaders into the new century." Summers had held out for some protections of retail investors, but on the whole he was equally ebullient about the new law, calling it "important legislation that will allow the United States to maintain its competitive position in this rapidly growing sector." Jim Leach, the chairman of the House Financial Services Committee, again stepped in and insisted on a provision that would authorize clearinghouses for swaps trades, forcing a little transparency, but the Treasury Department and the Fed never acted to create them.

The new law thus freed up what would later become a huge trade in the instruments that would lead to disaster, in particular credit default swaps. Much later on, Summers would argue that in the context of the times, the Commodity Futures Modernization Act was the best they could do. Regulators had no desire to use their authority anyway, and credit default swaps were barely in their infancy at the time the law was passed. They weren't even part of the debate, he said. But all in all, the new law was a remarkable fulfillment of many of the dreams of the era of Milton Friedman. Governments still reigned, but global finance was now free. Other nations, taking their cue as always from Washington, would follow suit, creating a framework that was really no framework: derivatives trade would be truly unencumbered. It had become perhaps the only totally free market on the globe. (That same Friday in December, again with the okay of the Treasury Department, Gramm also inserted a provision later called the "Enron exclusion" into the bill; it removed all public oversight and disclosure requirements for Enron online's energy trading operations. Enron had donated $100,000 to Gramm's election campaigns.)

Ironically, though no one could have seen it back then—certainly not Phil Gramm—it was actually the moment that marked the beginning of the *end* of the free-market era. What was to emerge, seven years later, as the worst economic disaster since the Great Depression was like a cancer that begins with the corruption of a single cell. Only in this case the cause was the corruption of a single bill that went all but unnoticed.

Somehow it was appropriate that no one was watching that day, because with the advent of the second Bush administration, and for the next eight years, very few people were monitoring the economy in a very concerned way. Our focus was elsewhere. After September 11, 2001— eight months into Bush's term—the 2000s were suddenly all about a tall, skinny bearded guy in Afghanistan who had orchestrated the most dramatic attack on continental U.S. soil since 1812, and then another fellow in Iraq who was not linked to the events in Afghanistan in any way but who seemed a handy villain. Bush seemed to think he could afford it all, and introduce permanent tax cuts as well. So lulled were Americans by then into thinking they had an indestructible economy led by unstoppable financial markets—and so repugnant, at the same time, was the idea of more taxes, more *government*—that even Alan Greenspan didn't raise a protest.

Greenspan knew better, of course, but he had always been a man who read the changing politics of Washington very well. After 9/11 he was also a man who felt he had the nation's welfare in his hands. Fourteen years at the Fed will do that. He urged his fellow Fed governors to keep interest rates low, the better to fulfill Bush's commandment to "keep shopping." Greenspan was later criticized, sometimes viciously, for this easy credit environment, which in retrospect gave the housing bubble a huge pump, but it was largely justified for those terror-haunted days. "It was right after 9/11, and we didn't know how badly the economy was going to get hit," said Gene Sperling, a close friend of Greenspan's.

Others in the Washington pecking order of regulators and lobbyists continued to take cues from the Great Greenspan. With the bracing wind of his libertarian ideology at their backs, they continued to espouse inaction and combined that policy stance with active lobbying against any other efforts at regulation. The Bush administration also orchestrated a fracturing of the financial regulatory structure, leaving each regulator weaker. In the summer of 2003, leaders of the four federal agencies that oversee the banking industry gathered to highlight the Bush administration's commitment to reducing regulation. They posed for photographers behind a stack of papers wrapped in red tape. Most held garden shears. But James Gilleran, Bush's nominee to head the Office of Thrift Supervision, brought along a chain saw and proudly brandished it for the cameras. The push for capital liberalization continued apace, as if nothing bad at all had happened in the 1990s. Despite the blowups, there was, both on Wall Street and in Washington, a sense that the economy worked better—that risk had been broken up, parceled out, and mastered. Regulators were not only ideologically predisposed to let things alone, they were benumbed. Things were working. The growing deficit was a problem that seemed far away, with ever cheaper debt.

The Bush administration saw financial deregulation as a national security issue as well. In its National Security Strategy of 2002, the administration praised free trade as a "moral principle" and called unambiguously for greater "international flows of investment capital to emerging markets"—as if crises such as the Asian contagion had never happened. On April 1, 2003, Treasury undersecretary John Taylor testified in favor of adding these provisions to free-trade treaties with Chile and Singapore, despite opposing testimony from Joseph Stiglitz and others. In 2003, Bush nominated none other than Mark Brickell, the bane of Jerry Corrigan's breakfast table and later the chief antiregulatory lobbyist on derivatives, to run the Office of Federal Housing Enterprise

Oversight, the weak, almost unknown agency that oversaw Fannie Mae and Freddie Mac. ("Like putting the fox in charge of the henhouse," one editorial writer said.)

Even as Bush moderated much about his foreign policy in his second term, the same was not true of his approach to regulation. William Donaldson, his first choice to head the SEC, had disappointed conservatives with his willingness to enforce regulation. One day, after Donaldson was ousted in 2005, Harvey Goldschmid, one of two Democratic SEC commissioners, was asked by his wife to name the "worst choice" he could think of from Capitol Hill to take over as SEC chairman. Goldschmid responded: "Chris Cox." His wife, it turned out, had been watching the TV and the news had just been announced: the choice was indeed Cox, who had sponsored that legislation back in 1995 to make it harder to sue securities firms and was, in the view of Goldschmid and others, another fox guarding the henhouse. Cox promptly aligned himself with two SEC commissioners even farther to the right than he was: Paul Atkins and Cindy Glassman.

Years later Barney Frank, the acid-tongued liberal Democrat who became chairman of the House Financial Services Committee, would talk about the deadening impact of that period. In Frank's view, the second Bush administration and the Republican-controlled Congress completed the task of "discrediting government" that Milton Friedman had begun so long before. "People forget, but from 2001 to 2007, we had the longest period of one-party control of the house and presidency since Lyndon Johnson," Frank said in 2009 as he sought to grapple with reinstituting regulation in the aftermath of the subprime debacle. "People say to me, 'Oh, you're going to give this [task] to these regulators, and they didn't do their job last time. I say, 'Well, yeah, because you appointed people who didn't believe in the job.'"

Bush had run as a "compassionate conservative," and his beau ideal was Ronald Reagan. Now the nation seemed to be living out Marx's observation that "all great, world-historical facts and personages" occur twice in history—the second time as farce. The supply-side ideas were back, but this time there was no restraint at all, no real debate. At least Reagan had been dogged by David Stockman, his budget director, and other fiscally responsible members of his party. A huge controversy erupted in 1982 when it leaked that Stockman had questioned Reagan's supply-side ideas and had been alarmed at continued tax cuts and ballooning deficits. As the 1980s played out, the Reagan revolution became more rhetorical than real. Reagan, described by Stockman as too "kind" and "gentle" to launch a revolution, could not himself bear to cut major government programs even as he stuck to his supply-side dream and tax-cutting ways. But others in the Republican Party pressed him to think about fiscal responsibility, and the GOP grew engulfed in bitter infighting between moderates and supply-siders. Leading members of the Reagan administration, including Stockman, Richard Darman, and then chief of staff Jim Baker, and the GOP Senate leadership argued in favor of tax increases to ease the deficit. The deficit wasn't healthy, but at least the debate about it was.

Twenty years later, when Paul O'Neill, Bush's first Treasury secretary—a Republican who was of that earlier generation—sought to stake out the same position and argue for fiscal probity, he found that he was all but alone.

11

The Canary in the Mine

P aul O'Neill was, in fact, a relic. An honest fiscal conservative from Pittsburgh, he had first come to Washington in the 1960s and then served as deputy director of Office of Management and Budget (OMB) under President Ford. After Ford lost the 1976 election to Jimmy Carter, O'Neill left Washington to embark on a brilliant corporate career, first at International Paper and then, from 1988 on, as chairman of Alcoa. He had entirely missed the era of free-market fundamentalism as it descended on Washington. Rooted in downtown Pittsburgh—which, while in Pennsylvania, is really a Midwestern city—he had resisted the era of deregulated finance that had given Wall Street the whip hand over the economy. O'Neill, like Stiglitz, was the product of a hardscrabble upbringing that made him mistrustful of bankers. Beyond that, he was too blunt for Washington, as he himself admitted. O'Neill had warned George W. Bush about this at their first meeting. "I like to say what I think, especially on subjects I've spent a few decades thinking through. In Washington these days, that might make me a dangerous man," he told the president-elect, who just laughed and hired him anyway.

But he *was* dangerous. It quickly became clear that not only did O'Neill speak his mind, he had not been tutored at all in the zeitgeist. Looking and sounding like a real-life Mr. Magoo, he came out with one verbal snafu after another. At one point early on O'Neill openly scoffed that he didn't need to consult the bond traders whom the Clintonites had sanctified. "I probably shouldn't have said it," O'Neill later recalled. "Someone said, 'Aren't you going to talk to people on Wall Street?' And

I said, 'Why would I talk to people sitting in front of flickering green screens?' But it's true. Why would I?" He was, again, reflecting the prejudices of an earlier era, when Wall Street investment banks were handmaidens to big business, not their taskmasters, and when they answered to the regulators in Washington. "I had spent fifteen years at the center of government thinking twenty-four hours a day about public policy matters across the Office of Management and Budget. I was pretty confident that nobody in Wall Street thought about things that I had," he said.

But now such sentiments had become sacrilege, and the statement cost O'Neill a lot of credibility.

It was soon apparent that Wall Street was returning O'Neill's contempt in kind. O'Neill was always an odd duck. At Alcoa he had insisted that his company stay out of the reckless use of derivatives after reading a 1986 book on the "new financial world" by Henry Kaufman, the Salomon Brothers economist then known as Dr. Doom. Kaufman wondered somberly—and far earlier than most—how regulators would be able to stay on top of a global financial system in which the role of banks had waned and new credit instruments, including then-exotic derivatives, were taking over. Said O'Neill: "When I first started being concerned about broad patterns developing in financial markets it was in the early 1990s. Henry Kaufman's book rang true to me. From the kinds of things that investment bankers were saying to me, I thought they were all lunacy. So I wouldn't let our financial functionaries at Alcoa do any of that exotic stuff, the third- and fourth-order derivatives." One of O'Neill's assistant Treasury secretaries, Sheila Bair, recalled him telling her that "when he was CEO of Alcoa he would make them go over every derivative position they had, and if he didn't understand it they wouldn't do it." He also had little use for investment banking in general. "When I was there, I honestly didn't buy the idea that investment bankers really had very much to offer," he said. "We had plenty of people inside International Paper who had a good education in finance. And they could do acquisition and asset sales better than investment banking houses. I was told we needed them for 'a comfort opinion.' I said, 'We're paying a bloody fortune for comfort.'"

O'Neill also had a hands-on pragmatist's view of markets. He was a kind of Jerry Corrigan of the corporate world, believing that "people need to be protected from themselves." At Alcoa, he had required that his twenty-six different businesses in forty-three countries produce, every

Friday, a "one-computer-screen" report on important developments in their areas the previous week. "It gave me fingertip sensitivity on what was going on in the world. I had this vast feeder of information. I knew better than anybody in government what was going on in the world economy." When he looked at the information-gathering and analysis systems at Commerce, Labor, and Treasury, he was appalled. "I said this is pathetic. A lot of this stuff is six months old."

He really rolled into action after the collapse of Enron. "I called Sandy Weill—he was then running Citigroup. I said, Sandy, what are your credit card billings, slow payment and late payments and default data? I'd like to have them every day. He said, fine. I called Rick Wagoner at GM, said I need to know what your daily sales are." O'Neill was creating a data-mining operation on the U.S. economy not unlike what he had done at Alcoa. "One of the things I was advocating was to require that CEOs of listed companies certify everything every three months, to make sure that what every intelligent investor needs to know is included and it's all true." Wistfully, he added, "By 2005, we would have had it in place. I think we would have pulled the trigger on it."

Not surprisingly, O'Neill also hired people who were inclined to take a more Corrigan-like approach to finance. Among them was Bair, a lawyer from Kansas and a former Commodity Futures Trading commissioner, who upon taking office as assistant Treasury secretary for financial institutions in 2002 grew worried about looser lending practices. Prompted by Senator Paul Sarbanes, Bair read the report that Summers's Treasury Department and Housing and Urban Development had prepared in the last months of the Clinton era. The report recommended that the Fed use its powers to write rules on lending—a point being pushed by Fed governor Ed Gramlich, who was a friend of Bair's. But the Fed was still refusing. Appalled by this, Bair sought to impose "best practices" on the lending industry, including rules that would require documentation of a borrower's ability to repay, and limiting refinancing to prevent "loan flipping." Bair had solid Republican credentials; she had gotten her start in Washington as counsel to Senator Bob Dole. But Bair also found that she was shouting into the wind. After getting nowhere, she soon left the administration (though she would return in 2006 as head of the Federal Deposit Insurance Corporation.

O'Neill was a classic example of what economist Thorstein Veblen once lionized as a technocrat, the kind of professional who should be entrusted to run the economy. He'd befriended many Republicans over the years whom he had thought of as like-minded, among them Alan Greenspan and Dick Cheney. In 1988, George H. W. Bush had offered him Defense; he humbly declined, saying he'd just started at Alcoa, and he recommended Cheney. Cheney returned the favor twelve years later, but now was no time for technocrats, and O'Neill could seem to do no right—especially when it came to the now-outmoded idea of fiscal responsibility.

In the spring of 2002, after 9/11, O'Neill had the temerity to suggest that perhaps another tax cut was not a great idea. "I believed there was still a prospect of another 9/11," he told me later. "The first one cost us one hundred or two hundred billion dollars," he said. "We needed money to fix Social Security and Medicare." Things got especially rough after the 2002 midterms, which the Republicans won handily. When Cheney pushed relentlessly for more tax cuts, and O'Neill worried aloud in a meeting about the rising deficit, Cheney barked that "Reagan proved deficits don't matter."

O'Neill, the author Ron Suskind wrote, "was speechless. Cheney moved to fill the void. 'We won the midterms. This is our due,' he said." Seated at the right hand of a Republican president, working at the pleasure of a vice president who had been his friend and, he thought, his ideological ally, O'Neill found himself instead in an alien world. The movement that had begun with the more responsible ideas of Milton Friedman was now in the hands of an administration in which movement politics, not economic management, would predominate. During the Bush administration, wrote one of the original Reagan supply-siders, Bruce Bartlett, supply-side economics "became distorted into something that is, frankly, nuts—the ideas that there is no economic problem that cannot be cured with more and bigger tax cuts, that all tax cuts are equally beneficial, and that all tax cuts raise revenue."

In keeping with the zeitgeist, the whole axis of opinion had continued to move rightward: If the Clinton Democrats were now fiscal conservatives, then the Republicans would be more passionate supply-siders than the Reaganites had been. O'Neill committed one of his biggest errors when he frankly admitted that Clinton had left things in good shape. "The Clinton administration pursued a really responsible fiscal policy," he told me. "It's true the economy was limping from the evaporation of the dot-com nonsense, but as we were going through

2001 the economy was not terrible. Interestingly enough, much to consternation of the economic types, even after 9/11 we didn't take as big a shot as people thought."

When O'Neill looked over his shoulder for the one supporter he felt sure would be behind him—his old pal Alan, the fiscal schoolmarm of the Clinton years—he found that the Fed chief wasn't with him either. O'Neill and Greenspan had known each other since 1968, and the two worked closely during the Ford administration, when O'Neill had been at the OMB and Greenspan had been chairman of the Council of Economic Advisors. Greenspan had been on the board of Alcoa when O'Neill was recruited to become chairman, and afterward he would stop by the Fed for long talks with Greenspan whenever he was in Washington. "One of the things that bound us together is that we're both analytic and numbers people," O'Neill recalled. "It was a great joy to be engaged with Alan. I've known a few data mavens in my time, and he's in the top rank."

But Greenspan, his old friend, left O'Neill swinging in the ill wind of the Bush team's tax cut fervor. Greenspan, who had campaigned so effectively for reining in the deficit during the Clinton years, suddenly decided he didn't want to be seen as holding out against the latest wave of supply-side economics. "When I was making my arguments about the right and not-right things to do about tax policies, he was quiet," O'Neill said.

The cold reception that O'Neill encountered paralleled, to some degree, what GOP moderates such as Colin Powell, Brent Scowcroft, and Senator Chuck Hagel of Nebraska faced in the national security realm. They no longer recognized the party they had grown up with. "Realism," the traditional stance of the Republican Party, which depended on strong defense married to restraint and carefully cultivated alliances, was gone with the wind. Post-9/11, it was all unilateralism and hubris. As Scowcroft described to me the new Bush team's attitude shortly before the Iraq invasion of 2003, a lot of it was about fixing what they saw as the squishy multilateralism of Bill Clinton and forthrightly embracing America's obvious destiny as the "hyperpower." "They think that the United States has been in a Gulliver-like position for a long time, tied down by the Lilliputians [the rest of the world] from doing the things that we think are right. . . . This is no time for caution, it's time to abandon your allies, your friends, and just go for it." It was time, in other words, to reassert American power.

Yet before long, the president who had sought to reassert American power was presiding over its hollowing out on two fronts, said many critics. Among the critics, of course, was Joe Stiglitz. The long, bloody slog of Iraq was the more visible front of the drain on U.S. power. But behind the scenes the tax-cutting and deregulatory ideologues and derivatives termites were at work slowly undermining its infrastructure. It was a danger that, at the time, no one perceived, though O'Neill was certainly worried. Unsound finance could doom great powers every bit as much as conquering armies. "Behind each great historical phenomenon there lies a financial secret," the British historian Niall Ferguson wrote later. Imperial Spain amassed vast amounts of bullion from the New World, but it faded as a power while the British and Dutch empires prospered because they had sophisticated banking systems and Spain did not. Similarly, the French Revolution was made all but inevitable by the machinations of an unscrupulous Scotsman named John Law, whom the deeply indebted French monarchy recklessly placed in charge of public finance. "It was as if one man was simultaneously running all five hundred of the top U.S. corporations, the U.S. Treasury and the Federal Reserve System," Ferguson wrote. Law proceeded to single-handedly create the subprime mortgage bubble of his day with French public debt. When the debt bubble collapsed, the fallout "fatally set back France's financial development, putting Frenchmen off paper money and stock markets for generations." Wilhelmine Germany, meanwhile, came up short in World War I "because it did not have access to the international bond market," Ferguson wrote.

Was the United States now, similarly, allowing its power to hang on a thin reed—its financial dependency on the rest of the world, particularly China? Larry Summers, now back at Harvard, called it a "financial balance of terror" in a speech. U.S. consumers overbought goods and overborrowed from China, and the Chinese in turn accumulated vast dollar surpluses that they plowed back into Wall Street investments, thereby supplying profligate Americans with the finance we needed to consume and sustain ourselves as the lone superpower. No one wanted to disturb the relationship, because it would be devastating for both economies, and so the world went on somehow, just as it had during the Cold War balance of terror. But how long could a great power last as a debtor to another nation across the world whose interests often clashed with its own? And what would the cost to the United States ultimately be?

As Stiglitz would later write from his new high-profile perch at *Vanity Fair* magazine, lamenting not just the "war of choice" in Iraq but the failure to move the country away from oil or invest in education or social welfare, opting instead for more huge Reaganesque tax cuts: "A young male in his 30s today has an income, adjusted for inflation, that is 12 percent less than what his father was making 30 years ago. Some 5.3 million more Americans are living in poverty now than were living in poverty when Bush became president," Stiglitz wrote savagely. "Up to now, the conventional wisdom has been that Herbert Hoover, whose policies aggravated the Great Depression, is the odds-on claimant for the mantle of worst president when it comes to stewardship of the American economy. Once Franklin Roosevelt assumed office and reversed Hoover's policies, the country began to recover. The economic effects of Bush's presidency are more insidious than those of Hoover, harder to reverse, and likely to be longer-lasting."

Social equity, unfair tax cuts, above all a sense of balance—it's what worried Paul O'Neill as well. But O'Neill got no hearing for these deeper worries. He had little sympathy on the outside either, in the markets. Robert Rubin and even Larry Summers were tough acts to follow. All most people saw with O'Neill was his Mr. Magoo side. Early on he helped to send the dollar into a tailspin with an ill-considered departure from Bob Rubin's mantra in support of a "strong dollar." O'Neill hadn't quite abandoned the strong dollar, but like his boss, George W. Bush, he wasn't especially good at nuance, and he had tried to make the sensible argument that the value of the dollar was simply the result of sound policy. ("We are not pursuing, as often said, a policy of a strong dollar," he said. "In my opinion, a strong dollar is the result of a strong economy.")

At another point O'Neill, dutifully trying to echo Cheney's view of deficits, dismissed the U.S. current-account imbalances as "meaningless" in the face of America's attractiveness as a source of investment. That was close to being economically illiterate: in fact, the vast amounts of capital flowing into the United States—into asset-backed securities, among other things—were arriving because Americans were consuming and borrowing, not because there were great investments here. No matter how hard he tried, time and again his ungoverned tongue got him in trouble with the markets. "Every time he got on TV, we would all say 'Don't talk!'" said one Wall Street trader.

The end came quickly. When O'Neill was dumped unceremoniously at the end of 2002 for daring to express public doubts about Bush's tax-cut-and-spend approach to government, almost no one mourned his departure. No liberal hero, he still found himself in the same boat as people like Stiglitz and Brooksley Born.

O'Neill's immediate successor, John Snow, a rail executive who seemed to have no discernible impact on any policy, lingered on through the first year of the second term, but he was seen as an ineffectual advocate of what were effectively unsustainable policies, and he was dumped as well. And as the budget deficit built through the mid-2000s, with an economy sustained only by the astonishing real estate market, George Bush needed a superstar to allay Wall Street's growing concerns. The Greenspan era was coming to a close, and the man the Bush team was coalescing around as his replacement, an obscure economist named Ben Bernanke, wasn't a superstar in anyone's eyes.

Ben Shalom Bernanke had grown up in a small Southern town— Dillon, South Carolina—and like Stiglitz, he was part of that internal Jewish diaspora that assimilated itself throughout the United States, all the while maintaining its tribal customs in small synagogues. And like Summers, Stiglitz, and Greenspan, he soared academically. Bernanke looked a lot like Alan Greenspan on paper. Both were child prodigies at math—and musicians—and both men were acolytes of Milton Friedman. The great man himself, Friedman, in one of his last interviews before he died, in late 2005, told Charlie Rose that he felt good about Bernanke, that he was sure Bernanke would "continue in Alan Greenspan's path."

Beyond that, Bernanke had distinguished himself, and arrived at the precipice of the Fed chairmanship, by playing the eager acolyte to Greenspan's view of the markets and the Fed's role. His ascent in Washington was part accident, as is usually the case. As a Princeton economist, he and his longtime collaborator, Mark Gertler, had presented a paper in 1999, during the dot-com bubble, arguing against a strategy of using interest rates to deflate asset prices using interest rates. The paper did defend the Fed's use of other tools such as regulation, especially in markets in which there was high leverage (not a major problem during the tech bubble that Bernanke and Gertler were addressing). But it caused some controversy: MIT eminence Rudiger Dornbusch attacked it, saying the Fed could do much more, monitoring loose credit on the way up in a bubble, and supplying credit on the way down. Still, the one man who counted then was Alan Greenspan, and he was impressed with Bernanke. "As we were filing out of the room Greenspan just happened to walk near us and said quietly as he passed: 'I agree with you,'" said Gertler. "That had us in seventh heaven."

Bernanke had in effect supplied scholarly ammunition to Greenspan's doctrine of noninterference. Bernanke too had resisted the idea of the chairman giving his irrational exuberance speech. Later Glenn Hubbard, Bush's chairman of the Council of Economic Advisors, recommended him for an opening on the Fed Board, and he performed as a loyal Bushie would be expected to. True to form, in 2002 Bernanke declared that "monetary policy cannot be directed finely enough [to prick bubbles] without risk of severe collateral damage to the economy." Greenspan was so certain of Bernanke's views that, when he handed off the Fed to him, he gave him only one piece of advice: When you have lunch with somebody, always arrange it so they sit with their back to the clock. That way you can see what time it is. After eighteen years, that was all Greenspan had to say.

Bernanke had hidden strengths—an almost preternatural calm married to a powerful intellect—that would become known and appreciated only later. Even as a teenager he seemed to have a calming influence on all those around him. His high school friend from Dillon, John Braddy, described a school trip when he and Bernanke were in Washington just after Martin Luther King Jr.'s assassination in 1968, and riots had broken out. "We were standing on the Capitol steps watching the smoke and fire from the riots. We had to be escorted out of the city. Being from the South, that really made an impact on us. But we never had a problem in our small town, and one reason is that Ben helped. He wrote several articles for the school newspaper about the future need for progress and integration."

There are few times in world affairs when one man of consequence perfectly meets the moment he has prepared for his entire life, and that fact changes history. Within several years Bernanke would become such a man. But at this point he was still just another compliant figure in George W. Bush's Washington, a conservative economist so mild and quiet in temperament—his voice sometimes had a slight tremor—that Bush was not sure he was ready to replace Greenspan, though Bernanke had become the leading candidate by 2005. Bush had named Bernanke as Fed governor in 2002 and then made him chairman of his Council of Economic Advisors in June 2005. Everybody liked him, but Bernanke did not look like anybody's image of a chairman, not after the Greenspan era. Sure, brains counted for a lot, but in positions at the top, imagery is vital. The image of a six-foot-seven Paul Volcker, chomping mightily on his cigar, helped in Ronald Reagan's Washington when he fought a lonely fight to vanquish inflation. Greenspan too, despite the constant double-talk, was a tall, athletic figure of authority.

So Bush needed a powerful voice at Treasury, a man who could really talk to the Street. This was one of the sensible bits of advice conveyed to him by his new chief of staff, Josh Bolten, who proceeded methodically to rid the administration of some of its more extreme ideologues. And when it came to the economy, Bolten knew exactly where to find a superstar: at his old company, Goldman Sachs. "Government Sachs," as it was sometimes known, was the most powerful and prestigious firm on the Street. It had been the spawning ground of Robert Rubin, the greatest Treasury secretary since Alexander Hamilton. And its current chairman was another powerhouse, Henry Paulson Jr.

12

The King of the Street

Square-jawed and gravelly voiced, Hank Paulson looked the part that Josh Bolten wanted him to play. He was just the sort of man George W. Bush liked and needed by his side. Paulson brought an intensity to everything he did. As an offensive tackle for Dartmouth in the late 1960s, he earned the nickname "the hammer." Paulson, who had been a high school wrestler, was known for leaping off the snap quickly and driving his head and shoulders into a defensive lineman's gut. The result was that Paulson, who was six-foot-one and weighed a scant two hundred pounds, often took much larger men out of the play. "He had this amazing ability to use his body. He would fire out of his stance and hit those Harvard tackles really low," said Bill Calhoun, who captained the 1966 Dartmouth team. "The funny thing was, when I would hear him in front of Congress, he would sound just like he did in the huddle. His own Hank intensity."

Paulson made All-Ivy and All-East (as well as honorable mention All-American), and his approach to football became his approach to life. Representative John Spratt, a South Carolina Democrat who as a young Army captain shared a Pentagon office with then Navy captain Paulson after the latter had been recruited from Harvard Business School, remembered him the same way. "He was always the hard-charger, the Dartmouth tackle who would play all-out in every play." At his first budget briefing for then deputy Defense secretary David Packard, Paulson was so keyed up about getting the presentation right that he forgot everything else. When he took off his overcoat upon arriving at the

Pentagon, he discovered he didn't have on his suit jacket. "We had to run up and down the D ring to find him a jacket," said Spratt. "The thing about Paulson is he brought an enormous amount of energy to everything he did."

It made him the consummate deal maker on the Street: always strike first. After he joined Goldman Sachs and rose quickly to become chief operating officer—he'd reluctantly agreed to move from Chicago to New York—Paulson won power at Goldman in a fierce coup. It was just the sort of thing that builds legends on Wall Street. After Jon Corzine, then CEO, appeared to err by committing the firm to a bailout of Long Term Capital Management without consulting the executive committee, Paulson forced Corzine's ouster with the help of John Thain and John Thornton, whom he made co–chief operating officers while he took the CEO spot. Paulson then pushed through the firm's initial offering and earned an average of $100 million for himself and each of the other 220 Goldman partners. Just like that, Paulson became the top man at the most prestigious firm on the Street. Once again, he had leaped off the snap and taken a rival by surprise.

But in many ways Paulson didn't fit the usual stereotypes of a Master of the Universe. He was almost mind-bogglingly inarticulate for someone who had risen so high in the corporate world; a conversation with Paulson was always a confusion of mental stuttering, replete with unfinished sentences and new sentences rising like uncertain phoenixes from the ashes of the old half-articulated ones. But that was part of Paulson's disarming charm. He put on no airs. He was a former Eagle Scout and a nonsmoking, nondrinking Christian Scientist who had stayed married to his first wife, Wendy (they were college sweethearts) and, even when he was at Goldman, he liked to spend weekends near his mother in his hometown of Barrington, Illinois, a Chicago suburb. In a culture of conspicuous consumption, Paulson was known for wearing penny loafers and a plastic Casio watch. Paulson, the passionate conservationist, filled his office with pictures of wild animals and predatory birds. Friends and subordinates alike came to admire him for his integrity and his eagerness to jump into every issue and get to the facts. One of Paulson's first jobs was as an aide to John Ehrlichman in President Richard Nixon's White House. In 1973, when he thought the president was lying, Paulson quit, recalled his old friend Walt Minnick, who also worked in the White House at the time.

Paulson was, in other words, exactly the opposite of the straw man most anti–Wall Street writers decry. He didn't act out of cartoon malice and greed; he served Wall Street's interests because he seemed to honestly believe that was the best way to serve all of America's interest. He understood that he was the heir to a tradition, one that went back to J. P. Morgan himself. During the Panic of 1907, Morgan had been the Rock of Wall Street, the man who calmly told the head of the New York Stock Exchange that he dare not close early in order to prevent panic selling and then called in his fellow bankers and told them they had to pony up money to keep the Exchange afloat. That world no longer really existed. Morgan, after all, was not only virtually a one-man Federal Reserve in his time—the Fed didn't come into being until five years later—but he actually controlled huge sectors of the economy: the railroads, the top three insurance companies, U.S. Steel. In subsequent eras, top bankers also had a sense of responsibility for the overall health of the financial system, people like Lewis Preston of JP Morgan and Walter Wriston of Citibank.

The difference was that while in the old days firms like JP Morgan had possessed a sense of noblesse oblige about the U.S. economy, Goldman had never matured into that role. It couldn't really afford it. In the post-Milken era, the elite of the Street had become vastly more diffuse, and the pickings much slimmer. As Morgan Stanley had learned, you simply couldn't make enough money at traditional investment banking, giving advice to favored clients and underwriting initial public offerings. The new game was to set up major trades for big-moneyed clients such as hedge funds and become a market maker, playing both sides of a transaction. Providing "liquidity" in these markets was, in the view of firms such as Goldman, the new social responsibility they had to bear. Proprietary trading, once frowned upon in the best firms, also became a necessity.

And whereas Wall Street banks once had a stake in the loans they made, and private partnerships like Goldman onced staked their own capital, the securitization game dissolved any sense of liability that firms had for the success or failure of their products. Along with the dispersion of risk, the idea of a corporate conscience—at least over preserving system stability—grew so diffuse that it no longer really existed. This was happening even as systemic risk began linking everyone up. It was a danger sign: while the consequences of the actions of individual banks were increasing in significance for the entire system, their corporate ethics were shriveling into nothingness. The outcome was a growing and alarming mismatch between Wall Street's vast and growing power over the economy and its utter lack of conscience, especially since incentives were being created that would motivate traders to actually blow up the system, though this would not become apparent until later.

If Goldman sat atop the pecking order, it was largely because it was better at this new game than any other firm was. Its corporate ethos was to be more predator than protector. It became known as the savviest and most prestigious firm on the Street in part because it had no scruples about simultaneously betting against products it was selling. Goldman justified this by saying that it had more sophisticated customers, like big institutional and professional investors, who understood the game themselves and didn't mind if Goldman placed hedges against the very investments it was touting to other clients. It was more of a hedge fund mentality than anything else.

Rather than feeling themselves obliged to preserve the stability of the system, top firms like Goldman were consumed with making money off of it. And in this era, that meant coming up with the best ways of lobbying Washington to back off. It was no accident that Goldman came to dominate the Wall Street–Washington nexus. JP Morgan had flourished in an earlier laissez-faire era when Washington dared not interfere with Wall Street; Paulson rose to power in an era when the thing to do on Wall Street was to gain influence in Washington so you could tell it what to do and shoo it away. This became especially necessary as the era of global competition grew intense. Goldman wanted its top people serving in Washington; it was Goldman that had produced Rubin at Treasury, another former chairman, John Whitehead, as deputy secretary of State, and Josh Bolten as chief of staff.

So Paulson, good corporate team player that he was, enthusiastically fulfilled the new role of King of the Street. He battered away at the regulators, creating more space for Goldman and the other top Street firms to increase profits. He became a leading champion of the push for more and faster change, citing the intense post–Cold War competition with the Europeans for new markets. In 2004, Paulson led a delegation to Washington to argue for permission to use much greater leverage in the market bets the firms could take. The big five banks—Goldman, JP Morgan, Merrill Lynch, Lehman Brothers, and Bear Stearns—all wanted to remove the capital they were required to use as a cushion against downturns and invest it. They argued that European regulators were insisting on a different kind of supervision, one that demanded a new complex formula to calculate exposure rather than simple, straightforward tools like capital ratios. They had to compete in that market, Paulson and the Wall Streeters argued.

It was, oddly enough, a chance for the SEC to grab some control back. Under the Gramm-Leach-Bliley Act repealing Glass-Steagall, the SEC had been given no oversight over investment bank holding companies. Now, under the new rules Paulson and the others had asked for, the SEC was given new powers to conduct regular bank inspections (while the capital ratios were dropped). But in the end the SEC simply let the inspection process flag, and the new approach to much bigger bets of capital became another concession to self-regulation. Like the Phil Gramm amendment four years earlier, it was the sort of arcane event almost no one paid attention to—a fifty-five-minute meeting of the SEC, and this was the last item on the agenda.

No one dissented from the change, except an obscure consultant from Middle America—Valparaiso, Indiana—named Leonard Bole, who noted in a letter to the SEC that a similar concept of self-regulation, without capital standards, had failed to protect Long-Term Capital Management (LTCM). "Nobody from the SEC contacted me," said Bole.

Paulson was happy to make lobbying trips to Washington, but by mid-2006 he wasn't eager to go there to work. He had no desire to serve out the last grim years of a deeply unpopular president. His reputation had never been higher on the Street, and he had just watched the reputations of the previous two Treasury secretaries get trashed. Among those who advised against it was his Goldman partner John Whitehead, an old Washington hand. "This is a failed administration," Whitehead said. "You'll have a hard time getting anything accomplished." But Josh Bolten was insistent and kept sweetening the pot, eventually agreeing to terms that allowed Paulson to take virtual control of the Bush administration's economic policy.

By the time he moved into Robert Rubin's old haunt, the Greek Revival palace next to the White House, in early July 2006, Paulson had a growing sense of dread. He knew the market was overheated and risk was horribly underpriced. He wasn't alone: credit default swaps issued by firms such as AIG, which offered protection against a market drop, were flying around the world like confetti. Early in the 1990s, it had been Goldman that had written one of the first warning reports on OTC derivatives, drafted by Jerry Corrigan, of course. As a cushion, Goldman kept vast amounts of liquidity on hand—a "lock box," as Paulson described it, with $50 billion in Treasuries at the Bank of New York.

In his first meeting with George W. Bush that July, talking in that gravelly voice the world would come to know—"it was like a thousand-dollar bill was caught in his throat," a Bush aide would say—Paulson told the president that they were going to suffer some kind of market turmoil. He didn't know the extent of it, but they'd better get ready for it. Paulson suspected the economy was in a another bubble; he thought if it burst there would be a test of the credit default swaps market and whether the regulated institutions had enough margins to pay them off. Were these institutions—the traditional banks and insurance companies—too exposed to the hedge funds? Paulson knew the hedge funds were "much bigger" than they had been then, and he was concerned about their use of credit default swaps. (In truth, the LTCM problem had largely fixed itself in the hedge fund world: no hedge fund was being allowed to operate again without margins, the way Merrill Lynch chairman David Komansky had allowed John Meriwether to do).

Paulson was also aware that other investment banks were getting in deep, especially Lehman under its CEO, Richard Fuld. Paulson didn't have much use for the rapacious Fuld, who had taken another old white-shoe firm and turned it into his personal hedge fund. Paulson respected Fuld for rescuing Lehman from the dead after Travelers had spun it off in 1994, but he was known on the Street as a wild man with "nine lives." Back when Mexico was bailed out, Fuld was buying Mexican Tesebonos (treasury bonds) at 18 percent and they were funding it with commercial paper and hadn't hedged it, and they survived that. In 1998, Lehman was on the brink again, but they seemed to always be able to pull through.

So, careful man that he was, Paulson promptly had Treasury conduct intensive audits of all the regulated financial firms and their exposure to the hedge funds—did they have enough margins? He also had his

Treasury people work on clarifying how cash settlements might work in a crisis. He even held "war games" with the British on what might happen if the global payments system went down, telling his colleagues, "There's no sense in trying to predict what will be the spark that lights the fire."

Paulson certainly didn't know that the world he had helped to create was about to blow up in his face. And the rest of the world was soon to find out just how far he was from the kinds of "kings of the Street" who had comprehended the whole system, from JP Morgan onward. Paulson had always been a guy who lived from deal to deal, never stopping or stepping back to comprehend the whole. As in football, every play was different from every other play. Every intervention was different. Now Paulson was mainly worried about hedge funds. He was thinking about a new LTCM. He was in some ways fighting the last war. It would be another man, the Mutt to Paulson's Jeff, a slight, mild-mannered fellow who might have made a good water boy for the Dartmouth offensive line, who would later show Paulson the way forward—Ben Bernanke.

More than most in Washington, Paulson was an honest man; he admitted to me frankly later on that he just wasn't paying much attention to this slicing and dicing of mortgages all over the world. Goldman had a relatively small presence in the subprime market—indeed, was hedged more heavily against a downturn than just about anybody. "I didn't tend to understand the retail market, I just wasn't close to it," Paulson said. Paulson, the onetime King of the Street, admitted he wasn't even very familiar with the "SIVs," or structured investment vehicles, that high-gambling investment banks and banks were now using, as the subprime mania reached its height, to borrow short-term and make long-term investments in mortgage-backed CDOs (collateralized debt obligations) off their balance sheets. The reason for this was simple: SIVs were a way for regulated banks to pile up investments without worrying about capital requirements from regulators. This was the world that later became known as the "shadow banking system." Thanks to securitization, loans that were once the province of the traditional banking world were now being bundled and sold worldwide through a shadow—or unregulated—world of investment banks, hedge funds, money market funds, and other entities, often through SIVs.

During this period of twenty years or so, the shadow banking system had actually grown larger in size than the traditional banking system, though to what extent would become known only later on. The problem was that there was no one in authority who was monitoring the shadow banking system or protecting it against a crash. It was truly a free market, unencumbered by government. Traditional banks had deposit insurance and guarantees from the central bank to protect them against bank runs in the event of a downturn. The shadow banking system did not—except that, as everyone was to find out only after it was too late, the federal guarantees of the traditional banking system would soon have to be extended to the wild world of shadow banking.

And Paulson had, frankly, bigger concerns. The Chinese were artificially depressing their currency, the yuan, making exports more expensive for U.S. businesses and further enlarging the trade imbalance between the two countries. On a trip in the spring of 2007, he became the latest in a series of U.S. Treasury secretaries—Rubin was hardly the first—to press for the liberalizing of the markets that Beijing had promised to trade representative Charlene Barshefsky when it joined the World Trade Organization in 2001. In a speech to Shanghai financial officials in 2007, he warned that China risked trillions of dollars in lost economic potential unless it freed up its capital markets. "An open, competitive, and liberalized financial market can effectively allocate scarce resources in a manner that promotes stability and prosperity far better than governmental intervention," Paulson said.

So under Hank Paulson, Treasury's reversion to the Goldman Sachs view of the world was complete. Soon it was as if Bob Rubin had never left.

Rubin himself was, by that time, still comfortably ensconced at Citigroup up in New York. Ever generous to his former acolytes, he began to bring in all his old aides, among them David Lipton and Michael Froman. Rubin even lured Stanley Fischer, the former deputy managing director of the International Monetary Fund, as vice chairman. As the Bush administration dug the United States further into the red, Rubin helped to set up a foundation intended to champion fiscal responsibility. He relished the golden standard he had set during his Treasury tenure, the standard by which every successor was measured, usually unfavorably.

Rubin was beginning to worry, just as Paulson was, that things were getting out of control in the wider markets. He spoke out against excessive leverage levels, and the underpricing of risk. But the lure of Citigroup had been in large part that Rubin wouldn't have to go back to what he once did at Goldman, worrying every trade and investment. As he wrote in his memoir, he'd always longed for an unstructured life, dreamed of it in times of stress. His year at the London School of Economics had been the greatest time of his life, when he "continued to explore—in my limited way—the strain within me that identified with the beat generation and its expatriate predecessors of the 1920s and '30s in Paris."

Sandy Weill was no fool; he coldly used Rubin as cover for the completion of his dream, the dismantling of Glass-Steagall, and then continued to run his own ship. That was okay by Rubin, whose impact on the firm was barely detectable, according to accounts from several insiders at Citigroup. "He was always off fly-fishing somewhere when we wanted him to meet clients," said one former Citigroup executive. Even when he was at meetings, apart from his brief turn as kingmaker, some members of the Citi board of directors recalled being struck by Rubin's lack of interest in the firm's governance.

Things changed somewhat after Weill was finally forced into retirement in 2003. Before he left, Weill had set up his protégé and close friend, Chuck Prince, a lawyer by training, as his successor. A novice in the world of trading, Prince badly needed Rubin's advice, and Rubin would often pad down to the chairman's office in his stocking feet for a chat. But the sort of broad strategic advice that Rubin was giving to Prince was not, frankly, very different from the kind of advice everyone else was handing out at the time: you needed to take on more risk if you were going to earn the double-digit returns that were, by that point in the mania, the quarterly expectation for every major firm on Wall Street. Rubin had been a risk arbitrageur, after all, and traditional banking was a tiny-margin business. "Chuck was totally new to the job. He didn't know a CDO from a grocery list, so he looked for someone for advice and support," a senior Citi executive told the *New York Times*. "That person was Rubin. And Rubin had always been an advocate of being more aggressive in the capital markets arena. He would say, 'You have to take more risk if you want to earn more.'" Still, Rubin never got into too much detail; he was the first to admit that the trading business had moved way beyond his understanding in the years he had been away. Nor did Prince ever catch up to the games his traders were playing; all he knew was that Citigroup had to be a part of it. Prince would later become infamous for pleading with regulators to step in and limit leverage amounts because he couldn't, as CEO, do it himself—not while every other bank on the Street was making monster profits off the practice. "As long as the music is playing you've got to get up and dance," he said.

Rubin was mainly focused on fishing, and Paulson was focused on everything but the tidal wave that was slowly beginning to gather out in the heartland—the wave that a few people such as Roy Barnes saw coming. It was a wave composed of little ripples of foreclosures accumulating from all over the country as the frauds and mortgage scams fell apart, and indigent or front borrowers defaulted.

But it wasn't just Rubin and Paulson who lacked foresight. The greatest minds in economics didn't see the wave coming either. They certainly never imagined that the theoretical world they had created was about to be destroyed by it.

13

Last Gathering
of the Faithful

I n late August 2005, Robert Rubin flew out to Jackson Hole for the
annual conference of the Federal Reserve Bank of Kansas City. Larry
Summers went too. For the pallid men (and increasingly, women) of
numbers, the Wyoming retreat had become a treasured interlude in the
sun every year. For two days the world's most prominent economists,
central bankers, and financiers don open-collar shirts and jeans in the
gorgeous surrounds of Grand Teton National Park and imagine themselves to be a little more like Clint Eastwood than Caspar Milquetoast. It
is, as one said, a lovely weekend of "taking long hikes while talking about
monetary policy."

But this was a special year, a special moment. They had all come to
celebrate an era, the magnificent eighteen-year-tenure of Alan Greenspan.
In keeping with the theme of the event, titled "The Greenspan Era:
Lessons for the Future," economist after economist sang the praises of
the maestro of monetary policy, and the astonishingly long period of prosperity over which he had presided.

It was Summers's moment too—just as it was Bob Rubin's. The key-
note speaker, of course, was Rubin, who spoke elegiacally of the "truly
remarkable relationship among Alan, Larry, and me" and harked back
to their great moment of mutual discovery of one another: the deficit-
reduction plan of the early Clinton administration.

For Summers, the Jackson Hole weekend was a joyful reaffirmation. It had been a tough year for Summers, who was then in the final stages of his troubled tenure as president of Harvard University. Like Geithner at the New York Fed, Summers had gotten the job partly on the recommendation of Rubin, a trustee, who assured the Harvard Corporation that his former protégé had the requisite social and political skills to represent America's most prestigious university to the world. But the "new Larry" had never completely taken root. After leaving the Treasury Department, he had arrived at Harvard in 2000 like a returning hero, bringing an entourage. Yet somehow the old sardonic Larry Summers, too clever and colorful for his own good, kept making headlines. First, he offended African American scholars by questioning the scholarship and work habits of the author and critic Cornel West, who promptly left for Princeton. Then, at a casual forum with other students in January 2005, Summers floated the idea that there were three possible hypotheses for why there were so many more males than females in high-end science and engineering positions. He was just being Larry, as always, thinking aloud, trying to provoke the students to further thought and debate. As Summers later explained, he was just synthesizing the scholarship that the organizers had asked him to discuss, and he warned his listeners, "I'm going to provoke you."

But it was a provocation that went too far, apparently, when he suggested that one reason might be a "different availability of aptitude at the high end" between men and women. There were gasps in the audience. One participant, Nancy Hopkins, an MIT biologist and a Harvard graduate, actually got up and walked out, telling the *Boston Globe* later that if she hadn't left, "I would've either blacked out or thrown up." After another attendee posted the Summers comments, the controversy erupted nationally. It was all a bit too much for a hallowed school whose presidents had always been models of academic propriety. For some at Harvard, Summers was a bracing truth teller, which after all is what a university education is supposed to be about. But for most it was too much controversy for one Harvard president. "There was a sense of not just a barbarian at the gate, but a barbarian in Mass Hall," recalled Richard Bradley, who wrote a harsh book about the Summers tenure at Harvard. "Here was a guy who had seemed all too anxious to get to Washington and when he got there seemed to internalize the values and priorities of that culture. And brought them back with him, along with chauffeur and press secretary and a chief of staff."

One irony of the controversy over female aptitude involved a woman whom Summers never met, an African American Ph.D. in applied math named Iris Mack. She had earlier raised questions to him about derivatives trading at Harvard Management Company (HMC). A New Orleans native, Mack said she once had aspired to be an astronaut, but she was devastated when her friend and mentor, Ronald McNair, was killed in the 1986 *Challenger* explosion. So Mack went into finance and found work at Enron, where she was also paid to worry about trading risk. She saw a lot of it. Afterward she moved on to HMC—hired once again as a "quant," a math whiz whose task was to help Harvard analyze the mind-boggling complexities of derivatives.

Mack said she was appalled that her male boss, Jeff Larson, didn't understand what he was getting into. She wrote e-mails suggesting the same. After she felt she was being ignored—in one message, Larson told her she was wrong and to watch her "tone"—she decided to write a private letter to Summers. Mack wrote that the HMC's use of derivatives was "frightening . . . much worse than anything I have seen—even at Enron!" In a series of e-mails, Mack asked that the exchange be kept quiet. She said she was worried about being exposed as a whistle-blower—"especially due to the fact that several individuals have been terminated from HMC when they raised concerns about such issues." Summers's chief of staff, Marne Levine, assured Mack that her letter remained "confidential," according to one of the e-mails.

A little over a month later, however, Mack was called into the office of the head of HMC, Jack Meyer. On his desk, she said, were all of her e-mails.

Mack was promptly fired.

(Five years later, the HMC trader about whom Mack had mainly raised questions, Jeff Larson, lost $350 million of the university's money when his hedge fund, Sowood Capital Management, became one of the first hedge funds to implode in the subprime disaster. And by 2009 Harvard had lost a huge portion of its endowment.)

For Summers, the women-in-science controversy didn't go away. On March 15, 2005, the Harvard faculty of Arts and Sciences passed 218 to 185 a motion of "lack of confidence" in the leadership of Summers, with 18 abstentions. A second motion that offered a milder censure of the president passed 253 to 137, also with 18 abstentions. The end for Summers came after yet another huge scandal erupted involving Summers's former protégé, Andrei Shleifer, who was found liable by a federal court in 2004 for conspiracy to defraud the U.S. government while leading a Harvard economic reform program in Russia in the 1990s. Shleifer allegedly had invested in Russia at a time when he was the State Department's contracted adviser. Federal prosecutors charged that Shleifer and his wife, hedge fund manager Nancy Zimmerman, violated State Department conflict-of-interest restrictions by investing in Russia beginning in 1994; the university was later forced to pay $26.5 million to settle the civil case and Shleifer settled for $2 million. Once again, Summers's penchant for personal loyalty to protégés may have done him in (though he later said his personal affection for shleifer had nothing to do with it). At a tumultuous faculty meeting the room buzzed with disbelief as Summers repeatedly said he didn't have enough knowledge of the Shleifer affair to comment on it. It was at that moment, said author Richard Bradley, that Summers lost the university. He resigned. His presidency became the shortest at Harvard since the Civil War. (Oddly enough, bearing out Summers's faith in him, Shleifer himself survived in his job at Harvard and became one of the most cited economists in the world, ranking just after Joe Stiglitz.)

All in all, it was a very dispiriting time for Summers, who perhaps had seen his appointment as a triumphal closing of the circle after he was rejected by Harvard as an undergrad applicant. Even as evidence began to emerge, for example, that perhaps the Washington Consensus didn't have a monopoly on wisdom, Summers exhibited a certain defensiveness about the issue. At a guest lecture he delivered at the business school in early 2002, Summers harshly criticized a paper cowritten by a newly minted Ph.D., Rawi Abdelal, who had gently suggested that Malaysian prime minister Mahathir Mohammad's decision to impose capital controls during the Asian crisis may have been right after all. Some economists had already begun arguing that the tactic had worked—Malaysia's economy was performing well—but Summers trotted out all his old arguments about crony capitalism. Brandishing the Abdelal paper before his audience of MBA students and academic colleagues—now his subordinates—Summers suggested that they didn't know the real world the way he did. "In my experience, capital controls don't work," Summers said. "They're always a bad idea." (Abdelal later commented to me: "It was a little annoying in the sense that we were trying to have a Socratic dialogue. This was a Harvard Business School case study, which is supposed to present both sides. It's not like there's science and truth all on the side.")

Summers's career had taken a sour turn. But there were two things he could be sure of. His tenure in Washington. His economy. "Whenever

Summers is asked, what are you most proud of, he says it's the period that contributed to sustained economic growth," said an old associate.

He was an ex–Treasury secretary and member of the Committee to Save the World. No one could take that away from him.

Out at Jackson Hole, Summers was in the audience as Rubin harked back to the glory days. Speaking to a rapt crowd of Greenspan fans, Rubin remembered his abrupt baptism of fire as Treasury secretary when, even before he'd been confirmed, the Mexican peso crisis had engulfed them all. "Alan, with his experience and standing, easily could have taken a preemptive attitude toward the new boy on the block," Rubin said. Instead, they dealt with the crisis as equals and partners. Later Greenspan came up to the stage for a discussion at the luncheon, and the two men genially needled each other, knowing they both occupied a special place in the pantheon of American financial heroes. When a reporter, Greg Ip of the *Wall Street Journal*, mischievously asked Rubin about Greenspan's defense of the Bush administration's 2001 tax cuts— which Rubin had opposed in a *New York Times* op-ed—Rubin, ever the gentleman, swept aside any notion of continuing discord. Greenspan had been "terrific" on fiscal soundness, and his endorsement of the tax cuts was actually very nuanced and qualified, Rubin said.

"What do you think, Alan?" Rubin asked.

"When's the last time I ever disagreed with you?" Greenspan replied.

"You disagreed with me on financial modernization," Rubin shot back, "and then you waited until I left town, which was not the most gracious thing to do."

The crowd loved it—they knew the disagreement had been minor, a matter of regulatory turf. This wasn't a clash of titans; it was more a tender tweaking between titans.

Even some of those who had been dissidents during the 1990s joined in the celebration of Greenspaniana. Among them was Princeton's Alan Blinder, who had left the Fed—and Washington—in 1996 when he realized that he would never have much say at the Fed under the one-man show that was Greenspan. Blinder and a Princeton colleague delivered a paper graciously extolling the chairman's historic recognition of productivity growth, which many other economists had missed and which contributed to a very effective monetary policy. Beyond that the "Greenspan era" had been "amazingly successful," Blinder wrote, through "wars in Iraq in both 1990 and 2003, a rolling worldwide financial crisis from 1997 to 1998, the biggest financial bubble in history [he meant the dot-com bubble], an amazing turnaround in productivity growth after 1995, and a deflation scare in 2003." Greenspan was certainly not perfect, Blinder conceded, but after all even Babe Ruth used to strike out. "The financial markets now view Chairman Greenspan's infallibility more or less as the Chinese once viewed Chairman Mao's," Blinder wrote. It seemed a backhanded compliment: even the Chinese no longer thought of Mao as infallible. "What will Greenspan's successor find when he opens the proverbial desk drawer?" Blinder asked.

Amid the congratulations, Greenspan himself played his customary role as the lugubrious doubter—especially when it came to the prospects for the housing market. The old man was, as always, even in his final hours in office, worrying the data, picking them apart. And he had begun to rethink his assessment of the housing market from a year earlier. Perhaps it was not so sound after all, he said. What he had no doubts about was the system. "Nearer term, the housing boom will inevitably simmer down," he said. "As part of that process, house turnover will decline from currently historic levels, while home price increases will slow and prices could even decrease. As a consequence, home equity extraction will ease and with it some of the strength in personal consumption expenditures. The estimates of how much differ widely." His admirers didn't make much of his newfound gloom, which seemed calculated to cover himself if a downturn followed his planned departure from the Fed in early 2006. The downturn would come, of course; that was the nature of capitalism. But if it came, it could be handled.

There was one very sour note, however. At a forum on the last day, Raghuram G. Rajan, the chief economist of the International Monetary Fund, presented a paper on possible dangers ahead. Rajan was an Indian-born microeconomist who studied emerging markets, like Stiglitz, and he knew that what America's economic elites had derided as the foibles of those markets was closer to home than they realized. Still, he'd been considered a safe choice when the Kansas City authorities asked him to assess financial development during the Greenspan era. After all, Rajan was "a member of the fraternity," as he later said. He was a University of Chicago man, and he had cowritten a book that many free marketers loved. It was called *Saving Capitalism from the Capitalists*, and argued that the biggest problem in the global economy wasn't free markets but businessmen who tried to manipulate and rig them. "Capitalism's biggest political enemies," Rajan and his coauthor wrote, were "the executives in pin-striped suits extolling the virtues of competitive markets with every breath while attempting to extinguish them with every action." The book praised the move away from excessive regulation over time toward a more liberal trade. It was Rajan who had done some of the key work Greenspan liked to cite in arguing that Glass-Steagall was unnecessary, who had showed that in fact the banks hadn't abused their relationship with their securities underwriting subsidiaries in the period leading up to the Depression.

Rajan had gone into the Jackson Hole project thinking he would write one of those papers about "the wonders of financial innovation over time." After all, the IMF by this time had fully bought into the idea. "There is a growing recognition that the dispersion of credit risks to a broader and more diverse group of investors . . . has helped make the banking and wider financial system more resilient," the fund's much-noted Global Financial Stability Review would conclude in 2006. Rajan had also expected to extol the U.S. banking system—and the global financial system emanating from it.

But as he began looking at the data, he "started getting worried," he said.

Rajan grew especially uneasy when he began examining the IMF's data on risk ratios for the banks. Banks were supposed to be the calm brains at the center of the financial system; securitization of risk was fine as long as the banks could come in and supply liquidity and rescue things if the markets went bad. That's what had happened during the Long-Term Capital Management crisis. The commercial paper market had died, but "people ran to the banks and the banks could then lend to the guys that were hurting, the industrial firms, the investment banks," Rajan said. And if in fact the banks were getting rid of risk now by selling it off to investors around the world, then the banks should be getting safer.

But when Rajan looked at the latest data on "distance to default" for the banks—a standard measure based on the volatility of their assets—he saw those risks had gone up, not down. Something was very wrong. How could that be, if the risk was getting laid off on the rest of the

world? The data showing that banks were getting riskier at the same time
as they were fobbing off all this risk to others could mean only one thing:
the system as a whole was getting riskier. Two plus two had to equal four.
And that led to another conclusion: "If banks are in fact taking on all
these risks," Rajan said, "what happens if the system has a problem, are
people going to run to banks? And if they can't lend it out, if they freeze,
the whole system freezes."

Why were the banks behaving this way? Rajan told the audience—among those listening was Greenspan himself—that he'd found
evidence of a lot of disturbing "perverse behavior" suggesting that
banks and other financial firms weren't always looking out for their
best interests in the kinds of assets they were taking on. He didn't fully
understand right away that the trend had a great deal to do with the
fact that banks were no longer just banks and that traditional banking
values were in eclipse; that banks were now giant finance conglomerates, and many bank holding companies had bought up and absorbed
the major nonbank lenders—part of the shadow banking system, in
other words—that were engaged in the shabbiest practices. Citigroup,
for example, had purchased Associates First Capital in 2002 for $31 bil-
lion, even though both the Justice Department and the Federal Trade
Commission were investigating the company for abusive lending practices at the time. But Rajan did realize that the data he was seeing fit
in with some of the stories he had been reading in the papers about
companies that had edged their way into what used to be banking—the
enormous business that AIG, for example, was doing in credit default
swaps. And he knew that because of the compensation structure of
the financial system, bankers and investment managers had incentives
to take risks that were concealed from investors. If they concealed the
real risks and got high returns, they looked smart next to their rivals at
some other fund. And the easiest risks to conceal were the so-called
tail risks—in other words, the risks that were by far the least likely to
occur—those of catastrophic system failure. That's what AIG's financial
products group in London was doing.

Another form of perverse behavior that he saw a lot of, Rajan said,
was "the incentive to herd" with other investment managers for fear of
being seen to be underperforming. And herd behavior can "move asset
prices away from fundamentals." Both forms of perversity can reinforce each other during an asset bubble, he said. At the height of the

mania, investment managers are more willing to shrug off the low proba-
bility that asset prices will "revert to fundamentals abruptly"—plummet,
in other words. At the same time the knowledge that all the other managers are herding around the same risks "gives them comfort that they
will not underperform significantly if boom turns to bust," Rajan said.
He added that "an environment of low interest rates" is particularly worrisome as the search for higher yields goes on.

Though couched in gentle language, it was an implicit indictment
of much of the hands-off approach to finance during the Greenspan
years—and a stunningly clear warning of the disaster that lay just over
the horizon. Rajan was questioning the rationality of markets and the
giant institutions that ruled them. He was questioning the decisions of
an entire era, from the early push to open up markets to "hot" capital
flows, to the cumulative impact of avoiding regulation of any of the new
derivatives instruments, to the growth of financial conglomerates that
had long since left their Fed and OTC and OCC regulators behind.
Rajan was telling his audience, in effect, that they might not be special—
that the financial ailments of emerging markets, which the Committee to
Save the World had handled so smoothly, might be cropping up on their
own home turf. "The usual story was that emerging markets have had
these big problems over the last few years because of horrible infrastructure, horrible regulation, not enough disclosure," Rajan recalled later
on. But that couldn't be true of the developed world, and certainly not
the United States. It had "checks and balances" that made it immune
to the lunacy of the boom. No one seemed to understand, yet, just what
a hollow thing the "checks and balances"—the regulatory structure—
had become in an era when mistrust of government ensured that every
policy decision would come down on the side of less rather than more
supervision.

The reaction of the crowd was, for the most part, muted. They were
all scholars, after all. But Rajan saw it in the stiffened body language and
averted eyes after the session, as he approached longtime acquaintances.
There was a certain wounded defensiveness, especially with Greenspan
right there. "People understood some of these patterns and could see it,
and they were hoping it didn't amount to anything bad," he said. "It was
hard to reverse even then what was going on in the housing market. And
at that point it was probably easier to play ostrich." Certainly, he wasn't
the only one who saw signs of a real estate bubble. But in keeping with

the Greenspan view of these things, there was a casual sense that when this one burst they, the central bankers, would be able to fix it just as they had done after the dot-com bubble.

Now Rajan was saying, don't be so sure. "I had rained on the parade," he said. "Obviously people were upset with that."

Well, there was upset, and then there was *really* upset. During the usual discussion period, Donald Kohn, Greenspan's loyal vice chairman, was polite. Kohn genteelly rejected Rajan's critique by sketching out the "Greenspan doctrine." On balance, the "changing financial technology, such as the growing ease of housing equity extraction," he said, improved the stability of the system. "By allowing institutions to diversify risk . . . and to improve the management of the risks they do take on, they have made institutions more robust," he said. All in all they've made the financial system "more resilient and flexible—better able to absorb shocks." Of course, Kohn said, markets don't always "get it right." Greenspan didn't quite believe that either. "However, the actions of private parties to protect themselves—what Chairman Greenspan has called private regulation—are generally quite effective."

The real Greenspan doctrine was the idea that the market was made up of very smart people, with reputations and wealth to protect. They're not going to blow it. Their self-interest wouldn't allow it. They can take care of themselves. Regulators were guys who hadn't gone to the best colleges or graduated high in their class; they were always going to be two steps behind. They were going to do more damage than good. The "fallacy," said Rajan, was that because of the herding problems and distorted incentives he had pointed out, "very smart people can do pretty crazy things."

To be sure, he didn't think the worst would happen. "What I wanted to do was to say that even sophisticated systems can be fragile. I was trying to say we need more clever regulation. What people did not buy at that time was that the system could fail. . . . They did not accept the premise that these smart guys on the Street could actually make these kinds of mistakes."

For some of those present, those who had championed and pushed hard for the current system, Rajan's critique had been too severe. He had attacked the heart of Greenspanism. His apostasy could not be allowed to stand, and Don Kohn had been far too kind. So when the floor was opened for discussion, Larry Summers was the first to stand up. Describing himself as a "repentant Tobin tax advocate," Summers spoke of how much he had learned from Greenspan, and then launched into an attack on Rajan, saying he found "the basic, slightly Luddite premise of this paper to be largely misguided." It was dramatic language for such a decorous forum, and some of those listening started in their seats at the word "Luddite." The old Larry, slash-and-burn Summers, was back in force. He was, in effect, ridiculing Rajan, who Summers seemed to be suggesting wanted to roll back financial innovation and return to Beaver Cleaver banking. Summers pulled out his favorite analogy about progress: comparing the development of finance to transportation systems and jet engines, upgrading it for the ears of his fellow economists. Transportation had moved from a primitive system whereby people provided their own power—they walked—to using tools they owned themselves, like horses. Then they relied on intermediaries, for example stagecoach lines. Over time, the transportation system was centralized into airports and train stations. As a result, accidents when they occurred were much larger and more serious. But the "overwhelmingly positive" thing was that overall substantially fewer people died. Summers allowed that, as in transportation with the FAA, some more regulation might be considered. But he warned that too much of it would do damage to all the positive things happening in finance.

Some who were there, such as Yale economist Robert Shiller, thought it was a fair point that Summers was making. You couldn't hold back innovation. "To some extent I felt sympathetic," Shiller later said. "One thing Summers and I agree on is that financial innovation matters." At the same time Shiller, of all people, appreciated the argument that Rajan was making, since the Yale professor had been sounding warnings about the real estate bubble. And he knew what it meant to go up against the common wisdom.

Shiller was, like many economists, a tad abstracted and not always ready for prime time—but he had been sounding this warning again and again. And to many he became almost as annoying as Stiglitz had been in the 1990s. The year before, Shiller had gone to a conference in Washington with the chief economist at Freddie Mac, who was giving a presentation. Shiller asked him what kind of home price declines he was considering in his calculations. "He said we've considered as much as

13 percent. 'What if it falls more than that?' I said. He said it's never fallen more than that, at least not since the Depression. That was the mode of thinking."

And when Shiller raised his concerns at the New York Fed, he found himself abruptly terminated. "I'd been advising them on monetary policy for fourteen years, until Geithner came and terminated me after one meeting. A young lady called me and said Mr. Geithner wants to rotate the panel. It's important to get new voices." Shiller was replaced by Geithner's old colleague Ted Truman—another former member of the Rubin Treasury and Greenspan Fed—free marketer Robert Barro, and former Federal Reserve economist Catherine Mann.

Rajan himself was stunned by the reaction. He knew the Jackson Hole event was supposed to be a celebration of Greenspan, but he had been happy that he'd been able to come to the conference with something substantial to say. "The thing an academic fears the most is not so much controversy but not having anything useful to say," he recalled. But after Summers attacked him, he said, "I thought I was being accused of the wrong thing. I was being accused of in a sense being a Luddite and wanting to go back. But I wasn't calling for boring banking." Just a little common sense and caution.

To an extent Rajan didn't fully realize, however, he had violated what had become the fundamental rule of the zeitgeist: do not question the financial markets. He had become just another heretic.

In November 2006, Milton Friedman died at age ninety-four, and the *New York Times* asked Summers, of all people, to write an appreciation. It was an appropriate choice, a way of showing how the great economist's influence had extended to all ends of the spectrum. Summers wrote how, when he was growing up in "a family of progressive economists," Friedman was "a devil figure."

"But over time, as I studied economics myself and as the world evolved, I came to have grudging respect and then great admiration for him and for his ideas." He still had issues with Friedman. There were areas like rising inequality and global climate change that "require that the free market be tempered instead of venerated." But today, Summers wrote, it was clear that Friedman was the most dominant figure in modern economics. That was especially true in finance. "At the time Mr. Friedman first proposed flexible exchange rates and open financial markets, it was thought that they would be inherently destabilizing and that governments needed to control the movement of capital across international borders," Summers said. "Today we take it as given that free financial markets shape finance."

After twenty years of free-market fervor, the stage was set. The world of the mid-2000s had become one of overleveraged banks too big to regulate and trillions of dollars' worth of derivatives bets that no one had track of—which in turn were helping to accelerate huge flows of capital coming in from abroad—and a Fed and government regulators who weren't aware or weren't watching. Much of this unleashing of freedom, in the post-9/11 era especially, was being done in the name of national security and the national interest. But most of all it was in the service of an indomitable zeitgeist.

14

Blown Away

I t all came true, of course, what Raghuram Rajan said—though two
more years went by before things began to seriously come apart. And
Rajan had been far too conservative in his worst-case fears. As he
later admitted, he did not come close to seeing how deep the problems
really were. No one did, actually, and Larry Summers, with his artful
analogy to plane crashes and the progress of transportation, was about
as wrong as it is possible for a human being to be—disagreeably so, since
he had insulted Rajan in public about it. The problem wasn't that accidents were now like plane crashes: less frequent but more "spectacular"
than they had been in the days of the horse and buggy. The problem
was that the entire transportation system was about to go up in smoke.
And after two decades in which this system—global finance—had been
allowed to grow and ramify into new exotic realms, with deep interconnections that no one on earth was following, there was really nothing that
anyone could do about what was going to happen.

A few in New York and Washington got a whiff of something coming,
though none could see the size of the conflagration. Among them was
Tim Geithner, who had taken over as president of the New York Federal
Reserve in late 2003. Though Geithner actually owed that job to Robert
Rubin, his old mentor, he had retained something of an immunity to the
pull of Wall Street, and he was blessedly free of intellectual arrogance.
Geithner had been one of the few who had said no to Rubin and to
Citigroup. He was still a government man, a pragmatic policy wonk, and
he opted to go to work instead for the International Monetary Fund in

Washington. There Geithner continued his lifelong habit of competence and caution—and of not tampering with the system too much. When Anne Krueger, the number two person at the fund, proposed a bold plan in 2003 to bring Wall Street and other global banks together with their debtor countries in order to discuss debt relief, Geithner resisted implementing it. He was reflecting both the views of the U.S. government, which resisted the Krueger plan, and Wall Street, observers said. "The financial sector was not going to support it, and Geithner didn't want any part of it. He simply left it to his deputy," said one former IMF official.

Rubin's fondness for his former protégé and the enormous influence he still wielded in the financial world had made all the difference when the job of New York Fed president came open. Rubin pressed Geithner on the search committee—"Who's Geithner?" the head of the committee, Paul Volcker, barked at first—and he got the job. Geithner fit in well at the Fed. Even though he was reluctant to change things too much, behind closed doors, he had never fully bought the adulation of markets. And by 2006 Geithner had become a kind of Corrigan lite. In fact, he consulted with Corrigan on cleaning up payment and settlement systems in the event of default.

At the International Monetary Fund—a pocket of foreign sedition three blocks from the White House—concern had risen for years about America's giant capital imbalances. "The United States was absorbing two-thirds of global savings," said Ken Rogoff, who was then chief economist at the IMF. "By any metric the U.S. was out of the bounds of historical experience." The Bush administration continued to pooh-pooh the trend. It was the same old hubris: if we're borrowing a lot, it must be something that the rest of the world is doing wrong. "The U.S. would say, well, 'We have no policy lever to pull,'" said Rogoff. "We're running big deficits but you don't want us to slow growth. There's nothing we can do that's healthy to stop it."

Over at the Fed a few blocks to the south, Greenspan, the data hound, noticed something peculiar in the numbers. There was a correlation between the rate of mortgage refinancings and the size of the current-account deficit. That meant that vast amounts of money were flowing out of the country to support all that housing borrowing, and it meant that the securitization market making that possible was huge. It was a stark warning sign of just how out of control the mortgage market was, but to do something about it required that Greenspan and the

Bush team worry about the current-account deficit. They didn't. In April 2007, John Lipsky, an American who had recently come from JP Morgan to be deputy managing director of the IMF, gave a speech endorsing Greenspan's view that the current-account deficit would have a "benign" resolution.

Still, there were more and more doubters within the broader financial community. In the spring of 2005, Gerald Corrigan, over at Goldman, suddenly became aware of the extent to which the derivatives market was running out of control. He discovered that the credit default swaps market had developed the habit of selling off or "novating" trades away from the original counterparty to an alternative counterparty without consent. "I was shocked when I realized the extent of this problem," Corrigan recalled. If you were Goldman Sachs and your original counterparty was, say, JP Morgan, and at some point along the course of the swaps contract Goldman or Morgan no longer liked the trade, they would simply sell off to another party willing to take up the swap obligation, like a hedge fund. The original counterparty wouldn't even realize until payment was due that they were no longer dealing with Goldman or JP Morgan but an entirely new third party, a hedge fund they hadn't know anything about. "That is about as bad as it gets," Corrigan said. "It defies the most sacred principle of banking, which is to know your customer, know your counterparty." So Corrigan mounted his hobbyhorse one more time, and in October 2005 he pushed through a new set of rules that forbade passing on or novating trades without the explicit consent of the original counterparty. Some two thousand firms signed on. It was a small victory for transparency, and it would help in a small way later on. But it wasn't enough.

Meanwhile, some of the smarter hedge funds began to divine that the subprime mortgage securitization market was heading for a major fall. In September 2006, at the semiannual conference held by financial journalist James Grant, hedge fund maestro Paul Singer delivered another early warning, calling the subprime market a scam for the ages; and he correctly identified the rating agencies as culprits at the heart of it. Singer—known for his acerbic wit—declared, "Through the ages humans have tried to spin gold from lead. To make silk purses out of sows' ears. To take dung and call it roses. But the time has finally arrived when this has been accomplished. This magical process is about taking risky, crummy, tag-end home mortgage loans made to people, many of whom cannot afford to buy their homes nor service the loans at other than extra-special, temporarily low interest rates, and to create from this dross securities of the highest and purest rating." A number of his fellow hedge fund managers promptly bet on a downturn, but the alarum never spread beyond that elite club.

Singer, though notoriously publicity-shy, was concerned enough that in April 2007 he and Jim Chanos, the hedge fund manager who had alerted journalists to the problems with Enron in 2001, appeared at a meeting of the G7 finance ministers to warn that a systemic financial collapse could occur. Later that year German chancellor Angela Merkel, then head of the G7, had the temerity to propose at a summit that international banks supply authorities with more information about their transactions. She "got her head handed to her by Bush and [then British chancellor] Gordon Brown and Paulson," said Ken Rogoff.

At Moody's Investors Service, the premier rating agency, Ilya Eric Kolchinsky, the managing director of the derivatives group, was also getting very worried. Kolchinsky was another math whiz who'd trained as an aeronautic engineer but went to work for Moody's in 1993 when, like other hard-science types after the Cold War, he couldn't get a job. Toward the end of 2006, he started to see things he didn't like or fully understand. "Things didn't feel right. I couldn't put my finger on it. There were some weird mortgage products like option ARMs. It seemed like people like mortgage brokers no longer had the incentives to do the right thing. I kept asking, 'Is this okay?'" he recalled. "But people who were smarter than me, Ph.D.s, told me not to worry about it." Kolchinsky, however, kept raising concerns about the kinds of ratings Moody's was giving to increasingly dubious bundles of mortgages. In September 2007, after he intervened to stop a rating on a deal that he considered to be badly inflated, Kolchinsky was dismissed from the company's derivatives group.

Sheila Bair, newly installed as head of the Federal Deposit Insurance Corporation in 2006, was getting a bad feeling as well. Upon returning to Washington after a four-year hiatus raising her family in Amherst, Massachusetts, she quickly realized that the problem of predatory lending identified in that 2000 Treasury-HUD report had "gone completely mainstream." She almost immediately became a vocal advocate for tightening up underwriting standards for the banks, but by the time she got up to scale it was already too late. The housing market was deflating and the economy was already going into recession. Even Paul O'Neill, watching from retirement in Pittsburgh, was fretting. In June 2007, he called one of the businessmen he'd gotten to know over the years, Angelo Mozilo of mortgage lender Countrywide, and told him he was really worried.

O'Neill said he was "prepared to make some phone calls. . . . I think we need to get the Treasury and Fed to create a huge liquidity pool, making it available to people like you to call back securitized debt obligations out there, and sort the underlying mortgages into legitimate single-As, double-As, and so on. . . . I'm worried you're going to have to call back these things. Angelo said, 'Can't do it, it's too complicated, Paul.' I said if we don't do something like that, then I think we're going to be in position where all that stuff ends up being valued zero. He said, 'We just can't do it.'"

Even Leo Melamed, Milton Friedman's most passionate supporter in Chicago, was finding that he agreed that derivatives needed to be regulated. Melamed had quietly agreed with Brooksley Born back in the late 1990s. The problem wasn't futures trading on his Chicago Mercantile Exchange; it was utterly unregulated trading off exchange. It was the big Wall Street firms, led by Goldman Sachs, that wanted this and that mainly opposed her. A lot of Melamed's viewpoint had to do with self-interest, of course. The Chicago exchanges were scared that over-the-counter trading in New York would cost them business, which is exactly what was happening. Born wanted only to see derivatives trading done more on exchanges like Melamed's. "Our customers, Goldman Sachs, Merrill, they opposed it," said Melamed. In the end he went along with what his biggest customers wanted. "We were getting enough not to try to rock the boat," Melamed said.

And so for the most part Washington and Wall Street went sailing into the catastrophe.

It began expectedly and innocently, with the slow deflation of the housing bubble. The housing mania had hit its height in 2006. Too many buildings were being constructed, too many of them put on the market. As inventories of unsold homes started to pile up, the prices of houses started to drop. As prices dropped, all those vulnerable and indigent and fraudulent borrowers who had taken part in the great subprime confidence game—they couldn't make payments, but they banked on their ability to refinance on the basis of higher prices—began to default in droves. Treasury data later showed that the default rates on loans issued in 2005, 2006, and early 2007 were much higher than those originated in previous years. That showed how poor the quality of the lending had become as the mania grew for new assets to bundle and as savvy short-selling hedge funds like Magnetar began to play their stealthy game of soliciting and bundling especially bad debt so they could create CDOs that were certain to fail. The spreading stain of defaults led in turn to a slew of bankruptcies of subprime nonbank lenders that had been issuing mortgages to these people indiscriminately.

Still, no one got too excited. For the authorities—Paulson, Bernanke, and Geithner—it looked like just another pricked asset bubble. They'd shown they could handle those, after all. Bernanke continued a line he had been taking since August 2005. "I think it is important to point out that house prices are being supported in very large part by very strong fundamentals," he said. The view still prevailed that prices in the housing market, even if they were falling in some places, weren't set on a national basis.

Many months into 2007 they thought the crisis was manageable, that it was still made up of local or regional "pockets." After all, there was only about $100 billion in subprime loans out there. As late as March 2007, when *BusinessWeek* presciently warned that the troubles in the subprime industry might cause "pain" to spread to "a broad swath of hedge funds, commercial banks and investment banks that buy, sell, repackage and invest in risky subprime loans," Bernanke was still knocking down the idea, insisting that the subprime issue was "likely to be contained." Giving congressional testimony in May, he said he saw only a "limited" impact of subprimes on "the broader housing market."

But the systemic infection that had spread for twenty years while almost no one was watching was just starting to reveal itself. In July 2007, two long-troubled hedge funds at Bear Stearns—both funds called themselves High-Grade—folded as it became clear they had bet heavily and in a highly leveraged way on subprime-backed securities. The collapse sowed doubt as it became clear that the Bear Stearns funds had also invested in a lot of highly rated bonds and CDOs. Why were those defaulting as well? Was there a problem with the ratings? Other forms of credit? Perhaps it wasn't just subprimes after all. The hedge fund managers, Ralph Cioffi and Matthew Tannin, had known how loaded up they were with defaulting debt, but they reassured their customers in conference calls and e-mails. That later became the basis of a criminal indictment against them for securities fraud, but in truth absolutely no one knew what was coming (which later became the heart of Cioffi's and Tannin's successful defense at trial; they were acquitted). The uncertainty spread rapidly.

The watershed day—the day that transformed a deflating housing bubble into an unprecedented systemic crisis—was August 9, 2007. In the early morning hours, when New York was still asleep and many top market players and government officials had headed off for vacation, the French bank BNP Paribas came out with a stunning announcement. It said it would stop investors from withdrawing money from three funds because it could not determine the market for their holdings. "The complete evaporation of liquidity in certain market segments of the U.S. securitization market has made it impossible to value certain assets fairly regardless of their quality or credit rating," the bank said in a statement. All of a sudden everyone seemed to realize at once that the markets were frozen. Nothing was liquid. The system could crash. Panic gripped every trading desk. The European Central Bank meanwhile issued an unusual statement saying it was making a huge flood of new lending available, indicating that no one trusted anyone's holdings any longer.

Back in Washington, initially Bernanke's Fed was befuddled. Anxious investment managers phoned both the European Central Bank and the Fed and realized that not only had the two not been talking to each other but they were pointing fingers at each other as well, each saying the other didn't know what it was doing. The prices of gold and U.S. Treasuries were rising rapidly, indicating a soaring fear of default on everything from asset-backed securities to commercial paper. Even the banks were reluctant to lend to each other. Everyone was abruptly afraid of what everyone else had on their books. A flood of liquidity dried up overnight. "You had a turn that was unimaginable twenty-four hours earlier," Greenspan said.

Gradually, like a landscape emerging from a fog, the hidden interconnections in the system began to reveal themselves. The shadow banks were funded by commercial paper, but now commercial paper was much more expensive to issue. Everyone saw that the real banks were going to have to bail out the shadow banking system, and people thought it would be like it had been so many times in the past, going back to

J. P. Morgan's 1907 rescue. But then it wasn't. For the banks—and stunned authorities—it suddenly felt like they were on the *Titanic* and had discovered that there were only enough lifeboats for a small percentage of the passengers. They had nothing close to the kind of capital they needed to cover the shadow banking system that had grown up almost entirely untended by regulators. At almost every turn the Fed and other regulators were taken by surprise. They had all pretended, for the better part of a generation, that they were getting rid of risk. But all they had done was to hide risk.

Above all, what no one seemed to realize was that for the best and brightest of Washington, these were their own policy choices over two decades coming back to haunt them. The vast profits of Wall Street had been driven by a formula that multiplied lots of complexity—which gave one a high profit margin—with huge amounts of volume. The complexity was made possible by derivatives, and the volume came from giant amounts of leverage. When Rubin, Greenspan, and Summers had ignored the concerns of Cassandras such as Brooksley Born, they set in motion the first part of the profit equation, the OTC derivatives explosion. When Hank Paulson led his fellow CEOs to demand more leverage, he made possible the second part of the equation, the multiplying of debt.

Now a generation's worth of profound misconceptions and all the policy errors that followed were coming home to roost at once. So was the misguided idea of "post-plumbing" central banking and regulation, the increasing reliance on the good sense of the bankers and financial firms that so characterized the Greenspan era. Starting with the failure of Bear Stearns, the problem many banks were having was a lack of liquidity as the market froze up; if they'd had the capital reserves they needed to tide them through the crunch, they might survive. But again, the regulatory art of Jerry Corrigan had been lost. The regulators realized they knew very little about the inner workings of the CDO and asset-backed commercial paper market, or the shadowy links between all these players. It was a free-for-all. And it was far too late for anyone to catch up.

An unfolding crisis is marked by nothing so much as denial, great amounts of it. The beginning of 2008 began the long process by which investors kept fleeing to safer ground. A constantly receding—and eroding—wall of denial was put up against the rising tide of defaulting mortgages—and the derivatives trades that, to an extent no one realized yet, tied everyone together. The great confidence game of passing on securities to the next guy was grinding to a halt and beginning to collapse on itself. As credit tightened, interest rates rose, making it all the harder to meet those adjustable rate mortgages. More defaults occurred. Countrywide, the mortgage lender, announced on August 15 that defaults in its subprime loan portfolio had risen dramatically, and it had a huge backlog of unsold mortgages because the securities market had stalled. That created another downward spiral, causing more defaults.

No one realized yet—and it would be quite a while before they did—that there really was no safer, higher ground.

There was a lull, as the Fed and other central banks responded. Now the hunting down of the weak began, again fed by the uncertainty of what everyone had on their books. It was a little like the Asian crisis or the Tequila Effect; just as the electronic herd of investors had gone after the next weakest economy then, now the ectoplasmic monster, that pool of hot capital, went after the next most vulnerable bank. Bear Stearns was something of a pariah on the Street, having refused to participate in the rescue of Long-Term Capital Management in 1998. That reputation, combined with fears that the firm was overloaded in CDOs, ensured that Bear would continue to be treated like a leper on the Street. Its stock steadily dropped, helped by short sellers, and the amount of capital Bear had flushed over into saving the hedge funds finally took its toll in March 2008. Bear CEO Alan Schwartz phoned Jamie Dimon, the head of JP MorganChase, and told him they were a few days from failure. Dimon was queasy about the amount Bear had in mortgages, so Hank Paulson kicked in with a guarantee after consultations with Black Rock, one of the superexclusive Wall Street investment advisory firms he used as a sounding board.

Here was where the true meaning of the crisis began to be apparent. Why couldn't Bear Stearns fail? So many other great investment banks had failed in the past, made a big mess, but the system went on. Dillon Read. Drexel Burnham Lambert. Barings. Bear was, like them, a medium-size investment bank. The government scurried to force Bear into a shotgun marriage with JP Morgan, and after Morgan absorbed the failing firm at a startlingly cheap $10 a share, Geithner finally explained why he had been so concerned. In testimony before the

Senate a few weeks later, he essentially acknowledged it was all because of derivatives—specifically Bear's counterparties in those trades. Had they decided the trades with Bear were no longer safe, they would have rushed to liquidate the collateral they held against those positions, triggering another wave of selling. Because of the explosion in derivatives and the linkups through securitization, firms that might have been permitted to disappear in another era, as recently as Barings had, became hooked inextricably into the new, derivatives-linked matrix of global finance. The lifting of Glass-Steagall had allowed all of them to get into the business together, with no firewalls that meant anything any longer; and derivatives had supplied the gasoline. A nearly free capital market had created its own antithesis. Firms that were created by and thrived on this free market no longer had to play by free-market rules. Every firm had a plethora of other firms dependent on its health, posing a devastating systemic risk.

Citigroup owned seven nonbanks that had taken enormous amounts of supersenior debt on their own books, and the risk models weren't working at all. And then another unforeseen pitfall of the Glass-Steagall repeal emerged. As the subprime market began to falter in 2006 and 2007, the banks had begun to buy up the asset-backed securities deals that their investment banking arms could no longer sell to the world. They were hidden off the books, but they were owned by the banks nonetheless.

Soon it began to emerge that almost every Wall Street firm and bank had its dark secret rooted in the shadow banking system. They all had some obscure time bomb ticking in an off-balance-sheet closet at the heart of the building, one that few executives at the top seemed to know about or even understand until it was too late. For Bear Stearns it was those two hedge funds and their mortgage trades. For AIG it was credit default swaps. At Citigroup, which absorbed the largest losses, it was the near-fatal discovery that it had issued an instrument called a "liquidity put" to many of the purchasers of its supersenior CDOs. A "put" is, again, a hedge against a market downturn. In this case, the put allowed buyers of Citi's supersenior CDOs to sell them back to Citi at original value. It had seemed a safe hedge because of the extreme unlikelihood that the put would be exercised for such safe CDOs. When those puts were exercised in the crash, Citigroup announced billions in losses. CEO Chuck Prince resigned.

No one was more clueless about what was unfolding underneath him than Bob Rubin, the man who had so personified the best and brightest of the post–Cold War world. Rubin later said he didn't even know what a liquidity put was, much less did he monitor them as they were being sold by Citigroup. To him the liquidity put was a mere footnote in a $2.3 trillion balance sheet. And the fact that he didn't know what it was proved the point he consistently made: he had deliberately avoided having any operational control of the kinds of businesses Citigroup was getting into, and he had designed his role that way. So in the ten years he was there, I asked Rubin in the fall of 2008, did he ever recommend specific areas of business to get into, specific financial instruments to the CEO or other execs with line authority? "Never," he said. He then paused, in his usual humble and deliberative way, and added: "Once I did say that I thought the company was underrepresented in the commodities area. I noted that Goldman and JP Morgan had oil trading operations and Citi didn't. I recommended it, certainly discussed it. But even there I wasn't deciding on what the company should do."

He elaborated: "I just wasn't close enough. I can discuss conceptually mortgage-backed securities. But when you get to granularity of today's instruments, I was more than fifteen years away from it." Another deliberative pause. "Actually, I'm probably close to twenty years beyond which I had a granular knowledge [of financial details]." Rubin admitted things had gone way beyond what he remembered. Way back in 1984, he had hired Fischer Black. But that was only one of many trends he had set in motion without fully understanding their consequences. It was amazing how much Rubin had helped to orchestrate. The opening up of capital. The repeal of Glass-Steagall and the gradual takeover of traditional banking by investment banking and then the trading mind-set. The quant revolution. The use of stock options as pay. All had now reached a flood tide underneath him at Citigroup. "What a lot of people thought was that the valuations had gotten excessive, but virtually nobody saw the kind of perfect storm that developed," he said.

For those whose reputations and credibility would be shattered by the catastrophe, the way to hold on to some shred of dignity was to call it a "perfect storm," as Rubin did, or a "hundred-year storm," as Greenspan later described it. No one could have predicted it, in other words. That became everybody's favorite rhetorical conceit. But for all of these former lions of finance, this was just a way of masking their ignorance.

During the Great Depression, the failure of regulators had been largely ideological. It wasn't that they didn't understand the 1929 market crash, the nature of it; it was that they believed the market should work itself out. This was different. Yes, there was the ideological resistance to government intervention, especially from the White House. But what was more important, those in government simply didn't comprehend the system they had created. Hank Paulson, Ben Bernanke, and Tim Geithner, the three men in charge of stanching the panic, had failed to see that through decades of encouraging U.S. financial firms to become as big and active as possible, these firms had become unfathomably big and active. Bernanke tried all the old tools—he lowered interest rates several times, and opened up a discount window to banks. He tried some innovations too, offering banks loans on their failing CDOs. None of these significant efforts would be big enough.

But Paulson was mainly the man of the hour: the master deal maker needed to push the stronger banks to buy the weaker ones. To Paulson, the solution to any economic problem was to turn it over to the geniuses on Wall Street, even when the problem was the geniuses on Wall Street. Paulson was, again, a transactions guy. You do one transaction and then you move on to the next one. That's what dominated the early stages of the crisis. There was no strategic overlay. Through it all he was just reacting. Geithner, by contrast, was starting to think systemically: after Bear, the New York Fed proposed something called a Consolidated Asset Management Trust, which would dispose of bad assets in an orderly way. The economy might be in trouble, homeowners stuck on a sinking ship, but the only solution they could see was getting financial firms back in the black by having the government absorb their losses.

By the time Paulson got around to thinking about it, it was too late. Fannie Mae and Freddie Mac were toppling around him. Asset values had already tumbled too far.

The entire financial system was now infected. As even the nation's most prestigious banks revealed their losses on assets once thought to be safe, investors grew more scared, which caused the market value of the assets to plummet further. Still, there was another lull after the Bear collapse, as banks stopped lending and shored up their capital.

Paulson loved to quote Warren Buffett's line: "When the tide goes out you can see who's swimming naked." Paulson understood, as well as anyone, that Lehman was the next most naked bank. Paulson knew its CEO, Richard Fuld, quite well, knew he was a wild man with "nine lives." When Lehman started to collapse, everyone talked about how sad it was to see, but also how predictable. Fuld had risked the firm before, so many times that Paulson, then at Goldman, and other more conservative Wall Street CEOs were often aghast at the trades he made. Back when Mexico was bailed out, Lehman had been deep into buying Mexican Tesobonos (Treasury bonds), funding it with commercial paper and they hadn't hedged it. Fuld had survived that. In 1998, Lehman was again on the brink because they were relying on commercial paper and they couldn't roll it over, but they seemed to always be able to pull through.

Now Fuld was in denial about his firm's true condition, Paulson saw. All through the spring the Treasury secretary practically held Dick Fuld's hand, talking with him regularly on the phone. The conversations escalated from urging Fuld to merely raise more capital, to urging him to raise capital with "strategic" (minority) buyers, to pleading with Fuld to find an outright buyer after Lehman announced a disastrous $3 billion third-quarter loss in June. Paulson knew that the firm's fourth-quarter earnings, which would come out in mid-September, would be at least as bad. Fuld wasn't easy to persuade, constantly demanding too-generous terms every time he sought a buyer. When he raised equity, he wanted it to be a premium. When he converted stock, he wanted the price to be too high. When he talked with buyers, he was also asking for too steep a price.

By the summer of 2008, Paulson knew Lehman's balance sheet was so grievously under water that he didn't think anyone would come forward to buy it.

During the summer, there was another lull, a kind of sitzkrieg. At the Jackson Hole conference in late August, the economists gathered at the home of former World Bank president Jim Wolfensohn. Many expressed hopes things had abated. But unknown to most of them, a new wave of disaster was already hitting Washington. Paulson had come back from a trip to China in mid-August to find that, to his astonishment, Fannie Mae and Freddie Mac also had giant holes in their balance sheets. He and his team, aware that Lehman's fourth-quarter earnings were going to be coming out and they were going to be grim, announced on Sunday, September 7, that they were seizing control of Fannie and Freddie. There was much praise for the move, except on the Right, where the criticism of government intervention targeted Paulson in particular.

But that weekend was nothing compared to the following one. The final run on Lehman had begun, and investors were not assuaged by the Fannie and Freddie bailout. Paulson, Bernanke, and Geithner decided to divide up responsibilities. Paulson made another run at Fuld, trying to force him together with Ken Lewis of Bank of America. No go: Lewis couldn't believe the size of the hole in Lehman's balance sheet and went after Merrill Lynch instead.

At the same time, Paulson was getting calls from AIG, the insurance giant, which was telling him it was short $15 billion. Washington Mutual was on the edge of failure. The European governments were continuing to shovel out bailouts. Paulson, Bernanke, and Geithner were desperately trying to put their fingers in a dike that was simultaneously springing numerous new leaks. There were vastly more leaks now than they had fingers.

On the weekend of September 13 they holed up at the New York Fed, with Bernanke conferenced in from Washington and another Fed governor, Kevin Warsh, acting as his proxy. There was no posh paneled boardroom, the kind of place that J. P. Morgan and his fellow plutocrats might have gathered in back in 1907. The great command center of the rescue effort was, literally, the "attic" of the Fed—on the thirteenth floor, interestingly enough. The building was going through a two-year asbestos removal, so Paulson, Geithner, Warsh, and staffers found themselves stuck all weekend in a makeshift conference room. "The furnishings were like a Ramada Inn in Toledo. They had those square carpet tiles that lift up when you walk on them," one participant said. All the banking CEOs were kept milling about downstairs in the large boardroom on the bank's main floor, the area that is open to public touring, and every now and then an emissary would be sent down to them. The food was as squalid as the surroundings, he said—"hot, steamy and disgusting." Sometimes catered, sometimes from the Fed's kitchen, it was a smorgasbord served in large metal trays reminiscent of "one of those Korean deli buffets, with the sternos under them."

Every two hours Warsh would run down to another conference room and give the waiting Bernanke an update, along with Fed vice chairman

Don Kohn and Scott Alvarez, the Fed's general counsel. Many of them were aware that it would be a consequential weekend, no matter the outcome. "Lehman changed the business of banking coming out of that weekend," said one participant. "It was different from what happened with Bear Stearns. Bear Stearns was a basket case but it wasn't seen as a business model question. It was just a bad apple. But during the ten days going into the Lehman weekend, it became increasingly clear that the business model [investment banking] and balance sheet problems were endemic. These institutions were chronically overleveraged for this environment. They didn't have the liquidity they needed."

But of course it was more than a mere "business model" problem. The regulators and CEOs gathered at the Fed building that weekend were, in the end, bearing witness to a failed idea, though it would be a long time before that was clear to anyone.

A final attempt at getting a Lehman buyer failed. The problem that Paulson, Bernanke, and Geithner faced was that only traditional banks, under the old federal laws, could be simply taken over by the government; there was no law that lets the federal government do the same with investment banks. There was only a provision in the Federal Reserve Act, Section 13.3, which allowed "lending with collateral to the satisfaction of the Federal Reserve Bank" under "unusual and exigent circumstances." Both Paulson and Bernanke later said that no one, including the Fed Board (which would have to approve such a loan), could have honestly concluded that such "collateral" existed in Lehman's case, not with a $50 billion hole in its side. What assets Lehman owned, in other words, were drowned in its liabilities.

In the hours preceding that weekend, they were each increasingly uncomfortable they were not going to have any buyers. Friday night, there were still hopes that Bank of America wanted it, despite Ken Lewis's dithering and his well-known interest in Merrill. "By Saturday morning, sitting in Tim's office, Hank and I both had the same view: 'You know what, it looks like they [Bank of America] could flake out on us.' And they did," said the participant. It wasn't a well-kept secret that Lewis had coveted Merrill for years. And so late on Saturday, when it was clear that Merrill too was going to sink no matter what happened with Lehman—that if Lehman were bailed out, Merrill would be he next target of sellers—Paulson took Merrill's CEO John Thain aside and told him he'd better try to sell his company to Lewis.

But Britain's Barclays had expressed strong interest in Lehman. There were different "workstreams" going on at the same time, with a separate group of lawyers working on bankruptcy. No one got much sleep, with the CEOs going back to their homes in Greenwich or Bridgeport, and Geithner and Paulson to their hotels. When Barclays suddenly expressed interest on Saturday, the CEOs were called in again. "We would get updates during Saturday, that the hat was being passed," the participant said. "The central issue was not could we raise all of the money we needed down there, because we could with a little regulatory persuasion, I'll tell you. It was how much would be needed. They could all afford a fixed amount check, but not a variable check. They could handle X billion, but it might be 5X, and they needed certainty. One said, we can afford this, but not an open-ended commitment. . . . On Sunday morning, they said okay, we're there [pitching in for Barclays]. But Hank, he's not coy. He would give them real-time updates during the weekend of the status of the talks—more so than I would have thought prudent. He said to all these guys, in real time, 'There is no buyer.' They were disappointed. They knew if they could just write a couple billion dollar check to make the problem go away they would have."

Paulson himself helped create the image that lingered out of that fateful weekend—that he simply was not going to do another bailout, not after he'd caught flack from the right about Fannie and Freddie. At a tense news conference after Lehman went down, he infamously declared that he "never once considered that it was appropriate to put taxpayer money on the line in resolving Lehman Brothers." But others say that attitude was just a tactic to get the scared bankers to come together and save Lehman themselves, knowing they would be each rocked by the market fallout if they didn't. "Yes, Hank had gone on record going in, saying, 'We did the last one, you the private sector are going to have to do this one.' But he was doing that totally for negotiating purposes. If there was a hole after [a bid came in, like the $29 billion JP MorganChase asked them to fill for Bear] we passed the hat downstairs [to the big banks gathered there] we would fill the hole." According to another source at the Fed, "He didn't want to be explicit about the reason. In that fragile time, the secretary of the Treasury didn't want to say, 'We didn't have the authority [because of Section 13.3].' He didn't want to expose the government's weakness. Better to make it look like it was a matter of principle."

In the end, they heard from Barclays on Sunday morning that they weren't getting the British regulator, the Financial Services Authority, to go forward with it. So Cox and Geithner called the FSA. The British authorities weren't going to say no, they weren't going to disapprove it. They just weren't going to approve it either. Paulson had received a warning call on Friday also from the finance minister, the chancellor of the exchequer, Alistair Darling, basically putting up flags. "To be totally blunt, they [Barclays] wanted to do it the whole time and the government wouldn't let them," said the Fed official. "I remember Hank coming back and telling Tim and me that Darling had said to him, 'We're not importing your cancer.'"

Coming from the only other nation that had championed fully free financial markets, it was a devastating pronouncement. Wall Street, with Washington's proud encouragement, had spent a generation humiliating and besting Britain's finest merchant banks, such as Barings. Now a quarantine was being placed around the Street—and the American system.

So that was it: Lehman was going down. Geithner, with graveyard humor, cracked that they all needed to "lay foam on the runway" for the crash. The fall of Lehman, Joe Stiglitz would later write, was to market fundamentalism what the fall of the Berlin Wall was to communism.

But there was literally no time to pause and take stock of this epochal event, for once again the crisis took a dramatic turn that no one had predicted. On Monday, September 15, after Lehman filed for bankruptcy, the $62 billion Reserve Primary Fund, a money market mutual fund, became the first in decades to "break the buck" because of its investment in Lehman's short-term debt securities. Money market funds specialize in high-quality, liquid debt securities, and they aim to at the very least never lose money, keeping their net asset value at $1 a share. The near failure of the Reserve Primary Fund represented the moment of maximum panic in the markets. If all the money markets started suffering redemptions, then the money markets would have called in their trillions in loans to the banking and nonbank sector. To an extent much greater than the government realized, the money markets had been buying the commercial paper of major corporations. Suddenly, Fortune 500 executives were calling the Treasury Department to say they faced imminent liquidity problems.

The failure of a few big banks got all the attention, but corporations facing liquidity problems were the real crisis. The next forty-eight hours could easily have led to a total financial breakdown and almost certainly a depression.

It almost happened. On Thursday, September 18, institutional money managers sought to redeem another $500 billion. Paulson intervened directly with these managers to dissuade them from demanding redemptions. Nevertheless, investors took out another $105 billion.

On Friday, Paulson announced a temporary program through which the Treasury would use the $50 billion in the Exchange Stabilization Fund to protect investors in money market mutual funds from any losses should their fund break the buck during the next year. Bernanke, meanwhile, announced that the Fed would expand its emergency lending efforts to allow commercial banks to finance purchases of asset-backed paper from money market funds. That also helped the funds to meet demands for redemptions. Both these moves seemed to quiet the panic, at least in the money market funds. No others broke the buck in the end.

But then AIG came crashing down. It turned out that the obscure London-based financial products division of the giant insurance company, making ingenious use of the parent's golden AAA-rating, had sold $500 billion worth of credit default swaps around the world without anyone knowing (certainly not the tiny and ineffectual Office of Thrift Supervision, which AIG had opted to go to as a regulator after the insurance company bought a small S&L). All of sudden AIG needed $85 billion in bailouts to pay off its counterparties—the same big banks that were sinking because of their own trades with others. The market started to tank again. Soon this biblical-size flood left but a single island of investment in a sea of red: Treasury bills. By late autumn they had become so sought after—even considering questions of U.S. solvency— that there was talk of a T-bill bubble. Treasury rates on three-month bills actually went negative—in other words, investors were paying the government to invest in them—for a period.

Ben Bernanke, more than anyone, now saw how deeply the system had been infected. Finally, he knew what needed to be done. That same week he decided he'd had enough of the ad hoc responses they'd been pulling together for a year. He called Paulson and told him they had to get more systematic about their approach. It took a while for Paulson, with his deal-making mentality and his long decades of Wall Street thinking, to understand that the problem was the financial system itself. Earlier in the fall, Paulson had turned down a proposal by Berkshire

Hathaway's Warren Buffett, PIMCO's Bill Gross, and Goldman Sachs's Lloyd Blankfein to set up a method for buying toxic assets. ("We had to put the fire out first," Paulson's former spokeswoman, Michele Davis, told me later, adding that there was also a question of how the participation of major private investors would be received by the public at that early juncture.)

For Bernanke, by contrast, it was as if his life had been leading up to this moment.

Ben Bernanke, like Joe Stiglitz, had emerged from humble circumstances that had given him a taste of how the nonelite America lives, and how finance connects up with the real economy. As a boy in Dillon, South Carolina, he had hung out at his dad's drugstore, waited tables at South of the Border—a roadside attraction on Interstate 95—and played sax in a high school garage band. He'd always had common sense. The similarities between Bernanke and Greenspan were, in fact, fairly superficial. While Greenspan spent his early career at Ayn Rand's side and running a Wall Street consultancy—as a pure market man, in other words—Bernanke made his grade at Princeton as a scholar studying the greatest market failure of modern times: the Great Depression. The main reason for the depth of that crisis, he ultimately concluded in a study that is still famous among economists, was that in the critical three and a half years between the 1929 stock market crash and FDR's New Deal, which began in March 1933, the Hoover administration allowed a third of the nation's banks to go under. Had that not happened—along with the Fed's disastrous decision to keep interest rates high—the Great Depression might have remained a not-so-great recession. "To understand the Great Depression is the Holy Grail of macroeconomics," he had written in the opening sentence of "Essays on the Great Depression."

He had spent a brilliant academic career doing just that, and now, he said, "I was not going to be the Federal Reserve chairman who presided over the second Great Depression. . . . For that reason, I had to hold my nose and stop those firms from failing." Bernanke's work on the Depression, Ken Rogoff later said, was "really important in helping him to think outside the box."

First in small steps, then in giant leaps, Bernanke began to correct the mistakes of the Greenspan era. In July 2008—far too late to make a difference in the subprime scandal—Bernanke announced a new "Regulation Z," which finally created some commonsense lending rules such as forbidding mortgages without sufficient documentation. Now Bernanke began to expand the Fed's lending powers in unprecedented ways. He doubled the Fed's balance sheet—the amount it spends—to $1.6 trillion as he flung open new lending windows to everyone from commercial businesses to other governments across Europe. So fast did Bernanke move that at one point early in the rescue, House Financial Services chairman Representative Barney Frank, an irrepressible wit, told him: "People are referring to you as the Loan Arranger, with your faithful companion Hank."

Now it was Bernanke who moved to take dramatic action after Lehman fell. Bernanke told Paulson they had to go to Congress to get legislative approval for a huge fiscal bailout, according to two sources familiar with the conversation who would describe it only on condition of anonymity. Paulson agreed. Afterward, the two differed on the focus of the $700 billion plan. Bernanke all along wanted a direct capital injection into the banks—the financial equivalent of an adrenaline shot to a stopped heart—as the best way to halt the bank panic. But that would mean partial nationalization, anathema to the free marketers in the White House and Congress. Paulson held out for an alternative scheme to buy up distressed mortgage securities from the banks. The problem: no one could figure out how to price the securities in a way that wouldn't either sink the banks or rob the taxpayers.

To the astonishment of both Bernanke and Paulson, the first version of the bailout plan failed to pass the House on September 29, and the markets took yet another plunge: 778 points, the largest single-day point drop ever. Paulson had asked for virtually unlimited authority to disperse funds to banks—it could not be questioned even in the courts, the language read—and House members found themselves besieged with e-mails demanding defeat. As Paulson scrambled to push for another vote, House Speaker Nancy Pelosi announced that she was getting ready to leave town for the weekend after Lehman's collapse and would be back Monday. Bernanke quietly told her, "We may not have an economy on Monday." After the markets tanked yet again (and Britain injected its own banks with capital, starting the trend), the bailout passed on a second vote on October 3, and Paulson finally endorsed the Bernanke plan for direct capital injections on October 13. Yet even on the day he announced the plan, the Treasury chief continued to proclaim his reluctance to partially nationalize the banks.

The remaining investment banks, Goldman Sachs and Morgan Stanley, swiftly asked to become bank holding companies, meaning the government would guarantee their liabilities as well.

George W. Bush, meanwhile, was confused about what his Treasury secretary was actually doing. Bush had hoped to deliver a series of "legacy speeches" that fall to trumpet eight years' worth of achievements. Among them was a robust economy. Now he simply listened, astonished, as Paulson told him that the government was going to have to intervene in the economy in an unprecedented way. Later on Paulson said that "the president was very engaged. We talked with him regularly. He used me as a wartime general here. He trusted me." But Bush's speechwriter, Matthew Latimer, said that Paulson was sending mixed signals. As Latimer told it, the president didn't seem to understand that Paulson was planning on bailing out the banks by paying more for their toxic securities than they were really worth. "After finally getting the speech draft turned around and sent back to the teleprompter technicians, we trudged back to the Family Theater, where the president rehearsed. In the theater, the president was clearly confused about how the government would buy these securities. He repeated his belief that the government was going to 'buy low and sell high,' and he still didn't understand why we hadn't put that into the speech like he'd asked us to. When it was explained to him that his concept of the bailout proposal wasn't correct, the president was momentarily speechless. He threw up his hands in frustration. 'Why did I sign on to this proposal if I don't understand what it does?' he asked."

Conan O'Brien's joke that fall got some laughs. "George Bush is the only one happy that we're going into a big depression," the comedian cracked. "Now he can check off the tenth and final thing on his bucket list."

Bush went along with it all, of course. "I readily concede that I chucked aside some of my free-market principles when I was told by chief economic advisers that the situation we were facing could be worse than the Great Depression," he said. He never spoke about his free-market principles again.

There was no longer patience or time for ideology, in fact. The global financial system was literally hours or days from collapse. Major governments began to take over their banks as it became clear that the banks did not have anything close to the amount of capital they needed to support the shadow banking world. So searing had been the Lehman experience that no one had any compunction about using the word "bail-out" any longer. On September 29, the British government nationalized Bradford & Bingley, a major lender. The following day the government of Ireland—which during the go-go 1990s had become known as the Emerald Tiger—guaranteed the deposits of all its banks, and Germany, Luxembourg, and Belgium combined to save Dexia. Holland national-ized Fortis Bank Nederland. By October 7, the Royal Bank of Scotland was within hours of collapse; the next day Britain announced it would inject 25 million pounds of capital into its banks, taking direct equity stakes. The fewest changes occurred in Japan, which had already taken control of most of its major banks in the 1990s, and in China, which had refused to open up its banking and financial sector to all those global capital flows. The West, some Chinese officials began archly observing, was no longer much of a model to them.

Paulson, Bernanke, and Geithner ultimately did something similar to what the Europeans had done. On October 14, Paulson gathered the heads of the nine biggest U.S. banks at the Treasury Department and gave them an offer they couldn't—weren't allowed to—refuse. Paulson told them the government was going to use the TARP (Troubled Asset Relief Program) funds to take direct equity stakes in their companies. Richard Kovacevich, the CEO of Wells Fargo, demurred at first. Why should his company sign its freedom (and his compensation) away to the U.S. Treasury when, unlike many other banks, it hadn't overloaded itself with risky mortgage-backed securities? It didn't matter. Paulson wanted all the top nine banks to take the capital injection, so that investors and other bankers making loans wouldn't retaliate against the ones that took the government funds. The strong could not be allowed to stigmatize the weak. It was as close as U.S. policy has ever come to socialism, and it was, in the ultimate irony, the end result of an era of free-market mania. Though the banks were permitted to retain their managers and oversee their own affairs, the injection of government into the bank-ing system on this scale had never happened before in the history of U.S. capitalism, not even during the Depression. Two days later, in a speech to the New York Economic Club, Bernanke gave the real answer to why no one else would be allowed to go under the way Lehman had been. "We have a very big 'too big to fail' problem" now, Bernanke said, involving "too many firms that are systemically critical" to the nation's financial health.

Later on, many on the Right would contend that the real problem was the role of Fannie Mae and Freddie Mac—government, in other words. During the subprime mania, the two government-sponsored entities ended up buying more subprime mortgage-backed securities than any other institution, abetted by the Bush administration, which gave them low-income credits to do so. Fannie and Freddie are government sponsored, but they're run by shareholders looking for a substantial return. It was Wall Street that had driven them and just about everyone else in the world to take risks, but Fannie and Freddie didn't go nearly as far out on a limb as other lenders, and they hadn't actually created derivative products themselves.

Those critics were looking for a way to keep the most ardent capitalists from taking the blame, but in the end, the doomsayers were vindicated. Robert Shiller of Yale and a few others were later credited, deservingly, with perceiving very early how serious the housing bubble was getting. Nouriel Roubini of New York University was justly credited with seeing that the housing crisis would lead to a broader credit crunch. Some economists, such as Ken Rogoff, also saw early on that the mania of the 2000s was just the latest iteration of an unwarranted faith in the ability of financial markets to correct themselves. The implicit faith that the world once placed in the global financial system we were the primary authors of was all but gone. It was, Warren Buffett said, "an economic Pearl Harbor." But it was unlikely that some ultimate victory would come now as it did in World War II.

For others around the world, especially governments in Europe and Asia, there was no small amount of schadenfreude at the comeuppance delivered to Wall Street, though their economies would suffer from it too. The left-leaning Europeans, especially, had warned of the terrible consequences of "letting market forces rip," as France's Socialist prime minister, Lionel Jospin, had declared in the late 1990s, saying it would "spell the end of Western civilization in Europe." Angela Merkel, a centrist, had also tried to stop the tide, and so had others. Such leaders had watched helplessly as their top corporations knuckled under to Wall Street and "Anglo-Saxon" finance; they had watched helplessly as the antiglobalization movement started, and their corporations, hearing the investment bankers' siren song, sought to list on the New York Stock Exchange or the Nasdaq. And now the true price of American hubris had come due. "What the disaster in Iraq did to U.S. prestige in foreign policy, this disaster has done to America's stature in the global economy," said Angel Ubide, a Spanish economist who directed global economics at Tudor Investment Corporation.

It would not be clear until many months afterward just how close the world had come to another great depression. In a speech in Chicago a year later, Christina Romer, the chairwoman of the Council of Economic Advisors, said the blow to public confidence from those harrowing months of 2008 was actually much worse than what happened in 1929. "The collapse in wealth was far more dramatic," Romer said. "All told, household wealth fell 17 percent between December 2007 and December 2008, more than five times the decline in 1929." Yet it would be even longer before people understood how deep the crisis was, how it was a crisis of the entire system, and how the roots stretched back to decisions made in the mid-1990s and beyond, to the early 1980s. Global finance had been allowed to develop and grow unhindered for nearly two decades. The Reagan revolution had at last had its laissez-faire experiment, and it had brought the world to the precipice of a global depression.

Oddly enough, it was left to Christopher Cox, Bush's hapless SEC chairman, to pronounce the final verdict in that grim autumn of 2008: "The last six months have made it abundantly clear that voluntary regulation does not work," he said.

But it was left to the man who had presided longer than anyone else over the free-market revolution, Alan Greenspan, to pronounce the final verdict on the era they had all authored—to deliver what one blogger called his "maestro culpa." At a hearing of the House Committee on Oversight and Government Reform that October, the aging former Fed chief professed his "shocked disbelief" that the nation's greatest banks hadn't protected themselves and their shareholders. "I made a mistake in presuming that the self-interests of organizations, specifically banks and others, were such that they were best capable of protecting their own shareholders and their equity in the firms," Greenspan said. Now, he added, "the whole intellectual edifice has collapsed." The committee chairman, Henry Waxman of California, asked: "You found that your view of the world, your ideology was not right, it was not working?"

"Absolutely, precisely," Greenspan said. "You know, that's precisely the reason I was shocked, because I have been going for forty years or more with very considerable evidence that it was working exceptionally well."

The presidential election of 2008 was exceedingly close until mid-September. That all changed the moment the financial markets took their terrifying tumble, and the investment banks that had dominated Wall Street for a generation disappeared in the wink of a calendar month. "We were three points ahead on September 15 when the stock market crashed. Then the election was over," said Steve Schmidt, chief strategist for the Republican candidate, John McCain, in a postmortem a year later. The U.S. electorate seemed to realize, all at once, that it wasn't just their financial institutions that were going bankrupt. The Republican Party and its ideas about markets were bankrupt as well. McCain's chief economic mentor, after all, had been none other than Phil Gramm—at least until Gramm, blunt-spoken as always, belittled America as a "nation of whiners" in mid-2008. (He was quickly deep-sixed by the McCain campaign.) The voters seemed to have the same realization, in other words, that the Democrats sitting in the audience at Reagan's first budget speech in 1981 had had—the party that had let all this happen no longer had any remedies.

McCain demonstrated that his ideological cupboard was bare in the most embarrassing way: on the day of the Paulson bailout plan, he avoided endorsing it while blasting his Democratic rival for his ties to Fannie Mae and Freddie Mac. A few days later, McCain announced he was suspending his campaign to fly back to Washington to help *pass* the rescue bill, and he called for a postponement of the first presidential debate. Obama wryly responded: "It is going to be part of the president's job to deal with more than one thing at once." Just as abruptly, McCain resumed campaigning—and showed up at the debate. Obama simply kept his counsel and kept on campaigning, making McCain look jittery by comparison. McCain's campaign also tried to game the moment, calling chief of staff Josh Bolten and urging him to stay away from specific proposals, Matthew Latimer later wrote. Instead, McCain wanted Bush to hold an emergency economic summit in Washington, with McCain in attendance. But it fooled no one. Nothing was decided, and Obama left the meeting shaking his head.

Obama's calm in the face of the economic crisis may have tilted some undecided voters his way. But he had no real ideas of his own about the financial markets. During the campaign, he had given a major speech at Cooper Union in New York that called for regulatory reform, but it was mostly a grab bag of nostrums and it didn't shift many votes his way.

Now, however, Bush's crisis was about to become Obama's crisis. It wasn't immediately clear who would become his field general, his Hank Paulson. But a few front-runners began to emerge even before the election. On September 19, 2008, with just a little over a month to go before the election, the candidate convened an emergency meeting of his new brain trust in a small room next to a basketball arena at the University of Miami, Florida. It was a remarkable gathering for a candidate who, during the primaries, had relied largely on an obscure, baby-faced University of Chicago economist named Austan Goolsbee. Now Obama needed big guns and experienced crisis managers. It was all happening too fast. With Obama in the room were Bob Rubin, Larry Summers, and Paul Volcker, as well as Laura Tyson, Clinton's Council of Economic Advisors chair; Gene Sperling, Clinton's national economic adviser; and Dan Tarullo, also a key Clinton go-to man on trade and G8 issues.

Also making his first—and as it turned out his only—appearance as a member of Obama's inner circle was Joe Stiglitz, who was piped in on a conference call with Warren Buffett and Obama's would-be vice president, Joe Biden. The topic at hand: what to make of Paulson's $700 billion rescue plan, which was to be announced later that day. For Obama, it was a comfort to have Summers there especially, briefing brilliantly as always, a participant said. Summers had been there, after all, during the Asian crisis, the peso crisis, and the ruble crisis. "There's a comfort level in having someone able to say, 'This is a little like what we faced ten years ago,'" the participant said. And after Obama won and scrambled to pull together his administration, he wanted advisers who knew what they were doing. There was no time to think too deeply about the ultimate causes of the catastrophe. The only question seemed to be: who would be in charge when the crisis landed in his lap on January 20?

15

Geithner Cleans Up (with Bernanke at His Back)

L arry Summers was a "mess" in the days before President-elect Obama's announcement of his new Treasury secretary in late November, said one friend. He was madly e-mailing around for the latest buzz. Summers had badly wanted the Treasury job again, but "he could feel the shift toward Geithner. He was hearing all the stories about how they'd bonded, Geithner and Obama," said another long-time Summers acquaintance. For the erstwhile MIT wunderkind who had once been so sure of himself, it was a humbling prospect to realize that he might be eclipsed by his former subordinate. Summers had been bitterly disappointed at getting to serve as Treasury secretary for just eighteen months at the end of the Clinton administration; Rubin, because of the Asian crisis and the Lewinsky scandal, had felt obligated to stay on longer than he had planned. After Summers's undistinguished year-and-a-half tenure marked mainly by his support of the Commodity Futures Modernization Act, and then his Harvard debacle, returning to his old job at Treasury would have been a chance for redemption.

For a time, it looked as if Summers might just get the post again. Cerebral and deliberative himself, Obama clearly loved the brilliant-briefer side of Larry, and so Summers quickly moved to the forefront, nudging aside the president-elect's longtime campaign adviser, Austan Goolsbee. Obama proved to be quite ruthless that way; after he had defeated Hillary Clinton for the Democratic nomination, he coldly marginalized the inexperienced advisers who had loyally supported him when he was a mere insurgent against the Hillary juggernaut and hired many of her best and longest-serving advisers. And Obama brilliantly neutralized Hillary by making her secretary of State.

As the Democratic campaign had heated up, Summers had begun to reinvent himself as a market skeptic and a full-blown Keynesian populist. Never mind his high-handed dismissal of Rajan at Jackson Hole, the grand salutes to Alan Greenspan and Milton Friedman. Summers became an old-style Democrat again, and with that combination of political cunning, analytical brilliance, and policy savvy he had become known for, he called out the Bush administration for its errors. "The pendulum will swing—and should swing—toward an enhanced role for government in saving the market system from its excesses and inadequacies," Summers wrote in his much-read column in the *Financial Times*. He pushed for a major deficit spending package. Most astonishing of all, he began to sound like Robert Reich, the populist Labor secretary who had lost every battle in the early Clinton administration. (This was according to the new president himself, who told David Leonhardt of the *New York Times*: "The fact is that Larry Summers right now is very comfortable making arguments, often quite passionately, that Bob Reich used to be making when he was in the Clinton White House.") Ever the master of both sides of an argument, Summers became a Reichian champion of the middle class, forgotten during the Bush years.

"In retrospect, the fact that 40 percent of American corporate profits in 2006 went to the financial sector, and the closely related outcome—a doubling of the share of income going to the top 1 percent of the population—should have been signs something was amiss," Summers wrote.

"I don't know quite what to make of it," Reich himself commented. He and Summers had been discussing macroeconomic issues since the mid-1980s, Reich said, and "frankly he had never been interested in distributional questions." Joe Stiglitz, always eager to point out the errors of his longtime rival, recalled that Summers had supported a cut in capital-gains taxes during the Clinton administration—"the worst possible policy" if one is looking to distribute income more equitably, he said.

Summers was, of course, now grappling with the very problems that Stiglitz had warned of so long before and which he had dismissed at the time. The forgotten middle class had been forgotten long before George W. Bush came along. The Clintonites had simply decided there was nothing to be done about the vicissitudes of global markets—the markets would, in the end, discipline themselves—and they had let the markets rip much as the Reaganites had done. In the process they had forced a middle class that had once been sustained by industrial jobs to maintain its lifestyle in the only way it could: with debt. Now the payment had come due. Average Americans had been induced and encouraged to take on more and more loans, more and more credit card debt, so they could continue to play a role in the world that they, and their country, could no longer afford: consumer of last resort. They had enriched the rising nations, first Japan, then China, with their consumption.

The new president, who was just catching up on a lot of these issues, declared that Summers's ideas on income inequality and boosting the middle class would "be the foundation of all my economic policies." But the would-be new Larry kept getting tarred with memories of the old Larry. He was just too colorful and provocative, as Bob Rubin had warned. All those piquant comments, especially those about women and math, would inevitably come out again at his hearing. Summers had acquired another liability that might hurt him as the backlash against Wall Street mounted: after leaving the Harvard presidency, he had earned $5 million giving strategic advice to D.E. Shaw, a giant hedge fund, and hundreds of thousands of dollars more giving speeches to Wall Street firms. Above all, for a president who had promised change, a Summers Treasury nomination would send the wrong signal that Obama was simply reappointing Clintonites to their old positions. That could prove an embarrassing spectacle at a time when the new administration needed to take command right away. In the end, Obama went with Geithner, who would provide both a fresh face and at the same time, like Bob Gates at Defense, would bring some needed continuity in a time of crisis. Geithner had been part of the autumn rescue team but had managed to come away largely untainted by it.

Summers had to settle for what seemed, at the time, a vague role as head of the old National Economic Council. During the Clinton administration, the NEC post had been only a secondary stepping-stone, so it almost seemed like a demotion at first. But in many ways it was a godsend for Summers. He would quietly consolidate power as Obama's chief economic adviser while Geithner caught all the anger in the early months.

And there was a lot of anger.

The first two months of the new administration were little short of a disaster for Geithner. The straitlaced civil servant was forced to admit within days of Obama's inauguration that he had failed to pay all his taxes. He won confirmation by a vote of 60–34, but it was the closest tally for any Treasury secretary since World War II. That put Geithner—who was publicity-shy even in normal times—at a moral disadvantage when he should have been a dominant voice dictating policy to Washington and Wall Street. "Because of the tax issue, he couldn't come off being too strong-voiced," said a former senior official at the New York Fed who knew Geithner well. "The problem was, by treading softly people said he didn't have the gravitas."

Geithner had always been a staff man, the backroom guy. Suddenly he was the cynosure of every market player and government minister at a time when the abyss was still in sight. But he wasn't ready for prime time. Often relaxed behind the scenes, with an ebullient and sometimes giddy sense of humor, Geithner tightened up in front of the cameras. He was the anti-Rubin, utterly ill at ease when he knew all eyes were on him. In the face of a terrifying global crisis, the boyish-looking Geithner came off as unsophisticated. Though he spoke well, Geithner sometimes slurred his syllables like a teenager rushing through an oral report in class so he could return to his seat. He had an unfortunate tendency to blush noticeably, as he did when someone asked him about *People* magazine's selection of him as one of its "50 Most Beautiful People." And he appeared to be learning to read a teleprompter on the job. Geithner hadn't "played the center ring until now," David Axelrod, Obama's chief strategist, explained sympathetically. "There is a bully pulpit, a theatricality to the role that is unlike any role he's held before." Beyond that, Axelrod told me, "this guy was appointed a general and dropped in the middle of a full-scale war. It takes a little while to get your bearings."

Over the first weeks of the administration, as the markets continued to show no confidence in a revival, the attacks on him grew ever more savage. Bloggers began comparing Geithner to little Macaulay Culkin, joking that he was "home alone" at the undermanned Treasury. The comedian Bill Maher put up photos of Geithner alongside a deer in the headlights and suggested that President Obama ought to just hire the deer. "Quite simply, the Timothy Geithner experience has been a disaster," Representative Connie Mack announced in early March, calling for his resignation "for the good of the country."

It wasn't entirely his fault. Obama himself first set Geithner up for a fall when he raised expectations to absurd levels over the Treasury secretary's February 10 rollout of his plans. Geithner, Obama declared jovially on February 9, would be "terrific" the following day in announcing "some very clear and specific plans for how we are going to start loosening up credit once again." He wasn't terrific. He was terrible. Once again, he looked like a terrified forest animal. The plans were vague and thin. Geithner knew at the time that the paucity of his very cautious, still-evolving scheme would upset the markets, but there was nothing he could do about the president's premature enthusiasm. Then, as he sought to bring in hedge funds and private equity firms to bid for toxic assets, Geithner found himself undercut once again by Obama, who sought to get ahead of the outrage over AIG's bonuses by ripping into Wall Street and ordering his Treasury secretary to find a way to recover without permitting them.

He was also plagued by what many critics say was a tendency to overpromise. In interviews, he invoked his experience in Tokyo as a Treasury attaché in the early 1990s—pledging to avoid the timid response of Japan after its bubble burst, and to apply "overwhelming force," an economic Powell doctrine. The markets were underwhelmed when they didn't see a big, detailed plan right away. Geithner argued that if you added up all of Treasury's programs, along with the record $890 billion stimulus plan, he had used as much force as he could, and just about as fast as he could.

Finally, toward the end of March, Geithner began to look steadier as he delivered the long-awaited details of his scheme to save the banking system by auctioning off those toxic mortgage assets, newly euphemized by the Treasury as "legacy" assets. While the program remained controversial, the promise of a payday "dazzled" Wall Street, the *New York Times* reported. ("We hadn't seen that word before," noted one bleary-eyed but satisfied Treasury aide.) A few days later, Geithner revealed the most dramatic plan for regulating finance since the Glass-Steagall Act of 1933. Among other things, he called for broad regulation of derivatives trading, nonbanks, and hedge funds—precisely the kinds of reforms that, the last time Geithner had been in Washington in the 1990s, the Treasury Department avoided. Most of all, Geithner seemed, at long last, to take charge: even his congressional testimony sounded more assertive.

Bit by bit, the mood of the country went from a desperate and pervasive fear that financial stocks might drop out of sight altogether—leading to a depression after all—to a steady rebound in financial securities. Whereas for weeks after the inauguration there was a real danger the major banks would all collapse at once and become government wards, even massively mismanaged Citigroup inched its way back from a penny stock to the $3 range. "The fever broke," White House chief of staff Rahm Emanuel told me at the time. The steadiness of character that Obama had so identified with when he met Geithner—"the bandwidth on his emotions is very small," as Emanuel put it—began to reassure the markets. After two months of wondering and waiting, the major elements of Geithner's and Obama's vision for recovery were in place: an $895 billion stimulus; the Term Asset-Backed Securities Loan Facility scheme to resurrect the securitization market; the housing-mortgage rescue. And Geithner's public-private partnership to create government-backed "funds" intended to bid for the toxic assets on the banks' books. Above all, the stress tests on the major banks laid to rest arguments about taking them over.

And fortunately for Geithner, Bernanke had his back. Though his interest-rate toolbox was all but empty, the Fed chairman managed to find yet new ways of acting with striking speed and force. Bernanke began printing more money on a large scale to fortify the financial sector, committing himself to buying $300 billion of Treasuries and committing an additional $750 billion to mortgage-backed securities. Bernanke then made another dramatic move, announcing for the first time that the Fed would provide loans to investors willing to buy toxic assets.

Summers also renewed his efforts at restraining the lesser angels of his nature. Chastened by the comeuppance of a financial industry whose interests he once championed, scorched by his experience at Harvard, Summers no longer conveyed the sense of certainty that once had seemed so central to his persona. "I suspect over time there's maybe a little less of the brusqueness that people experienced when I was younger," he told me cautiously. "That's probably not an uncommon thing as people get older. It may also be the seriousness of the issue and the problems led to a greater sense of uncertainty on everybody's part." His new colleagues agreed that it was a remarkable change from the scruffy Treasury undersecretary who used to treat important legislators like the hapless foils he once trampled as a national debate champion.

"There is a difference in him in the sense that, when he starts to make a comment, he says, 'Now I could be wrong but . . .' I feel the old Larry would not say 'I could be wrong,'" Christina Romer, the new chairwoman of Obama's Council of Economic Advisors, told me. "That also goes for his economics ideas. There is a sense that things are hard and we could be wrong." Obama quickly picked up on the tendency people always had to poke fun at his foibles, Summers's penchant for putting numerical estimates on things. "The president likes to play with that: 'Are you 83 or 82 and half percent sure?'" said Romer. "Then someone else will say 'I'm going to channel Larry and say I'm 77 percent sure.'"

Summers would continue to maintain, well after the crisis, that he had never been a full-blown advocate of deregulation. "I think the record will show that from the time I became Treasury secretary I was highly aggressive on predatory lending issues," Summers told me in early 2009. There was some truth in this: Summers was one of the first major officials in Washington to issue warnings about the flaws at the heart of Fannie Mae and Freddie Mac—the fact that they were "enterprises that borrow with quasi-government guarantees for private benefit, with the benefits passed on primarily to shareholders," as he put it.

When I went over to the White House to profile Summers in the early months of the Obama administration, along with my colleague Evan Thomas, we asked him about his changed views about regulation. With a wry smile, Summers related an anecdote, as economists are wont to do, about the great and newly fashionable John Maynard Keynes. "Keynes famously said of someone who accused him on inconsistency, 'When circumstances change, I change my views. What do you do?'" Still, Summers allowed that "there's no question that with hindsight, stronger regulation would have been appropriate" before the financial crash. "There certainly were people who were earlier in seeing some of the dangers," he said, though he didn't say who. He added, "Large swaths of economics are going to have to be rethought on the basis of what's happened."

That was true too. But there were also the large swaths of economics that had been simply ignored over the past quarter-century, starting with the warnings of dissidents such as Joe Stiglitz and Hyman Minsky about the dangers of financial markets and too much unregulated capital. It was no surprise that, despite such tentative admissions of failure from officials like Summers, an undercurrent of smoldering anger ran through everything that happened early in 2009. Many Democrats were mystified by some of Obama's choices to fix the economy and the financial system. Somehow, those who had let the catastrophe happen were once again running the show. It wasn't just that Summers and Geithner had returned; so had Mary Schapiro and Gary Gensler, two more Robert Rubin acolytes whom Obama nominated to run the Securities Exchange Commission and the Commodity Futures Trading Commission, respectively. Schapiro had failed to assert control over derivatives trading as the head of the CFTC in the mid-1990s, a time when it was already beset with fraud and manipulation.

Later, when Schapiro was running the Financial Industry Regulatory Authority (FINRA) in the 1990s, she also missed Bernie Madoff's Ponzi scheme and R. Allen Stanford's alleged mini-Madoff scam. According to the wire service Reuters, associates of Stanford's, as was the case with Madoff's family, even served as advisers to FINRA, the industry's ostensible "self-regulator" (though it was widely seen as a joke in the industry). In both her previous jobs, Schapiro had followed a pattern: she tended to aggressively investigate relatively minor violations while failing to see the hippopotamus-size frauds in the room. Gensler's past efforts to block derivatives regulation were no secret. At a congressional hearing on May 15, 1999, Gensler said he "positively, unambiguously" agreed with his boss (then Treasury secretary Summers), in his testimony to the committee opposing additional regulation of the institutional over-the-counter derivatives market. Gensler went on to argue that the "vibrancy and importance" of the global over-the-counter derivatives market "put the burden on those who are suggesting changes and further regulation . . . before we tamper on some of the successes of this marketplace for the economy."

What was Obama thinking when he appointed these people— starting with Geithner and Summers? The new president wanted, above all, to practice a "ruthless pragmatism," he said; he was only interested in competence and experience, and Geithner and Summers had handled financial crises before. In his inaugural address, Obama proclaimed "an end" to the "worn-out dogmas that for far too long have strangled our politics." He said he wanted to move beyond "stale political arguments. . . . The question we ask today is not whether our government is too big or too small, but whether it works." Obama, in interviews at the time, wasn't very interested in discussing his ideology or philosophy; instead he sounded like a man at the head of a clean-up crew standing in the middle of post-Katrina New Orleans. Whatever works, we'll do it, he told *60 Minutes* at one point, and we'll throw out what doesn't. He said he didn't care if the idea came from "FDR or Reagan."

In truth, he didn't really have either option any longer, as far as the economics profession was concerned. There were no sweeping models left to explain what had happened. The era had come full circle. Just as the New Deal and Keynesian thinking had once been discredited, a quarter-century later Friedmanism and Reaganism had overreached to absurd lengths. "All gods fail, if one believes too much," said Martin Wolf of the *Financial Times*, perhaps the preeminent financial columnist of the era. Economists should have realized, Wolf said, that "just as Keynes's ideas were tested to destruction in the 1950s, 1960s, and 1970s, Milton Friedman's ideas might suffer a similar fate in the 1980s, 1990s, and 2000s." And in the face of the obvious failure of both gods of economics—both Friedmanism and Keynesianism—pragmatism seemed the only answer. "The Keynesians were romantic about the possibilities of governments. The free marketers were romantic about the possibilities of markets," commented economist Rob Johnson. "But the policies in neither camp have much validity at this point."

That left a sort of conceptual vacuum. And so for many people, pundits and policy makers both, the old regime and the old intellectual constructs—compounded of Friedmanism, Greenspanism, and Rubinism—continued to dominate by default. "Call me naïve," Paul Krugman wrote, "but I actually hoped that the failure of Reaganism in practice would kill it. It turns out, however, to be a zombie doctrine: Even though it should be dead, it keeps on coming." The target of Krugman's ire was the prairie fire backlash to the bank bailouts that ultimately killed the "public option," a government alternative to private health insurance. The public option had been inspired by Stiglitz's work, said Peter Orszag, Obama's budget director. But with deficits spiraling out of control, it was seen as an intervention too far. It was dropped.

What the smaller-government movement missed entirely, of course, was that the enemy was them. Milton Friedman and Alan Greenspan, the apostles of free-market absolutism, had helped to precipitate the largest government intervention into the markets since FDR. It was a bigger one, actually, since the New Deal hadn't taken over banks for longer than FDR's brief "holiday." In all, the federal government spent $4.6 trillion of taxpayer funds in direct loans to Wall Street companies and banks, purchases of toxic assets, and support for the mortgage and mortgage-backed securities markets through federal housing agencies, the Center for Media and Democracy reported. And in the end, as the free-market era reached its apogee under George W. Bush, it was clear that no economic progress had been made at all. The decade of the "aughts," the *Washington Post* wrote, actually had been for naught: it had been a lost decade. There had been net-zero job growth, which was unprecedented; no previous decade as far back as the 1940s had seen job growth of less than 20 percent. During the 2000s, economic output rose at its slowest rate of any decade since the 1930s. "The past decade was the worst for the U.S. economy in modern times, a sharp reversal from a long period of prosperity that is leading economists and policymakers to fundamentally rethink the underpinnings of the nation's growth," Neil Irwin of the *Post* wrote.

Yet no one—least of all Barack Obama, who was already turning his attention to health care—seemed terribly interested in probing into the deeper causes of the catastrophe.

Among those who were stunned and disappointed by this restoration of the old guard was Joe Stiglitz, who kept waiting for the phone to ring in his spacious floor-through apartment on Riverside Drive, not far from Columbia University. Stiglitz, after all, had seen Obama's potential early. Back in 2007 he had been telling foreign officials that Obama was going to be president. But the call never came. "Who knows why? Obama has been choosing center-right people," said someone close to Stiglitz. No one doubted that Stiglitz's longtime enmity with Summers was a factor, though Summers denied it. (Summers, for the record, rejected the notion of a rivalry with Stiglitz and expressed his respect for Stiglitz's academic work, telling me, "I've got huge admiration for Joe as an economic thinker.") The worry now, Stiglitz said, was that led by Summers, "the Obama administration has put together a team which will not be zealous in trying to reform the financial system and regulatory structure." Even close associates of Summers expected him to take a minimalist approach. "He's very much a market man," said David Gergen, the GOP strategist whom Bill Clinton had hired in the early 1990s and Summers later brought in to help him with his Harvard presidency. "He will come out more on the side of lighter regulation."

Another Democratic dissident emerged on the scene as well: Paul Volcker. He was eighty-two now, and the famous six-foot-seven frame was bent. For Volcker, it was somewhat ironic to find himself cast in the role of an opponent to the new administration. He had been one of Obama's earliest supporters. Volcker had never before endorsed a presidential candidate—except for the time he'd urged his fellow Jerseyan, Bill Bradley, to run in 1988. To his surprise, the Obama team didn't do much with his endorsement. People weren't really talking about the economy as much back then. It was only the beginning of the deflation of the mortgage bubble, and Obama and Clinton were engaged in a fierce fight over each other's credibility and suitability for high office. But by the summer and fall of 2008, as the subprime disaster began to dominate the headlines, Volcker's phone started to ring and that distinctive 302 area code (Chicago) began to pop up. There were late-night calls with the candidate, and the Obama-ites rolled him out for the cameras. "They obviously decided I could be some kind of symbol of responsibility and prudence of their economic policy," he said, with a knowing smirk on his face. After Obama won, however, Volcker didn't hear much until February when the new president made him head of a largely cosmetic "Economic Recovery Advisory Board," which hardly ever met. "We're the economic policy equivalent of Obama's BlackBerry," keeping the president supplied with fresh ideas, said one board member hopefully.

Volcker talked to the president only sporadically. And once again he found himself largely ignored—and feeling a little bit used. Summers said he was happy to work with Volcker's board as an "independent" group, but with a hint of the old acerbic Larry, he noted that it was "not going to be a source of policy." (When there was a delay in convening the board in the early months of the administration, some of its members wondered suspiciously whether Summers was behind it.) And as the months dragged on in 2009, Volcker began to let it be known that Obama was perhaps not quite as much of an "agent for needed change" as he ought to be.

Volcker traveled all over the country to deliver a series of speeches pushing for even more fundamental reform of the financial system— parting ways with both the administration and most of Congress. Volcker wanted commercial banks that enjoy federal guarantees on their deposits to be legally barred from heavy risk taking and proprietary trading in derivatives—which is another way of saying that he wanted America's major banks to stop acting like hedge funds, as they did before the financial crisis. "I would like to draw a line there and say that's the heavily regulated part of the market. They shouldn't be doing risky capital market stuff," he told me. "They should not be large proprietary traders. They should not operate their own hedge funds or equity funds. Then the rest of the market I'd leave with some degree of regulation, but much less intense. And I'd try to create an environment that says bailing out nonbanks would be unlikely."

As the months passed and the promised fixes languished, Volcker grew more and more outspoken. He began to graduate from criticizing risky trading to questioning almost everything new that Wall Street had created in the last twenty years or so. Beyond John Reed's ATM, Volcker asked at a conference in Britain, what had all these new products like derivatives really added to the economy? "Wake up, gentlemen!" Volcker told his fellow regulators. "I can only say your response is inadequate. I wish that somebody would give me some shred of neutral evidence about the relationship between financial innovation recently and the growth of the economy, just one shred of information. I am getting a bit wound up here."

By the time of the Jackson Hole meeting in August 2009, none other than the eminent economist Stanley Fischer began endorsing some of Volcker's views, saying, "We seem to be taking it for granted that we should go back to the structure of the financial system as it was on the eve of the crisis." Fischer, now the governor of the Bank of Israel, had been one of the most powerful economic officials of the 1990s— number two at the International Monetary Fund during the era of the Washington Consensus bias in favor of deregulation. After leaving the IMF, Fischer became vice chairman of Citigroup—the corporate embodiment of the too-big-to-fail problem. So it was all the more remarkable to hear him apparently jumping to the other side of the issue—and implicitly criticizing his old comrades-in-arms Bob Rubin, Larry Summers, and Tim Geithner. Fischer's experience at Citigroup had been unhappy, and it had convinced him that banks didn't have to be "financial supermarkets." There just were no synergies to be achieved from banking and selling insurance at the same time—and at the same time there were many, many dangers.

Democrats on the Hill were upset by the setup of the new administration as well. Many were driven by a sense of having been Cassandras about financial disaster in the past. Like the aging John Dingell, Senator Byron Dorgan of North Dakota had warned in 1999 that "massive taxpayer bailouts" would result from the repeal of Glass-Steagall. As the crash unfolded in the fall, Senator Maria Cantwell of Washington sat aghast in front of the TV in her Senate office, watching. For Cantwell it brought back memories. Not long after her arrival in D.C. in 2001, Enron had imploded. Energy speculators wielding complex derivatives had gouged her constituents in Washington State out of $1 billion. The federal government, she thought, had done little since then to prevent fraud and manipulation. Cantwell knew something about business—she had made millions as an executive at RealNetworks during the dot-com boom. And she was concerned that the administration, filled with men who had supported financial deregulation during the Clinton administration, didn't have the stomach to impose the kind of tough reform she thought Wall Street required.

So, along with a small group of insurgent Democrats in the Senate, she began pushing for a meeting with President Obama to make her case.

Months went by before it happened. The meeting occurred in April only after Cantwell and Vermont's senator Bernard Sanders, perhaps the most left-leaning member of the Senate, used their senatorial prerogative and put a "hold" on the confirmation of Gensler to head the CFTC. The call from the White House finally came in late March. Cantwell and her confederates—Carl Levin of Michigan, Byron Dorgan of North Dakota, Dianne Feinstein of California, Jim Webb of Virginia, and Bernie Sanders— sat down with Obama and the senior members of his economic team.

"I told the president I was concerned that the administration had people in charge who had missed all this before," Cantwell said. It was an awkward moment: two of the officials that Cantwell and her allies came to complain about—Summers and Geithner—were sitting right there. Yet one by one, the other senators echoed Cantwell's concerns. Obama's appointed officials and nominees were products of the system that had brought us this economic grief; they would tinker but in the end leave Wall Street mostly intact. "Some of the people around the president needed to be given a push," said Levin. Cantwell was worried about loopholes that would permit traders and firms to keep trillions of dollars of derivatives trades in the shadows, escaping regulation, by defining them as "customized." But Cantwell remained skeptical that the Obama team would hold the line against the Wall Street lobby. "Do I think they've become true believers? No, I don't," she told me.

Summers, for one, continued to hold out against more dramatic action, and he continued to be as colorful as ever in making his point; in a meeting with congressional Democrats, he compared calls to dismiss the management of the bailed-out banks with George W. Bush's de-Baathification program in Iraq, saying too many good executives would be lost just as too many able Iraqi officials had been eliminated from postwar governance in 2003–2004.

Still, there was some evidence of a shift in views—and genuine contrition. When he finally got to attend his confirmation hearing, Gary Gensler expressed some regrets about his past performance and said he had seen the light. He now wanted something close to what Brooksley Born had been pushing for ten years earlier: derivatives "should be brought into mandated centralized clearing and onto exchanges," he declared (actually, all Born had wanted to do was to question whether such rules should be put in place). "Looking back now, it is clear to me that all of us—all of us that were involved at the time, and certainly myself, should have done more to protect the American public through aggressive regulation, comprehensive regulation," Gensler said.

Geithner also said he was committed to a whole new regime of regulation. But he continued to be dismissive, often profanely so, of critics who railed against the more controversial aspects of his plan for a public-private partnership creating government-backed "funds" to conduct an auction for bad assets. Among those critics was Paul Krugman, who said the plan was another rich giveaway to Wall Street that wouldn't make banks more solvent. Geithner scoffed at their proposed alternative, what he called "preemptive nationalization of the big institutions," saying his critics had no idea what they were talking about. The government didn't have the resources to do more, Geithner said, not with political outrage so high. And Washington couldn't just take over banks that were not technically insolvent yet. "We would end up killing the institutions and having the government assume right away all those basic losses. . . . There's no feasible way we could get in and out quickly. It's like the roach motel. You can check in, but you can't check out."

That sounded like an excuse for more minimalism, but Geithner said AIG was a good example of how difficult nationalization would be as the administration sought to make fixes at the same time as it was bringing the economy back from the abyss. "The government took 80 percent of the thing as a condition for initial intervention. They replaced management, changed the composition of the board—they might call that nationalization," Geithner told me. "We did that because they couldn't operate. They were on the brink of default. Look at what's happened. They've had the [healthy aspects of their] business bleed away."

"You can't solve it that way," said Geithner.

How did he plan to solve it? The same way the government had in the past: turn to Goldman Sachs. Geithner assigned two more ex-Goldman men to fix the vast mess their colleagues helped to create: Steve Shafran, a former favorite of Paulson's, and Bill Dudley, Goldman's former chief economist and the successor to Geithner as head of the New York Fed. Shafran and Dudley were given the mind-bending task of resurrecting the market for securitized assets, an effort to lure the private market back in to bid on the toxic securitized assets that still sat like dead weight on major banks' balance sheets. Geithner's chief of staff was Mark Patterson, Goldman's former chief lobbyist in Washington. In the fall of 2009, another Goldman man, Adam Storch, was named chief operating officer of the SEC's enforcement division.

Geithner, of course, was only following the habit of his entire career: move cautiously, and don't cause any pain to corporate balance sheets. Oddly enough, the chief political operatives at the Obama White House, such as chief of staff Rahm Emanuel, were arguing that politics demanded a tougher stance with the banks. Summers also argued that if the banks failed the "stress tests" they were being given, a more robust takeover might be in order. But Geithner was firm that his middle course was the only way—they needed to get the banks healthy, not break them up, and Summers ultimately backed him. Still, over at the IMF, the consensus among economists was that Geithner and Summers were missing an opportunity. "This was the time for big-bang reform in the financial sector, but Geithner is not the man to do it," said one of them.

As the economy stabilized and Wall Street began paying the government back, Geithner's cautious approach began to win equally cautious plaudits in Washington. By April 2010 he himself was writing in an op-ed in the *Washington Post* that the nation was "close to turning a page on this economic crisis." Geithner boasted that "the overall cost of this crisis will be a fraction of what was originally feared and much less than what was required to resolve the savings and loan crisis." But then, with an odd leap of logic, he conceded that "the true cost of the crisis" must be measured by "the millions of lost jobs, the trillions in lost savings and the thousands of businesses closed" due to the recession. There was no acknowledgment of the deeper ailments brought about by a Wall

Street–centered economy. It was left to historians to speculate on what might have been: a determined effort to break up a plethora of overlarge institutions and restructure the entire system to create new incentives for lending over speculating.

Obama kept saying in speeches that the key to finally restoring health to the economy was to restore investor faith in the markets. No one wondered why that faith should be restored when the people who were most prescient about the hazards of unregulated financial markets were still standing on the outside of the administration, while those who let the catastrophe happen were once again running the show. Over at the SEC, the number one regulator of Wall Street, Schapiro made clear she, too, was taking a minimalist approach. Bill Singer, a former attorney for the National Association of Securities Dealers who became a leading critic of regulators, called Schapiro an "incredibly competent and qualified individual." But he added: "My ultimate concern with Mary Schapiro is, we cannot afford to have the new SEC chair come in with a bucket of whitewash and a bucket of plaster. We need a wrecking ball." Among her first hires was Robert Khuzami, an ex-prosecutor, as head of SEC enforcement. He used to work for Deutsche Bank, one of the biggest culprits in the subprime-mortgage disaster.

Nothing demonstrated Singer's point better than the SEC's own astonishing report on its failures to detect Bernie Madoff's two-decades-old Ponzi scheme. In the days immediately after Madoff's arrest, some enforcement experts I talked to speculated that the errant financier might have been an honest investment manager for much of his career. They said it was likely that he started scamming his investors only after he found himself underwater at some point and got desperate. After all, they reasoned, no one had ever gotten away with a Ponzi scheme for so long, more than twenty years. (The eponymous Charles Ponzi himself was discovered after only two years.)

But the inspector-general (IG) report explained how Madoff did it: sheer regulatory incompetence over two decades, through several SEC chairmen, both Democratic and Republican. The Madoff Ponzi scheme was a relatively simple scam. All anyone in enforcement ever had to do over the years was to obtain documents showing that wily old Bernie wasn't doing any trading at all. They never did. Perhaps the most startling line in the report was about how easily Madoff could have been discovered very early, sparing thousands of people the anguish of losing much of their life's earnings. In 1992, the SEC received credible information that a Madoff "associate" had been conducting a Ponzi scheme. But the agency focused narrowly on the associate and "never thoroughly scrutinized Madoff's operations even after learning that the investment decisions were made by Madoff and being apprised of the remarkably consistent returns over a period of numerous years that Madoff had achieved with a basic trading strategy."

And it wasn't because what Madoff was doing was so complex: all the inspectors had to do was check whether he was making the trades he said by getting records from the Depository Trust Company, a third party; in other words, all they needed to do was corroborate what the alleged suspect was telling them, which is standard operating procedure for any local police department investigating a burglary. Instead they simply asked for Bernie's records and went away. "Had they sought records from DTC, there is an excellent chance that they would have uncovered Madoff's Ponzi scheme in 1992," the IG report concluded.

Time and again, the SEC examiners simply didn't follow leads or failed to comprehend what was being said to them. Beyond that, the SEC examiners were repeatedly intimidated by Madoff, who at one hearing grew "increasingly agitated" and attempted to "dictate to the examiners what to focus on in the examination and what documents they could review." When the investigators reported this encounter to their superior, "they received no support and were actively discouraged from forcing the issue," the report said.

Schapiro issued a statement saying that "many changes we have made since January will help the agency better detect fraud" and that she had "begun to hire new skill sets." But the return of Schapiro and the old crowd raised a practical as well as an ethical issue. In truth, the SEC was never going to be the tough old watchdog it had once been under the Stanley Sporkins of yore. With the advent of electronic trading (which Madoff himself did much to make happen) and vastly richer globalized finance, the markets spun out of the orbit of the SEC and its fellow agencies such as the Commodity Futures Trading Commission. The markets had grown so huge in sophistication, so complex, and so well compensated that the regulators were simply overmatched. And so they would remain. The SEC and the CFTC, along with other regulators, were chronically understaffed and depended on whistle-blowers to tip them off. What was needed instead was a brand-new culture combining government supervision and a new form of self-regulation—mainly by encouraging smart whistle-blowers in the markets such as Harry Markopolos with Madoff, and Jim Chanos, the hedge fund manager who rooted out Enron's fraud, with rewards.

But why whistle-blow if you believe the people on top are the same ones who ignored you the last time? There was, ultimately, a "moral hazard" problem to many of the choices Obama made. The reascendancy of Schapiro and Gensler seemed to demonstrate that, as a regulator, it doesn't pay to put yourself out on the line or listen to whistle-blowers. Instead, it pays to move with the herd. That's what had gotten us into all this trouble in the first place.

So the dispute reopened an old wound at the heart of the Democratic Party, one that first arose when the Clinton administration's market-friendly policies riled the party's liberal base in the 1990s. Obama himself was still getting up to speed on it, suggested Michael Greenberger, Brooksley Born's former deputy at the CFTC. "He didn't run for president to fix derivatives," said Greenberger. "When he brought in Summers, Geithner and Gensler he just thought he was getting the best of the best. I don't think he understood that within the Democratic Party there was a great split over regulatory philosophy." Cantwell agreed that Obama may have been just getting up to speed. His response to her complaint at the White House was merely to tell her he'd study up. "The president said he needed to know more about it," she said.

At bottom, the debate had two sides. On one side were those who wanted to fix the financial house we had. On the other were those who thought we should knock the house down so we could build a brand-new one—a new Wall Street. The keep-the-house-intact crowd was led by Geithner and Summers. They wanted serious fixes to the Wall Street system—new rules and regulations to repair the old house and ensure that it doesn't burn down again in the future—but they didn't much want to change its structure. Having giants like Citigroup and Bank of America dominating the landscape was okay with them, as long as those giants followed the new rules. On the other side of the debate were critics such as Paul Krugman and Paul Volcker and Sheila Bair, chairwoman of the Federal Deposit Insurance Corporation—and Joe Stiglitz, of course, sitting up in New York—who thought the old house was structurally unsound. They believed that not only couldn't we solve the present crisis by merely tinkering with the old house, but we'd assuredly find ourselves in another crisis down the line if we didn't dismantle it entirely—starting with the nationalization of and then forced breakup of the biggest and most troubled banks, like Bank of America and Citigroup. The more deep thinking of these critics, like Stiglitz, also believed that the old house was hopelessly lopsided, that it had skewed the economy pathologically in favor of Wall Street and the wealthy.

The house would, in the end, remain largely intact.

16

Too Big to Jail

To Arthur Levitt Jr., it seemed only right and proper that he should assume *some* responsibility for the catastrophe. Sure, most of the worst things had occurred on Bush's watch, but Levitt knew there had been missed opportunities during the Clinton years, when he had been in office. Levitt, chairman of the Securities and Exchange Commission during all eight years of Bill Clinton's presidency, was as much a man of Wall Street as Robert Rubin and Alan Greenspan were, but now he was rethinking everything.

Levitt's desire for candid self-assessment was unusual for Washington. Politicians and public officials in the nation's capital generally hate to admit to error. The bigger the mistake, the more they are reluctant to confess to it. They are all ambitious people—that's how they got to Washington in the first place—and they are terrified that such confessions will come back to haunt them at their next confirmation hearing or in their next election, that their carefully cultivated careers could be destroyed in one blow.

Levitt was different. Tall, lean, and white-haired, he seemed inordinately comfortable about saying where he went wrong and saying it publicly; perhaps because he was already in his late seventies, and his career in public life was almost certainly over. Still, even as a younger man Levitt seemed to have an extra measure of integrity. He had come from unremarkable circumstances—Brooklyn-born, an English major at Williams College—and had bounced around from marketing magazines to selling cattle before settling in at a young brokerage that eventually became Shearson Loeb Rhoades, and then as chairman of the American Stock Exchange. But his guiding light had always been his father, Arthur Levitt Sr., the Mr. Integrity of New York State politics. Levitt Senior had been the state comptroller six times and had won his last election by the largest plurality in the history of New York elections. Arthur Levitt Jr.'s mother had been a schoolteacher. So Levitt had been tutored in personal and moral accountability by the best.

What lingered most disturbingly in Levitt's mind was the way they had all joined together to destroy Brooksley Born back in 1998. "It was something that bothered me a lot and I thought about it a great deal," he said. Yes, they had all had legitimate reasons for opposing her at the time. Jim Leach was worried that Born's Commodity Futures Trading Commission would be hopelessly inadequate to the task, and that the solution should come from new legislation. Levitt, along with Rubin, Greenspan, and Summers, was concerned that an abrupt attempt to regulate over-the-counter derivatives would have cast a legal shadow over the trillions of dollars' worth of contracts that were already out there. And Born was, well, a pain. "She was a very difficult personality," Levitt told me later. "It may well have been that the proposal was ill thought out. Rubin and Greenspan were probably right in saying there were outstanding contracts thrown into uncertainty," he said. "But we could have grandfathered those and said that thenceforward we were going to regulate them. We could have taken that opportunity to refine it. To make it forward looking. I think that the explosive growth of a product that was unlisted and unregulated should have occasioned greater reaction."

Brooksley Born, after all, had only tried to raise the curtain a little on a market that, even back then, was a dark force raging out of control. She had seen into the fallacy of a self-regulating market. She had understood that neither Wall Street nor markets were to be trusted. Give the woman a little credit for prescience, show a little graciousness. That's all Arthur Levitt, a gentleman to his core, was doing.

But Larry Summers, who still anticipated a confirmation hearing as chairman of the Federal Reserve in his future, apparently didn't see it that way. Shortly after the November 2008 election, when he and Levitt had been called into a meeting on the crisis with House Speaker Nancy Pelosi, the two of them were walking out of the conference room together when Summers quietly told him, "I read somewhere you were saying that maybe Brooksley Born was right." Levitt seemed flabbergasted; he had been quoted as saying that in one of the papers, wondering whether they'd been too hard on her. Summers went on.

"But you know she was really wrong," he said, according to someone who overheard the conversation, which Levitt later confirmed. "Her plan was no good. And we offered a different plan."

In truth, there had been no other plan, at least not one that anyone ever tried to enact. (Summers was probably referring to a vague recommendation, bandied about in 1998, to get the SEC to regulate derivatives broker-dealers, which never came to light.) In subsequent interviews with journalists (including me), Summers also declined opportunities to credit Born with any special foresight. And he grew upset when journalists or critics harped on the regulatory failures only, delivering up a brilliant array of causes for the crisis. "The extent to which this crisis was made in insufficient regulation, in excessively lax monetary policies, in the surge of global capital inflow that was set to blow up bubbles, in the natural proclivity of the private sector to periodic excess, and the sense of risk aversion at close to zero after twenty-five years on an up escalator—what the relative importance of those factors are can be very much debated," he told me. "But there's no question that with hindsight, stronger regulation would have been appropriate."

Presumably, Summers was giving the new president the same measured assessment. No doubt he was saying that there were too many things that could be "debated," that they needed to be very slow and careful in how they proceeded. Above all, they should not throw the baby out with the bathwater, undo too many of all the good things they had done the last time he, Summers, was in Washington in the 1990s.

Oh, they had reason to be so cautious, Summers and Geithner, the other ex-Rubinites. Maybe it was just too big a task, with economic recovery still hanging in the balance, to change Wall Street in fundamental ways, to try to wrest control of the economy again from the all but untouchable financial elites who controlled it. There would be a great flurry of activity in the first year of the Obama administration, and most of it would merely skim over the surface of things. Congress would eventually enact some serious reforms. But the administration would resist all major structural changes proposed in Congress—especially a rule forcing the big banks to "spin off" their derivatives operations into separately capitalized entities—every step of the way. The Clinton administration's former deregulatory brigade, now reincarnated as Obama-ites, would, in the end, decide not to tamper too much with the world they had helped create. They would accept "too many givens," said one senior Fed official who was distressed by the minimalist approach being taken to regulation. The Obama team seemed to go on the assumption that you couldn't roll back Wall Street from what it had become, though what it had become was close to being ungovernable. Despite a new "resolution authority" that allowed the government to liquidate failing financial firms, the firms would remain too big to fail and very probably too big to regulate. The big banks would buy up the failing nonbank lenders, even with all of their bad lending habits and legal liabilities. The restructuring of Citigroup, vaguely promised in exchange for the bailout money, would take place only on the margins. The rating agencies would keep their old business models, exchanging their assessments for payouts from the companies they were rating—Eric Kolchinsky, the former Moody's managing director, alleged in hearings in late 2009 that *even into the year after the crisis* the firm continued to deceive investors by inflating ratings on dubious securities. Banks and investment banks would resume proprietary trading, in derivatives and everything else, with great fervor.

Although U.S. taxpayers had saved Wall Street and now owned part of it, Wall Street was back to earning record profits by late 2009—and awarding itself even more bonuses than its top executives had received in 2007, before the crash.

No serious effort was made by the government to use its leverage as the dispenser of bailout money and the holder of preferred stock in the banks to change their behavior. The Obama administration did nothing to induce greater lending or better behavior, or reorient pay packages so perhaps some of our greatest minds wouldn't go into useless financial engineering but instead would begin to consider real engineering.

Nor would there be a flood of prosecutions, as there had been after the S&L crisis, or during the insider-trading scandals of the 1980s, when Michael Milken and Ivan Boesky had been led off in handcuffs. True, it was clear by now that Wall Street had been playing a giant confidence game with the world, disguising bad and often fraudulent mortgages as highly rated securities, selling scam derivatives by the trillions of dollars. There were fitful efforts to investigate some, particularly Lehman Brothers for allegedly cooking its books—allegedly hiding $50 billion in debt in the late stages of the bubble. Goldman, Morgan Stanley, JP Morgan, and others were investigated for allegedly setting up CDOs to fail. But Wall Street's defense was collective guilt. Everyone was involved, and no one knew how bad it would get, or how serious the risks really were. "Look at

Lehman, Merrill, Citi, Wachovia," said Carl (Chip) Loewenson, a former assistant U.S. attorney who helped prosecute some of the big insider-trading cases in the 1980s and now defended white-collar criminals. "They just got killed. Unless you're going to say they were all in one big conspiracy, or they all coincidentally happened to have identical conspiracies, the only reasonable explanation is they all got blindsided by a thousand-year storm." The only CEOs who had resigned were those who had no choice because their companies disappeared (James Cayne of Bear Stearns, Dick Fuld of Lehman, and John Thain of Merrill Lynch) or who were shown to be such astonishing incompetents that their boards had no choice but to can them (Stanley O'Neal of Merrill and Chuck Prince of Citigroup).

Character was indeed fate. And now the character of the men who were running Washington was playing itself out in the fate of the nation. They were well-meaning but cautious people, the Obama-ites, always looking over their shoulders. And what they saw over their shoulders was a giant—Wall Street—that could not be changed. The financial system itself had been deemed too big to fail. Even more significantly, no one in power in Washington dared to broach the fundamental issue: the extent to which the dominance of the financial markets within the capitalist system during this freewheeling era—the fact that finance had come to hold the whip hand over labor and the manufacture and production of "real" goods and services—had corrupted capitalism itself.

Finance had once been a means to an end: the growth of the real economy. Banking had once served industry and services. Even in the robber-baron era, when J. P. Morgan and a few other lions of Wall Street controlled a lot of the real economy, they had sought to add value; they had created growth and jobs. Now finance had become the end, and the real economy was subservient to financial services, which had become one of the country's most vibrant exports. And it wasn't just venture capital finance any longer but casino-style finance. By the end of 2009, over-the-counter derivatives trading had climbed back up to more than $600 trillion. Of that amount some $230 trillion was controlled by four banks: Goldman Sachs, JP MorganChase, Morgan Stanley, and Bank of America. That meant speculation would continue to go hand in hand with, and even to dominate, sober investment. "At some point in our recent past, finance lost contact with its raison d'être," European Central Bank chief Jean-Claude Trichet said in 2010, when it became clear to the Europeans that the Obama administration had no real interest in fundamental change. "Finance developed a life of its own. . . . Finance became self-referential."

As long as this pathological state of affairs continued, the questions of global growth and social welfare would continue to depend on Wall Street and the enduring fallacies of free-market finance. The manias and panics that so easily dominated finance would continue to infect the world economy.

What was also becoming clear was that although Washington had facilitated the rise of Wall Street over the past generation, Washington and Wall Street no longer understood each other. In late April 2010, Carl Levin's Permanent Subcommittee on Investigations held a series of revelatory hearings. Drawing on a voluminous collection of internal Goldman e-mails and other exhibits, Levin and the ranking acting cochair, Senator Susan Collins of Maine, tore into an array of current and former Goldman mortgage traders over their behavior during the final stages of the financial catastrophe. "Was Goldman honest with its clients about what was happening in the markets?" Levin asked imperiously. The internal communications among Goldman executives about the various deals they were peddling—including one called Timberwolf, described in a Goldman e-mail as "one shitty deal"—showed that what they were telling themselves and what they were telling their clients were two completely different things. Daniel Sparks, the former head of Goldman's mortgage department, repeatedly declined to say that he had acted in the clients' best interests. "You knew it was a shitty deal," Levin told Sparks, repeating again and again a word seldom heard on the record from high public officials. "How much of that shitty deal did you sell to your clients?" Sparks refused to say. When Collins asked him whether he felt an obligation to "act in the best interest of your clients," Sparks couldn't answer that directly, either. "I had a duty to act in a very straightforward way and very open way with my clients," he responded, prompting gasps of incredulity in the room.

It was a kind of Mars and Venus moment. The senators and the traders were simply talking past each other. As Senator Jon Tester put it: "It's like we're speaking a different language here." To Sparks, he was making an obvious distinction: Goldman had an obligation to act mainly in its own best interests, not its clients'. Goldman now existed mainly to supply its clients with products to buy, and during the bubble, the riskier (or more high-yielding) those products were, the better. Caveat emptor. (Never mind that voluminous internal e-mails uncovered by Levin's committee showed that Goldman wasn't terribly straightforward or open either; for example, it avoided sophisticated hedge funds as clients because they'd want to take the short side of many bad deals along with Goldman.) What seemed a shocking breach of ethics to Levin, Collins, and others in the hearing room was quotidian reality to the Wall Street men.

When he got up to testify, Goldman's CEO, Lloyd Blankfein, patiently tried to make the same case. Blankfein and Levin had both gone to Harvard Law School, but they too seemed to share nothing in common. Goldman, Blankfein pointed out, was a "market maker." That absolved the firm of any fiduciary responsibility for the deals it set up for its clients. Levin persisted, repeatedly trying to get Blankfein to concede that Goldman was morally wrong to bet on the sly against securities that it had touted as solid investments to its clients. No, Blankfein demurred, that wasn't how the financial system worked anymore. "There's been a change in the sociology of the business in the last ten to fifteen years," Blankfein explained patiently. "Somewhere along the line," he said, big clients stopped asking investment banks for good advice and started to seek them out only to set up deals for them—merely to under-write the transactions and be on the other side of them. That was why Hank Paulson was so determined in the late 1990s to push ahead with Goldman's initial public offering, transforming the firm from a private partnership into a publicly traded company: it was the only way Goldman could obtain the big-time capital it needed to create such deals. But the Goldman executives also believed that this move gave them carte blanche to shaft any helpless investor on the other side of those transactions. Liquidity was all. Nothing else mattered.

Not surprisingly, Wall Street continued to try to subvert the efforts by authorities in Washington to bring the dark world of over-the-counter derivatives trading—the only true laissez-faire market in the world—under some control. This was the most astonishing development of all in some ways. The revelation that no CEO of a major Wall Street firm had understood what his own traders were doing with derivatives was proof positive that Wall Street could not govern itself. It was also clear by then that derivatives and structured finance products traded off-exchange were a major source of Wall Street's profitability because they were not exposed to market and risk valuation; in other words, the market was rigged and full of scams, as Frank Partnoy had warned. It was clear that the parties coming out on the sour end of these derivatives deals were Wall Street's best customers—corporations, pension funds, money market funds. And it was clear that, unmonitored, derivatives could in fact blow up the civilized world.

So there was ample cause for Washington to take decisive action. Geithner and the Obama administration started out by insisting on a simple rule: all standardized over-the-counter derivatives must be traded on an open and supervised exchange, with the Securities and Exchange Commission and the Commodity Futures Trading Commission as the sole judges of what was standardized. That way authorities would know most of what was being traded and could make sure the major players weren't getting in over their heads. It was a good start.

But then, while the Obama-ites moved on to other things, like health care and budgets, the Street took over the process. The banks were careful. Knowing they were toxic in public opinion, they began a stealth lobbying effort to ensure that this wonderful profit center—derivatives trading—remained as free of government control as possible. A newly formed group called the Coalition for Derivatives End-Users began putting itself out on the front lines of the fight against legislation curbing derivatives. The group consisted of Wall Street's corporate customers, a who's who from Apple to Whirlpool, organized by the Chamber of Commerce, the National Association of Manufacturers, and the Business Roundtable. They were persuaded that going onto exchanges would mean higher costs for them; they'd have to post margins. Most of these corporations didn't seem concerned that they were paying much larger spreads than they might have if the derivatives hedges they bought were subject to open pricing on exchanges.

The lobbying met with some success, thanks in part to the deep reach that Wall Street now had in the Democratic Party, especially among a business-friendly group called the New Democrats led by Representative Melissa Bean of Illinois, who was listening to the free-traders of the Chicago Mercantile Exchange. And Barney Frank, who had been so leery of free capital flows back in the 1990s but was now the powerful chairman of the House Financial Services Committee, began to listen to the New Democrats, who often came from "red" or Republican-dominated districts. Everyone knew they had a tough midterm election in 2010, one that could depend on donations from the financial industry. Beyond that, the industry brought back some of the same key legal minds who had drafted the 2000 Commodity Futures Modernization Act, chief among them Edward J. Rosen, a shaggy-haired, soft-spoken

Oxford University graduate and the coauthor of a two-volume treatise on derivatives. It sometimes seemed as if the United States was no longer a republic but a "plutonomy"—a term invented by a trio of Citigroup analysts in 2006 as they tried to comprehend the huge and ever-widening income gaps in the country and the role of the superrich in dominating policy making in Washington.

The initial result of the first-ever attempt to legislate oversight of derivatives was riddled with loopholes. The administration didn't fight the changes. Indeed it overreacted to the failures of the Clinton approach to a number of key issues—health care, climate change, as well as financial reform—by deferring to Congress on the details. Obama was determined not to do what Clinton had done in trying to design his own legislation and force the finished package through a reluctant Congress, which resulted in the disaster of Hillarycare and the unratified Kyoto Treaty on climate change. That left the door open to a lobbying onslaught, especially as financial reform grew eclipsed in public attention by the issue of health-care reform late in Obama's first year.

But one man did carry the fight—Gary Gensler, President Obama's new head of the Commodity Futures Trading Commission. Like Arthur Levitt, the slight, balding Gensler had been, it seemed, quite sincere in his remorse. Gensler formed a close association with Brooksley Born's old deputy, Michael Greenberger—now a law professor at the University of Maryland—and almost single-handedly fought both the inertia of the Obama administration and the Wall Street lobby. He managed to quash loophole after loophole—especially one that would have allowed almost any firm that claimed it was hedging risk to avoid trading on an exchange.

Gensler was something of an odd bird; almost avian and nervous in appearance, he constantly radiated self-doubt about how he was perceived in Washington's ranks and what position he ought to be taking. But he was chastened by the months-long hold that Cantwell and Sanders had put on his nomination. Gensler, somewhat like Bernanke, had always had a foot in both worlds. Neither of his parents had gone to college, and his father ran a tiny cigarette and candy vending business in Baltimore. He rocketed out of the University of Pennsylvania and the Wharton School of Business into a successful career at Goldman Sachs— of course—and his mentor had been, of course, Robert Rubin. But after serving as Rubin's assistant secretary and then undersecretary, he hadn't

gone back to Wall Street right away; instead he'd gone to work for liberal Maryland senator Paul Sarbanes as his senior adviser. After Enron
crashed, it was Gensler who drafted the first version of what became the
Sarbanes-Oxley law, which even if it was watered down was at least a
start at improving the management of large corporations. Even Gensler
himself poked fun at the dual perceptions of him: "Is he the guy that
Paul Sarbanes tells us he is? Or is he the guy who's part of the team who
brought us the Commodity Futures Modernization Act?"

In the end, Gensler proved to be a tougher advocate of the administration's opening position on derivatives trading than the administration
itself. Even so, many exemptions remained in the new derivatives
bill—in particular, a provision excusing "end users" of derivatives from
regulation—and there was little doubt that Wall Street would be driving
truckloads of new, over-the-counter derivatives products through them
in the years to come.

Ben Bernanke was also a changed man. And the Fed was an utterly
changed place. Bernanke had undergone a battlefield conversion. He
turned Alan Greenspan's Fed upside down. He began by meeting with
consumer activist groups—what would have been considered an unthink-
able bit of slumming in the Greenspan years. He strengthened oversight
of lending. The Fed became activist central. He even called for amend-
ing the Federal Reserve Act to increase consumer protection. And he
began to question his earlier conclusion that the Fed should avoid target-
ing asset bubbles. Many economists would later realize their profession
had been overturned, that all the assumptions about efficient financial
markets had to go out the window and a whole new balance, a whole
new level of mistrust, was needed between government and finance.
But all that was going to take them decades to figure out in academia.
Bernanke had had to make split-second decisions on the same issues in
the fall of 2008 and winter of 2009. It was an amazing performance, and
whether you agreed with his decisions or not, you had to acknowledge
his phenomenal grit and presence of mind. His actions at the Fed, in
fact, dwarfed anything that was done on the fiscal side by either the Bush
or the Obama administration.

It was little surprise when Obama nominated him for a second term
at the Fed at the end of the summer of 2009. But as the months passed

and the economy languished at 10 percent unemployment, his position weakened as it became clear that there was no real channel for public outrage. Someone had to pay. As senators from both parties cast about desperately for a way to appease the outrage, Bernanke found himself continually saddled with the offenses of the Greenspan era, and it didn't help that Geithner wanted to give the Fed even more power to oversee the financial system. It didn't matter that he had grown in office, or that many of the financial institutions that were most troubled during the crisis were outside his supervisory reach, in part because of yet another action that took place long before Bernanke joined the Fed.

Student of history that he was, Bernanke had known what was coming. He had known there was a fair chance he would end up being the handiest villain, that all the anger would come crashing at his door as he sat for confirmation on Capitol Hill.

And now the anger was coming from both sides, from both the populist Left and a resurgent Right.

In a book published at the start of the crisis, the historian Niall Ferguson asked whether the modern globalized financial markets had become the new dinosaurs, whether things had grown too complex to survive. "Are we on the brink of a 'great dying' in the financial world—one of those mass extinctions of species that have occurred periodically, like the end-Cambrian extinction that killed off 90 percent of Earth's species, or the Cretaceous-Tertiary catastrophe that wiped out the dinosaurs?" he asked.

But these were dinosaurs that were being allowed to survive—fed on a diet of market faith that was now based more on hope than experience.

Now the biggest issue was the too-big-to-fail problem. The major players had all been saved (with the exception of Lehman and Bear Stearns), and Washington's policies were communicating this implicit message both to investors and to the rest of the world: we'll save them again someday. Why shouldn't they all start taking risks with the world's savings once again? Greenspan himself, his ideology shattered, was so bothered by the implications of the too-big-to-fail problem that he repudiated utterly what he had written nearly forty years before, as one of the contributors to Ayn Rand's 1961 book, *Capitalism: The Unknown Ideal*. Then he had derided antitrust law—"the entire structure of antitrust statutes in this country is a jumble of economic irrationality and ignorance," he wrote—and he praised Standard Oil's dominance of 80 percent of refining capacity at the turn of the century as something that "made economic sense and accelerated the growth of the American economy." Now Greenspan called for a breakup of the biggest banks for fear that, otherwise, the market system couldn't function. Greenspan was grappling with the same dilemma that Rubin had in the aftermath. "If they're too big to fail, they're too big," Greenspan said. "In 1911 we broke up Standard Oil—so what happened? The individual parts became more valuable than the whole. Maybe that's what we need to do."

Yet somehow the fundamental questions were never addressed. Obama appeared to be channeling Geithner, for the most part. "The president and his economic team explicitly decided not to break up all big financial institutions," Goolsbee said. Obama decided that the cause of the crisis "wasn't primarily about size. The most dangerous failures— Bear Stearns, Lehman—were not even close to being the biggest. You could have broken the largest financial institutions into, literally, five pieces and each of them would still have been bigger than Bear Stearns. The main danger to the economy was interconnection, not raw size." By the fall of 2009 the "jobless" recovery was well under way. No one mentioned the bailouts anymore. The Dow had made it past 10,000, and Barack Obama had moved on to health care, expending political capital that could have been used on financial reform. The horror movie that the financial system became seemed to be over. But as in one of those clichéd Hollywood endings, the monster in the story wasn't really dead, even if most people had forgotten about him.

The one man who seemed to understand this, if only sporadically, was Barack Obama himself. After a year of listening to Summers and Geithner—and watching as Wall Street guiltlessly awarded itself record bonuses while doing little to restart lending—the president finally seemed to have had enough. "Wait, let me get this straight," Obama said at a meeting in December. "These guys are reserving record bonuses because they're profitable, and they're profitable only because we rescued them," according to an economic advisor. "He was incredulous." By the beginning of 2010, a year into his presidency, he was sinking badly in the polls and had just suffered a jarring defeat in the Massachusetts special election to replace the late senator Ted Kennedy.

Obama was increasingly perceived as being on the wrong side of the issue. Now, prodded by his vice president, Joe Biden—like Stiglitz and

Paul O'Neill another product of a hardscrabble upbringing, in Scranton, Pennsylvania—the president began to rethink how to take on Wall Street. "We kept revisiting it," said the economic advisor. The one big idea that hadn't been adopted, that was still out there, was Paul Volcker's notion of barring federally insured banks from risky proprietary trading. Geithner and Summers still questioned whether it was feasible, but Obama pressed them in his typically legalistic, analytical way. "I'm not convinced Volcker's not right about this" the president said at one meeting in the Roosevelt Room. Biden, a longtime fan of Volcker's, piped up: "I'm quite convinced Volcker *is* right about this!" Maybe incentives did matter, as the economists never tired of saying. So Obama abruptly rediscovered. The day after his first anniversary as president, he stepped out in front of the cameras to announce his support for a "Volcker rule"—named after "the tall guy behind me," he said.

The problem was, it may have been too late. Obama, having put financial reform on the back burner, had already depleted most of his political capital. And the Wall Street lobby was ready once again to fight for itself. As they had done with the fight over OTC derivatives trading, the banks would seek to create loopholes that would allow them to do things as they have in the past. They would argue that the "proprietary trading" that Volcker wanted to bar them from was technically very similar to market making. Even as Obama made his announcement, administration officials conceded that, yes, firms "would be able to make markets, related to doing services for their customers," according to one official. On the side of the Wall Street firms was none other than Volcker's former protégé, Jerry Corrigan, who said it would probably prove difficult, if not impossible, to distinguish market making from proprietary trading. "I don't think it's practical to think you can slice and dice classes of activities in any meaningful way," Corrigan said.

But Obama had an even bigger problem than that. Wall Street was now global, and government was not. Unless the president could convince the other major financial markets around the world, such as London, to adopt the same rules, it would be easy enough for the behemoths of the Street to shift their headquarters and their over-the-counter derivatives and proprietary trading elsewhere. The key was to coordinate a global effort to bring these fully global markets under control. And that's what was missing.

Instead, as a crisis in the European Monetary Union (EMU) began to rage in 2010, the new administation found itself actually fighting against global reform—and for Wall Street.

Typically with European crises, Americans start out thinking that Europeans should fix them until we finally get dragged in. That's what happened in the two world wars of the twentieth century. But when it came to the euro zone crisis, it turned out that Goldman Sachs and other investment banks had already dragged us in years before. The banks' strategy dated back to the 1990s, when countries such as Greece and Italy, with chronic fiscal deficits, were eager to join the European Monetary Union but couldn't match the standards of budget discipline imposed by the 1992 Maastricht Treaty (which created the EMU). So Wall Street helped these countries hide their true national indebtedness, at a high price. Goldman and other firms sold the governments swaps and other complex instruments that made government borrowing appear to be something else, such as a currency trade or an asset sale. The Greek government was like a hapless credit card holder who is mortgaged to the hilt. Athens sold everything, from airport landing fees to lottery revenues, to Wall Street and then took on impossible debt at exorbitant rates. Its fiscal deficits were still there—only now, because of the extra interest, they were larger. So it would cost Greece much more to dig out. And the government had fewer options now beyond hoping for a bailout, making the crisis more acute.

Greece was mostly to blame for its fiscal profligacy. But it was, for the most part, just another "end user" like the corporate patsies whom Wall Street lobbyists had trotted out to argue against exchanges. In some cases, such as the swap deal Italy did in the late 1990s in order to defer interest payments on a bond issue, allowing it to squeak into the EMU, such instruments may have helped in the long run—assuming the euro zone and Italy's place in it remained intact. But by pulling the wool over the eyes of investors, many such deals "led governments down the wrong policy path of avoiding to take strict measures to rein in their deficits and debt," said Gikas Hardouvelis, an Athens-based economist who documented Greece's transactions with Wall Street.

It was not unlike what had happened in previous currency crises—Mexico in 1994–1995 and Asia in 1997–1998. In those earlier cases it was the local banks, not the governments, that cut quiet swaps deals to juice their income. When Mexico decided in December 1994 that it would try to devalue the peso by just 10 percent, hundreds of millions of dollars of off-the-books derivatives deals turned the effort into a market rout. All of a sudden Mexico's major banks were hit with margin calls from U.S. banks, taking Mexico's central bank by surprise. The result was a $50 billion bailout orchestrated by Washington—the first of many, with Wall Street the main beneficiary nearly every time (though to be fair, the U.S. Treasury ultimately made a profit from Mexico's paybacks, too). The Asian crisis played out similarly, with Asian banks also badly hit. These too were precursors to the latest crisis that had gone ignored. (After the markets began to attack Greece in 2010, Gustavo Piga, an Italian economist who first warned about such derivatives deals in the 1990s, recounted to me how he had been rediscovered by the media. "I got no phone calls for the past nine years. All of a sudden the bomb explodes and everybody's on the case.")

But the Obama administration while it was clearly pressing for greater global regulation, also began kibitzing on Wall Street's behalf, taking the banks' side against Europe, which erupted in 2010 over the U.S. financial industry's role in helping countries like Greece disguise their debt. As the G7 and G20 nations continued to disagree, further squabbles broke out between Geithner and his European counterparts. The Treasury secretary warned against protectionism that would harm U.S. private equity and hedge funds. And Wall Street began to relax once again.

17

Larry and Joe (Again)

No one had thought longer or harder about how to discipline global finance than Joe Stiglitz. Watching the rollout of Obama's economic team on TV with his longtime collaborator at Columbia, Bruce Greenwald, Stiglitz was deeply upset that he wasn't there. He strongly suspected that Larry Summers had somehow blackballed him. But even then, Stiglitz had remarked as he and Greenwald sat together: "Larry's the only one of all of them who's smart enough to know how to fix this." Stiglitz and Summers shared little in common save for enormous brainpower, yet somehow that was enough for Joe—if only Larry could be persuaded to do the right thing. ("They hate each other like poison," Greenwald told me at the time. "But they do respect each other.")

As the months went by, the hoped-for phone call from the White House never came. Stiglitz had a pretty good idea why. It wasn't just that he and the president's chief economic adviser didn't get along. It was the persistence of the zeitgeist. "America has had a revolving door," Stiglitz said. "People go from Wall Street to Treasury and back to Wall Street. Even if there is no quid pro quo, that is not the issue. The issue is the mindset."

Still, there was some reason for hope. Barack Obama, a constitutional lawyer and community organizer from Chicago, held no brief for Wall Street. And Obama was nothing if not acutely sensitive to criticism that he didn't welcome dissent. If there was one thing the brilliant and dynamic new president took pride in—that his advisers never ceased marveling over—it was Obama's relentless insistence on thrashing every issue out thoroughly, even if it took months. And so he directed Summers to convene a dinner of dissenters on the economy. He would take them on and win them over just as he had the rest of the country— and the world.

Just as he saw that Volcker was winning adherents on his proprietary trading idea, Obama knew that one of his most vociferous critics in the early months was this troublesome economist he had briefly welcomed into his fold, Joseph Stiglitz. Despite his early vote of confidence in Larry, Stiglitz had grown more and more open with his disagreements as the minimalism of the Obama team became apparent. In March, he declared that Geithner's and Summers's bailout plan amounted to an "ersatz capitalism" in which the banks' investors and creditors would feel no pain, fobbing off all their errors of judgment on the taxpayers. Obama, in a revealing interview with the *New York Times'* David Leonhardt in May 2009, grew notably defensive about the makeup of his economic team, which had been increasingly criticized for the narrowness of its views and experience. Leonhardt noted that Obama had said before the election that he had thought a lot about the Clinton administration's economic debates, and that he wanted to have a "vigorous debate" in front of him by "a Robert Rubin-type" and a "Robert Reich-type."

"Clearly you have a spectrum of Democrats within your economic policy team," Leonhardt probed gently.

"But I don't have Paul Krugman or Joseph Stiglitz," Obama shot back, filling in the unspoken part of the question. It was then that Obama offered up his revelation that, in his view, the new Bob Reich was Larry Summers. The president added, "Keep in mind, though, I mean, I have enormous respect for somebody like Joe Stiglitz. I read his stuff all the time. I actually am looking forward to having these folks in for ongoing discussion."

So it was that one morning in late April 2009, Stiglitz's wife, Anya, got a call from Larry Summers's office. Anya, a vivacious former journalist, was on her back taking a Pilates class in Central Park at the time. She looked at the phone next to her with some difficulty and saw 202 pop up with no phone number attached. That usually meant the White House. No big deal, she thought. People often called her when they wanted to talk to Joe, because even though he had spent four decades figuring out how the global economy worked, he hadn't quite gotten the hang of voice mail. (Anya had even recorded his cell-phone greeting: "He doesn't listen to his messages, so if you want to talk to him, keep calling.") When she picked up, an aide to Summers was on the line looking for Joe. Anya said she'd pass on the message—then went back to work on her abs. Anya figured Summers was just calling to complain, as he sometimes did, probably about the ersatz capitalism piece this time. "I thought, Larry—he's just going to yell at Joe," Anya said. But the Summers aide called back a little later, more insistent. It turned out the president wanted Joe to come to dinner—that same evening, Monday, April 27. It seemed a bit odd, particularly when they found out that others invited to the dinner, including Krugman, Volcker, Ken Rogoff, and Alan Blinder, had been asked the week before.

The only explanation for the last-minute invitation was that dinner had been arranged before Obama made his remark to the *New York Times* about having Stiglitz over to the White House. Stiglitz believed that Summers had kept him out of the administration, and probably wasn't eager to have him over for dinner (charges that Summers himself denied). But now that Obama's comment was out there in the blogosphere, Summers had little choice but to invite him to this event, even if it was last minute.

Stiglitz, of course, jumped on the next train.

The group met in the old family dining room of the White House. Representing the home team were Summers, Geithner, chief of staff Rahm Emanuel, and Christina Romer, chairwoman of the Council of Economic Advisors, Stiglitz's old job. Krugman, Stiglitz, Blinder, Volcker, and Rogoff represented a whole spectrum of dissenting views. Obama, who was in good spirits, quickly broke the ice as they sat down to dinner of roast beef. The president announced that the salad they were about to eat consisted of lettuce from the White House garden, which his wife, Michelle, had been working hard at cultivating. ("It was very good lettuce," said Blinder.) Obama then told the group that while it was not necessary to keep the meeting a secret, he didn't want the contents to get out. "I think he wanted to hear the arguments right in front of him," said Blinder.

Obama clearly had been reading his critics in the press. They went through all the arguments politely, with Stiglitz and Krugman arguing for nationalization of the banks. Obama spoke knowledgeably about Stiglitz's idea for creating a new global reserve currency to replace the dollar. The president argued that now was not the time because the United States needed the dollar to remain the world reserve currency in order to finance its trade deficits. (Stiglitz's argument was that the dollar's role as the world's reserve currency actually made those deficits worse, and kept U.S. workers uncompetitive to boot by keeping the dollar artificially strong; but Stiglitz was impressed nonetheless that the president seemed up on the subject.) It was all very decorous. Even Larry and Joe were fairly well-behaved—though, being Larry and Joe, they began to bicker at one point over how much of a knock-down price banks' toxic securities would go for, until Obama cut them off with a sharp look. "There wasn't any particular fireworks," Blinder said. "When you're around the table with the president of the United States, you're on your best behavior."

Yet Stiglitz came away feeling that the conversation was far less satisfying than the meal. This was the moment to talk about making fundamental changes to the economy, beginning with a redress of Wall Street. The worst of the crisis had passed. Almost nothing had been demanded of the banks—no quid pro quos—yet they were not lending; instead they were back to their old bad habits: selling and trading over-the-counter derivatives at a record pace.

Stiglitz had a whole slew of ideas for reform. While the Obama administration tried to induce the banks to lend more and develop workout programs for underwater borrowers, Stiglitz wanted to give mortgagees the same kinds of rights that indigent corporations get under Chapter 11 of the bankruptcy code, which would allow a judge to reduce the amount of mortgage in the same way he negotiates a reduced debt to creditors in a Chapter 11 proceeding. The financial industry hated the idea, but it was wealthy enough now to endure it. Everyone tut-tutted over the "moral hazard" of forgiving homeowner debt on bad mortgages—it would make mortgagees lazy and careless in the future, critics said. (The "Tea Party" movement was launched by CNBC reporter Rick Santelli's rant about this on camera.) Never mind that the moral hazard of bailing out the banks was likely far worse; the supposedly savvy financial mavens who ran the banks had made mistakes and taken risks that were often far stupider than the errors of judgment made by typical unsophisticated people who took out mortgages they couldn't afford.

Stiglitz, like others, was angry about Wall Street's resumption of its past pay and trading practices, as if nothing had happened. But he went further than most others in talking about a complete rethinking of pay and bonuses, tossing out the performance-based incentives that had only rewarded short-term sales and grossly twisted behavior. He wanted to fix corporate governance to wean it from Wall Street. Stiglitz even urged a new look at why credit card companies charged small businesses so much—1 to 2 percent—for every transaction. What was the reason for that? he asked: modern technology permitted an efficient, low-cost electronic payment mechanism that should cost pennies per transaction. It was yet another example of the way Wall Street seemed to have the upper hand over every part of the real economy.

Stiglitz had learned his own hard lessons from his time as a bomb thrower in Washington in the 1990s. He, like Obama, wanted solutions that might work—a smart populism. Stiglitz wasn't talking about Leftist populism in the tradition of Huey Long's "share the wealth" crusade of the 1930s or William Jennings Bryan's cross of gold speech, in 1899, when the Democratic candidate electrified a crowd by inveighing against the gold standard. But he understood better than anyone else what Washington's wise men had created over the past three decades and how deep the problems ran. Because of the income inequalities that had been created globally, money was not being efficiently and effectively used around the world. The growing income gaps meant that the rich had too much money, more than they could possibly spend, while the poor who were far likelier to spend it had too little of it. This kept global demand and therefore economic growth down. Another chilling effect on growth was that countries that had been burned by "hot money"—like the East Asian nations in 1998—began hoarding large reserves to protect them from the next attack. That too was money that went unspent and reduced economic growth. And all of it was in service to Wall Street's demands.

Stiglitz knew that only a reordering of "incentives"—economists' favorite word, and one he used often—would help shift the nation's best minds away from unproductive financial engineering and into more productive pursuits. He argued that something had to be done about all the out-of-work physicists and misguided math whizzes who had become Street quants inventing products that added no economic growth and baffled their CEOs to boot. They were America's future, but they had to be redirected. Wall Street kept saying that to reduce pay incentives and bonuses would cost the firms their best talent. Stiglitz's response was *Yes!* That's precisely the idea. Let's make banking "boring" again, and return it to its rightful place. "What kind of society is it in which a CEO says, 'If you pay me only $5 million, I will give you only a fraction of my effort. To get my full attention, you have to give me a share of the profits'?" Stiglitz said.

Yet somehow, even as the public outrage remained high, the anger had no channel and no champion. Whatever Obama did about Wall Street seemed to be reactive, like suddenly embracing Paul Volcker. He had gone to Copenhagen to try to take the lead globally on climate warming. He had even gone to Oslo to get his hometown, Chicago, picked for the Olympics (he failed). He had been awarded the Nobel Peace Prize in anticipation of his global leadership. But when it came to the financial sector, Obama seemed perfectly willing to leave things to his trusted lieutenants, Geithner and Summers.

All of this amounted to something of a mystery about the young president. There was so much passion and ambition in Obama's words, and so much dispassion and caution in his policy choices. Early in the Democratic primaries, in January 2008, Obama had stunned many of his supporters by praising Reagan as a transformational president—a contrast to the eight years of Bill Clinton, Obama added cuttingly. "Ronald Reagan changed the trajectory of America in a way that Richard Nixon did not and in a way that Bill Clinton did not," Obama said. "He put us on a fundamentally different path because the country was ready for it."

Yet at what would seem to be a similar historical inflection point— what should have been the end of Reaganism—the man who had now become President Obama was not ready to address the deeper ills of the free-market system.

Especially after Obama distracted himself with health care reform, the nation seemed to sink deeper and deeper into irreconcilable partisanship, with the Tea Party movement on the right and the slighted progressives of the left both fulminating against the new president. The Right reached a tipping point of too much government; the Left was appalled at Obama's willingness to gut the health-care bill in deference to the insurance industry. One of the few issues everyone on both sides of the political divide could actually unite on—the power of Wall Street and the too-big-to-fail problem—was lost in the political maelstrom.

The persistence of free-market fundamentalism infected the health-care debate as well. Here too Stiglitz's thinking was seminal. As he had divined so many years before, listening to his father at the dinner table in Gary, insurance just doesn't work well in a free market dominated by for-profit insurance companies. The reason, Stiglitz wrote, is that people who most want insurance are also the people who are likely to become ill or who are already ill; for-profit companies, knowing this, work equally hard to eliminate these customers or to minimize the care they can get (a concept called "adverse selection"). Despite that, the first thing to be dropped from the debate in President Obama's legislative triumph was the "public option." Never mind that it was probably the only measure that could really bring the insurance companies under control. The new Obama law, while a hard-won victory that created new federal restraints in insurance and extended coverage to the poor, still left the final determination of costs and coverage to the for-profit companies and their master, Wall Street.

Obama was clearly not pushing to be FDR or even trust-busting Teddy Roosevelt, who after the panic of 1907 had sent a long message to Congress calling for a variety of additional protections for ordinary Americans and for serious restraints on stock speculation. "There is no moral difference between gambling at cards or in lotteries or on the race track and gambling in the stock market," Roosevelt declared in words that sound quaint today. He called this his "campaign to make the class of great property holders realize that property has its duties no less than its rights." Again, so very quaint. Yet the first president Roosevelt's words, carried forward a hundred years, continued to address a fundamental inequality, a system of rigged markets, that still defined the U.S. economy in the second decade of the twenty-first century.

As for FDR, people tended to forget that along with sunny optimism— "Happy Days Are Here Again," his celebrated campaign theme song went— Roosevelt delivered a strong dose of justice upon taking office in March 1933. FDR gave that job to Ferdinand Pecora, a fierce New York prosecutor to whom Roosevelt granted carte blanche to investigate Wall Street's perniciousness. Pecora delivered big-time. He humiliated and forced the resignation of Charles Mitchell, the head of National City Bank (later Citibank), and oversaw a twelve-thousand-page probe into the causes of the Great Depression that gave birth to a new regulatory framework, including the Securities and Exchange Commission (Pecora was later one of its first commissioners). Other Wall Streeters were prosecuted, convicted, and jailed.

There was little of that now.

Obama had seemed eager at first to embrace Roosevelt's pragmatic approach in 1933. Obama knew that what the country needed, economically and politically, was not so much an organized program but a hodgepodge of bold experiments like the New Deal. "It is common sense to take a method and try it," FDR said back then. "If it fails, admit it frankly and try another. But above all, try something." Yet to achieve that FDR had sought out a large range of ideas. "Roosevelt had everyone throwing stuff at him in the New Deal. He was notorious for asking two or three people to work on the same thing," said Michael Greenberger, Brooksley Born's former deputy and another Stiglitz ally who was kept on the outside. "Stiglitz is too good a mind to be thrown out to pasture during the worst crisis since the Great Depression."

Perhaps the most bizarre thing was that at a historical moment when a broad and deep rethinking of economics was obligatory, the president's menu of policy options was narrower than Bill Clinton's had been, much less FDR's. "Our ruling intelligentsia in economics runs the spectrum from A to A minus. These guys all talk to each other, and they all say the same thing," one leading Washington critic said to me. Stiglitz knew that an occasional dinner really didn't amount to a sincere invitation to dissent. Whatever else you wanted to say about Clinton and his long tack rightward in the 1990s, he, Joe Stiglitz, had at least been a part of the debate then, and he remembered fondly the "Socratic discussions" of that period. This was a mere dinner. As they parted, he said, Obama "made it clear he wanted to keep hearing from us—and he said he knew he would, in the media."

All of it made for a strange disconnect as the twenty-first century entered its second decade. In Barack Obama's Washington, Joe Stiglitz was clearly little more than an afterthought. But wherever he went elsewhere around the world—Europe, Asia, Latin America—Stiglitz found that he was received like a modern-day oracle. "Here in New York we can't get a table at a fancy restaurant, but in the rest of the world there's this insane celebrity," Anya Stiglitz told me. By the time the crisis was all over, after thirty years of warning about the fallacies of free-market fundamentalism, Stiglitz had become the most cited economist in the world.

His work was referred to more than any other, according to authoritative data compiled by the University of Connecticut.

"In Asia they treat him like a god," said Rob Johnson, a top economist for the Senate Banking Committee and a former managing director for George Soros's hedge fund, who occasionally traveled with him. "People walk up to him on the streets. He's a cultural hero." At a speech in 2007, Malaysian economist Andrew Sheng turned to Stiglitz and thanked him, to loud applause, "on behalf of everyone in Asia" for standing up to the International Monetary Fund, which made serious errors during the Asian financial "contagion" of 1997–1998. Said Sheng: "I think he is the nearest thing to Keynes there is in the current crisis."

Indeed, to many of his admirers around the world, Stiglitz now stood out as a figure of almost Keynesian prescience. The subprime mortgage disaster had supplied almost tailor-made proof of Stiglitz's ideas. The subprime scandal had been all about people who knew a lot—such as mortgage originators and Wall Street derivatives traders—exploiting people who had less information, like borrowers and global investors who bought up subprime mortgage-backed securities. "Globalization opened up opportunities to find new people to exploit their ignorance," Stiglitz said. "And we found them."

In the broader area of theory, Stiglitz's stature was titanic. Even Ken Rogoff, his old antagonist at the IMF, had come around to his way of thinking, at least to some degree. As Rogoff told me later, "The heart of the crisis was U.S. borrowing from abroad and the failure of U.S. authorities to recognize that we weren't as special as we thought we were, and these inflows corrupted our system. We made most of the typical mistakes other countries make when all that money's coming in." The systemic issues that Stiglitz had raised over the last two decades, going back to capital-account liberalization—the issues that had been thrown back in his face again and again—were now the rubble of Wall Street.

Yet rather than using Stiglitz's prestige around the world to lead a charge against the global power of finance, Obama largely ignored him. Indeed, it sometimes seemed the world was now divided up into Larry and Joe spheres of influence. Summers still ruled Washington, with Obama leaning heavily on his advice about Wall Street, while Stiglitz flew around the globe advising other nations' leaders. French president Nicolas Sarkozy invited him to a conference on rethinking globalization, and the Chinese government endorsed Stiglitz's idea for a new global reserve system to replace the U.S. dollar as the world currency. According to Fang Xinghai, the head of the Shanghai Financial Authority, Chinese prime minister Wen Jiabao was influenced by Stiglitz's work, especially when "he talks about economics of poor people." Said Fang, "His ideas have a big following."

The disconnect was echoed in the halls of Congress and academe. Back in the world's biggest economy, especially in academia where so much of this had started, "Chicago ideas" remained the dominant paradigm even in the years after the disaster. Milton Friedman's influence lived on—so much so that liberal-leaning economists complained that they could no longer get published in the major economic journals. Chicagoans still had control of many of the key editorial positions, a neat bit of historical justice for the happy warrior.

In response, in the spring of 2010, renegade financier George Soros and Rob Johnson brought together some of the leading lights of the market-skeptic school—including Stiglitz, of course—to talk about ways of taking back the economics profession. The inaugural gathering of Soros and Johnson's Institute for New Economic Thinking, held in the same stately surround where John Maynard Keynes developed his general theory—King's College at Cambridge University—was planned as a kind of tea party of its own. It was the opening shot in what was certain to be a bitter war for the commanding heights of economics. Yes, economists had learned a few things since the Great Depression—at least when it came to crisis response. The fiscal and monetary measures taken by the Fed and the Bush and Obama administrations in the critical months of late 2008 and early 2009 clearly showed that. But the point of the conference was that if we were to understand how badly wrong markets really made things, a much bigger discussion needed to take place. The market failure of the Depression had produced a wholesale rethinking of economics, culminating with Keynes's general theory. A similar rethinking should have been occurring now. It wasn't.

The eclectic group therapy session convened by Soros and Johnson in Cambridge included not just economists but a remarkable array of leading philosophers, scientists, journalists, financial experts, and respected financial bloggers. Again and again, the sharpest observers at the conference drove this point home: rational models of economics didn't work because there were too many unknowns to justify them. There was no real equilibrium in the real world. The models didn't compute. Literally. Even Kenneth Arrow, who codesigned the best-known mathematical proof of a market-clearing equilibrium, which earned him the 1972 Nobel Prize, told me that too much of economics was misled by "an implicit omniscience. It was not that economists thought there was no uncertainty, but there was a belief that you could understand the consequences of uncertainty." It just wasn't true: the people who made up the economy—that is, the people who became investors, savers, and consumers—were simply burdened with too much faulty or incomplete information to make truly rational decisions most of the time. So the very foundations of modern economics needed to be rethought. The dominant alternative paradigm, called New Keynesianism, had merely grafted Keynesian countercyclical concepts like fiscal stimulus on top of the old rational-markets theory. "We need better theories of persistent deviation from rationality," as Stiglitz summed it up.

During one session, J. Doyne Farmer, a physicist at the Santa Fe Institute, bluntly warned the economists that unless they abandoned their false scientific pretensions—their "physics envy"—economics would fail to take advantage of the enormous computing power that was now available to it. By using these new technologies, researchers could better map human economic behavior, similar to how we track climate change or the weather. But for that to happen, the profession had to create "much more complex models," Farmer admonished, and economists couldn't get there by sticking to the simplistic dogma that markets self-stabilize.

But little of this was impinging on the thinking in Washington. Back on Capitol Hill, the Republican Party seemed almost immediately to revert back to the party of Goldwater (and Friedman) in opposition to Obama, standing united against "big government" on the issues of stimulus, financial reform, and health care. Two decades of runaway Reaganism had ironically cued a Keynesian comeback. But no one seemed to be picking up the irony of these constant historical cycles; everyone simply took up their old cudgels. The Republicans seemed to respond to the latest ideological stimuli as they always had, by rooting around in their closets for their Barry pins. No one seemed to have learned anything.

What was most disappointing of all, perhaps, was that there didn't even seem to be a great deal of soul-searching anywhere in Washington officialdom, apart from Arthur Levitt, Gary Gensler, and a few others.

Brooksley Born was treated to a flurry of attention after the crisis bottomed out in the fall of 2008. But she was semiretired by that time and, demure as ever, she declined to lead a movement for reform or even to utter anything that sounded remotely like an "I-told-you-so," to me or to anybody else. Born was given the John F. Kennedy Award for Courage up at Harvard, and was turned into the subject of an admiring

PBS documentary. She was also asked to serve on what was billed as a latter-day Pecora Commission. It would have been a neat bit of historical justice had Born been asked to chair the commission, of course, but House Speaker Nancy Pelosi opted to give the job to one of her political cronies, former California treasurer Phil Angelides. A well-meaning man who seemed somewhat out of his depth, Angelides promptly decided to call in the biggest Street CEOs for his first big hearings on Capitol Hill in early 2010.

Oddly, however, Born was slated last of the ten commissioners to ask her questions at the hearing. That's the position usually reserved at congressional hearings for the most junior member of the panel. Reporting on the event for *Newsweek*, I couldn't get a straight answer from commission staff on why one of the few people in Washington who really predicted and understood the dangers to come had been so seemingly marginalized. It seemed akin to batting A-Rod ninth in the opening game of the World Series. Further inquiries revealed that Born was not entirely happy about starting things out with the CEOs. Born would have preferred to build a case more carefully. She wanted to question junior witnesses first, including key people at the Wall Street firms, and only then confront the CEOs with detailed questions about their practices. Bringing in the CEOs first as a headline-grabber and asking them gentle opening questions, one observer told me, was like "making Richard Nixon the first witness in the Watergate hearings." Born was overruled, just as she had been in 1998, but sadly for the country, she was proved right once again. After the hearing, when JP Morgan chairman Jamie Dimon was asked why the CEOs hadn't been more apologetic, he responded that questioners have to be "very specific" about what they want him and the others to apologize for. They weren't.

As for Brooksley Born's nemesis from a decade ago, by the late fall of 2008, Robert Rubin had virtually gone undercover. His time at Citigroup was ending, but he couldn't quite grasp it right away, couldn't see that his golden reputation had turned to dross. As media accounts gave Rubin a double-barreled blast of blame—both for his performance as Treasury secretary and his performance at Citigroup—he indulged in some rare self-pity. He simply couldn't believe what was happening. He seemed startled and hurt when I asked him whether he might be asked to leave, launching into an anecdote about how CEO Vikram Pandit had just that morning come by his office to ask for some advice.

He resigned three weeks later. In truth, Rubin had come to be resented throughout the organization. It was no accident when, just before the Democratic convention, Citigroup made the first move toward pushing Rubin aside when it was announced that he would give up the chairmanship of the board's executive committee. The announcement was cast as a mere bureaucratic reshuffling, part of the company's decision to do away with the committee and fold its work into its nominating and governance committee, headed by Richard Parsons. In truth, it was intended as a humiliation by senior Citi executires, who thought Rubin no longer deserved the respect he was accorded and wanted the Democrats gathering in Denver to know that.

Rubin never acknowledged responsibility, even though some of his old acolytes suggested that it would help his plummeting reputation if he did. Still, at a hearing of the Financial Crisis Inquiry Commission in April 2010, with Born seated on the dais in front of him, Rubin did finally acknowledge her. In an offhanded way, while in the middle of his answer to another question from another commissioner, he remarked, "Commissioner Born is right about derivatives regulation." That was all. Born was startled. For more than a decade he had never said word one to her, and he wasn't even looking at her now. But his admission was something.

Rubin and other former senior Clinton officials remained adamant that the subprime disaster never would have happened on their watch. The deregulatory recklessness of the Bush administration had gone way beyond what the Clinton administration would have allowed, they said. "We were already worried about the GSEs [government-sponsored enterprises], worried about predatory lending," said one former senior Clinton administration official. "Do you think that if we had seen figures showing that 50 percent of mortgages had no money down, we would have just ignored that?" Beyond that, Rubin felt that he was being blamed for trading decisions at Citigroup that he'd had no part of: so what if he had urged the company to get into higher-risk businesses? It had been broad strategic advice, nothing more. "It's as if he had advised the government to be more fiscally disciplined, and then someone had cut the navy in half, and he's blamed for it," said one Rubin loyalist. When I spoke to him for the last time, giving him another chance to rethink the decisions he'd made over the years at the NEC, Treasury, and Citigroup, he was the same old Rubin. There was the same endearing self-reflection, the impressively deliberative pause. Sure, in hindsight, there were things he might have liked to change. But that was just Monday-morning quarterbacking. No, he said, there really wasn't much that he would have done differently at the time.

In the months after he left office, Hank Paulson holed up at the Johns Hopkins School of Advanced International Studies (SAIS) to write a book. After a career building a pristine reputation as a great Wall Street banker, Paulson knew that his career henceforth would be judged largely by what he did, or didn't do, in one year, 2008. And he knew he was battling the tide of already settled historical opinion. He was painfully aware of what had become the common wisdom on him: that he was the shaky quarterback who fumbled some of the big calls and let the crisis get away from him. He was determined to show that, no, this was all wrong, that he did all that he or any Treasury secretary could—especially when it came to Lehman—during that critical nine-month period. There was a certain amount of pathos to the way Paulson was sitting there at SAIS, continuing to work in a city he had resisted coming to in the first place, scrambling to write his book and interviewing old colleagues to get his narrative right. Paulson, the ex-football jock, was behaving like the athlete who has just been beaten for the first time in his life in a big game and can't bring himself to leave the field; he was reliving the critical plays over and over.

Around the world, the prevailing view was that the United States might never regain the prestige it once had enjoyed. Thanks to American advice and the American-sponsored world system, the free marketers of Wall Street had been able to undermine, to misdirect, the genuine and unmatched ability of capitalism to create wealth. They had rigged the system. It was one reason that, in the aftermath of the crisis, one of the few issues in Washington that seemed to unite a bitterly partisan Congress was that the United States had a serious "too-big-to-fail" problem. Democrats deplored Wall Street's outsize role in the real economy and its lobbying influence, and conservatives were appalled at the way the capitalist system had been undermined and rigged in favor of big banks that introduced so much moral hazard into the markets.

Yet neither side seemed to have the power or the will to take on the systemic disease that underlay it all—the infection of the U.S. economy by finance—and they weren't getting much help from President Obama.

It was this enduring state of affairs—the fact that America's leaders could not even now, at this late date, grapple with the fundamental economic pathology they had created—that ultimately cost the United States so much of its credibility in the wake of the crisis. "Can we, those of us in the rest of the world, go on financing the deficits of a leading world power without having any say? The answer is clearly no," said French president Sarkozy. Many major nations began to defiantly go their own way; some, like Brazil, emulated Malaysia and imposed capital controls. But the rebellion would be slow in coming. America's record deficits would continue to be financed by buyers of Treasury bills around the world. In the year after the financial catastrophe, the G20 group of nations, which included China and other major developing nations, won a kind of battlefield promotion. The G20 would now be seen as the world's preeminent economic forum, eclipsing the hoary Group of Seven, which had been meeting since the 1970s to decide on interest rate and currency policies for the world. (Precrisis plans for an expansion of the G7 into a G14 were junked.) But after the disaster, the governments of the G20 nations, like the officials in Washington, would be leery of proposing dramatic changes because no one wanted to upset economic recovery. No one wanted to offend the financial markets.

Even so, something profound had changed. The last decade had seen multiple disasters and missed opportunities emanating from Washington—the diversion away from Afghanistan to Iraq, the long period of fiscal, regulatory, and financial recklessness, the squandering of global leadership over climate change and the carbon-based global economy. As a result, other countries were no longer interested in looking to Washington as a model, and Obama didn't do enough to change minds, to deliver up sufficient substance to go with his soaring rhetoric. Leaders abroad were sympathetic; there had been an initial period of giddy hopefulness around the world after his inauguration; and they knew that Obama was largely engaged in cleaning up the Augean stable's worth of disasters that Bush left him. But foreign financial officials kept waiting for something more from the president while the urgency of the crisis ebbed away. Certainly, higher capital requirements for banks should be required, but how much higher should they be? Yes, we would like to see more derivatives trade done on standardized exchanges or clearinghouses where it can be monitored—but how rigid is that requirement going to be?

As with so many other issues he dealt with, like health care and climate change standards, Obama ended up deferring to Capitol Hill to fill in the details, and the old Wall Street lobby was back in full force, this time arguing cleverly from the perspective of keeping consumer choice rather than the interests of the banks. "The rest of the world is concerned that all we'll do is straighten the paintings a little bit and fix up the furniture and say we're fine," said Ken Rogoff. "You hear a lot of concern in Europe that the U.S. has exercised too much restraint [in confronting] Wall Street." Out on the front lines with the dissidents, of course, was Stiglitz. In October 2009, Stiglitz flew to Istanbul for the fall meetings of the IMF and the World Bank, and he was struck by the outright contempt he encountered. "There was a real discounting, a dismissal, of our advice. They think we have the politics of a banana republic," Stiglitz said.

The U.S. Senate did try to respond. Spurred by the perception that it looked helpless and weak against the Wall Street lobby—and encouraged at long last by Obama, who was equally concerned about his reputation—the Senate had made real progress on regulation by mid-2010. It pushed through laws that walled off swaps transactions at banks and restricted proprietary trading, a version of the Volcker rule. It gave the SEC discretion to ban other swaps that looked like mere gaming bets on whether deals—or whole nations—would fail (preserving the swaps function for its proper use as a hedge against future price or interest-rate changes). It narrowed the definition of derivatives "end users" to legitimate corporations, making it likelier than ever that most derivatives deals would be done on clearinghouses and exchanges, under regulation.

But the fundamental structure of Wall Street hardly changed. On the contrary, the bill that Obama called "the toughest financial reform since the one we created in the aftermath of the Great Depression" effectively anointed the existing banking elite. The major firms got to keep the biggest part of their derivatives business in interest-rate and foreign-exchange swaps. "The bottom line: this doesn't fundamentally change the way the banking industry works," a former U.S. Treasury official told me as the bill passed in the summer of 2010. "The ironic thing is that the biggest banks that took the most [bailout] money end up with the most beneficial position, and the regulators that failed to stop them in the first place get even more power and discretion."

And the Obama-ites continued to be cautious. They sought to keep the language of the giant new law, the successor to Glass-Steagall, as vague as possible in order to preserve flexibility for future regulators.

Their argument was that, as Geithner put it in a letter to a congressman about proposed new limitations on leverage taken by banks, setting such things down in writhing might endanger banks' future business. "We do not believe that codifying a specific numerical leverage requirement in statute would be appropriate," Geithner wrote. Doing so, Geithner suggested, would "produce an ossified safety and soundness framework that is unable to evolve to keep pace with change." And change, of course, financial innovation, was still deemed good.

This attitude was, oddly enough, a pitfall of having a smart cookie like Obama in the White House. Obama was just smart enough to convince himself that he and his successors in Washington could keep up with Wall Street in the future, no matter that the past had suggested otherwise. No matter that, as happened during the Greenspan-Clinton-Bush era, we saw that regulators outsmarted by the Street could easily undo regulations with little public debate, depending on which way the political and ideological winds were blowing.

So the insurgency against U.S. leadership would continue, but it would be evolutionary, not revolutionary. It would be a question of changing the voting-right structure at the IMF so that Washington was no longer so dominant; of holding secret meetings—from which Americans were excluded—to design a strategy of gradually displacing the dollar as the reserve currency by moving to assorted "baskets" of other currencies, (even though the leading alternative, the euro, grew more troubled than the greenback). That effort was led by the Chinese, but even they had to be very careful: to bring their own economy back to health, the Chinese continued to buy Treasury bills in an effort to suppress their currency and maintain their export strength.

What seemed indisputable, however, was that America's Cold War triumphalism had finally run its course. The United States had come out of the Cold War so full of hopefulness and promise. Over the ensuing twenty years, the United States had lost ground in military projection, manufacturing, moral authority, and technological innovation. And now we had to confront the fact that something essential about America's traditional role in the world—as its locus of wisdom, its lodestar for behavior—had irretrievably slipped through our fingers. The shattering of the free-market fantasy was of a piece with the debunking of the neocon pretensions about the unlimited projection of U.S. power. The ideals we relied on and espoused so passionately during times of life-or-death struggles—during the fight against fascism and during the Cold

War—were certainly not dead. But it was clear they were irreparably tarnished, revealed to be full of fallacies, and they were no longer sufficient as a basis for governing the global system.

In both politics and economics, the age of certainty is over. One thing still seems fairly certain: Wall Street's continued dominance of the U.S. economy. Propelled into the lead by a generation of Washington policy makers, the Street seems destined to stay ahead of them—and largely out of our control.